BATTLEGROUND
THE FAMILY

BATTLEGROUND

THE FAMILY

VOLUME 2 (H–Z)

Edited by Kimberly P. Brackett

GREENWOOD PRESS
Westport, Connecticut • London

Library of Congress Cataloging-in-Publication Data

Battleground : the family / edited by Kimberly P. Brackett.
   p. cm.
   Includes bibliographical references and index.
   ISBN 978-0-313-34095-6 (set : alk. paper) — ISBN 978-0-313-34096-3 (vol. 1 : alk. paper) — ISBN 978-0-313-34097-0 (vol. 2 : alk. paper)
1. Family—Encyclopedias.   I. Brackett, Kimberly P.
   HQ515.B38   2009
   306.8503—dc22   2008038759

British Library Cataloguing in Publication Data is available.

Copyright © 2009 by Greenwood Publishing Group, Inc.

All rights reserved. No portion of this book may be reproduced, by any process or technique, without the express written consent of the publisher.

Library of Congress Catalog Card Number: 2008038759
ISBN: 978-0-313-34095-6 (set)
      978-0-313-34096-3 (vol. 1)
      978-0-313-34097-0 (vol. 2)

First published in 2009

Greenwood Press, 88 Post Road West, Westport, CT 06881
An imprint of Greenwood Publishing Group, Inc.
www.greenwood.com

Printed in the United States of America

The paper used in this book complies with the Permanent Paper Standard issued by the National Information Standards Organization (Z39.48–1984).

10 9 8 7 6 5 4 3 2 1

CONTENTS

Guide to Related Topics   *ix*

Series Foreword   *xiii*

Preface   *xv*

Entries:

Abortion	1
Addiction and Family	9
Adversarial and No-Fault Divorce	15
African American Fathers	24
Arranged Marriage	33
Attention Deficit Hyperactivity Disorder (ADHD)	40
Battered Woman Syndrome	49
Benefits of Marriage	56
Biological Privilege	63
Birth Control	67
Birth Order	76
Breastfeeding or Formula Feeding	81
Changing Fertility Patterns	89

Child Abuse	98
Child Care Policy	105
Child Support and Parental Responsibility	112
Childbirth Options	117
Childfree Relationships	125
Children as Caregivers	134
Cohabitation, Effects on Marriage	139
Common Law Marriage	145
Corporal Punishment	152
Cosleeping	157
Covenant Marriage	163
Culture of Poverty	167
Dating	177
Day Care	185
Deadbeat Parents	191
Developmental Disability and Marital Stress	196
Divorce and Children	201
Divorce, as Problem, Symptom, or Solution	206
Domestic Partnerships	215
Domestic Violence Behaviors and Causes	221
Domestic Violence Interventions	228
Elder Abuse	239
Elder Care	247
Employed Mothers	252
Extramarital Sexual Relationships	257
Family and Medical Leave Act (FMLA)	265
Family Roles	269
Fatherhood	279
Fictive Kin	285
Foster Care	289
Gay Parent Adoption	297
Grandparenthood	304

Grandparents as Caregivers	311
Homeschooling	319
Housework Allocation	326
Infertility	333
International Adoption	346
Juvenile Delinquency	355
Mail Order Brides	363
Mandatory Arrest Laws	369
Marital Power	375
Marital Satisfaction	383
Marriage Promotion	394
Mate Selection Alternatives	400
Midwifery and Medicalization	405
Mommy Track	414
Motherhood, Opportunity Costs	418
Nonmarital Cohabitation	423
Only Child	431
Overscheduled Children	436
Parenting Styles	443
Pet Death and the Family	450
Plural Marriage	457
Poverty and Public Assistance	464
Premarital Sexual Relationships	472
Prenuptial Agreements	478
Preparation for Marriage	485
Religion and Families	493
Religion, Women, and Domestic Violence	499
Remarriage	504
Same-Sex Marriage	515
Sibling Violence and Abuse	521
Stay at Home Dads	526
Surrogacy	532

Teen Pregnancy	543
Transition to Parenthood	552
Transracial Adoption	558
Wedding and Eloping	567
White Wedding Industry	572
Bibliography	579
About the Editor and Contributors	617
Index	625

GUIDE TO RELATED TOPICS

DATING AND RELATIONSHIP FORMATION
Cohabitation Effects on Marriage
Dating
Fictive Kin
Mate Selection Alternatives
Nonmarital Cohabitation
Prenuptial Agreements

DOMESTIC VIOLENCE
Battered Woman Syndrome
Child Abuse
Domestic Violence Behaviors and Causes
Domestic Violence Interventions
Elder Abuse
Mandatory Arrest Laws
Religion, Women, and Domestic Violence
Sibling Violence and Abuse

ENDING PERSONAL RELATIONSHIPS
Adversarial and No-Fault Divorce
Divorce and Children
Divorce, as Problem, Symptom, or Solution

FAMILY AND OTHER INSTITUTIONAL CONNECTIONS
Biological Privilege
Child Care Policy

Culture of Poverty
Foster Care
Homeschooling
Marriage Promotion
Poverty and Public Assistance
Religion and Families

FAMILY FORMATION OPTIONS
Changing Fertility Patterns
Childbirth Options
Gay Parent Adoption
International Adoption
Midwifery and Medicalization
Surrogacy
Teen Pregnancy
Transracial Adoption

FAMILY WORK, FAMILY CRISES, AND CAREGIVING
Addiction and Family
Children as Caregivers
Elder Care
Grandparents as Caregivers
Housework Allocation
Juvenile Delinquency
Pet Death and the Family

FERTILITY AND SEXUALITY IN RELATIONSHIPS
Abortion
Birth Control
Extramarital Sexual Relationships
Infertility
Premarital Sexual Relationships

PARENTING AND CHILD REARING ISSUES
African American Fathers
Attention Deficit Hyperactivity Disorder (ADHD)
Birth Order
Breast Feeding or Formula Feeding
Child Support and Parental Responsibility
Corporal Punishment
Cosleeping
Deadbeat Parents
Fatherhood
Grandparenthood

Only Child
Overscheduled Children
Parenting Styles
Transition to Parenthood

RELATIONSHIP AND MARITAL PROCESSES
Benefits of Marriage
Childfree Relationships
Developmental Disability and Marital Stress
Family Roles
Marital Power
Marital Satisfaction

TRADITIONAL MARRIAGE AND ITS ALTERNATIVES
Arranged Marriage
Common Law Marriage
Covenant Marriage
Domestic Partnerships
Mail Order Brides
Plural Marriage
Preparation for Marriage
Remarriage
Same-sex Marriage
Wedding and Eloping
White Wedding Industry

WORK AND FAMILY LINKS
Day Care
Employed Mothers
Family and Medical Leave Acts (FMLA)
Mommy Track
Motherhood, Opportunity Costs
Stay-at-home Dads

H

HOMESCHOOLING

Homeschooling is enjoying increasing popularity in Westernized countries around the world, including South Africa, Israel, and Canada. In the United States, an adequate understanding of the homeschooling movement requires an understanding of compulsory public education. Because this topic may be contested between different interest groups (educators, legislators, politicians, and parents), a critical stance is warranted when reviewing statistics regarding the academic performance of homeschooled children. Factors that could strongly qualify statistical findings are often not detailed when advocates present data, or may be under-emphasized when studies are publicized.

HISTORY

America has valued education from the time of its first colonists. In Puritan times, the supervision of children's education was considered the responsibility of the family, and in particular, the father. Although the Plymouth Colony would take 40 years to establish a school, the faster-growing Massachusetts Bay Colony opened a school in 1636, roughly 7 years after obtaining a royal charter. In 1647, the Old Deluder Satan Act required families in settlements of certain sizes to provide reading and writing education to the children. Families were financially responsible for this charge, but the towns were subject to fines if the families there did not comply. This was an important law because it highlights that the community, rather than individual families, was responsible for the form of education. Homeschooling was still important because children often began learning to read at home or under the instruction of a literate neighbor.

Enactment of compulsory education laws began in industrializing states, where the lure of factory jobs brought many rural and immigrant families. The middle and upper-middle classes supported the legislation, not only from their fear that unwashed, unsupervised, and impoverished youth would degrade their society, but also out of a growing public support for the poor. Those opposed to compulsory education included parents who needed their children's earnings as well as those with libertarian leanings. Compulsory attendance laws, first enacted in 1852, were at first rarely enforced because local school officials were charged with, but not compensated for, enforcing them. As public schools accommodated ever-larger student enrollments, a bureaucratic, rules-based discipline emerged in the classrooms. Standardized punctuality, regularity, obedience, and silence from pupils were expected and rewarded. Coupled with this was increasing commitment from teachers to institute a set of factory-like rules to help manage the classroom. After Reconstruction, southern states (except Tennessee) were forced to institute free public schools as part of their states' constitutions in order to be readmitted to the Union, which was the first interference of the federal government in the schooling policies of states.

Although illegal in most states by the 1970s, homeschooling is now legal in all states, as well as the District of Columbia. Homeschooling is either explicitly mentioned as a type of private education or it is included under statutes designed for religious and private schools. It is estimated that the number of homeschooled students has virtually tripled in the years from 1990 to 2001 (Collom 2005) to perhaps as many as 1.35 million at present (Cooper and Sureau 2007). The movement, originated by those on the political left and Libertarians in the 1960s and 1970s, has grown into a powerful grassroots movement now more politically diverse and often led by social conservatives.

Court rulings in favor of homeschooling have often cited the first amendment rights to religious freedom. Perhaps for this reason the public may often assume that parents home-school due to their religious beliefs. States that do not have particular homeschooling statues include rules about homeschooling in their rules on private or alternative schools.

PARENTAL MOTIVATIONS FOR HOMESCHOOLING

Although religious freedom was often cited in the early days of homeschool acceptance, researchers now find several motivating factors for parents of these children. Several factors are identified related to parental choice of homeschooling, finding that concerns about academic and teaching standards are the most influential. Although some parents do show concern about values degradation in the public schools, this is not always accompanied by a strong religious faith. For example, some parents are concerned about school violence, low educational standards, and whether their children can get their special needs met in the public schools. One Canadian study examining the motivations of 203 families found none that reported religion as their primary motivation for choosing to homeschool. It is still the case, however, that the majority of homeschool families are Evangelical Christians. Homeschooling parents are likely to believe that they should be active in their roles as parents and that they are effective at teaching. Whether this is an artifact of having homeschooled or a factor motivating the choice is not clear.

Homeschooled families are notoriously difficult to locate. Because many states do not require that homeschooled children register with public agencies, it can be impossible for researchers to discern whether they have obtained a reasonable response rate. If only 1 percent of the homeschoolers are sent questionnaires, for example, and then only 50 percent of those are willing to complete and return the surveys, it is unlikely that the researcher's sample will be representative of the population of homeschooled children or their parents.

One researcher examined home charter school students, who are required to take standardized achievement tests but aren't strictly homeschooled, and have an actual campus, unlike the traditional notion of homeschool. The response rate was high and the results were intriguing. It was found that minority parents and parents with a spouse involved in the teaching were more likely to be motivated by criticism of public schools. He also found that parents with higher levels of reading achievement are more critical of public schools. Homeschooled children in higher grades did better on the assessment instruments than did those in lower grades. The most stunning finding, however, was that there were no meaningful differences between the performance of children by race or class. He writes "student race also has no statistical relation to achievement here. The two great divides that public school children face—race and class—are inconsequential for student achievement among home-educated children" (Collom 2005).

Two other investigators claim that parents decide to homeschool based on the quality of education they expect to be able to give relative to the quality of education that the public school offers. If they believe that they can give better quality, they are more likely to opt to do it themselves. The same investigators also claim that the more widely distributed income is in a school district, the more likely there are to be homeschooling parents, and that stricter regulations on homeschooling are associated with a decrease in homeschool enrollments. Where the state requires testing of homeschooled children there are fewer enrolled at home. They also found that in districts where more women are employed there is a lower probability of public schooling, and suggest that this is because those families have more income and are able to send their children to traditional private schools. Also, the more money that is spent on children in public schools the less likely parents are to choose homeschooling. Finally, they note that where there are high concentrations of Catholics in a school district, there is a higher proportion of children enrolled in private school relative to homeschool. In other words, Catholics may be more likely to choose a private school when making nonpublic schooling decisions (Houston and Toma 2003).

ARGUMENTS

One argument against homeschooling is that the teachers are largely unqualified; without degrees in education. Some studies, including those noted below on student performance, suggest that homeschooling teachers are just as effective as salaried teachers. Homeschooling may be better for precocious children, because less time is spent on the curriculum, and more time can be allotted for the child's particular interests. It has noted that the lower student-teacher ratios may be a determining factor in the performance of homeschooled children on standardized tests.

STUDENT PERFORMANCE

Some researchers have argued that homeschooled children have higher levels of academic performance than children educated in public schools. But any research findings, and particularly those concerning issues that are highly charged politically, should be able to answer some basic questions.

QUESTIONS TO ASK ABOUT THESE RESEARCH STUDIES

Did a lot of people or only a small percentage of people respond to the questions in each category? This matters because there might be something special about homeschooling families that make them less likely to respond to questions about their education choices. Perhaps public school families are more likely than homeschooling families to respond to these studies. For example, if only 10 percent of homeschooling families responded, it would be very difficult to say that we really know very much about homeschooling families. That would mean that for some reason we don't yet understand, the vast majority of homeschooling families share some trait that makes them less likely to want to answer the questions of researchers. And this trait might be the very one that would reveal the underlying differences between homeschooling and public schooling families. In other words, we may be able to say a lot with a healthy sense of confidence about groups that have high response rates, or large percentages of completed questionnaires returned. But if the group has very low response rates, we don't end up knowing very much about the group, but only about the few who returned the questionnaires. If one group has an extremely low response rate compared to the other group, as may be the case with homeschooling and public schooling families, it may be impossible to compare them in a meaningful way.

In fact there is usually a low response rate on homeschool research. This may be because the families are more suspicious of outsiders, because they disapprove of questionnaires, or for some other reason. We can't even know for certain why they have refused if they do not respond. But for whatever reason homeschooling families are less likely to use standardized achievement measures such as exams using multiple choice questions, and unless the school districts require that homeschooled children be registered, it may be impossible to estimate the number of children who are homeschooled in an area. If they are not required to register, the researchers do not know what the response rates are.

Do the children in the study have parents with similar incomes and education levels? Factors such as parents' income and parents' education are extremely important to know when making predictions about how well a child will perform in an academic setting. One researcher has noted that the two most popular articles that are used to prove the superiority of homeschooling over public schooling are biased because they don't take this into account. That report claims that in both those studies the parents of the homeschooled children were more educated, had higher incomes, and had fathers who were much more likely to be employed than did the public schooled children. So the children in homeschooling families already started with an advantage, even before their families decided not to use public schooling. In general, children whose parents are better educated and who have higher incomes and higher rates of employment for the fathers do well academically whether they are schooled at home or in public schools.

This report also tells us that it is reasonable to assume that the homeschooling families may be more interested in their children's education than average families. That is because homeschooling requires so much work from parents. When parents take an active role in their children's education, whether at home or in public schools, we should expect high achievement from the children. While homeschooling parents must be motivated and involved this is not necessary for parents of publicly schooled children.

Are the students in the studies matched? Homeschooled children have academic advantages. They enjoy small classrooms, individualized attention, close parental involvement, and above-average family background characteristics. With all those advantages, their academic gains should be even better than current research shows. So we should ask whether the research studies are comparing public school students in crowded classrooms and poor family backgrounds with homeschooled students. In other words, is it being schooled at home that makes the difference in academic performance or is it having individualized attention from the instructors that matters most?

COMMUNITY/SOCIETY CONCERNS AND CRITICISMS

Although homeschooling is considered by many to be a private matter, it has become a powerful force in the public sphere. Homeschooling parents are voters who make a point to tell their legislators what they want.

Democracy

Since Plato's time, social thinkers have agreed that leaders must be educated. Because democracies place power in the hands of their citizens, education of the masses is extraordinarily important. But this is an area of much disagreement. Some argue that homeschooling is merely one more educational option. But others note that it is an option that only a few families can afford, that is, only those families who can afford to have a parent at home, not working. This argument also states that it's not good for competition to exist in children's educational "options." Public schools cannot compete with the tiny classrooms found in homeschools.

The families most likely to leave unsatisfactory schools for homeschooling will take with them a pool of students whose presence as peers could improve education for all. This argument says that homeschooling is just a part of a much bigger trend in the United States; privatization. Privatization is a process in which private groups take over public services. But privatizing education is bad for us as a group because it prevents us from all participating together in the discussion of how we want our country's education to proceed. By making education private, we make it into something we can buy or sell—a commodity. If all public goods and institutions that were begun to make this a better society become commodities, then we may not really be true citizens anymore; we will be just consumers. This calls into question whether we have a true democracy.

The parents may argue that it is their right to homeschool without interference from the government, but parents must obey outside authorities in many situations. For example, they may be prohibited by law from neglecting their children, and they may not abuse them, even if they believe it is their right to do so. Why, we may ask, should parents have any more rights to educational choices than they do to disciplinary choices?

Fairness

Homeschoolers sometimes sue for access to public educational facilities. When they sue for the rights to participate in school sports and other extracurricular activities they typically lose their cases. It is paradoxical that they sue to use public goods at the same time they demand to have their individual rights away from the public resources.

Culture

Homeschooled children, while not social misfits, may be less likely to experience the diversity of mainstream U.S. society. Although they do participate in social outings, that is not the issue here. The issue is whether parents choose homeschooling as a way to limit their children's exposure to values, beliefs, and behaviors that are different from their own. In other words, in our culturally diverse society, homeschooled children learn to reproduce their parents' beliefs and practices, even if these are extremely different from those of our general culture. For example, if their parents are racist, they will be more likely to reproduce the racism if they are prevented from participating in the broader culture. U.S. society celebrates individual choice, but because homeschooled children may not be exposed to the diversity present in public schools, their own adult choices may be limited. This is because they will have had limited exposure to the possibilities available to them. Universal education is one way that our society insures that we all start out on an equal footing. Homeschooling leads to a situation in which an individual's family background is the primary factor in determining future success in life. In other words, homeschooling insures that we do not start out on an equal footing.

Health

Some studies suggest that homeschooling parents are less likely to have their children immunized than parents of children enrolled in either public or private schools. This is because homeschooling parents are less likely to believe that vaccines are safe or that the government is telling the truth about them. Parents must have their children vaccinated before they are allowed to enter public or private schools. Requiring these vaccines is the main way that health care authorities make sure that we will not experience outbreaks of deadly and crippling diseases from the past. Some states have procedures to ensure that even homeschooled children receive vaccinations, but most do not. It is possible (although not demonstrated at present) that homeschooled children may be more vulnerable to diseases from which other children are protected by vaccinations. It is also possible that children schooled at home have a lower risk for certain common diseases because they may be less likely to be exposed to them.

Welfare of Children

Children may suffer in other ways through homeschooling. One small study has suggested that children with attention deficit hyperactivity disorder may do better in home than in public or private schools. It is suggested that this is because students in homeschools get individualized attention. In fact, because the student-teacher ratio is so low in homeschools, another problem is avoided. Teacher certification courses involve learning some type of classroom management. Classroom management is necessary when classes are large, but home educators do not need these skills because classes are small. For this reason, the problem of uncertified teachers in homeschool environments is moot. Also, some argue that parents are the people best qualified to determine what will most help their children, and to identify their individual needs. So homeschooling might be better on all these counts.

Yet homeschooling can also make it possible for child abuse and neglect to flourish. In those places where families are not required to register their homeschooled children, the children may never have regular consultations with public officials. Abuse and neglect may go unnoticed by authorities in these situations. While these examples may be few, that they exist at all is a source of concern for many critics of the homeschool movement.

See also Attention Deficit Hyperactivity Disorder (ADHD); Parenting Styles; Religion and Families.

Further Reading: American Homeschool Association. http://www.americanhomeschoolassociation.org/; Brabant, Christine, Sylvain Bourdon, and France Jutras. "Home Education in Quebec: Family First." *Evaluation and Research in Education* 17, nos. 2/3 (2003): 112–131; Collom, Ed. "The Ins and Outs of Homeschooling." *Education and Urban Society* 37, no. 3 (2005): 307–335; Cooper, Bruce S., and John Sureau, John. "The Politics of Homeschooling-New Developments, New Challenges." *Educational Policy* 21, no. 1 (2007): 110–131; Duvall, Steven F., Delquadri, Joseph C., and D. Lawrence Ward. "A Preliminary Investigation of the Effectiveness of Homeschool Instructional Environment for Students With Attention-Deficit/Hyperactivity Disorder." *School Psychology Review* 33, no. 1 (2004): 140–158; Green, Christa L., and Kathleen V. Hoover-Dempsey. "Why Do Parents Homeschool?" *Education and Urban Society* 39, no. 2 (2007): 264–285; Home School Legal Defense Association. http://www.hslda.org/; Houston R. G., and E. F. Toma. "Home Schooling: An Alternative School Choice." *Southern Economic Journal* 69, no. 4 (2003): 920–935; Kennedy, Allison M., and Deborah A. Gust. "Parental Vaccine Beliefs and Child's School Type." *Journal of School Health* 75, no. 7 (2005): 276–280; Lyman, Isabel. "Homeschooling: Back to the Future?" The Cato Institute, 1998. http://www.cato.org/pubs/pas/pa-294.html; National Home Education Network. http://www.nhen.org/; National Home Education Research Institute. http://www.nheri.org/; Sheehan, Michele. "Dancing With Monica: Personal Perceptions of a Home-School Mom." *Roeper Review* 24, no. 4 (2002): 191; Urban, Wayne and Jennings Wagoner Jr. *American Education: A History.* New York: McGraw Hill, 1996.

Carolyn F. Pevey

HOUSEWORK ALLOCATION

The word "housework" normally refers to the unpaid labor done inside, or as a part of, the home. Housework includes not only household chores such as cooking and cleaning, but also child care, caregiving for elderly dependents, supervision and entertainment of family members, coordination of routines and family rituals, preparation and planning for events, and generally managing home and family life. In addition, many scholars recognize that household labor also includes the provision of indirect economic support. A spouse who manages the household and rears children makes it possible for the other to attend school, gain valuable work experience, and climb up the occupational ladder. When a wife is employed and has to come home to complete the bulk of housekeeping chores, it is often termed the second shift.

The central debate in this area is the question of how unpaid labor is distributed among family members. Consistently, researchers find that wives, even those employed outside the home on a full-time basis, perform significantly more housework than husbands. The consequence of this is that wives and mothers, especially those who are employed, feel tired, anxious, overworked, and undervalued. Husbands grow accustomed to an unfair division of labor and may seldom recognize their wives' contributions as work. The unpaid work done by wives and mothers is taken for granted and for some is assumed to be a natural consequence of women's nurturing and nesting nature. Religious conservatives, especially those who are biblical literalists, stress that women and men are innately distinct from one another and that women are naturally inclined to care for others and cultivate family life.

Sons and daughters witness and experience the unequal division of labor in their families of orientation and consequently model this in their own relationships. Thus, a gendered and unequal distribution of household labor is perpetuated, unchallenged, and over time is viewed as natural and normal. A further consequence of this pattern is that employers may feel justified in paying women less because they assume that all women will assign priority to home and family, thereby putting less time and effort into their occupations. In addition, women may choose occupations that they view as more flexible or less demanding so that they may accommodate the needs of their husbands and children. Women are more likely to choose part-time or flex-time employment and to work closer to home. Husbands rarely have to make such a choice between the demands of career and those of family.

In the United States, the housewife role is imbued with contradictions. Girls are often encouraged, subtly or explicitly, to pursue a domestic course in life. This is reinforced through toys, books, mass media, and parental socialization. On the other hand, unpaid labor is not regarded as real work and women who stay home to raise children are, perhaps, one of the most powerless groups in our society. Past and present studies of women's well-being find that the homemaker role is disadvantageous to women. Compared with their employed counterparts, women who stay home suffer more from depression, anxiety, and poor physical health.

OVERVIEW OF WOMEN AND WORK

It is difficult to discuss and understand contemporary patterns in housework without first considering the historical trends in paid and unpaid work. It is generally believed that American women have always borne a greater share of the burden for domestic work. Historical records reveal that during colonial times, some tasks in and around the home were more often performed by either men or women. Men performed the heavy, agricultural work of the fields and barn while women performed tasks such as spinning and weaving, making lace, soap, shoes, candles, and transporting water. However, before industrialization, most goods were produced in the home or nearby and all family members participated in the production of goods to some extent, even children. Families were primarily economic units where members spent a considerable amount of time engaged in essential tasks, such as the production of food. Because modern conveniences were unavailable and food surpluses uncommon, all members of the family participated in domestic labor and the divisions between women and men, as well as adults and children, were not as common as they are today.

In colonial America, women were not excluded from working outside the home. Colonial women engaged in a great variety of occupations, such as shopkeepers, crafts workers, nurses, printers, and teachers. Women also acted as physicians and midwives in all of the early settlements. In the South, slave women worked in both the private and public spheres.

The so-called ideology of separate spheres, a belief system regarding the proper and natural roles of women and men, emerged first in England and then spread to the United States around the time of Industrial Revolution. Women were thought to be inherently weaker, more submissive, and more adept at domestic work whereas men were considered stronger, more competitive, and more comfortable in dangerous situations that may arise outside the home. With the creation of new types of jobs, the roles of women and men became increasingly distinct, with women being encouraged to devote most of their time and energy to the private, domestic sphere.

Despite the growth of this belief system, women as well as men were invited to work in the factories during the early years of industrialization. Most women employees were young, single, and well-educated for the times. The work of women was highly valued and encouraged, in part because men continued to perform most of the heavy labor on farms. Women's employment accelerated during both World Wars. It was during this time that married women entered the labor force in sizable numbers. Women worked as switch operators, tool makers, lumberjacks, and stevedores. However, after the war ended, there was a shift in cultural norms and women were encouraged to return to their traditional roles as wives and mothers. This shift occurred as a response to the growing fear that women would compete with men for jobs.

As the economy strengthened, the necessity for all family members to work lessened. During this time, men earned a family wage, therefore wives' wages were increasingly thought to be unnecessary. A new cultural ideal for women emerged during the mid-1800s and continued into the early-1900s known as the "cult of true womanhood." Women were applauded for fulfilling what was viewed as their natural role; that of domestic work and caregiving. Husbands with nonworking wives gained prestige, and wives acquired status via their working husbands. Furthermore, middle-class wives were now in a position to acquire the status of lady, a title normally reserved for the most elite women of society. Unmarried and minority women continued to have higher rates of labor force participation.

While the image of Rosie the Riveter took hold during the 1940s, the ideology of separate spheres reemerged strongly during the 1950s and 1960s. Popular television programs glamorized stay-at-home mothers and women were encouraged to seek fulfillment through marriage and motherhood. Middle-class women who wished to pursue careers felt their femininity was called into question. Nevertheless, women's labor force participation rates continued to rise in the 1960s and 1970s, creating what some refer to as a stalled revolution. While the women's movement expanded opportunities for women outside the home, it did not change the ideologies or expectations of men to a great extent. Contemporary studies reveal that husbands often resist their domestic obligations through feigning incompetence or performing tasks incorrectly—a type of playing dumb.

CHILDREN AND HOUSEHOLD LABOR

The greatest difference between wives and husbands in time spent in paid and unpaid work occurs when their children are under three. Even couples with relatively egalitarian marriages often find that the division of labor becomes quite segregated with the birth of the first child. When children are born into a marriage, women tend to work less outside the home and more inside the home. Only about 35 percent of married women with children under the age of six work full-time, but most of them do work at least part-time. Furthermore, women are much less likely today to interrupt their employment because of children. Interestingly, older children often perform more housework than do fathers.

Mothers report being responsible for the daily tasks associated with rearing children, while fathers are more likely to parent on an as-needed basis. Thus, women may be more likely to experience parenting as hard work, while men are more likely to describe parenting as fun and to view parenting as a temporary distraction from their primary obligations. Younger and more educated men perform more housework than do other men. Generally, these men hold less-traditional gender role attitudes. Employment status and relative earnings influence husbands' share of housework. Husbands of employed wives perform more housework than husbands of nonemployed wives, although the distribution is still far from equitable. Husbands whose earnings far exceed their wives do less housework than other husbands. The recent increase in men's contribution to domestic labor is primarily in child care, especially of older children, not in housework typically described as feminine. When fathers do watch children, they often do so in the absence of other activities or obligations whereas mothers watch children while shopping or attending to household chores. Culturally, it is assumed that good fathering is measured through good providing; thus, men are unlikely to experience conflict between their occupational and familial roles. On the other hand, good mothering is defined as being constantly available and accessible to children. Consequently, working mothers are very likely to experience conflict in their paid and unpaid work obligations. Indeed, a strong commitment to paid work on the part of mothers is likely to be viewed as incompatible with good mothering.

In recent years, there has been a slight increase in the amount of housework performed by men. However, it is likely that this increase in husbands' contribution to housework is actually the result of a decrease of the wives' contribution resulting from their employment; this results in a relative increase in husbands' contribution. Otherwise stated, less housework is being done in total by dual-earner couples. Therefore, women and men may feel that some of the household work is simply left undone.

It is still common for husbands as well as wives to describe men's contributions as helping out. Some fathers even describe time spent with children as babysitting. Descriptions such as these reinforce the belief that housework and child care are inherently and inevitably women's work and that wives whose husbands participate in these roles are the beneficiaries of their husbands' generosity.

RACE, ETHNICITY, AND SOCIAL CLASS

African American and Latino men perform a greater share of housework than do white men. In large part, this is due to the economic necessity for many African American and Latina wives to work outside of the home as well as wage similarity between women and men of color. African American and Latino families are more egalitarian than white families, and more so than most stereotypes suggest. In terms of expressed beliefs, working-class couples often prefer a more traditional division of labor, although they are more likely than middle-class couples to have an egalitarian division of labor. Middle-class couples, on the other hand, are more likely than working-class couples to express a preference for an egalitarian division of labor, while maintaining a traditional division of labor. When comparing various types of intimate relationships, lesbian couple households appear to be the most egalitarian of all. This is most likely due to gender role ideology as well as wage similarity.

CONSEQUENCES OF THE UNEQUAL DIVISION OF LABOR

Despite the fact that women have entered the paid labor force in increasing numbers since before the turn of the twentieth century, it is well-known and widely accepted that American women continue to bear the brunt for work done inside the home. Several studies have computed the difference between men and women in terms of time spent in unpaid labor. Wives spend two to four times as much time in domestic labor as husbands, and this is true even when wives are employed. One consequence of the increase in women's labor force participation rates and the rise in dual-earner couples with children is that parents are more likely to work different shifts, alternating the responsibilities for child care somewhat and spending less time as a couple.

Most marriages today are dual-earner, meaning that both husbands and wives work outside of the home for pay. Nevertheless, women spend more time each week in housework and childcare, and the difference is significant enough that scholars now acknowledge a so-called leisure gap between American husbands and wives. Married women, especially those with children, have substantially less free or leisure time than their male counterparts. Like paid work, unpaid work is differentiated based upon conventional, gendered assumptions. Some tasks are considered women's work, while others are thought to be more masculine. Although there is this dividing of household tasks along gender lines, women perform the majority of the most time-consuming and least discretionary responsibilities. For instance, women do most of the food preparation, shopping for groceries, laundry, dish washing, clean-up, and child care, while men are more likely to do household repairs, yard work, and to play with children. Laundry is the task most often performed by women, with women doing about seven times as much. Women are more likely to multi-task in the household; they prepare meals while watching and entertaining children. Wives are also the kin-keepers of families, planning and coordinating family routines and rituals such as holiday get-togethers with extended family members. Thus, women work even when it appears to others that they are not working. They carry the psychological burden for anticipating and organizing family work. In short, men generally have more flexibility to participate in personal interests and to not work when they are at home. Married men actually create as much household labor as they perform. Indeed, married women spend more time in household work than do single mothers.

Sociologists now refer to the combination of wives' paid and unpaid labor as the double day or second shift, comprised of housework and child care. The demands of housework are monotonous and continuous, leaving married women with little time for personal hobbies, friendships, or relaxation. Women's obligation to the second shift reveals our culture's reluctance to relinquish them from what is seen as their primary role, even when they are successfully involved in other nondomestic pursuits. The second shift performed by wives has significant implications both for wives' well-being as well as for marital quality. In one well-known study, it was reported that many married women, especially those who were mothers, talk about sleep the way a hungry person talks about food. Married women who are just beginning their families are especially vulnerable to stress and lack of sleep.

HOUSEWORK AND MARITAL QUALITY

On average, men report higher levels of satisfaction with their marriages than do women. Marital quality is compromised when spouses hold divergent views on gender roles. Wives generally make more compromises and adjustments in marriage and this is reflected in their lower marital satisfaction scores. The most distressing role combination for spouses is the combination of a traditional husband and a modern or liberal wife.

It comes as no surprise that those wives in households with an equitable division of labor report higher levels of job satisfaction and well-being. These women are less anxious and have fewer depressive symptoms than other women. It may come as a surprise, however, that husbands who participate more equally in the division of household labor also report higher levels of well-being. Husbands who share more equally in housework report happier marriages, less anxiety, and higher levels of satisfaction with their sex lives. Men who resist social change and attempt to maintain conventional gender roles report high levels of distress.

OPTIONS AND STRATEGIES

Recognizing that they will most likely be unfairly burdened by domestic responsibilities, some women may opt to delay marriage or parenthood. Highly educated, successful career women are the most likely group to remain single, marry late, and remain voluntarily childless.

Highly paid, dual-career couples may elect to hire outside help to offset some of the burden for housework and childcare. Unfortunately, this option is not available to most working-class couples or single mothers. Furthermore, the responsibility for locating and screening housecleaners, baby-sitters, and nannies falls to wives, thereby constituting another inequity. Also, a large proportion of domestic workers and nannies are lower-income women of color. Thus, reliance on such services continues to reinforce gender inequality for another class of women.

See also Children as Caregivers; Employed Mothers; Family Roles; Marital Power; Stay at Home Dads.

Further Reading: Coltrane, Scott. *Gender and Families.* Thousand Oaks, CA: Pine Forge Press, 1998; Coltrane, Scott. *Family Man: Fatherhood, Housework, and Gender Equity.*

New York: Oxford University Press, 1996; Focus on the Family. http://www.family.org; Hesse-Biber, Sharlene, and Gregg Lee Carter. *Working Women in America: Split Dreams.* New York: Oxford University Press, 2000; Hochschild, Arlie Russell, and Anne Machung. *The Second Shift: Working Parents and the Revolution at Home.* New York: Viking, 1989; McGraw, Philip. http://www.drphil.com; National Organization for Women. http://www.now.org; Padavic, Irene, and Barbara Reskin. *Women and Men at Work.* Thousand Oaks, CA: Pine Forge Press, 2002; Schlessinger, Laura. http://www.drlaura.com.

Susan Cody-Rydzewski

INFERTILITY

Most persons take their fertility for granted and expect that conception will occur naturally and easily when they choose to pursue pregnancy. In reality fertility and child bearing can be a difficult and painful phenomenon for many couples who attempt to become pregnant. This situation is known as infertility and the rates of infertility have been increasing in the United States in recent decades, although definitive explanations for the increase are lacking.

Infertility is a diseased condition of the reproductive system, usually diagnosed after a couple has experienced one year of unprotected sex, with well-timed intercourse, and failed to conceive or if a woman suffers from multiple miscarriages. Infertility is not a condition that only affects women, it also affects men. Lack of ability to conceive can be related to either partner's health deficiencies. It is a disease that not only affects a couple physically, but it also affects them emotionally.

There is considerable controversy surrounding the question of infertility. Not only are there physiological aspects to infertility, but emotional and social aspects as well. Couples must find ways to manage problems with infertility or they will suffer relationship consequences. Some persons would argue if a couple is infertile, it was not in life's plan for them to have children. They should, according to some, remain childless. In opposition are those who favor the sometimes costly and painful medical interventions.

Other controversial issues associated with infertility include both internal and external pressures. Internal pressures are associated with the idea of immortality and someone to carry on the family name and heritage. For women, internal pressure is associated with the idea of a ticking internal clock. As mythological as the concept may seem, it is very real according to physicians. External pressures stem from society. As a society, we still have a pro-natalistic approach when considering family and what we define as family. If you have no children society thinks that there is something wrong with you. You are not within the defined norms of family in society if you have no children.

Time is another controversy related to infertility. In recent years people have delayed child bearing in pursuit of their own progress and goals as individuals. This delay could be potentially costly to a couple's fertility. This controversy can be directly related to or correlated with the economy; more women today work and pursue education than ever before. It is important to note, however, that infertility affects people of all socioeconomic levels with no distinction between races, ethnicities, or religious predispositions.

WHO IS FERTILE?

As a method of evaluation doctors consider a couple infertile if they have been trying to conceive through unprotected intercourse for 12 months with no success and the female is under 35 years of age. This is known as subfertility. In some cases a couple may have one child already and are having difficulty conceiving another, this is known as secondary infertility. If the female is over 35 years of age, and the couple has not conceived after 6 months of unprotected intercourse, they too are considered infertile. Females incapable of reaching term in pregnancy are considered infertile as well. Healthy couples in their mid-20s have a greater chance, one in four, of conceiving in one year's time than do older women. This ability to conceive is known as fecundity.

INFERTILITY DIAGNOSIS IN AMERICA/EPIDEMIOLOGY

The Centers for Disease Control and Prevention indicates that 1 in 8 couples are infertile; 7.3 million Americans are not able to conceive. This is approximately 10 percent of the reproductive age population. Thirty-five percent of infertility is due to the female and another 35 percent is due to the male. The remaining cases are either unexplained or involve problems with both partners. There are four types of infertility, the male factor, the female factor, and two unexplained factors. The American Society for Reproductive Medicine indicated common health factors that lead to infertility are age, sexuality, tubal diseases, endometriosis, diethylstilbestrol (DES) exposure, smoking, and alcohol use. It is important to receive early diagnosis because several intervention methods may eventually result in a successful pregnancy. Over time nearly one-half of infertile couples will conceive.

FEMALE REPRODUCTION

Understanding female infertility involves understanding the female reproductive system. It is complex to determine infertility in females because although their systems are alike, not every woman's system functions in the same way.

An individual trying to conceive needs to understand exactly how her system functions. Basic biology and reproduction is important to know and understand when considering the problems of infertility. For an individual to get pregnant she must understand the complex cycle of her body's rhythm.

Ovulation is the most fertile time in a woman's cycle. The hypothalamus gland in the brain regulates functions in the body, everything from hunger to the libido. For the purpose of reproduction the hypothalamus gland controls endocrine functions. The hypothalamus releases a chemical messenger called follicle stimulating hormone releasing factor (FSH-RF). FSH-RF tells the pituitary gland, also located in the brain, to execute the next step. The pituitary gland then secretes the follicle stimulating hormone (FSH), and a little luteinizing hormone (LH) enters into the bloodstream that causes the follicles (where the eggs are) to begin to mature. When the follicles mature they release the hormone estrogen. The follicle ripens in a seven-day period and releases more estrogen into the bloodstream. Estrogen causes the lining of the uterus to thicken and the mucous of the cervix to change. When the level of estrogen rises the hypothalamus gland releases large amounts of hormones from the pituitary gland, known as the LH surge. This surge of LH triggers the most mature follicle to burst open and release an egg. This is called ovulation. The prevention of pregnancy with birth control pills utilizes medications that block the LH surge, thus inhibiting the release of the egg.

Prior to ovulation a woman's cervix secretes an abundance of fertile mucous, which by character is a stretchy substance. This substance is important because it helps facilitate the sperm's travel to the egg. Daily mucous testing is used to monitor the most fertile time of the month, along with basal body temperature.

Once ovulation begins, about 14 to 16 days before the menstrual flow, the blood supply to the ovary increases and the ligaments contract, pulling the ovary closer to the fallopian tube. This allows the egg, once it is released, to enter into the fallopian tube. After ovulation, basal body temperature rises by about 0.4 degrees Fahrenheit. Tracking basal body temperature elevation can provide helpful information about the day of ovulation.

Once the egg is released it lives for 24 hours. Once inside the fallopian tube the egg is carried along by the tiny hair-like projections called cilia toward the uterus. A woman can become pregnant from intercourse with a fertile male for about 7 to 10 days in the middle of her cycle. Fertilization occurs if the sperm are present as the live egg reaches the uterus. The corpus luteum (yellow body) forms in the ovary from the ruptured follicle where the egg is released. As it heals it produces the hormone estrogen and progesterone in larger amounts which are necessary for maintenance during pregnancy. If any breakdown occurs in the process, the possibility for infertility increases.

FEMALE FACTORS IN INFERTILITY

A couple who has experienced infertility will be evaluated by a physician. This evaluation includes an analysis of each partner's health and medical history. The evaluation of both individuals is similar. A physical examination, an evaluation of the reproductive hormones, and other analyses of the reproductive organs is performed. Medical history is an important part of the physical examination. The notation of history of menstrual cycle, pregnancy, birth control, sexually transmitted diseases, and surgical procedures are important for analysis. A physician will take into consideration such fertility inhibitors during his analysis as medications, sexual patterns, other significant health problems, lifestyles, and work environment.

As the discussion of the common tests below indicates, identification and treatment of infertility is very complex and costly, leading some to question whether the desire of a couple to conceive is enough to warrant expensive medical tests, particularly those covered under insurance and Medicaid. The physical examination of a woman includes a thyroid, hair distribution, breast, and pelvic examinations. When checking the thyroid, the doctor will examine the thyroid with fingers, feeling for any abnormalities. If there is excessive hair growth on the face and body, this might indicate the presence of male hormones. Breast examination includes observation of size and shape. The breast might also be squeezed to see if any liquid comes out of the nipple. This liquid could be an indication of the presence of increased prolactin, a hormone that prevents ovulation. The physical examination can conclude with a pelvic examination to inspect the cervix. The physician is looking for signs of unusual growths, sores, discharge, or infection. A pap smear is conducted to check for cervical cancer. Cervical mucous is examined for possible infections.

Additional Testing for Females

Ovarian Function Tests

Ovarian function tests are a series of blood tests taken to determine certain hormone levels. Day 3 FSH tests are taken on day 3 of ones menstrual cycle to measure the level of FSH. If there is an increase in FSH it could be an indication that there is a decrease in the production of good-quality eggs and embryos. Day 3 estradol tests measures the amount of estrogen in one's blood. A high level of estrogen could indicate poor egg quality. Inhibin-B levels tests are tests that determine if inhibin-B is being produced at too low a level. Both inhibin-A and inhibin-B are hormones secreted by the gonads (by seroli cells in males and the granulose cells in females) that inhibit the production of FSH by the pituitary gland. The inhibin also plays a role in the control of gametogenesis as well as embryonic and fetal development. Inhibin-A is elevated in the blood serum of women carrying fetuses with Down syndrome. Finally, to complete the ovarian test a trans-vaginal ultrasound is performed several days after the LH surge to determine if ovulation has occurred.

Luteal phase testing includes additional blood tests and a biopsy. Plasma and progesterone levels are tested through blood tests in the last part of the female's menstrual cycle. High levels of progesterone indicate that ovulation has occurred. Hormone tests measure the amount of prolactin, androgen, and thyroid stimulating hormones. An endometrial biopsy is performed after day 21. This test involves taking small pieces of tissue from the uterine lining. These tissue samples help to determine if the lining of the uterus is thick enough for a fertilized embryo. The results will indicate endometrial development.

A postcoital test (PCT), performed mid-cycle and shortly after intercourse, tests and evaluates the quality and quantity of cervical mucous. Additionally, it documents the presence of live, motile sperm in the mucous.

EVALUATION OF REPRODUCTIVE ORGANS

A series of x-rays, scopes, and ultrasound examinations are conducted on the reproductive organs. Hystreosalpingogram (HSG) is an x-ray procedure that is performed in the first half of the cycle by using a water- or oil-based dye to identify any structural abnormalities in a woman's uterus or fallopian tubes. A hysterscope is a tiny telescope mounted with a fiber optic light. It is used to examine uterine abnormalities if such have been indicated by the HSG.

Laparoscopy is a surgical procedure performed under general anesthesia before or around ovulation. This procedure gives the doctor a clear view of the pelvic cavity, which includes ovaries, fallopian tubes, and the uterus. The laparoscopy will allow the doctor to intervene if a problem is recognized. If adhesions or endometriosis is discovered, a laser may be attached to remove growths.

Sonohystogram is an ultrasound that utilizes saline to inflate the cavity of the uterus for careful observation. Vaginal and abdominal ultrasounds are used to visualize the uterus and ovaries. They are also helpful to monitor the growth of follicles on the ovary during the cycle to detect fibrosis or ovarian cysts.

OTHER FACTORS

Abdominal factors that infer with infertility are called peritoneal factors. Two of these problems include pelvic adhesions and endometriosis. Pelvic adhesions are thick fibrous scars that can result from a past infection, particularly by a sexually transmitted disease. Such infections as pelvic inflammatory disease or infection following abortions or prior births create scaring. Previous surgeries can also leave behind scars. Complications from appendicitis and certain intestinal diseases can also result in pelvic adhesions. Endometriosis, when uterine tissue is located outside of the uterus, results in pelvic adhesions. When endometrial tissue implants itself in other areas of the pelvis it creates an irritation. This irritation, tissue, and bleeding create scarring.

Pelvic adhesions contribute to infertility because they block the fallopian tubes. When the fallopian tubes are blocked, the ovum is prevented from traveling down the fallopian tubes from the ovary. It also prevents sperm from traveling up the fallopian tubes from the uterus. Ultimately, this blockage can prevent a blastocyst, a thin-walled hollowed structure from which the embryo develops, from entering the uterus where it implants. The outer layer of blastocyst cells gives rise to the placenta and other supporting tissues needed for fetal development. At the same time, the inner cell mass cells gives rise to the tissue of the body.

Uterine factors contributing to infertility include tumors, other abnormal growths within the uterus, chronic inflammation of the uterus, abnormal structures of the uterus, and a variety of endocrine problems (problems with the secretion of certain hormones) that prevent the uterus from developing the thick lining necessary for implantation by the blastocyct.

MALE REPRODUCTION

Male reproduction is equally as complex as female reproduction. Hormones released by the pituitary gland also regulate the male system. FSH stimulates sperm production in the testicles while LH stimulation produces testosterone. The spermatozoa then develop through several stages, gaining motility after 24 hours. Stored in the epididymis, at ejaculation the sperm pass through the vas deferens, which assists in their expulsion. Sperm must be motile, morphologically sound, and plentiful in order to fertilize the egg. Any disruption in the male reproductive cycle can lead to problems with fertility as well.

MALE FACTORS IN INFERTILITY

The most important factors in determining male infertility are illness and sexual history. Such illnesses include mumps after puberty, hernia repairs, athletic injuries to the groin, and history of un-descended testicles. Sexual history plays an equally important role. Such things as possible sexually transmitted diseases (STDs), urinary tract infections, prostatitis or ejaculatory problems, impotence, certain prescription medications, as well as excessive smoking, drinking, or drug use can effect sperm quality.

To evaluate male factors physicians generally conduct a physical examination, semen analysis, and reproductive hormone evaluation. Reproductive hormones include FSH, androgen level-testosterone, and protactin. Additional sperm analysis testing takes into account sperm antibodies, sperm penetration, and cervical mucus penetration test. Physicians are looking for the sperm count, ability of the sperm to swim, velocity of forward progress of the sperm, size and shape of the sperm, total semen volume, and the liquefaction of the semen, or the ability of the semen to go from gel-like state at ejaculation to a liquid state.

PHYSICAL EXAMINATION AND TESTS

The physical examination entails observation of the hair growth patterns in the genital area, which should be diamond shaped, extending upward toward the navel. A general examination for abnormalities of the penis, scrotum, and testes is conducted. The examination concludes with the examination of the prostate.

Normally, semen analysis includes volume, sperm number, motility, forward progression, and morphology. Normal sperm number should be 200 million or more per ejaculation, and at least 50 percent or more should be motile. Additionally, there should be no significant sperm clumping or agglutination, no significant white blood cells or red blood cells, and no hyper-viscosity (thickening of the seminal fluid).

Semen analysis is usually done in a laboratory or physician's office where a man ejaculates into a cup. Within a few hours the sperm are analyzed. If the volume of semen is low this may indicate that the ducts are blocked or that there is some problem with the prostate gland. If a man's sperm count is below 10 million, which is considered poor, this could signal a problem. Sperm counts of 20 million or more are considered healthy as long as motility and morphology are normal. For motility and velocity two aspects are considered. Motility involves the number of active cells as a percentage of total numbers, and should be at least 50 percent active. Quality of movement is indicated by a rating of 0 to 4 with a score of 2 or more being acceptable.

A Kruger morphology test examines the shape and size of sperm head. Normal morphology is when 14 percent or more of the sperm heads are shaped normally. Otherwise normal men with less than 4 percent normal shape are considered to have a significant fertility problem. A liquefaction test of semen is used to indicate if ejaculate immediately coagulates into a pearly gel that liquefies within 20 minutes. Failure to coagulate and then liquefy may indicate a problem with the seminal vesicles. A too-thick or too-thin consistency in this seminal fructose can indicate a problem. If no fructose is present, a congenital defect in the vas deferens or seminal vesicles or obstruction of the ejaculatory duct is the problem.

ADDITIONAL SPERM TESTING

Analysis of sperm antibodies examines if the sperm movements are agile. If the sperm don't move well, the physician may order tests that can localize and quantify specific antibodies in the blood and on the sperm's surface. If there is a problem with antibody attachment, the following can be affected: if they stick to the head of the sperm, the sperm may be not able to penetrate; if they cover the tail of the sperm, the sperm may not be able to swim fast enough or in the right direction. A penetration assay is a test that evaluates the sperm's ability to break through the outer membrane of an egg and fuse with the egg cytoplasm.

A cervical mucous penetration test is a test conducted in the laboratory that uses cow's mucous to evaluate the sperm's ability to move through the women's cervical mucous. A physician may take cultures of semen and other cultures of the urethra to test for the presence of bacteria or other STDs.

In sum, male infertility is commonly associated with no sperm production or inadequate sperm production. Sometimes sperm cells are malformed or they die before they reach the egg. In rare cases, infertility in men is caused by genetic disease such as cystic fibrosis or a chromosomal abnormality.

Female infertility factors can include ovulation or other cycle disorders. Female infertility factors can include blocked fallopian tubes that can occur when a women has had pelvic inflammatory disease or endometriosis. Congenital abnormalities (birth defects) involving the structure of the uterus or uterine fibroids can be associated with repeated miscarriages.

EFFECTS OF INFERTILITY ON THE COUPLED RELATIONSHIP

Society plays a major role in the emotional state of couples who are having difficulty conceiving. According to the ascribed roles of society, women are caregivers, thus the assumption that she has a greater investment in being able to conceive. Women are more skilled at concealing the anger, fear, and resentment of infertility. Consequently, she takes responsibility for the problem, and often she attempts to face infertility alone, withdrawing from the partner. Some women in this position will become depressed. As infertility is often interpreted negatively by society and the individuals experiencing it, neither person knows how to comfort the other. Hiding their true feelings has significant effects on a couple.

Men in the role of the protector, problem solver, and provider often become helpless when infertility is an issue. They experience feelings of inadequacy, disappointment, and fear. The ability to father a child is rarely even considered, and just assumed to happen when the male desires. Men are trained to take charge and solve problems, so that emotional reactions are not acceptable. When men find themselves in a state of helplessness they may have difficulty expressing that to a partner. Infertility issues can affect a couple's self-esteem as well as their hopes and dreams for their future lives together, making it difficult to comfort each other. Because infertility is such an emotional subject, each partner will likely face emotional consequences.

Couples begin to feel a sense of inadequacy. Women describe feeling hollow inside and men feel like they are shooting blanks after failed attempts to get pregnant. They share a diminished sense of masculinity and femininity. The behavioral effects are numerous as well. Couples begin to feel that sexual intercourse is a chore, not a spontaneous act of love that takes place between two individuals; sex becomes like homework. Their entire lifestyles become dictated by schedules, appointments, and calendar dates. Couples experiencing infertility problems go through many emotional stages.

STAGES OF EMOTIONS

Some practitioners believe that couples go through various emotional stages when faced with the problem of infertility. Those stages are: realization and acknowledgement, evaluation and diagnosis, treatment, and resolution.

In realization stage, couples are shocked to realize that they can't get pregnant on their own. When they attempt to get pregnant after discontinuing birth control they become more and more anxious at each failed attempt. During this stage the feelings of frustration, anger, denial, guilt, shame, self-pity, and jealousy begin to occur. Disagreements about issues in the marriage become more obvious. Men may need convincing that intervention and treatment are necessary. To cope with these emotions couples need to communicate their feelings openly, make appointments to see physicians, and embrace their mixed emotions.

The second stage is evaluation and diagnosis. Couples experience mixed emotions in this stage. Although this is a very stressful time, it should offer the couples hope because they will find out what their health problems are and what solutions may be available. Because the couples have to record all their behaviors and coordinate their sexual activities on a schedule to assist the doctor in evaluating the problem, couples may sense a loss of control. Couples generally develop a sense of resentment for couples who are pregnant or those that have children. Sexuality starts to diminish as spontaneity is no longer an option. To conquer these emotions, couples need to maintain good communication. They should also become educated on infertility by learning as much as they can. Joining a support group and keeping all doctors appointments should help them cope with stress and emotions. Couples who don't receive the proper amount of support can find themselves growing apart as they handle the situation in their own way. By the time a couple reaches the third stage, treatment, they may feel that infertility is dominating their lives. To become pregnant with schedules and timetables becomes very demanding.

To add to the frustration, anger, and resentment that each may be experiencing, now the mates have to deal with the emotions associated with hormonal treatments. These drugs generally magnify the emotions already present. There is an increasing sense of vulnerability and sensitivity and couples often feel like other aspects of their lives have been put on hold, waiting for the conception. They may begin to resent intercourse, thinking more of it as a chore than something to strengthen their relationship. They might also experience feelings of self-punishment (e.g., maybe we don't deserve a child) of feelings of self-blame (e.g., if only we'd done this or that, then we would have a baby). Handling these emotions requires counseling and support. Again, communicating frustrations, instead of holding emotions in, helps to keep stress manageable. Couples should attempt to have fun sex, not so-called baby-making sex.

The final stage is resolution. Once a couple reaches this stage they have endured intense emotional and physical strain. This gives the couple a sense of renewed self-esteem and confidence because they have survived this traumatic experience. Their emotions range from exhaustion and a need to move on to a realization that you cannot control every aspect of your life. Some couples feel relieved that they will not have to endure the strenuous schedules anymore. Other couples feel a sense of closeness and have more empathy for the other person's problems. As they deal with conception or not conceiving, they gain some sense of normalcy in their lives. Those who are unable to conceive either decide to try again later or explore other options for having a family like specialized treatment or adoption.

THE CONTROVERSIES

All of the testing, trauma, and invasion of privacy beg the question, why don't people just give up? The question of parenting creates a dilemma stemming from many personal and societal controversies. Controversies surrounding infertility are of several different types. Some originate with the couple's desire to have a child. Perhaps it relates to their ideal image of family life or the ways that they see themselves. Some controversies over infertility relate to the larger societal and cultural expectations on couples to parent. Both areas prompt questions about the causes of the infertility, the acceptability of childlessness in a marital relationship, and decisions to seek medical intervention.

Whose Fault is it?

Historically, the question of fault has been central in discussions of infertility. The fault was assumed to be with women, as the bearers of children, whose failure to become pregnant must mark a fundamental problem with their physiology, or even their psychology. In biblical times, for example, women who were barren were ostracized and bore their shame alone. In more recent years, the question of fault has become less accusatory, but no less important. Women are stereotypically still thought to be the problem more often than men.

The partner diagnosed with the problem may choose to undergo expensive and sometimes painful treatments. The assignment of fault is important for knowing what medical intervention to seek. However, this can lead to feelings of letting the partner down, being inadequate, or broken. If the inability to conceive results from previous infections, such as STDs or abortion complications, the placement of blame can create relationship problems. Given that males and females have very similar rates of infertility problems, it is important that one not be more readily blamed as the source of problems

The problem of infertility has become more controversial in some ways because we live in a time in which couples are waiting longer to have children. When issues of lifestyle choice are invoked, the debates can become quite heated. Some camps are less sympathetic to childless couples because they argue that it is their own selfishness that led to the problem. Had they had children when they were younger, they may not have had conception difficulties. The deferment of bearing children is due to fulfilling other life ambitions, obligations, and commitments. Critics suggest that couples just want to have it all and that is impossible. They have to choose and they chose unwisely. Here again women receive more blame than do men. Author Sylvia Ann Hewlett suggests that this is resulting in an epidemic of childlessness.

Increases in women's participation in the job market have been blamed for accompanying increases in infertility. Beginning in the early twentieth century, increased numbers of women in the labor force lead to increases in the age at which women decided to bear children. Society's transition from a manufacturing-centered economy to a service-oriented economy demanded a supply of women to work. In 1940, less than 20 percent of the female population age 16 and older participated in the labor force. By the year 2006, that figure had risen to 59 percent compared with 79 percent of men. Women of childbearing age have the highest rates of labor force participation. The year 1980 marked the first time that the number of full-time working women exceeded the number of full-time stay-at-home mothers. Families could not survive on one income and found themselves in need of dual-income households.

Women, bolstered by the equality strides of the Women's Movement, began to delay childbearing because of the rewards associated with the independence of working, including pride, self-worth, and an identity apart from their husbands.

The long-term economic benefits also played a role in the decision to work. The desire for education can not be overlooked in women delaying childbearing.

While on average women are around age 25 at the time of their first birth, the numbers of women delaying well into and beyond their 30s has seen a dramatic increase in the last 20 years. This has been credited with the increasing rates of infertility seen today. Some alarmists have suggested that the most important issue facing married Generation X couples is not waiting too long to attempt conception. The fecundity rate indicates that one-half of women in their 20s will conceive within three months. For women in their early 30s the comparable data are that one-half will conceive within five months, and for women in their late 30s, one-half will conceive within nine months. There is evidence that fertility declines significantly past age 35 because an older woman's eggs, all of which are produced before her birth and age as the woman ages, are more prone to problems.

In addition to maternal age, blame has been directed toward environmental contaminants like chemicals and radiation that can build up in the body over time and lead to difficulty conceiving. While this may be beyond the control of the partners, waiting seems to exacerbate the problem. Another lifestyle element that can lead to blaming is the scarring from a sexually transmitted disease.

Another controversial question arises regarding whose fault infertility is. For some fundamentalist Christians, infertility is seen as God's punishment of a couple or perhaps part of his plan for them. This explanation might retain some blame on the couple, as they search for explanation in a past transgression, but it also absolves them of some of the self-doubt. It provides a coping strategy.

Is It Okay for the Relationship to be Childless?

Pressure to bear children comes from both internal and external sources. The internal pressure centers on the biological need to reproduce and not become a genetic dead end. It may also arise from a sense of what is the right thing to do. For example, the lack of a child to carry on the family name marks the end of their family linage. Birth of a child tends to give people the idea that they are immortal as a part of themselves will live on in the child.

External pressures come from the pro-natalist society in which we live. Ours is a society that places a great deal of emphasis on couples having children. There is a negative stigma attached to being married without a child; or being a couple who has been in a long term relationship and not had children. It is against the norms of society. There is a significant percentage of the United States population that would not describe the couple as being a family unless they had at least one biological or adopted child. The presence of children in a marriage goes a long way toward defining that marriage within the norms of the culture. Many persons suggest that the primary reason to marry is to have and rear children. Biblical pronouncements such as "be fruitful and multiply" abound and couples take them to heart, so that infertility may cause the couple and observers to question the quality of the marriage. A question that young married couples often hear is, "when are you going to start a family?" This seemingly innocent question tells us much about what we expect of married adult persons and what constitutes acceptable behavior.

Studies conducted by the University of Michigan and Wayne State University reveal that infertility creates stress that has the effects of increased marital conflict, decreased sexual self-esteem, decreased satisfaction with one's own sexual performance, and decreased frequency of sexual intercourse. Furthermore, infertility has both indirect and direct effects that decrease evaluations of life as a whole, self efficacy, marriage, intimacy, and health. The negative affects on life quality of females is greater than that of males, again demonstrating how infertility is more of a blow to women than to men.

Researchers further believe that the affects of infertility cause emotional problems. Initially, it was believed that infertility was created by psychological problems, now it is believed that infertility causes psychological problems, although this cannot be definitively proven. This question of whether biology or the couple's stress over not conceiving is the source of the infertility has been debated for some time. It certainly is true that biological research on aging eggs and sperm have indicated that conception does become more unlikely. However, the general happiness of infertile couples declines as their efforts to conceive fail. The most significant drop in the quality of life is seen in cases involving depression in women. This is an indirect effect of infertility. The ability to socialize, work, maintain relationships, and self-esteem issues become an additional burden in conjunction with infertility. Couples often find it quite difficult to interact with friends who have children.

When fertile persons learn of the infertility difficulties of the childless, they are likely to feel pity as they surely cannot be happy without children. While it is more acceptable to be childless (without children due to infertility) than childfree (without children through personal choice), neither are considered ideal. Couples with fertility problems can easily find themselves being asked highly personal questions to which they must determine how to respond appropriately. Does one wish to share the information regarding infertility, offer a witty retort, or ignore the question altogether? Many websites offer advice to couples about how to respond to the curiosities of those who wonder why they have not yet begun to parent. Other topics that are covered include handling unsolicited advice such as "you just need to relax" or "go on vacation."

Should We Look to Science for Solutions?

Couples who are infertile often look to science as a way to solve the problem. As increases in reproductive technology have made conception at later ages more successful, more couples take advantage of them. This is, however, quite controversial. At what age should persons be ineligible for fertility assistance? Is there a point when a couple is simply too old to parent? For some younger couples, who want everything in a hurry, have all other avenues been examined first?

Fertility drugs can have some unwarranted side effects. In cases where multiple viable embryos are fertilized, should a couple elect to abort some of them to give the remaining embryos a better chance to become full-term babies? Or should we follow the example of Kenny and Bobbi McCaughey, whose premature septuplets captured national attention? For some couples infertility is just a matter of donated sperm or eggs, but questions about the acquisition of these can arise. Sperm banks have been around for many years, but the harvesting of a healthy woman's ova for surrogate use or implantation in an infertile female is relatively new and remains controversial. One particularly interesting aspect of egg donation is the cost.

Some couples turn to science first for a solution, and when that is not successful or prohibitively expensive, they consider adoption. One of the biggest concerns with adoption, however, is the extremely small numbers of infants available in the United States.

It has been suggested that if a couple is infertile, it is a clear indication that they were just not meant to be parents. It is God's plan for the couple. Technology today can allow any couple to test, question, and challenge this theory. However, there are some who believe that trying to challenge what they think is the presence of God's wisdom is not practical. The medical intervention in infertility may be considered a sin in some conservative groups. The only acceptable solution to the problem is prayer.

CONCLUSION

Infertility is a life-altering realization for couples. It can lead to psychological turmoil as well as financial difficulty given the cost of infertility treatments. This psychological turmoil can lead to emotional discomfort. A couple may find it stressful as they journey from evaluation to treatment in their efforts to conceive. When initial efforts for conception fail, couples might find themselves utilizing a reproductive specialist. Reproductive specialists assist with aggressive conception methods like hormone stimulation, artificial insemination, and in vitro fertilization. Couples facing infertility have many options for conception. The question usually is whether they can endure the steps it will take to conceive. With infertility being covered in some portion by insurance companies, infertility problems today are more manageable, although infertility itself raises many challenging questions about the definition of family, the role of women in society, and reliance on science.

See also Childfree Relationships; International Adoption; Surrogacy; Transition to Parenthood; Transracial Adoption.

Further Reading: American Pregnancy Association. "What is Infertility?" 2007. http://www.americanpregnancy.org/infertility/whatisinfertility.html; Beer, Alan E., Julia Kantecki, and Jane Reed. *Is Your Body Baby-Friendly? Unexplained Infertility, Miscarriage, and IVF Failure*. LaSalle, Ont.: AJR Publishing, 2006; California Cryobank, Inc. http://www.cryobank.com; Domar, Alice. *Conquering Infertility*. New York: Penguin Books, 2002; Endometriosis Association. http://www.endometriosisassn.org; Feminist Women's Health Center. "Menstrual Cycles: What Really Happens in those 28 Days?!" http://www.Fwhc.org/health/moon.htm; Fertile Thoughts. http://www.fertilethoughts.com; Hewitt, Sylvia Ann. *Creating a Life: Professional Women and the Quest for Children*. New York: Miramax Books, 2002; interMDnet Corporation. "The Doctor Will See You Now." 2008.

http://www.thedoctorwillseeyounow.com;IVF-Infertility.com.http://www.ivf-infertility.com/; RESOLVE: The National Infertility Association. http://www.resolve.org; Saake, Jennifer. *Hannah's Heart: Seeking God's Hope in the Midst of Infertility.* Colorado Springs, CO: NavPress, 2005; Toth, Attila. *Fertile vs. Infertile: How Infections Affect Your Fertility and Your Baby's Health.* Tucson, AZ: Fenestra Books, 2004.

Nataylia Ketchum

INTERNATIONAL ADOPTION

International adoption, also known as transnational adoption or intercountry adoption, is the process of a prospective adoptive parent seeking and obtaining a child for legal adoption from a country other than that of the parent's citizenship. For residents of the United States, children are available for adoption from over 50 countries. However, U.S. residents are ineligible to adopt from Canada, Australia, and Western Europe. Residents of the United States adopt more children through intercountry adoption than do the residents of any other nation. The practice has garnered more attention in recent years as Hollywood celebrities flaunt their adoption-created families. Parents in the United States are turning increasingly to international adoptions as a way to create their families. Since 1971, more than 330,000 children have been adopted from foreign countries. Recent numbers indicate nearly 23,000 international adoptions by American parents in 2005 (www.travel.state.gov). Comparably, in 1994 there were approximately 8,000 international adoptions.

The dramatic rise in international adoption can be attributed to war, poverty, and the lack of social welfare in the children's home countries. Factors in the United States that contribute to the increase in international adoptions are a disinclination toward foster care adoptions, perceived difficulties with domestic adoptions, and preference toward adopting infants in lieu of older children. As fewer healthy white infants became available in the United States, parents seeking children with these characteristics began to look elsewhere. Additionally, prospective parents in the United States have a greater amount of expendable income compared with couples from other developed countries. These financial resources are necessary because an average international adoption processed through a private agency can easily cost between $7,500 to $30,000, depending on the child's country of origin and adoption service used (www.statistics.adoption.com).

INTRODUCTION

In the United States, the vast majority of children who are in need of adoptive parents are older children. Statistics on the ages of children adopted in the United States gathered in 1998 by the Adoption and Foster Care Analysis and Reporting System (AFCARS), showed that fewer than 2 percent of children that were in need of adoption were two years old or younger. For families seeking an infant, international adoption is increasingly becoming the answer. Most international adoptions are of infants and toddlers, with the majority of these children adopted from China, Guatemala, Russia, and South Korea. The number of children adopted from each of these countries varies from year to year, but these countries have been generally supportive of international adoptions. Increased infertility rates have also played a role in the rise in international adoptions. Infertility rates have been on the rise as more and more couples in the United States choose to postpone having children until later in life. For some of these couples, their goal of having a family can only be realized with an adoption.

With the large number of internationally adopted children entering the United States each year come many challenges concerning cultural socialization, developmental delays as a result of poor health, and potential behavioral issues. The language barrier alone causes many of the educational and social problems faced by children adopted from other countries. Additionally, these children sometimes face medical issues. According to the *International Adoption Guidebook,* children who are adopted from other countries are at risk for numerous medical conditions with the five most prevalent being hepatitis, HIV, fetal alcohol spectrum disorder, reactive attachment disorder, and sensory integration disorder. This creates special challenges for these families once they have navigated the bureaucracy to add the child to their family.

BACKGROUND

The history of international adoption in the United States began in earnest after World War II and continued during the early Cold War years. These two events served to globalize the adoption market as the plight of orphaned children overseas became more visible to Americans. Many of the orphaned children were the byproduct of relationships between U.S. soldiers stationed in foreign lands and local women. The story of these half-American children who were often cruelly treated in their home countries attracted the attention of people back home in the United States.

Many of these early international adoptions were the result of religious motivation. Lutherans, Catholics and Seventh Day Adventists were among the many religious groups that mobilized to facilitate international adoptions. Religious groups were also responsible for the formation of such organizations as the League for Orphan Victims in Europe (LOVE) and the American Joint Committee for Assisting Japanese American Orphans. The goal of these groups was twofold. Benevolence definitely played a huge part in that these people genuinely wanted to help with the plight of the orphaned children. Secondly, they could make healthy infants available to Americans who wanted to adopt.

Religious conviction to provide assistance was not the sole reason for international adoptions. Many American couples who wanted children of their own were pleased to discover areas such as the newly created West Germany where thousands of healthy children had been abandoned as a result of the war. The first families to adopt these children were military families stationed abroad, but the story quickly spread to the American media. In 1949 *Readers' Digest* published an article chronicling one of these families in an article entitled "Our International Family." In the 1950s, U.S. citizens were allowed to adopt children in foreign courts in absentia. These proxy adoptions were a popular way to adopt internationally, making it easy for parents to do so. Many child welfare advocates disliked this type of adoption because they felt it lacked regulation. The chief of the U.S. Children's Bureau at the time, Katherine Oettinger, believed that internationally adopted children were more likely to suffer abuse and disruption because their adoptions did not adhere to even minimum standards. Oettinger argued that while the government, philanthropies, and parents all respond to the idea of rescuing helpless children from likely deprivation (their hearts were in the right places), problems that exist in adoption are significantly harder to resolve in adoptions that span the ocean.

Beginning in the 1990s, Americans started adopting children from Central and South America. Guatemala has been very high on the list maintained by the State Department of countries that provide large numbers of children for adoption by American couples. Due to the end of Communism in countries such as Romania and the former Soviet Union, there has also been a dramatic rise in the number of adoptions from these countries. At the end of the Cold War, the United States sent numerous news correspondents to document social life in these places. Human interest stories served to publicize the plight of these children. Many times the children were living in deplorable conditions, lacking basic medical care. As a result, American couples began adopting these children in record numbers. In 2005, there were 4,639 Russian children adopted by American families (compared to 12 children of Russian origin adopted in 1991). By 2002, children from China, Russia, South Korea, Guatemala, and Ukraine accounted for 75 percent of foreign adoptees.

POPULAR INTERNATIONAL ADOPTION COUNTRIES

South Korean Adoptions

The Korean War (1950–1953) began the largest wave of international adoptions. In 1955 Harry Holt, an Oregon farmer and his wife Bertha, were so touched by the situation of the orphans from the Korean War that they adopted 8 of these children from South Korea. This story sparked widespread media interest around the country and many other Americans became eager to adopt these children. In response, the Holts created Holt International Children's Services, which as of 2007 had placed around 60,000 Korean orphans into American homes.

Foreign adoptions became so prevalent after the war that a special agency was created under the Ministry of Social Affairs in South Korea. In the 1950s the majority of children adopted overseas were the mixed-race children of Korean women and American male service members. These children were referred to as the dust of the streets, and were often treated cruelly in Korea. Eventually the practice of adoption became so widespread in South Korea that not only mixed-race children were sent for adoption, but children of poverty-stricken families were put up for adoption as well. South Korea became the largest supplier of children to the United States and other developed countries. Since the end of the Korean War, over 200,000 Korean children have been sent overseas for adoption, 150,000 of them to the United States. To this day, Koreans comprise the largest group of adoptees in both the United States and Western Europe. Because unmarried Korean women often face a severe social stigma for nonmartial births, they are likely to put their children up for adoption because this makes the women eligible for substantial financial support.

Vietnamese Adoptions

In the 1970s the Vietnam War was responsible for another wave of international adoptions by American families. In 1975 Operation Baby Lift brought 2,000 Vietnamese and mixed-race children to the United States for adoption during the final days of the war. Critics questioned whether this hasty evacuation was in the best interest of the children. The most contentious point was whether these children were technically orphans who qualified for adoption. This operation was plagued with lost and inaccurate records, casting a negative light on international adoption. In several well-publicized instances birth parents or other relatives later arrived in the United States requesting custody of children who had already been adopted by American families. This effort was also criticized as another example of American cultural imperialism.

Guatemalan Adoptions

As previously stated, Guatemala has become a popular country for adopting American couples; however, the number of Guatemalan adoptions is set to dramatically decrease due to a pronouncement from the president of Guatemala, Oscar Berger. He has announced, according to the Guatemalan Department of State, that effective January 1, 2008, all intercountry adoptions will be suspended. Due to this announcement, over 5,000 Guatemalan children who have already been matched with prospective adoptive parents will be without a family. This effectively leaves them in a state of uncertainty because they no longer have contact with their birthparents and also have no hope of being united with their adoptive parents in the foreseeable future.

Unfortunately, due to the instability in Guatemala, many agencies can no longer offer Guatemalan children a refuge with American parents. Guatemala is considered a third-world country and they do not have the financial resources, as in other countries, to support these children for the expected extended period of time it will take until adoptions are reopened. One of the primary reasons that so many children were available for so long in Guatemala relates to high levels of poverty where birth parents may not be able to adequately care for all of their children and perceive adoption as a way to better their child's life. There has also been a long-standing concern that many Guatemalan children offered for adoption were actually stolen from their birth parents who did not wish to tender them for adoption. As a result of this, recently Guatemalan children entering the United States via adoption have been subject to DNA testing to ensure that they are, in fact, eligible for adoption and that they were not kidnapped from their birth parents.

Chinese Adoptions

China routinely has a high number of children adopted by U.S. parents. This is due in part to China's one-child policy. In the 1950s Communist Party Chairman Mao Tse-Tung encouraged Chinese families to have as many children as possible because he believed that this would strengthen the country. As a result, a huge population boom occurred. In the 1970s, however, the Chinese government began to fear that there would not be enough food or other resources for its growing population and something needed to be done to curtail the birth rate. This is how the one-child policy came into existence. In 1979, the Chinese government determined that Chinese couples residing in urban areas could only have one child without penalty. If these couples had more than one child they could receive jail time, pay heavy fines, and be ostracized from the community (china.adoption.com). If they chose to have only one child they, and the child, would be rewarded.

Additionally, China is a country where baby boys are revered and baby girls are seen as burdens on society. Inheritance and ties to the ancestral family are passed along the male line, so parents have a preference that their one child be a son. This is a very important element in Chinese society. As a consequence of the preference for male heirs, there are many more baby girls to be adopted than baby boys. Historically, female fetuses were more likely to be aborted and some female infants were killed by their parents. Rather than becoming the victims of infanticide, many times baby girls in China are abandoned in temples and hospitals or in subways or railway stations. When found, these children are taken to orphanages where they can become eligible for adoption. While Chinese law permits adoption of both male and female children to international parents, statistically many more female than male children are available. Despite the adoptions by U.S. families and other foreign parents, the problems facing female infants in China remain severe.

Former Soviet States and Adoption

In the early years of this decade, the former Soviet States, including Russia and Ukraine, were competing with China for the place from which the most children were being adopted by Americans. More recently, however, the numbers of children being adopted from Russia have declined significantly. One of the reasons was a stricter enforcement of adoption standards and additional required paperwork instituted by the Russian government. Also, adoptions were to be handled in a uniform way. Additionally, in 2006 the Russian government required a registration and re-accreditation for all foreign not-for-profit organizations operating in the country. This included adoption agencies. So there was a time, at least, where few agencies were available to assist clients. Some agencies are again being permitted to conduct business, although the accreditation process is slow moving.

On the social policy front, Russian President Vladimir Putin signed into law in late 2006 measures designed to enhance families in the country. In particular, subsidies for having additional children have meant that parents may be receiving support to care for their offspring rather than offering them for adoption when they are unable to provide for them. While some of this may have been done to sustain population growth, it might also have been the result of increasing Russian nationalism. Skepticism of American motives for adopting so many Russian born children can not be discounted.

BENEFITS OF INTERNATIONAL ADOPTION

There are many challenges that parents face when attempting to adopt internationally. But the benefits may outweigh the difficulties in many cases. Among the most attractive reasons for international adoption is that the children are legally available for adoption before being advertised or listed with agencies. This means that there is very little chance that birth parents will change their mind and take back the child at the last minute, as has happened with some open adoptions in the United States.

While the bureaucratic aspects of international adoption make it unlikely that one can adopt directly at a child's birth, as can happen in open adoptions in the United States, nearly one-half of the children who are adopted internationally are under the age of one when they meet their new parents and almost all are under the age of four. This factor is very appealing to American parents who would have many options for domestic adoptions if they preferred older children, but few when they prefer the youngest children.

There is a tremendous variety in the children that available for adoption. They are from different countries, of different ages and genders, and they have many different needs that adoptive parents might be able to fulfill. This variety means that parents can generally find the child with whom they will have the best fit. Multicultural families lead to greater tolerance and acceptance, supporting the politics of community and unity. Famous adoptive parents Angelina Jolie and Brad Pitt have such a multicultural family. Parents who have adopted children from poor countries often cite the opportunity they have to provide for the underprivileged child as a motivating factor in their decision.

While many domestic adoption agencies have limitations on who is eligible to adopt, some foreign agencies have less stringent guidelines, perhaps permitting older parents or singles to adopt when other avenues for domestic adoption are closed to them.

CONCERNS OF INTERNATIONAL ADOPTION

Because everyone dreams of a healthy, happy child, potential adoptive parents need to recognize that they may not know about medical problems. While generally parents get information about the child's health, they rarely know about the birth parents' health and backgrounds. The concerns extend to whether any prenatal care was available or attained by the birthmother. Children who were cared for in orphanages may have some additional special needs related to mental health and adjustment as a result of the institutional environment, though these are often resolved relatively quickly upon arrival in their new home.

International adoption remains costly, but again this varies by country. Agencies usually provide a list of expenses up front so that prospective parents can plan accordingly. The costs, however, do limit those persons eligible to adopt in this manner. This has led to the suggestion that international adoption agencies sell children to the highest bidders who can pay for fees, travel, and sometimes extended stays in foreign locales. Extortion has even been reported with some agencies. These scams claim a child is available, send details about the child, and get a commitment from prospective parents who send money to the agency only to be told later that the fees have increased and more money is needed, or the child is no longer available.

Adopting internationally can be a time-consuming and tedious process. The Unites States Citizenship and Immigration Service (USCIS) is a federal agency within the Justice Department that is responsible for overseeing citizenship issues for foreign-born persons who wish to enter the United States, including children. The USCIS must provide permission for the adoptive child to lawfully enter the United States prior to the adoption being finalized in the child's country of origin. The average time frame for an international adoption is 12 to 18 months, but much of this depends on the country of origin and whether the U.S. paperwork is prepared properly.

Some persons do not like to travel abroad. Although the amount of time that one must spend in the country of adoption varies, it is usually for a minimum of one week. A challenge for travel, however, is when one doesn't speak the language and requires the services of interpreters. Generally part of the agency fee goes toward providing facilities and services for the adoptive parents while they are in the country.

THE STATE OF INTERNATIONAL ADOPTION TODAY

International adoption continues to be a subject that is fraught with questions and remains controversial. These questions are important as the number of international adoptions continues to rise. It remains to be seen whether international adoptions are in the best interest of the child. Even though conditions may not be perfect in their home country, would it not be of benefit to be raised in the culture to which one is born? Will the child suffer discrimination or have difficulty identifying with their American-born parents? With all of the millions of dollars spent on legal processing, could it be better spent to improve conditions in these countries so that adoptions are no longer necessary?

These questions, and others, remain unanswered. Although, they are very important to consider because there are hundreds of thousands of children, and their adoptive families, that would like to know the answer. While in the earliest years of international adoption the concerns expressed by adoptive parents and the general public were primarily about transitioning to the new family and adjustment, with an occasional question about transmitting cultural heritage, today the concerns are expanded.

The concerns have shifted to include legal, criminal, and ethical issues affecting both birth and adoptive parents and the children. The options for parents who would like to adopt internationally are many, but they are always in flux. For example, as countries' laws regarding immigration or their political regimes change they are more or less likely to permit children to be adopted to foreign families. Not only do policies, laws, and procedural requirements change in other countries, they change in the United States as well. The Hague Treaty on International Adoptions, when ratified by all Hague Convention nations, is designed to help ensure ethical adoption practices so that all parties will benefit and have their rights maintained. One of the primary goals was to prevent the abduction, trafficking, or sale of children through intercountry adoption. Additional provisions were designed to protect both the birth and adoptive parents' rights. The Intercountry Adoption Act of 2000 was passed in the United States to implement the provisions of the Hague Convention Treaty, ratified by the United States in April 2008. These provisions are forcing some changes in the ways that international adoptions occur. Specifically, agencies must have a national accreditation with consistent standards of practice, and there must be a mechanism for filing complaints.

As the procedure for international adoptions changes in response to the Hague Convention, this is a confusing time for those wishing to adopt internationally. As the nations adhering to the Convention change, so do those nations' policies. There are also some shifts in which of the countries are being explored by prospective American parents. In 2007, according to the U.S. Department of State, there were 1,255 Ethiopian children adopted by U.S. Citizens, a three-fold increase from 2005. Changing patterns of adoption will be interesting to monitor.

See also Fictive Kin; Gay Parent Adoption; Infertility; Mail Order Brides; Transracial Adoption.

Further Reading: Adoption.com. "Cost of Adopting," 2007. http://statistics.adoption.com/information/statistics-on-cost-of-adopting.html; Adoptive Families Magazine. http://www.adoptivefamilies.com; Berquist, Kathleen Ja Sook. *International Korean Adoption: A Fifty-year History of Policy and Practice* (Haworth Health and Social Policy). Binghamton, NY: Haworth Press, 2007; Cartwright, Lisa, Kay Kendall Johnson, Laurel and Barbara Yngvesson. *Culture of Transnational Adoption.* Durham, NC: Duke University Press, 2005; Center for Adoption Support and Education. http://www.adoptionsupport.org; Davenport, Dawn. *The Complete Book of International Adoption: A Step by Step Guide to Finding Your Child.* New York: Broadway Press, 2006; Falkner, Elizabeth Swire. *The Ultimate Insider's Guide to Adoption: Everything You Need to Know about Domestic and International Adoption.* New York: Wellness Central Publishing, 2006; Gray, Deborah. *Attaching in Adoption: Practical Tools for Today's Parents.* Indianapolis, IN: Perspectives Press, 2002; Internation Adoption Center. http://www.adoptionclinic.org; Joint Council on International Children's Services. Guatemala 5000. http://www.jcics.org (accessed November 2007); Knoll, Jean, and Mary-Kate Murphy. *International Adoption: Sensitive Advice for Prospective Parents.* Chicago: Chicago Review Press, 1994; Miller, Laurie C. *The Handbook of International Adoption Medicine: A Guide for Physicians, Parents, and Providers.* New York: Oxford University Press. 2004; National Council for Adoption. http://www.adoptioncouncil.org; Schwartz, Margaret L. *The Pumpkin Patch: A*

Single Woman's Adoption Journey. Chicago: Chicago Spectrum Press, 2005; Trenka, Jane Jeong. *Outsiders Within: Writing on Transracial Adoption.* Cambridge, MA: South End Press, 2006; Uekert, Barbara. *10 Steps to Successful International Adoption: A Guided Workbook for Prospective Parents.* New York: Third Avenue, 2007; U.S. Citizenship and Immigration Services. http://www.uscis.gov; U.S. Department of State. Bureau of Consular Affairs. http://www.travel.state.gov.

Hayley Cofer

J

JUVENILE DELINQUENCY

The role of the family, as a social institution, is to essentially prepare children for adulthood. To accomplish this task, the family is comprised of values and norms and different statuses and roles, all of which are devoted to achieving the goals of the family as well as that of society. However, this is no easy task. Families are often scrutinized when a child displays delinquent behavior. Of particular concern are the ways that families might promote or prevent juvenile delinquency. Among the areas of concern when examining the link between family and delinquency are traditional family values, child-rearing practices, the influence of the mass media, and parental responsibility.

However, social scientists have identified a variety of other possible factors that they believe contribute to juvenile delinquency. These other factors include: the lack of parental supervision; a lack of discipline; a lack parental monitoring; the lack of attachment to pro-social institutions like school, community, and church; low income; poor housing; a large family size; low educational attainment; associations with other delinquents; drug or alcohol abuse; and the criminal behavior of parents and siblings. Social scientists suggest that it is not just one single factor, but many factors in conjunction with one another, that increase the likelihood of juvenile delinquency.

JUVENILE DELINQUENCY

In the United States, juvenile delinquency is a social problem affecting families, communities, and society as a whole. Federal Bureau of Investigation (FBI) statistics show that violent crime accounts for approximately 12 percent and that property crime accounts for approximately 88 percent of all serious crime in the United States. The FBI's Uniform Crime Reports (UCR) estimate that 1,417,745 violent crimes and 9,983,568 property crimes occurred nationwide in 2006, with 10,472,432 people arrested for both types of offenses. Of those arrested in 2006 for violent and property crimes, 372,559 (approximately 23.5 percent of the arrests) were persons under the age of 18, and of these arrests, 119,810 (approximately 32.2 percent) were of persons under the age of 15 (http://www.fbi.gov/ucr/cius2006/data/table_38.html). Given these statistics, it is understandable why there is concern over juvenile delinquency.

Juvenile delinquency refers to persons under a state-established age limit who violate the penal code. This means the law breaking was done by a child. In the eyes of the law, the only difference between a criminal and a delinquent is the person's age, and the state-established age limit varies from state to state. In the eyes of the law, a juvenile officially becomes an adult at 16 in three states, at 17 in seven states, at 18 in 39 states, and at 19 in one state. Furthermore, delinquency is comprised of two parts. The first part includes property crimes like arson, burglary, larceny, and motor vehicle theft, while violent crimes include assault, robbery, rape, and murder, all of which would be considered crimes if committed by adults. The second part includes status offenses that are law violations that only apply to juveniles. This would include curfew violations, running away, and truancy. These status offenses are not violations of criminal law, but are undesirable behaviors unlawful only for juveniles. It is believed that these offenses, if not dealt with, may lead to more serious delinquent behaviors in the future.

Therefore, the juvenile justice system takes steps to correct the behavior of juveniles and to try to change their behavior before they get involved in more serious property or violent crimes. It is the goal of juvenile courts, and has been since the first juvenile court was established in 1899, to prevent delinquent behavior and rehabilitate juvenile offenders as apposed to just punish them. This is why juveniles are not labeled "criminal" and their hearings are conducted in an informal atmosphere where testimony and background data are introduced as opposed to a trial that simply determines guilt or innocence. In addition, the juvenile-court judge plays more of a parental role, reviewing the behavior of the juvenile offender in a less threatening environment than that of an adult criminal court. The juvenile court judge then determines an appropriate form of discipline, if any, and a course of action designed to prevent future delinquent behavior. Interestingly, many researchers believe that the majority of serious delinquent offenses are committed by a relatively small group of offenders and expect this delinquent population to maintain the antisocial behavior into adulthood.

ARENAS FOR DEBATE

Family Values

The debate over the family's role in juvenile delinquency covers a variety of areas such as family values, child-rearing, the influence of the mass media, and parental responsibility. The central focus of this debate is on the lack of traditional family values in a so-called traditional family. Conservatives believe that alternative family forms like single-parent families, blended families, cohabiting families, and gay and lesbian families fail to instill traditional values in children. They believe that the traditional family is the foundation for strong values, norms, and an overall healthy society. Therefore, they push for a return to the traditional family, where mothers stay home and fathers are breadwinners, with a focus on traditional family values. In addition, they encourage parents to spend more time with their children and focus more on the family's needs as opposed to the individual's needs. For them, anything that threatens the family is considered a social problem. As a result, they believe that living together without marriage (i.e., cohabitation), premarital childbearing, divorce, and single parenting are social problems that weaken society and place children at risk. Conservatives point out that children are most affected by these social problems in that these factors not only increase their chances of ending up in a single-parent family, but they also increase their likelihood of living in poverty and put them at a higher risk for divorce as adults. The solution, according the conservatives, is to abolish no-fault divorce laws and discourage couples from living together in low-commitment relationships that favor so-called me first values that support individualism over commitment.

Liberals, on the other hand, are more tolerant and supportive of the various alternative forms of families such as singlehood, cohabitation, single-parent families, blended families, and same-sex families. They believe people have the right to choose what type of family is right for them. They point out that family diversity is not new and that a variety of family forms have existed throughout history. In addition, liberals believe that this diversity is actually a solution to the historical problem of male-dominated households. They believe that the traditional family limits the opportunities of women and traps them in a male-dominated environment, which, in some cases, can be an abusive environment. According to liberals, alternative family forms are not the problem. The problem lies in the lack of tolerance for alternative family forms, in the push for the ideal traditional family (which discourages opportunities for women), and in poverty, that have a greater impact on women and children. Therefore, liberals feel the solution is to encourage more tolerance for alternative family forms, expand affordable child care programs so more women can work, and to enforce antidiscrimination laws so working women will be paid as much men.

Child-Rearing

Much of the debate over child-rearing in single-parent families is focused on the lack of parental supervision and the lack of guidance. Critics point out that in many cases single parents simply do not have enough time to meet the demands of adequate child-rearing because of the demands placed on them to be the breadwinner and head of household as well as still maintain somewhat of a personal life. Unfortunately, the result is that children may not receive the parental supervision, guidance, and the emotional support they need to develop into law-abiding adolescents. Consequently, more delinquent children come from single-parent families than two-parent families. Estimates are that children from single-parent families are about 10 to 15 percent more likely to become delinquent than are children with similar social characteristics from two-parent families (Coleman and Kerbo 2006). Children who are raised in an affectionate, supportive, and accepting home are less likely to become delinquents. Moreover, children whose parents model pro-social behavior in addition to adequately supervising and monitoring their children's behavior, friends, and whereabouts, as well as assist their children in problem solving and conflict resolution are less likely to engage in delinquent behavior. The bottom line is that parents have the ability to teach their children self-control, right from wrong, and respect for others, or they can teach their children antisocial, aggressive, or violent behavior. Therefore, children who grow up in a home with parents that are uninvolved or negatively involved are at greater risk for becoming juvenile delinquents.

Of course, critics of child-rearing in single-parent families are not simply advocating more discipline. If parental discipline is too strict or too lenient it can promote delinquency. There is strong evidence to show that children raised in single-parents families, specifically mother-only homes, are at a greater disadvantage than those raised in two-parent families. Single-parent neighborhoods, particularly with high levels of mother-only households, have a higher rate of delinquency because working single-mothers have less opportunity to adequately supervise their children, leaving them more vulnerable to the influences of deviant peers. Critics also point out that in addition to higher rates of delinquency, children reared in single-parent families, specifically mother-only homes, are more likely to live in poverty, to score lower on academic achievement tests, make lower grades, and to drop out of high school.

The Mass Media

Another area for debate is the influence of the mass media in juvenile delinquency. The concept of mass media refers to television, movies, music, video games, print media, sports, and the Internet. All of these have considerable influence over our attitudes and behavior, especially for those under the age of 18. Not surprisingly, the mass media is the most controversial agent of socialization because of how much it influences our attitudes and behavior. Because we live in a society that seems to crave violence, it is no surprise that these different forms of mass media cater to the desires of the public by producing violent television shows, movies, music, video games, and overzealously cover violent incidents in the news media. This excessive exposure to violence not only desensitizes us as a society, but for those in under the age of 18, these influences seem to have a number of serious effects. Some of the effects include: (1) *aggressive behavior:* media violence teaches children to be more aggressive so they tend to be less sensitive to pain and suffering; (2) *fearful attitudes:* media violence causes children to be more fearful of the world around them; and (3) *desensitization:* media violence desensitizes children to real-life and fantasy violence, making it seem a normal part of everyday life. Exposure to media violence also increases a child's desire to see more violence in real-life and in entertainment, influencing them to view violence as an acceptable way to handle conflicts.

Other studies link excessive exposure to media violence to health problems, alcohol and tobacco usage, sexual activity, poor school performance, and more. These studies show that the effects of excessive exposure include: (1) decreased physical activity, which leads obesity and other health problems; (2) photic seizures; (3) insomnia; (4) a decreased attention span; (5) impaired school performance; (6) decreased family communication; (7) increased sexual activity, which may lead to teen pregnancy and sexually transmitted diseases; and (8) an increased usage of alcohol and tobacco. Children ages 8 to 18 spend on average 44.5 hours per week (equivalent to 6.5 hours daily) in front a computer, watching television, or playing video games, so that by the time a child reaches age 18, he or she will have witnessed on television alone, with average viewing time, over 200,000 acts of violence which include 40,000 acts of murder (http://www.mediafamily.org/facts/facts_vlent.shtml). Children will view more than 100,000 acts of violence, including 8,000 acts of murder, by their first day in junior high school (Kirsh 2006). Given the frequency of exposure to violence, children's violence and delinquency should not be surprising.

All media violence is not equal in its effects, however. The violence portrayed in cartoons is most often presented in a humorous fashion (67 percent of the time) and is less likely to depict long-term consequences (5 percent of the time) (http://www.babybag.com/articles/amaviol.htm). Considering that the average preschooler watches mostly cartoons, this poses a greater risk for younger children because they have difficulty distinguishing between fantasy and reality. Therefore, they are more likely to imitate the violence they have seen. Researchers indicate that parents can be effective in reducing the negative effects of violent media viewing. Some of this can occur by parental understanding and utilization of television ratings. Other suggestions include watching television with one's child to permit discussion of difficult issues, turn the television off if the program is unacceptable, limit the time and type of programs watched, prescreen programs with a VCR, and explain the differences between fantasy and reality.

In summation of the effects of the mass media, Leonard Eron and Rowell Huesmann, psychologists at the University of Michigan who have studied the viewing habits of children for decades, found that the single factor most closely associated with aggressive behavior in children was watching violence on television. In testimony before Congress in 1992, they stated that "television violence affects youngsters of all ages, of both genders, at all socio-economic levels and all levels of intelligence. The effect is not limited to children who are already disposed to being aggressive and is not restricted to this country" (http://www.abelard.org/tv/tv.htm). It is interesting that this has been a major issue for decades and that many key people, including former Surgeon General Dr. Jesse Steinfeld, have testified in numerous hearings on the topic yet it is still a major issue.

Parental Responsibility

Parental responsibility is yet another area of concern regarding juvenile delinquency. Fundamentally, parental responsibility suggests that parents are to ensure that their children are protected, their needs are met, and their behavior is monitored. In addition, parents are responsible for socializing their children by instilling in them a sense of right, wrong, and the norms of society, helping them develop the skills they need to participate in society and shaping their overall development so that they are productive, law-abiding adolescents and adults.

However, when parents fail to ensure that their child or children develop into law-abiding adolescents, who is to blame? To what extent are parents responsible for their children's behavior? This has actually been an issue throughout our nation's history, and over time various types of legislation have addressed this specific question. Historically, the overall objective of these various laws was to require parents to provide the necessities for their children and to prohibit abuse or abandonment of minor children. However, due to the growing concern over juvenile delinquency, legislators have been prompted to expand laws regarding parental responsibility. More recently, parental responsibility goes beyond simply feeding, clothing, and loving your children. Recent laws hold parents accountable for their child's actions by imposing various sanctions, including possible incarceration, fines, community service, and restitution. In addition, many states have enacted laws that require more parental involvement in juvenile court dispositions such as hearings, court-ordered treatment, counseling, training, rehabilitation and educational programs, and probation. Unfortunately, there is not enough comprehensive research on this subject to fully understand the effectiveness of parental responsibility laws. Whether the laws accomplish their intended purpose and have an effect on juvenile crime rates remains to be seen.

CONCLUSION

Solutions to the problem of juvenile delinquency are varied and have shown limited success at reducing crime among youth. Perhaps the slow pace of change is the result of the different schools of thought regarding the origins of delinquent behavior working in opposition to each other. Family, as the primary institution for rearing children, has been targeted as both the cause of and a preventive measure for juvenile delinquency. For some constituencies, the solution is encouraging traditional two-parent families with traditional values while discouraging other families forms such as single-parent families, cohabitating families, and same-sex families. For others, the solution is tolerance of alternative family forms and more focus on the overall well-being of children regardless of their parent's marital status or sexual orientation.

Social scientists have determined that it is not just one single factor that increases the likelihood of juvenile delinquency, but rather many factors in conjunction. Of the many factors, advocates have determined that a healthy home environment is the single most important factor and that adequate parental supervision is the second most important factor in decreasing the likelihood of delinquent behavior. Understandably, parents play a crucial role in a child's moral development, so it is their job to instill in their children a good sense of right and wrong and to promote healthy development in a healthy environment. Therefore, adolescents who live in a home environment with a lack of parental supervision and monitoring, poor or inconsistent discipline, a lack of positive support, a lack of parental control, neglect, and poverty are more likely to engage in delinquent behavior. On the other hand, for those adolescent's in a positive home environment, which includes family support, nurturance, monitoring, and involvement, statistics show they are more likely to engage in prosocial behavior. In other words, children need parental affection, support, love, cohesion, acceptance, and parental involvement. When these elements are missing, the risk of delinquency increases.

See also Addiction and Family; Foster Care; Attention Deficit Hyperactivity Disorder (ADHD); Parenting Styles; Sibling Violence and Abuse.

Further Reading: Albanese, Jay S. *Criminal Justice,* 3rd ed. Boston, MA: Pearson Education, Inc., 2005; Babybag.com. "Facts About Media Violence and Effects on the American Family." http://www.babybag.com/articles/amaviol.htm; Brown, Kevin D., and Catherine Hamilton-Giachritsis. 2005. "The influences of violent media on children and adolescents: a public health approach." *Lancet* 365 (2005): 702–710; Caldwell, Roslyn M., Susan M. Sturges, and N. Clayton Silver. "Home Versus School Environments and their Influences on the Affective and Behavioral States of African American, Hispanic, and Caucasian Juvenile Offenders." *Journal of Child and Family Studies* 16 (2007): 119–132; Children and Television Violence. http://www.abelard.org/tv/tv.htm; Coleman, J. W., and H. R. Kerbo. *Social Problems,* 9th ed. Upper Saddle River, NJ: Pearson Prentice Hall, 2006; Focus on the Family. http://www.family.org/; Kirsh, Steven J. *Children, Adolescents, and Media Violence: A Critical Look at the Research.* Thousand Oaks, CA: Sage Publications, Inc. 2006; Media Awareness Network. http://www.media-awareness.ca/english/issues/violence/index.cfm; National Institute on Media and the Family. http://www.mediafamily.org/facts/facts_vlent.shtml; Office of Juvenile Justice and Delinquency Prevention (OJJDP): A Component of the Office of Justice Programs. U.S. Department of Justice. http://ojjdp.ncjrs.org/; Quinn, William H. *Family Solutions for Youth at Risk: Applications to Juvenile Delinquency, Truancy, and Behavior Problems.* New York: Brunner-Routledge, 2004; Quinn, William H., and Richard Sutphen. "Juvenile Offenders: Characteristics of At-risk Families and Strategies for Intervention." *Journal of Addictions and Offender Counseling* 15 (1994): 2–23; Siegal, Larry J., and Joseph J. Senna. *Essentials of Criminal Justice,* 4th ed. Belmont, CA: Wadsworth/Thomson Learning, Inc., 2004; Territo, Leonard, James B. Halsted, and Max L. Bromley. *Crime and Justice in America: A Human Perspective,* 6th ed. Upper Saddle River, NJ: Pearson Education, Inc., 2004; U.S. Department of Justice. "Crime in the United States, 2006." http://www.fbi.gov/ucr/cius2006/data/table_38.html; Wells, L. Edward, and Joseph H. Rankin. "Families and Delinquency: A Meta-Analysis of the Impact of Broken Homes." *Social Problems* 38 (1991): 71–93; Wright, Kevin N., and Karen E. Wright. *Family Life, Delinquency, and Crime: A Policymaker's Guide. Research Summary.* Rockville, MD: Juvenile Justice Clearing House, 1994.

Tonya Lowery Jones

M

MAIL ORDER BRIDES

A mail order bride is a woman who advertisers herself as eligible to wed. These advertisements are usually, though not exclusively, directed toward men in more developed countries such as the United States, Canada, Australia, and Western Europe. In some instances the men might advertise themselves as available husbands and list the social standing they can provide for wives. This is seen in the Philippines due to current prohibitions on women's advertising of themselves. In the United States, a famous outlet for men seeking wives in this manner is *Alaska Men* magazine.

During the early 1900s mail order brides were referred to as picture brides because the relationship may have been initiated by the man with only a picture of the bride. He would likely never have spoken to her face to face until she arrived in the United States. Today, the Internet may provide the picture, but the principle is similar.

INTRODUCTION

The phenomenon of globalization has led to more than just the integration of business and culture. It has afforded greater opportunity to people throughout the world. Along with the ease of transporting goods half-way around the world, it has also become much easier and increasingly common for people to migrate to foreign countries in search of the prosperity Western nations can offer. The desperate and destitute conditions brought about by political turmoil, economic downfalls, and extreme poverty have led many to take drastic measures to achieve this dream. Each year, thousands of women arrive in the Untied

States, mostly from nations such as the Philippines, Russia, and Ukraine. Drawn by promises of gainful employment, education, and a better, more comfortable life, these women seek a husband as a means of entrance into the United States. Often, the men are seeking partners who are willing to master the domestic sphere rather than those who seek entrance into the professional world.

Proponents of the industry assert that these services offer opportunities for women that would otherwise be unattainable. Participation in looking for a partner through this method is left up to the discretion of the women who make the decision to become involved. Women are also given the opportunity to meet men with different personalities and lifestyles with which they are not acquainted.

This path to citizenship has drawn criticism from various human rights organizations and recently from governmental agencies. Opponents argue that services such as those offered by mail order bride agencies are doing nothing more than exploiting impoverished, ill-informed women for their own financial gain. Because of the lack of regulation of the industry, women risk lives of slavery, abuse, and virtual imprisonment instead of the riches they were promised. This, many argue, amounts to nothing more than human trafficking, an operation more prosperous and treacherous than the infamous slave trade of the seventeenth and eighteenth centuries.

BACKGROUND

The mail order bride industry has existed, in various shapes and forms, for centuries, and has been a part of the American landscape since the colonial days. Early settlers, men seeking prosperity as the United States continued to conquer the West, found themselves sending back home requests for a bride to come and join them. Through the pioneer era, as a consequence of there being disproportionately more men on the frontier than women, men would write home or even to Europe in search of a wife. These women not only provided some of the comforts of home for the men, but much-needed companionship during very difficult times. Men's magazines contained advertisements for marriage brokers who could assist in finding a suitable partner.

In the early eighteenth century colonization of Louisiana, for example, King Louis XV sent French girls to wed Louisiana colonists. These girls where known as casket girls in reference to the small trunks that they used to bring their belongings with them. This somewhat primitive form of the industry has morphed into one of global proportion.

MAIL ORDER BRIDE AGENCIES

The functions of mail order bride agencies have adjusted as technology has revolutionized the world. Originally, contacts were made through pen-pal clubs in which men and women would be matched through agency officials and then communicate through letters. If both parties agreed that the relationship was something that they wished to pursue, then the agency would assist them in arranging a face-to-face meeting that would ideally result in marriage. In many locales this is still the case because the potential brides may be from very poor countries with little access to telephones, not to mention the Internet.

With the advent of the Internet and e-commerce, however, the process has been modernized. Pen pal set-ups still exist, but are now more often in the form of e-mails. Today, both parties have the chance to see pictures of the other and a description of their lifestyle, personality, and what they are looking for before a relationship begins. Although today's technology has enabled greater independence during this process, mail order bride agencies still hold a vital role in arranging meetings and beginning new relationships. Not only do they maintain the listing of available women through websites and notebooks, but they may help to complete some of the paperwork necessary to gain a temporary visa for the woman to visit the United States. Some agencies, such as A Foreign Affair, offer so-called dating tours where men who are seeking wives travel to different locations to interact with many different potential partners, perhaps making a love or like match at that time.

The costs vary by the agency used, but generally from first search through to marriage, the process costs roughly $10,000. In the United States it is estimated that there may be as many as 400 international marriage brokers. The industry is minimally regulated by only a few nations. While several nations have begun to consider enforcing minimum standards of practice, the movement to establish an international protocol is in its infancy. In the United States, the International Marriage Broker Regulation Act of 2005 (IMBRA) attempts to safeguard foreign women through several provisions. Brokers are now required to obtain their male clients' criminal histories, including sex offender status, which is translated into the woman's native language and is given to her. It also limits the number of fiancée visas that a man can petition for. Finally, if an engagement occurs, the woman must be given information about domestic violence resources.

THE PARTIES

It is difficult to determine the prevalence of foreign women who enter the United States as brides because there are few hard statistics available. Estimates are that 4,000 to 6,000, or less than one percent of marriages each year, are arranged through foreign agencies. However, at the time of the IMBRA it was estimated that 8,000 to 12,000 men were using brokers to find mates. Statistics also indicate that brokered marriages have a lower divorce rate compared to other marriages. When a marriage does occur, spouses apply for citizenship for the wife and minor children, if she brings any to the marriage. Investigations and personal interviews are utilized by the Immigration and Naturalization Services in an effort to determine the legitimacy of the relationships on the behalf of both the man and the woman. This is to ensure that it is a bona fide marriage, and not just a tactic to attain citizenship for the woman.

Often times, women seeking the assistance of mail order bride agencies sincerely believe that this is their key to a better life both for them and their

FILIPINO MAIL ORDER BRIDES

The majority of women who are married as mail order brides around the world each year are from the Philippines. This has been the trend for some years. In the 1970s the government of the Philippines was looking for ways to expand the economy. They realized that they had a surplus of workers who could travel to countries with a deficit of workers. Many Filipinos living abroad in this capacity were able to send monies home to significantly elevate the economic standing of their families and country. This pattern has continued such that the most profitable export from the Philippines today is people. While not all of the women who leave the Philippines are mail order brides, this group does contribute significantly. Despite laws banning the advertising for brides in the country and the official government policy condemning the practice, there is little enforcement because the agencies in question are located outside of the Philippines or because they advertise the available husbands; a practice that is not banned.

Exporting Filipinas for brides has existed in the Philippines since the 1950s; however it was accelerated and became a business following the Vietnam War. During the war, some 10,000 American soldiers per day visited the Philippines and many married the women that they met there. After returning home, sometimes friends would see the positive relationship and desire to marry a Filipina themselves. Friends and family members of the wife were often selected to come to the United States to marry the husband's friends. Formal matchmaking companies soon followed. The internet has proven to be a very useful tool in international marriage markets. Two of the websites that specifically focus on Filipinas are www.filipinaladies.com and www.filipinawives.com.

Today, the issues for Filipinas are similar to those of all mail order brides; avoid exploitation while you try to make a better life for yourself and your family. An organization known as the Gabriela Network hopes to help them do just that. This is an international nonprofit organization founded by a Filipina that aims to end the trafficking of women.

family members remaining in their home country. Overwhelmingly they are from countries in Southeast Asian, Eastern Europe and South America. Most are in their late teens or 20s and, just as in the Western world, are bombarded daily with media images of the riches available in other lands, including those of a financial, educational, and personal nature. These types of advancements are often unfathomable in their country of origin. In an effort to lure the man, the women often play into gender stereotypes of ultra-femininity. There are websites, such as www.goodwife.com, that provide information to these women about what American men desire in a partner.

Many of the men to whom this industry caters have sought out such services due to their dissatisfaction in relationships with women in their own culture. At the heart of this is usually value differences, primarily the emphasis modern women put on educational and occupational advancement as opposed to placing family life as their top priority. These men, primarily Caucasians, come from all walks of life, socioeconomic classes, backgrounds, and are generally between ages 30 and 60. They do tend to hold conservative political views. In many cases they are distressed with the independence of American women and are looking for a more traditional marital model. Social critic Marc Rudov argues that American woman make it too hard on American men, that they are too demanding, and are unwilling to fulfill traditional roles in the home. His website reflects the merging of twenty-first century hyper-sexuality with the gender role model of the 1950s.

While the majority of men seeking mail order brides are from Western Europe, North America, and Australia, it is a significant practice elsewhere. Currently a marriage brokerage system exists between Vietnam and Taiwan in which over 80,000 Taiwanese men have purchased Vietnamese brides in the last 10 years.

THE DEBATE OVER THE INDUSTRY

Support for International Marriage Brokering

Supporters of the mail order bride industry point to the large number of women who voluntarily register to participate in the programs as evidence of their legitimacy and social value. By providing a link to the Western world, they are simultaneously assisting them in improving their own, as well as their families', social position. They argue that without such services the women would have no escape from the hopelessness of poverty and oppression. Indeed, many of the women who have participated in the programs credit the agencies for exactly that. They are grateful for the opportunities that have been afforded them. Since their introduction to the Western world, they have experienced prosperity to the extent of being able to assist family members, either financially or with an ability to help them gain citizenship.

Another reason for appreciation that is often cited is the preferable characteristics of men in America as opposed to the men in their native country. American men, they claim, treat women better. They are more appreciative of how hard the women work managing the household, are more responsible citizens, and are less likely to be abusive or to drink excessively. Similarly, many have argued that these marriages are healthy for the U.S. economy and society as a whole. By finding wives who value the traditional roles of homemaker and mother, they assert that they are creating a positive and more stable environment for their children than is widely found in the modern dual-earner relationships.

The potential long-term courtship of a mail order bride and spouse can allow them a reasonable opportunity to know one another. Particularly in cases where men live in remote areas, they may have difficulty finding a partner locally. Likewise if he is shy or not a particularly good conversationalist, he may be much more comfortable expressing himself via correspondence.

Criticism of International Marriage Brokering

Criticism of the mail order bride industry often centers on the concern over the safety, well-being, and potential exploitation of the women who are involved.

Until quite recently, the lack of regulation has meant that men could participate without background checks or even a face-to-face evaluation to determine financial or psychological stability. Indeed, currently men are just required to disclose a criminal history, but not barred from meeting potential partners. Men who seek to prey on naïve women, it is argued, are strongly attracted to organizations advertising women available for relationships and even marriage. These women, unfamiliar with American customs or the English language, become largely helpless when they entrust themselves to men who have the capability to control their access to vital social, educational, health, and legal resources. Consequently, they become sitting ducks for whatever treatment the husband wishes to bestow upon his wife.

This inherent ease in seeking a partner, not for love but for self-gratification and exploitation, has led numerous global human rights organizations to label the mail order bride industry as a socially unacceptable form of human trafficking. Women can become coerced into participating through empty promises of safety and prosperity. Company officials are often aware of the potential dangers of marrying a man one knows nothing about. Unfortunately, these concerns are rarely relayed to the vulnerable women. In fact, it has been reported that women have been told by company officials that any attempt to seek legal or medical assistance would at best result in disbelief and would likely lead to deportation, although this is inaccurate. Layli Miller-Muro, founder and executive director of Tahirih Justice Center, has been concerned with these exact issues. Her organization was instrumental in writing the IMBRA after a Ukrainian woman came to her organization seeking help to escape her abusive American husband. Because women may know virtually nothing about the men because all of the information provided by the agencies is about the women, they are at a serious disadvantage.

Many men who have been accused of domestic violence against wives whom they have met through international matchmaking agencies claim that the charges were falsified solely as a means of gaining citizenship independent of a marriage. They have developed internet discussion boards to share their stories. They perceive themselves as the exploited victim, having given their love away only for it to be ultimately denied and to be accused of heinous crimes. If a marriage ends because of domestic abuse, the alien spouse can apply for a waiver which could possibly allow her to remain in the United States.

An emerging criticism of the dating tours, where men spend several days in a foreign country being introduced to many eligible partners, is that they amount to sex tourism rather than a legitimate attempt to find a suitable partner. In this case, it is argued, prostitution is just using a different name. Again the woman are exploited due to their hope for financial or lifestyle improvements.

CONCLUSION

Mail order bride agencies provide services which can serve a vital role in the lives of many women who have no other opportunity to seek asylum from a life of poverty and hardship. An unfortunate consequence of this is that the occasional woman will find not a loving husband but an abusive and exploitive relationship. It is a risk the participants take when they agree to participate. However, it has also been well documented that the agencies often do a poor job of honestly explaining the dangers to these women, or even worse, they refuse to admit that dangers exist. Because of the global expanse of the trade and the vast majority of providers, regulation of the industry has proven all but impossible. While more countries are considering, and even passing, legislation to monitor the programs, international standards of practice are far from a reality.

International marriage brokering, accelerated by the Internet, has become big business and is growing all the time. Not only is the industry growing, but it is moving away from the fringe of society and becoming more mainstream. Present estimates suggest that there are over 100,000 women around the world that are listed as available for marriage to Western men.

See also Arranged Marriage; International Adoption; Marital Power; Mate Selection Alternatives.

Further Reading: Constable, Nicole. *Romance on a Global Stage: Pen Pals, Virtual Ethnography, and "Mail-Order" Marriages*. Berkeley: University of California Press, 2003; Enss, Chris. *Hearts West: True Stories of Mail-Order Brides on the Frontier*. Guilford, CT: Two Dot Press, 2005; Larsen, Wanwadee. *Confessions of a Mail-Order Bride: American Life through Thai Eyes*. Far Hills, NJ: New Horizon Press, 1989; Minervini, Bibiana Paez, and Francis T. McAndrew. "The Mating Strategies and Mate Preferences of Mail Order Brides." *Cross Cultural Research* 40 (2006): 111–129; *In The Name of Love: Modern Day Mail Order Brides* (Film). 2005. Harriman, NY: New Day Films; Susie's Alaska Men Magazine. http://www.alaskamen-online.com.

Courtney Blair Thornton

MANDATORY ARREST LAWS

With the dubious distinction as one of the most common forms of violence in human history, domestic violence continues to disrupt lives and stir controversy in the twenty-first century. Also referred to as intimate partner violence, domestic violence has been both celebrated and condemned across time and cultures. As globalization continues to occur and various groups attempt to assimilate into U.S. society, domestic violence is destined to remain an important issue for generations to come because different attitudes toward domestic violence remain in competition in the culture. A wide range of tactics have been employed to reduce the incidence of such crimes, ranging from treating it as a private matter that is to be dealt with solely within the confines of a family to obliging the arrest of those accused. The former strategy, the standard historically, has all but vanished today while the latter, known as mandatory arrest, is thriving. Questions remain about mandatory arrest policies, including their origins, purposes and criticisms, as well as other intervention techniques that compete with these zero-tolerance statutes. Many religious texts, including the Bible and the Koran, have been interpreted as supportive of a male's domination over his wife. Centuries of so-called honor killings have been cheered by communities around the world who subscribe to the belief that a perceived violation of religious morals is justification for the violent murder of female family members. English Common Law of the 1700s introduced the rule of thumb law. This law allowed husbands to beat, or discipline as it was often referred to, their wives with a stick without fear of castigation, so long as the rod was no larger in circumference than the man's thumb.

For decades after such actions were no longer deemed socially acceptable, and were even publicly condemned, the legal system continued to turn a blind eye to domestic violence. Such unfortunate circumstances of battering were seen as private matters, ones in which police intervention served as more interference than intervention. With the passing of the Nineteenth Amendment, women not only gained the right to vote but also began to advance awareness of the seriousness of domestic violence. The decades to come brought about drastic changes in how both the public and policy makers looked at these crimes. Family courts were developed and abuse became legal grounds for divorce in New York. Police in Washington, D.C. were given the authority to make an arrest without a warrant in these situations, although they rarely exercised that ability. It was not until the 1980s, after significant gains to the social status of females had occurred through the Women's Rights Movement, that more restrictive legal consequences became expected policy. The primary means of such reform was through the implementation of mandatory arrest policies. This meant that law enforcement officers who arrived at a scene and determined that domestic violence had occurred, or was occurring, were required to arrest the offending party. These laws were enacted in much of the country and were designed to provide protection for the victim while simultaneously serving social justice.

Recently, however, such strategies have come under heavy criticism from the same victims' rights groups who once urged the passage of such laws. One illustration of the failure of such prevention and intervention strategies is the widely publicized case of professional football player and actor O. J. Simpson. Despite years of documented violence against his wife, Nicole Brown-Simpson, he was found not guilty of her murder and the murder of Ron Goldman. Two years after this verdict, however, he was found civilly liable for their deaths and ordered to pay $33 million to the victims' families.

DOMESTIC VIOLENCE: BASIC FACTS

The majority of victims in reported cases of domestic violence are women. For this reason, future references herein will refer to women but should be equally applied to any victim, regardless of gender. The spectrum of domestic violence is broad and includes physical, psychological, and sexual mistreatment or exploitation as well as forced economic, social, and spiritual isolation. Although expansive, all of these acts include some degree of intimidation, aggression, and trauma—often expressing an attempt to control. While some argue that one type of intimate partner violence is more damaging than another, it is difficult if not impossible to form a sound conclusion as to the difference in overall impact on the victims' psychological well-being. Indeed, it varies by intrapersonal and sociocultural factors.

In 2003, the Centers for Disease Control and Prevention (CDC) estimated that 2 million injuries and 1,300 deaths in the United States alone could be attributed to incidences of intimate partner violence. Although research has identified several characteristics that have been shown to increase the likelihood of a domestic violence situation, it is a problem that cannot be connected with a specific social, economic, or religious group. Rather, it is a vice seen across all reaches of the population. Parenting children before age 21 has been found to be a positive correlate, as has low socioeconomic status, low levels of education, and alcohol or drug use. Traits of the abuser include low self-esteem, mental illness, and a history of having been abused themselves.

The consequences of domestic violence are often overlooked by the public, discarded as relevant only to the individual. But, as new policies continue to be developed to address this problem, a thorough and empathetic understanding becomes increasingly important. In addition to physical injuries, many victims also experience long-term physiological difficulties, such as cardiovascular and gastrointestinal disorders. Domestic violence has also been related to symptoms of posttraumatic stress disorder (PTSD), an increase in suicide among females, and involvement in dangerous activities such as high-risk sexual behavior, use of mood-altering substances, and eating disorders. Because such costs could be used to endorse the belief that domestic violence is a personal issue, it is important to note the impact it has on the United States economy and society as a whole. The CDC estimates that the cost of these crimes exceeds $8.3 billion annually, in addition to the amount of workplace and household productivity lost. This cost is in medical treatment, police protections, and court resources.

CHILDREN AND DOMESTIC VIOLENCE

Unfortunately, children often witness the violence between their parent and the parent's partner. In fact, it has been found that the majority of men who abuse women also abuse children. It is therefore vital to weigh the impact of domestic violence on children when developing policies to address it.

Annually, more than three million children are the victims of abuse or neglect. The effects of these experiences are no less devastating than those suffered by the adult victims. A particularly debilitating injury specific to this population involves a disruption in early brain development that is often the result of severe trauma. Longitudinal studies have found that these children are more likely than children who neither witnessed nor experienced domestic violence to be involved in tumultuous relationships in adulthood, thus continuing the cycle of domestic violence and abuse.

MANDATORY ARREST: THE PARADIGM SHIFTS

In the 1980s, feminist groups pushed law enforcement agencies across the nation to examine alternative approaches to domestic violence that would have a more significant and lasting impact on the problem than traditional hands-off practices, such as allowing the matter to be resolved in private or suggesting a cooling-off period. One such jurisdiction was Minneapolis, Minnesota. Known as the Minneapolis Domestic Violence Experiment (1981–1982), the project was intended to determine whether mandatory arrest policies were more effective than current practices in reducing the rates of repeat offending.

The experiment was a joint venture between the National Institute of Justice, the Minneapolis Police Department, and the Police Foundation along with procedural recommendations by the psychological community to ensure the best possible response. The random assignment, or lottery, format required responding officers to apply one of three research interventions: removing the offender from the scene for eight hours, counseling the family on strategies for deescalating the situation, or actually arresting the offender. Follow-up interviews with victims were conducted by specially trained female interviewers to determine the extent to which they were satisfied by the intervention technique as well as what, if any, impact it had on continued violence in the relationship. Experts concluded from the Minneapolis Experiment, among others, that mandatory arrest policies were the most effective strategy for handling domestic violence situations because they simultaneously lowered the likelihood of repeat offenses and served to empower the victim by being attentive to her needs and sympathetic to her concerns for her safety and the safety of her nonoffending family members.

Since this experiment, many states have adopted mandatory arrest policies in an effort to increase public approval of their handling of intimate partner violence. Advocates claim that mandating the arrest of perpetrators protects the victim from further injury during the time immediately following the offense. By removing the victim from the decision-making process, a great deal of emotional distress is removed. The perpetrator may be less likely to blame the victim for his arrest, and perhaps be less likely to increase violence toward her at a later time. Proponents also claim that, due to the trauma and oppression they have faced at the hands of the abuser, women are unable to make an informed decision because their confidence and feeling of control over their lives has been attacked and crippled. Many women are satisfied with the police response when the offender is arrested and feel that law enforcement is truly concerned for their well-being. Conversely, other victims felt abandoned if they felt the offender was not treated harshly enough.

Mandatory prosecution policies often go hand in hand with mandatory arrest. The motivation for such legislation is similar to the rationale of law enforcement interventions; to empower the victims by proving that the justice system does indeed recognize the danger they face and will protect them from the perpetrator through any means necessary. Prosecutors in jurisdictions with hard so-called no-drop policies are required to pursue charges against all those accused of domestic violence, regardless of the victim's wishes. Protection of the public from a violent criminal is the primary concern in regards to such prosecutions, viewed as supreme to the concerns of a single person.

Many groups, including some victim's advocates and men's rights organizations, are upset with policies requiring the arrest of all those accused of domestic violence, claiming they are easily and often manipulated. While mandatory arrest laws have minimized the effect of police discretion on the outcome of a domestic violence situation, it is not uncommon for both partners to be arrested whether they were the aggressor, acted in self-defense, or were wrongly accused. On-sight evidence need not be found to substantiate claims of abuse in many states, and policies that require that the cases be prosecuted have dealt a handicapping blow to the legal system because time and manpower are spent on cases with little or no evidence supporting the charges.

Another criticism of mandatory arrest laws is that there are other, arguably more serious, crimes for which police are not required to make an on-the-spot arrest. Also, mandatory arrest does not allow for consideration of the victims' wishes. Police must arrest the offender even if the victim does not wish to press charges. For some, finding a way to come up with bond money for an unwanted arrest can be as damaging as the violence itself. Conversely, many women fear having their abuser arrested because of the threat of revenge upon his return to the home. As a result, they may choose not to report these crimes at all and, hence, not receive help because they see law enforcement not as an ally but as another controlling, authoritative figure. Additionally, many officers dread domestic violence calls because of the higher chance of injury to the officer in such a setting.

VICTIM EMPOWERMENT MODELS: A NEW PHILOSOPHY EMERGES

Victim empowerment models are becoming an increasingly popular form of domestic violence intervention being considered and implemented in many jurisdictions. The foundation of these strategies rests on making the victim feel as if he or she is in charge of the outcome of the situation, a position that often is entirely opposite of the deeply engrained victim mentality of someone who has been abused. Another research study in Minnesota, also during the early 1980s, was known as the Duluth Domestic Abuse Intervention Project. This experiment combined various community resources available to domestic violence victims including counseling, protective shelters, and legal advice so as to provide the most efficient response to this traumatized population. The findings of the Duluth Project led to an increased focus by corrections agencies on domestic violence offenders to decrease recidivism rates as well as highlight the unique needs of the victim. The goal was for offenders to offend less and victims to have all of their unique needs met by available agencies and resources.

The cycle of violence that often traps generations of families can be broken only through the determination of the victim(s) to learn from their experiences and prevent similar circumstances from surfacing in the future. Victim empowerment models respond to this sentiment. Often combined with soft-drop or victim-decided prosecution policies, the abused is encouraged to exercise control over many parts of her life which she may not have been able to do for quite some time. This can easily become overwhelming and it is common for women to be unable to follow through with charges and a trial the first time they attempt to do so. If the abuser violates her again, she is able to start the process anew with the knowledge that she was able to stand up for herself before. This leads to increased levels of confidence and a greater likelihood that she will seek restitution.

Victim empowerment intervention strategies have also been found to increase the public's confidence in the justice system by demonstrating empathy for the victim and determination in deterring future crimes. Researchers found in a 2003 study that victims who were allowed to drop charges against their offender were significantly less likely to suffer additional violence six months after the arrest than were victims who were forced to follow through with charges.

These techniques, much like mandatory arrest laws, have come under intense criticism. It is argued that women, frozen in the role of victim, are incapable of making an appropriate decision in regard to their safety and the consequences of their action or inaction. They may blame themselves or fear reprisal from the abuser and decline to have him arrested even if encouraged to do so by police. This often places officers in a delicate position where they must balance satisfying the wishes of an individual complainant and protecting the public.

CONCLUSION

There is little doubt that the United States, and indeed the world, has made tremendous strides in dealing more effectively with the epidemic of domestic violence. Law enforcement responses at the beginning of this century were almost nonexistent, sometimes perceived as condoning intimate partner violence and certainly keeping it in the private realm of family life. Through decades of activism by feminist organizations and victims' rights groups, both the public and the government have become aware of the enormity of the problem as well as the difficulties faced by those who find themselves in these relationships. In addition to the proliferation of domestic violence shelters and counseling centers offering emotional support and recovery, many legal statutes have been passed that have sought to offer much-needed assistance to these families. One such policy, mandatory arrest, has increased the faith of many victims in the criminal justice system by acknowledging their struggles and working to ease their plight. Still others criticize the strategy as continuing the controlling schema of the abuser by not allowing the victim to have input on the outcome of the situation. Other intervention strategies, known collectively as victim empowerment models, are becoming increasingly popular. They help to diffuse the primary criticism of mandatory arrest, that the victim has no power to determine the fate of the offender, by encouraging the victim to be the decision maker about whether an arrest is made or prosecution results. Supporters say that this allows victims to begin to take back control over their lives while critics argue that the victim mindset is not an appropriate one for making decisions that could potentially determine the fate of one's abusive partner.

See also Battered Woman Syndrome; Domestic Violence Behaviors and Causes; Domestic Violence Interventions; Religion, Women, and Domestic Violence.

Further Reading: Break the Cycle: Empowering Youth to End Domestic Violence. http://www.breakthecycle.org; Centers for Disease Control and Prevention. "Child Maltreatment." http://www.cdc.gov/injury; Centers for Disease Control and Prevention. "Intimate Partner Violence: Overview." http://www.cdc.gov/ncipc/factsheets/ipvoverview.htm (accessed May 15, 2007); Centers for Disease Control and Prevention. "Understanding Child Maltreatment, 2006." http://www.cdc.gov/injury; Ford, D. A., and S. Breall. "Violence against Women: Synthesis of Research for Prosecutors." National Institute of Justice. http://www.ncjrs.gov/ pdffiles1/nij/grants/199660.pdf; Geffner, Robert A., and Alan Rosenbaum. *Domestic Violence Offenders: Current Interventions, Research, and Implications for Policies and Standards.* Binghamton, NY: The Haworth Press, Inc., 2002; Han, E. L. "Mandatory Arrest and no Drop Policies: Victim Empowerment in Domestic Violence Cases." http://www.bc.edu/ schools/law/lawreviews/meta-elements/journals/bctwj/23_1/04_TXT.htm (accessed May 19, 2007); Legal Momentum, Advancing Women's Rights. http://www.legalmomentum.org; Mills, L. G. "Mandatory Arrest and Prosecution Policies for Domestic Violence: A Critical Literature Review and the Case for More Research to Test Victim Empowerment Approaches." *Criminal Justice and Behavior* 25, no. 3 (1998): 306–319; Minnesota Center Against Violence and Abuse. "History of Domestic Violence: A Timeline of the Battered Women's Movement." http://www.mincava.umn.edu/documents/herstory/herstory.html (accessed May 26, 2007); National Coalition Against Domestic Violence. http://www.ncadv.org; National Network to End Domestic Violence. http://www.nnedv.org; Roberts, Albert R. *Handbook of Domestic Violence Intervention Strategies: Policies, Programs, and Legal Remedies.* New York: Oxford University Press, 2002; Sherman, L. W., and R. A. Berk. "The Minneapolis Domestic Violence Experiment." *Police Foundation Reports* (1984); Shoop, J. G. "Children in Violent Homes Need Better Protection, Report Says." *Trial* 30, no. 11 (1994): 114–116; Support Network for Battered Women. http://www.snbw.org; VAWFV: Violence Against Women and Family Violence. "NIJ's Violence Against Women Research and Evaluation Program: Selected Results." http://www.ojp.gov/nij/vawprog/selected_results.html (accessed May 16, 2007).

Courtney Blair Thornton

MARITAL POWER

When most people think about marriage, they rarely consider that power differences between marital partners exist, and they are even less likely to believe that they matter for how couples construct their daily lives. Many family researchers, however, believe that the power balance in a relationship is critical for many aspects of marital success, including how the couple handles childrearing, finances, and even their sexual relationship. One of the biggest controversies in a discussion of marital power is the source of the power differences. Other questions revolve around whether power should be equally shared between spouses.

Research has focused on how power influences the decision making in personal relationships.

INTRODUCTION

Power refers to the ability that one person has to influence another. When you can influence someone else's attitude, behavior, or outcome, we say that you have power. Despite most marital partners' reluctance to talk about which partner holds more power in the relationship, perhaps ignoring the presence of power in a quest for equality, all relationships include a power component. Bosses have more power than employees, parents have more power than children, and husbands have more power than wives.

Power has been a key sociological concept since the beginning of the discipline. It has been defined in a number of ways and researchers have not always agreed about the most appropriate definition. Two of the approaches to the concept of power can be traced back to sociological founders Karl Marx and Max Weber. Karl Marx defined power in terms of class relations between the rich and poor and the relative economic power that each possessed. Max Weber on the other hand defined power as a person's ability to control people and to enforce one's will despite opposition or resistance. Weber's definition is based on social relationships and includes the ability to shape people's beliefs and values. Sociologists approach the study of marital power from both perspectives and each can contribute to an understanding of how power matters in personal relationships, especially marriage. More recent conceptions of power attempt to move beyond a strictly economic (Marxian) or relationship (Weberian) standpoint with regard to power between spouses. These researchers show how marital power is negotiated by the participants in the marriage and has led to significant consideration of whether there could be a marriage based on equality; a peer marriage.

MARITAL POWER AND GENDER INEQUALITY

Scholars may disagree on the specific economic or ideological antecedents of marital power, but most start with the assumption that variations in power are due to one's gender, with men having more power than women. One controversy within the study of social stratification, or how various characteristics are differentially valued by society, asks whether race, social class, or gender is the characteristic that results in the most prominent form of discrimination based on power. Race, a categorization of various physiological traits, the most visible of which is skin color, has been a stratification variable in the United States from the beginning of the nation. Social class refers to a person's standing as poor, in the middle, or wealthy, and is usually determined by some type of income measure. In the United States, those persons who are lower class and poor have the least amount of power. Gender is being masculine or feminine and is the social role that one is expected to play based on being biologically male or female.

Noted researcher William Julius Wilson studies the link between race and social class and argues that race is less significant than social class. Cynthia Fuchs

Epstein, however, finds that gender is the most fundamental, persistent and arguably the deepest divide in the world today. This divide is visible when looking at the extent of inequality women face inside and outside the family. Women's inequality relative to men can be found world wide. Women earn less income compared with men, women run a risk of being subjected to physical violence and emotional abuse by men, women are more likely to lack adequate heath care (large number of women still die in child birth), and women around the world are more likely to be illiterate.

SOURCES OF POWER

There are a number of different sources of power in marriage. It is important to remember that power must be given or granted to another person through interactions with them. It is quite difficult for someone to just take power or exercise more power without someone giving them permission to do so. For personal relationships this means that one partner permits the other to be in control of certain things. For example, if a wife does not like to discipline children, she may cede the power to do so to the husband by using the classic phrase "wait till your father gets home." While the expectation is that fathers are more powerful at discipline than mothers, this tactic reinforces that approach. Over time, the mother's power to discipline would decline significantly. The sources of power in relationships relate to the partners' interactions with each other as well as to the cultural expectations for who is in control. Common sources of power are economics, status characteristics like gender, cultural norms, physical attributes, and relationship dynamics.

Economic Power

Economic power influences inequality. This was a central concern of the work of Karl Marx and Fredrich Engels. They suggest that before the advent of capitalism and the presence of private property the division of labor within the family was based on communal sharing of responsibilities and resources. Communal division of labor and resources means that ownership and use of property belong to all members of the group equally. Capitalism and private property, however, lead to the creation of wealth that had to be passed on to future generations. The new wealth and the need to preserve the wealth for future generations required developing rules for a clear line of inheritance. Men wanted the line of heritance to pass from themselves to their sons. In order to make sure these men were caring for their biological sons, women were sexually controlled, marriage was monogamous, and the traditional nuclear family became standard.

Economic standing as a source of power relies on the concept of limited resources. Certain resources are more valued than others and everyone does not have access to the same resources. Men and women have historically had different resources. With men more likely to be working, they have enjoyed more financial resources than have women. Additionally, the resource of education that allows one to get a more lucrative job until recently has been more accessible to men.

The impact of resource distribution has been tested in the division of household labor literature. The idea is that because men have greater economic resources, their work outside the home is highly valued. Women, even when they work for pay, tend to earn less income in the marketplace, therefore their contributions outside the home are less valued. With men's higher economic value, they are able to be released from chores at home, thus they do less housework. Blood and Wolf in *Husbands and Wives* and Schwartz and Blumstein in *American Couples* present a theoretical argument that the division of labor in the household is related to resource distribution. The research became known as resource theory, and the authors speculated that the balance of marital power is established through exchanging resources between the husband and the wife. The person who brings more resources to the marriage, and is less dependent on the partner, will have greater power in the decision-making process. Thus, husbands traditionally have more decision-making power than do wives.

Gender Ideology

Marx focused on power defined in terms of access and control of economic resources; however, Max Weber approached power as a social relationship and the ability to influence one's beliefs and attitudes. Some scholars have continued the economic argument as the driving force behind marital power, but other scholars point to gender ideologies. Gender ideology refers to a person's beliefs and attitudes toward men's and women's roles and responsibilities concerning marriage and the family. Gender ideology is usually seen as either traditional or nontraditional, sometimes called egalitarian. Gender traditionalism gives men and women different responsibilities. Women's responsibilities are in the home and include housework and child care, while men are expected to be the primary wage earners, the ultimate decision-makers, and are seen as being more suitable for political leadership. Individuals who believe in gender egalitarianism strive for a more equal division of household and family responsibilities than one based solely on gender.

Religion plays an important role in influencing gender ideology. Religion offers a script that defines beliefs, norms, and values that are supportive of family beliefs. This script is reinforced in theological messages communicated by formal and informal means, and interactions and networking that occur with members of the church that all support the best model of family life.

The beliefs, norms, and values enforced in the script are conservative and liberal at opposite extremes and lie along a continuum between the two based on the church's approach to family issues such as gender roles, abortion, and sexuality. For example Jews, unaffiliated persons, and Episcopalians are on the liberal end of the continuum while Southern Baptists are on the conservative side of the continuum. Thus religion can have a significant impact on the ways that males and females view their roles within the family. This is quite evident through the Promise Keeper's Movement that encourages men to be the leaders in their homes and take back the formal authority that they are supposed to have according to biblical prescription.

Cultural Norms

Based on gender ideology, the culture transmits information about the proper roles of men and women, husbands and wives. With regard to expectations of power, cultural prescriptions indicate that the power is supposed to be held by men. A system in which males dominate is referred to as a patriarchy. This argues that men have a legitimate right to exercise power over women. In the most extreme form of patriarchy, males have life and death power over females. In the United States today, patriarchy remains the norm, though is has been tempered over time by the gains of the women's movement and equality legislation. Areas where we see the continuing influence of patriarchy is the tendency to give children, even those conceived and born out of wedlock, the last name of the father, and women's likelihood of taking the husband's last name upon marriage. Owing to the fact that men today are more likely to desire that their wife works than that she stays home, patriarchy may be transitioning into a more androgynous society in which roles are no longer totally defined as belonging to males or females, but should be fulfilled by the persons with the most skill or interest in performing them. One demonstration of this is a greater number of stay-at-home fathers today.

While never the norm in the United States, there have been societies in which women have held the majority of the power. The pattern in which women are the more powerful sex is known as matriarchy. In this instance, based on their biological birth characteristics, women have a legitimate right to exercise power over men. Anthropologists have suggested that women's style of power is different than men's in that women attempt to build more coalitions and elicit cooperation, rather than using force to attain their objectives.

Physical Attributes

One's physical size and strength are a source of power, particularly of coercive power. Given that husbands are typically physically larger, taller, heavier, and stronger than their wives, this is a source of power that enhances men's position. Unfortunately, the physical differences between husbands and wives means that should he use that physical strength for violence and physical aggression, he is more likely to injure her. The intimidation she may feel based on his size relative to hers may be enough to swing the power to him.

Appearance, however, is a physical trait that historically has been equated with women's power over men. A particularly attractive woman may use her beauty to influence the choices that her partner makes or even which partner she can form a relationship with. The stereotypical idea that a wealthy man, regardless of his looks, will be able to acquire a more beautiful woman does have some merit.

Relationship Dynamics

Within the relationship, couples may not discuss power very often for obvious reasons, but it plays a role in how they relate to each other. One of the ways

AFRICAN AMERICANS AND MARITAL POWER

The discussion of the distribution of marital power in the United States frequently surrounds white men and women; however, the distribution of marital power has been different for African Americans. Growing out of a legacy of slavery, African Americans traditionally have not engaged in the gender-driven division of labor. As a result of long-term discrimination and subsequent poverty, African American women have always worked for pay, requiring men to participate in the household and creating a more equal sharing of power and decision making.

Today, African American males are more likely to hold liberal attitudes toward gender roles and equal division of household labor. For example, African American males outperform white males in cooking, shopping, and caring for children. Despite the long-term sharing of power, some African American males are beginning to report more conservative gender ideologies. The increasing belief in traditional gender roles may signify a new trend that reflects changes in the economic resources available to African American males. More African American males have achieved a middle-class standing with the resources to support a wife in a traditional fashion and some men are becoming more traditional in the expectation of power sharing. Just as the Promise Keepers encouraged men to be responsible to their wives and families and aspire to traditional male roles the Million Man March, organized by the Nation of Islam and targeting black males, emphasized how African American men should be better breadwinners and providers.

---

that power operates in relationships is through the principle of least interest. The relative love and need that each feels for the other has a lot to do with the interaction. For example, if a wife perceives few options outside of her marriage, she may be more inclined to acquiesce to her husband's wishes. She loses power because if the relationship were to end, she would be in a difficult situation. For women who have been homemakers for most of their adult lives, the loss of the husband's income and standing would be traumatic. The partner that has the most options outside of the marriage (for love, financial stability, personal growth, etc.) is able to demand more from the other partner and has more power to set the tone for the relationship.

NEGOTIATING MARITAL POWER

Thus far we have illustrated how power in a marital relationship can be driven by either access to economic resources or by the ability to influence cultural beliefs. These factors are based on structure. Structural factors are external to the individual and can constrain and determine opportunities available for individuals. An ongoing debate in the discipline of sociology that is important for understanding the way that power works in marriage is called the structure versus agency debate. The structure side of the argument posits that humans are like robots that are nonthinking and act only within the society's structure. In other words, individuals must act in a routine way, and have little awareness that they are doing so. Contrary to the structural argument is the concept of agency. Rather than advocating that people act within the limits of structure, agency argues that individuals are capable of acting independently and exercising free will. An agency argument with regard to power suggests that power is not rigid or absolute, but fluid and defined within relationships, emerging within a certain context, and being created and re-created.

John Bartkowski, in the book *Remaking the Godly Marriage: Gender Negotiation in Evangelical Families,* argues that sociological research has presented marital power in evangelical families as a neatly packaged unified belief system with men wielding all of the power over women. However, he found the following three patterns of power negotiation within evangelical families: (1) husband headship/wifely submission—the husband could consult the wife, but the man had the final decision; (2) the moderates—submit to each other with both partners submitting to Christ; and (3) servant/leadership—the husband is the leader but also a servant to his wife. In the servant/leadership model husbands lead by discussing matters then reaching a final decision. These patterns suggest that there is a great deal of flexibility with regard to how individual couples negotiate their power, even when a model is provided. Ultimately, Bartkowski suggested that the patterns of power negotiation among couples are ambiguous and full of exceptions.

CHANGING GENDER IDEOLOGY

Support for individual coupled negotiations of marital power may not be surprising given how dramatically gender ideology changed during the twentieth century. Throughout the first half of the century, wide support existed for a traditional division of labor, in which men made the money in the workplace and women were responsible for household tasks and child care. In the last half of the century, researchers documented the shift toward a more egalitarian gender role ideology. Egalitarian attitudes started to increase in the 1960s, with married women, especially those with younger children, moving into the workplace. Beliefs about appropriate gender behaviors continued to liberalize for three decades, from the 1970s through the 1990s; however, a slowing of those changes occurred in the 1980s and 1990s due to what Faludi calls a "backlash" against equality.

Factors influencing a changing gender ideology can be divided into micro (on the level of the individual) and macro (on the level of the social structure) components. Individual changes in gender ideology show that men's attitudes have remained more conservative on gender issues and their attitudes have changed more slowly than women's. Other individual changes can be attributed to broader social change, including shifts in attitudes toward religious beliefs, political allegiance, socialization values, and support for civil liberties. In addition, other micro-level factors found to influence gender ideology include youth labor experience, educational attainment, and mother's gender-role attitudes.

Changing gender ideology can be attributed not only to changes in individual attitudes but also to changes in the makeup of the population due to births and deaths, or to historical and cultural contexts. Among the ideas supporting a structural change in gender attitudes is cohort replacement. A cohort is a group of persons of the same age and historic experience. Cohorts come of age in an historical context and are eventually replaced by younger cohorts who are raised in a different time within a different historical context. For example, cohorts who reached adulthood between 1985 and 1996 are the children of mothers who first entered the labor force in the 1960s and 1970s. Subsequently, the more liberal attitudes of the 1985 to 1996 cohort, persons who are negotiating marital power and decision making today, would be a result of their personal experience growing up.

FUTURE DIRECTIONS

One of the most contentious issues in discussions of marital power involves whether the power should or could be equally shared. Those who favor sharing say that the equality leads to a greater identification with the partner and stronger sense of fairness. However, couples who negotiate their own power arrangements may find it difficult to maintain and persons outside the relationship may question their choices. In her book *Peer Marriage: How Love Between Equals Really Works,* Pepper Schwartz interviewed couples who have created and managed equal relationships. Important elements of the peer marriage included putting the marital relationship first even before children and careers, having the marital partner as one's best friend, and developing a deep and true partnership based on equality, equity, and intimacy. Couples who choose a peer marriage must be constantly vigilant to avoid falling into familiar cultural patterns that divide power unequally.

Those in favor of a traditional arrangement, one that relies on a gendered division of labor, suggest that it is the best distribution of power because it has a long tradition of success. Among the more widely cited arguments is that a traditional division of labor is helpful for rearing children and takes advantage of men's greater earning capacity relative to their wives.

When discussing factors that influence marital inequality, one may wish to ask what society with more power equity would look like. It might be a lot like Sweden. Sweden has been described as the most egalitarian society on Earth and a leader in the modern women's movement. Equal rights for Swedish women has a long history with the right to an inheritance (1845), legal independence (1858), suffrage (1862 and 1918), university enrollment (1870), independence for married women (1890), political equality (1920s), sexual and reproductive rights (1930s), and access to equal education (1920s) coming much earlier there than in the United States. In addition to legal measures of equality, the family is less traditional with young adults more likely to cohabit than to marry, most babies born out of wedlock, and 70 percent of women with families holding full-time jobs. Some of these trends are no doubt the result of generous maternity and family leave policies by the Swedish government.

Despite the gains Swedish women have made, they still have not gained completely equal sharing of power. Swedish women still are more likely to experience employment discrimination (earning lower incomes than men), to work in traditional female jobs such as teaching, nursing, and social work, and are more likely to do more and carry the heavier burden of the housework than men. Even though Swedish women have not gained full equality, the family is certainly less traditional and gender roles are more egalitarian in comparison with other industrialized countries.

See also Battered Woman Syndrome; Employed Mothers; Family Roles; Housework Allocation; Mail Order Brides.

Further Reading: Bartkowski, John. *Remaking the Godly Marriage: Gender Negotiation in Evangelical Families.* New Brunswick, NJ: Rutgers University Press, 2001; Bartkowski, John. *Promise Keepers: Servants, Soldiers, and Godly Men.* New Brunswick, NJ: Rutgers University Press, 2004; Blood, R. and D. M. Wolf. *Husbands and Wives.* Glencoe, IL: The Free Press, 1960; Blumstein, Philip, and Pepper Schwartz. *American Couples: Money, Work, Sex.* New York: Simon and Schuster Adult Publishing Group, 1985; Brewster Karin, and Irene Padavic. "Change in Gender-Ideology, 1977–1996: The Contributions of Intracohort Change and Population Turnover." *Journal of Marriage and the Family* 62 (2000): 477–487; Collins, Patricia Hill. *Black Feminist Thought: Knowledge, Consciousness, and the Politics of Empowerment.* New York: Routledge, 2000; Epstein, Fuchs Cynthia. "Great Divides: The Cultural, Cognitive, and Social Bases of the Global Subordination of Women." *American Sociological Review* 72 (2007): 1–22; Greenstein, Theodore N. "Gender Ideology, Marital Disruption, and the Employment of Married Women." *Journal of Marriage and the Family* 57 (1995): 31–42; Hartmann, Heidi. "The Unhappy Marriage of Marxism and Feminism: Towards a More Progressive Union." In *Social Stratification: The Sociological Perspective,* ed. D. Grusky. Boulder, CO: Westview Press, 2001; Hertel, Bradley, and Michael Hughes. "Religious Affiliation, Attendance, and Support for 'Pro-Family' Issues in the United States." *Social Forces* 65 (1987): 858–883; Johnson, Leanor Boulin, and Robert Staples. *Black Families at the Crossroads: Challenges and Prospects.* San Francisco, CA: John Wiley and Sons, Inc., 2005; Nordstrom, Byron. *The History of Sweden.* Westport, CT: Greenwood Press, 2002; Schwartz, Pepper. *Love Between Equals: How Peer Marriage Really Works.* New York: Simon and Schuster Adult Publishing Group, 1994; Thornton, Arland. "Changing Attitudes Toward Family Issues in the United States." *Journal of Marriage and the Family* 51 (1989): 873–893; Wilson, William Julius. *The Declining Significance of Race: Blacks and Changing American Institutions.* Chicago: University of Chicago Press, 1978; Wilson, William Julius. *The Truly Disadvantaged: The Inner City, the Underclass and Public Policy.* Chicago: University of Chicago Press, 1993; Wright, Erik Olin, Karen Shire, Shu-Ling Hwang, Maureen Dolan, and Janeen Baxter. "The Non-Effects of Class on the Gender Division of Labour in the Home: A Comparative Study of Sweden and the United States." *Gender and Society* 6 (1992): 252–282.

Christy Haines Flatt

MARITAL SATISFACTION

Marital satisfaction is a measure of married partners' feelings of fulfillment from their relationship, their enjoyment of being a couple, and their continued commitment to one another. Some people fear that marital satisfaction among United States couples is in overall decline. One reason is that divorce rates from the second half of the twentieth century through today are unarguably higher than those of the first half of the century and earlier. Many people, linking this decline in stability with a decline in quality, lament the shift as evidence that high numbers of contemporary couples are experiencing dissatisfaction with the marital relationship. Opponents of this view argue that dissatisfaction rates were higher previously, although marriages were more stable, and the contemporary marriage climate is one of increased satisfaction with marriage for those who choose it.

A major distinction between marriage then and now is a trend away from a traditional form of marriage toward more egalitarian unions. At no point in time have all marriages been alike. In earlier periods, during which so-called traditional marriage was popular, some couples likely chose to have more equal responsibilities and decision-making power. Similarly, today when more couples choose equitable, or what they consider fair or balanced, relationships, many partners still uphold conventional ideals. However, the general movement in relationship types has been away from models based on father breadwinner/mother homemaker standards to newer models with dual-earners as the norm.

Before the controversy surrounding the evolution of marriage and whether or not it has produced more satisfied couples can be considered, an explanation of the various measures of marital success and a brief description of how marriage in the United States has changed over time are worthwhile.

MARITAL SUCCESS MEASURES

When discussing marital success, researchers and others often refer to marital stability, marital quality, and marital satisfaction.

Marital Stability

Marital stability is the most concise of these success measures because it is based on the longevity of the relationship. Stable marriages are those which remain intact, with the ultimate durable union being one that continues until the death of at least one spouse. Although this measure is widely used by those who study and write about marital success, it can be misleading because couples who stay together are not necessarily satisfied. In the view of many people, a long-term marriage is not really successful if the partners are miserable throughout that time. Yet one helpful indicator for marital satisfaction comes from stability's opposite, instability. While it cannot be assumed that all stable marriages are satisfying, it is safe to believe that the great majority, if not all, of those that end in divorce involve some level of dissatisfaction.

Marital Quality

The notion of marital quality is less distinct in its definition. When speaking of marital quality, researchers often refer to the partners' reported level of happiness and their positive or negative feelings about the experience of being married to one another. This measure might include many commonly studied correlates of marriage on which the partners rate themselves and their relationship, such as level of positive or negative interaction between them or level and frequency of conflict experienced. The terms marital quality and marital satisfaction are sometimes used as synonyms because these concepts have overlapping features.

Marital Satisfaction

Marital satisfaction is an indicator used for the positive feelings and fulfillment spouses experience as a result of being together, the opposite of which is marital dissatisfaction, a measure that identifies negative feelings and a lack of fulfillment. This concept is often related to some standard against which spouses judge their experiences and how they feel their relationship rates next to others they observe or hear about. Like marital quality, this measure depends on individuals' reports about themselves, their partners, and their marriages. For the purposes of this discussion, marital satisfaction will be used as a blanket term to encompass the ideas generally held under this measure as well as those used to address marital quality.

HOW MARRIAGE HAS EVOLVED

The expectations, structures, norms, and ideologies for marriage are constantly in flux and have changed considerably over time. One illustration of this is the varying legal representations of the marital relationship by Western culture over the last few centuries. Under the doctrine of coverture, which appeared during the Middle Ages, wives were defined as belonging to their husbands. They had no legal rights to own property and were expected to turn any wages earned over to their spouses. Marriage was seen as the melding of two people into a single individual—the husband.

In the 1800s many Married Women's Property Laws were passed by some states giving wives the right to own property and keep any wages they earned. During this time, the conception of marriage shifted to acknowledge the existence of both individuals and gave a degree of equality to each. From this arose the norm of the wife who served her husband, who in return provided for her. Throughout the 1960s and 1970s, other legal modifications affecting marriage took place. In general, these changes supported the emerging trends of more equalized relationships and spouses' shared responsibilities for economic, household, and childcare tasks. One important change during this period was the enactment of the first no-fault divorce laws by California in 1970.

On the whole, the evolution of marriage in the United States has involved two major shifts. The first was from the traditional, instrumental view of marriage to the more modern, expressive view. The instrumental view characterizing so-called then, or more traditional, marriages describes matrimony as a utilitarian and pragmatic undertaking. Partners form an economic union meant to provide for themselves physically and to meet the needs of society, including reproduction of the species. Under this instrumental doctrine, the idea of marrying for love is foolish. During the period for which this view was the norm, men and women were taught to be objective when choosing a mate, to look for a spouse who, for example, had a strong body for labor, a good hand for sewing, or a physique conducive to bearing many children. Following instrumental norms, people considered their marriages satisfying if the unions produced heirs, economic stability, and interdependence. Love and intimacy were likely appreciated by those who developed them, but these components were not considered requirements or ends unto themselves.

Relatively recently, so-called now, or more egalitarian, marriages have come to be characterized by the expressive view of marriage. This doctrine places primary value on the emotional satisfaction and intimate fulfillment couples gain from their interactions with one another. While social pressure persists for women to marry wealthy husbands or for men to seek wives who can keep a clean house, for example, a high number of people accept partners who offer few instrumental incentives. Furthermore, in today's culture most people believe that love is a natural prerequisite for marriage. Therefore, for contemporary marriage the major criteria for satisfaction are intimacy and emotional gratification between partners. These factors are so important that many people report that a loss of either would lead them to discontinue their relationship.

A second social shift affecting marriage has been from patriarchy to democracy within the family. Shown by laws such as the doctrine of coverture, Western culture, including the United States, has a long history of patriarchal dominance. This dominance pervaded society, giving males unquestioned authority in business, the courts, and the home. Women were considered second-class citizens, expected to defer first to the authority of their fathers and later to their husbands as the head of the household.

The system of patriarchy was slowly eroded as women gained more legal and social ground. However, it remained largely intact until the 1960s when several movements and changes came together to give women more power than ever before. This shift resulted from catalysts such as the Women's Movement, the availability of more educational opportunities for women, the invention and increased accessibility of contraceptives, especially birth control pills, and a dramatic rise in the number of women holding paid employment outside the home. As women gained more equal value in society as a whole, they began to expect more democracy at home as well.

MARITAL SATISFACTION: THEN VERSUS NOW

No two marriages have ever been exactly alike. Even when couples share the same ideals, perspectives, beliefs, and values, they interpret these elements differently and approach their relationships in subtly and significantly unique ways. Despite this, common characteristics can be identified among groups of married partners that create general categories under which they can be considered. Marriages of one period can be compared and contrasted with marriages of another in general terms. A current conceptualization is that unions of the recent past are fundamentally different than unions of today, resulting in the categorization of then and now marital models. As is the case with many social dichotomies, controversy exists over whether one form is better, meaning more satisfying and less prone to divorce, than the other. Supporters and detractors on both sides of this debate present a variety of arguments.

MARRIAGE WAS MORE SATISFYING THEN

A major contention of those who believe that marriages of the past were more satisfying and stable is that the movement of women into paid labor has been disastrous for husbands and wives. These proponents point to historical data showing that increasing divorce in the United States has coincided with the rise in women working outside of the home. In the traditionalist view of then marriages, husbands are expected to be the sole wage earners and women are expected to be homemakers. In fact, they view the latter role as the greatest source of value and fulfillment available to wives. Keeping a home and taking care of a husband and children is an expression of true femininity. The movement of women into the workforce has upset the traditional gender division of labor, and left a void in the home as some wives give primacy to wage-earning.

A more specific source of dissatisfaction cited by these claimants is that the movement toward working wives has caused partners to struggle with balancing work and family responsibilities. According to these proponents, conflicting loyalties for the husband and wife cause strain, stress, and overall dissatisfaction as each tries to manage multiple roles. Supporters point out that such a struggle was not present in then marriages when men and women upheld complementary roles, each caring for distinct elements of family survival. Husbands spent their days working in the fields, factories, and offices, earning the money needed to run the household. This undertaking was so demanding that it required the majority of their time. Wives, on the other hand, were responsible for maintaining the home and rearing the next generation. Thus, each sex could focus on separate life aspects, either work or home, without burdening one another with unnecessary concerns.

Additionally, then marriage advocates say complementary husband and wife roles increase satisfaction with the marital relationship. They believe spouses are more comfortable when expectations and responsibilities are clearly defined. One of their biggest criticisms of egalitarian relationships is that spouses are confused about what they need to do for their marriage to function smoothly. Roles are blurred and expectations can change suddenly, they claim, leading to disappointment and discord. In addition, men are conflicted today by contradictory social instructions about the right way to be a husband. Often, husbands find themselves torn between upholding norms telling them to take wives as equal partners with whom they can share the burdens and joys of supporting the family and other norms that tell them their place is as head of the household with primary financial responsibility for the family.

A final argument made by advocates of more traditional marriage is that people expect too much of marriage today. The contemporary notion of matrimony is that partners will be everything to one another. People expect their spouses to meet all their physical, social, and emotional needs. They suggest that couples of the past were more realistic in their expectations. In these marriages, partners were expected to provide many physical and some emotional benefits to one another, but this was in tandem with the benefits to be received from the community, friends, and other family members. Critics of modern marriages believe that many couples become dissatisfied when their relationships cannot measure up to the mythical be all, end all standard and are encouraged to seek satisfaction elsewhere when a current marriage does not meet their unrealistic demands.

MARRIAGE IS MORE SATISFYING NOW

Many researchers and claimants provide evidence that contemporary couples are happier and more satisfied than those of the past. A key reason for this, they feel, is the equality modern couples often experience. Current marriage advocates identify the movement of women into the workforce, the need to balance work and family, and the sharing of household responsibilities as strengths of now marriages that engender fulfillment and satisfaction.

The increased social power afforded to females as a result of paid labor is heralded by some as an overdue recognition of women's value comparable to men. While then marriage advocates believe homemaking is the ultimate expression of femininity and the truest source of female contentment, opponents propose that earning their own wage is much more gratifying for women. Many studies have found women who report that their work gives them pleasure, a sense of identity, and improved self-efficacy. Working outside the home empowers women, providing them positive feelings about themselves that carry over to the marriage. Following the saying that one cannot love another person unless one loves oneself first, it is reasonable that women who feel good about themselves at work feel good about themselves at home too and are better able to get along with their spouses.

Also in contrast to traditionalist claims, many people do not consider the need of partners to balance work and family as a catalyst for decreased satisfaction. Actually, some researchers, such as Milkie and Teltola, have found the opposite result in dual-earner families. These studies find that spouses gain a sense of accomplishment and success from negotiating multiple roles at work and at home. Contemporary society in general is encouraging, rather than condemning, of working parents and the dual-earner household is the norm. Couples who are able to do well at work while upholding household duties are likely to get a sense of satisfaction from meeting social expectations. Finding support for their lifestyle has positive implications for their marital satisfaction as well.

Furthermore, where then supporters see complimentary roles, now advocates cite inequality and suppression for wives. They believe that women in general cannot truly be happy as servants of their husbands. The system of patriarchy that is perpetuated by traditional marriage places wives in a subordinate social position. While they agree that marriages of the past were more stable, they point out that longevity does not necessarily indicate satisfaction. Wives in then marriages had fewer options for improving their situation and were overall unable to end their repressive unions. Happy or not, they were compelled by legal and social sanctions to stay with their husbands.

A characteristic of modern marriages thought to have positive implications for marital satisfaction is a decrease in family size. Married partners today, on average, produce far fewer offspring than previous couples. This may improve feelings about the relationship because spouses with fewer children experience less stress over the marital life course. Research has consistently shown that satisfaction decreases when a child is born because parents no longer have time for one another, they face increased financial burdens, and the stress of caring for offspring engenders more negative interactions between them. This effect compounds with each subsequent child. Moreover, the more children a couple have, the later in life they will share space with and be responsible for those offspring. Thus, the modern trend toward smaller family size has positive implications for the marital satisfaction of now couples when compared with then couples.

Finally, egalitarian marriage advocates point to couples' self-reports of their experiences in these relationships as evidence of improved satisfaction. A number of husbands and wives consciously choose to have more equal relationships than did earlier generations. These couples often say that they are happy with their high levels of intimacy and with sharing, as opposed to delegating, the majority of responsibilities in their lives. Most would not want to give up joint household care, child rearing, and decision making, as these efforts allow them to act as a team, to value each other's input, and to put the needs of the relationship before their individual desires.

CORRELATES OF MARITAL SATISFACTION

While the controversy surrounding then versus now marriages and which version produces more satisfied couples with better outcomes is often debated, many researchers choose to examine more general variables for marital satisfaction that relate to partners in any marriage type. A tremendous amount of research has been conducted to pinpoint the attitudes, behaviors, social characteristics, and other possible correlates of marital satisfaction. A comprehensive list of such factors is almost impossible to compile because researchers are continuously finding new areas to study. Some old areas are discarded only to be picked up again later. However, it is feasible to discuss a few of the more common correlates investigated.

Some of the most famous ideas about marital satisfaction have been put forth by John Gottman. Among the more influential is Gottman's proposal of the Four Horsemen of the Apocalypse for happiness in marriage. He identified four behaviors partners could engage in that are highly damaging to their relationship: criticizing the spouse, displaying contempt for the spouse, becoming defensive, and stonewalling (refusing to talk to the spouse). By conducting longitudinal studies with married couples, using both observational and self-report techniques, Gottman concluded that the four behaviors, especially when used in combination, devitalized relationships and produced high dissatisfaction.

A second prominent result of Gottman's research regards the ratio of positive to negative interactions between partners. According to many researchers some conflict is necessary for a healthy marriage. Perfect marriages in which couples never disagree are a myth. Thus, the presence of negative interactions is not necessarily detrimental to a relationship. Rather, it is the number of bad experiences versus the number of good ones that impacts a couple's overall satisfaction. Gottman proposed that for a couple to be happy in marriage, they need to have five positive engagements for every negative one.

Another well-researched area of marital satisfaction deals with the homogeneity of partners. Homogeneous partners are those who are alike in demographic and social characteristics. This means they are of the same racial, ethnic, or religious background, are from the same social class, have similar educational levels, and are near one another in age. Research has shown that when compared with heterogeneous spouses, homogeneous couples are better able to relate to one another and to get along. This increased harmony results from shared backgrounds, values, morals, and other fundamental expressions of self. For much of the history of the United States the vast majority of marriages were homogeneous unions. Contemporary marriages, however, are characterized by increasing heterogeneity.

Much interest has been directed toward the correlation between sexual satisfaction and overall satisfaction with a relationship, particularly the search for a link between sexual frequency and satisfaction. Some have reported that happier couples are those who have sex more often. This link has also been approached in the opposite manner, with some researchers indicating that being happy with one's relationship leads one to desire sex more frequently. Conversely, other findings indicate no direct relationship between intercourse frequency and satisfaction, noting that the quality of intimate contacts is more important than their frequency. Finally, a few who have investigated this area report that satisfaction is related more to how partners talk about sex than the act itself. Those couples who feel comfortable enough to be honest about their desires and feelings about intercourse and how they prefer for the experience to progress feel more positively about their marriage overall.

Another major correlate of marital satisfaction found in the literature is communication. Marriage is a series of negotiations and problems to be solved. In order for couples to maneuver through their everyday interactions, they must communicate. Some couples develop effective communication styles whereas others do not. Many spouses adopt an open approach to communication in which they feel free to express their opinions and feelings and to bring up whatever topics they desire. Other partners are more closed in their communication, meaning they sometimes censor things they talk about with one anther.

A number of communication behaviors have been found to be damaging to a marriage. These include Gottman's Four Horsemen as well as placating, whining, nagging, and being verbally abusive. Communication actions that positively affect marital satisfaction involve praising the spouse, speaking to one another with respect, and expressing love and endearment.

Communication is a crucial component of conflict management, another variable related to spousal satisfaction. According to research, some of the more functional conflict approaches are those in which couples address issues directly and with a desire to have their own needs met without necessarily denying their spouses' needs. On the other hand, using coercive communication in conflict, such as passive-aggressive strategies, personal attacks, and refusal to hear the other person's side generally decreases satisfaction with the union.

Finally, a number of studies have looked at the impact time spent together has on marital satisfaction. One such study reported that partners who spend 90 minutes of together time each day are often happier than those who spend less than an hour together per day. Furthermore, taking part in recreational activities as a couple is even more beneficial. Mere exposure to one another can have a positive impact on feelings about the relationship. Partners who spend time talking together about joint concerns as well as experiences while apart, such as one another's day at work, have higher satisfaction levels than those who converse less often.

For some time it was commonly believed that all satisfied marriages followed a similar structure and pattern and that dissatisfied marriages deviated from this model. More contemporary researchers, such as Cuber and Haroff, however, have determined that stable unions come in a variety of forms. This diversity makes determining exact correlates of happiness difficult. Satisfaction is relative; different individuals and couples define being satisfied in varied ways. Relationship characteristics that would lead some men or women to seek divorce are expected and even desirable to others. Therefore, no suggestions or techniques for improving satisfaction will ever work for all couples.

LIFE COURSE CONSIDERATIONS

Another way of looking at marital satisfaction is whether and how it changes over time. One popular method of illustrating this is the family life cycle model, first introduced in the 1950s. This model contains eight stages, each with unique implications for marital satisfaction. Stage one is beginning families. This stage, during which the wedding occurs and partners settle into their marriage, is thought to be highly satisfying. In stage two, childbearing families, the first offspring are born to the couple. As the financial burden and other stressors increase during this period, satisfaction decreases. The trend toward lessened satisfaction continues for stage three, families with preschool children, stage four, families with school children, and stage five, families with teenagers. The loss of satisfaction is connected to the high stress and financial worries found throughout these stages and peaking in stage five.

Stage six is families as launching centers. The implications for satisfaction here can be positive or negative. Increased satisfaction can arise as children leave home and spouses find renewed time for and interest in their relationship. On the other hand, many partners end up in a marital crisis as they are no longer able to relate after many years of focusing on the children rather than each other. The results of stage seven, families in the middle years, can be likewise variable. Retirement occurs during this stage for most people and couples find themselves spending more time together. This may revitalize the marriage for some while leading others to realize they do not enjoy being together as they once did. The eighth stage is aging families. The health of the partners has the biggest impact on satisfaction for this stage, with the poor health of one or both spouses causing potential strain. The family life cycle model ends with the death of one or both partners.

Although it has been widely used for decades, the family life cycle model has received much criticism. Critics argue that the model does not fit all couples. For example, they claim it is often not applicable to now marriages resulting in nontraditional, modern families. They feel it is also not realistic for the lower classes that do not progress through the stages in the same way as the other classes, or for divorced or remarried individuals, as the model does not allow for stopping movement through the stages with one relationship and beginning again with another.

More general explanations of changing marital satisfaction over the life course exist, arising from the work of researchers such as Norval D. Glenn. One common theme among these is that the presence of children decreases the positive feelings between husbands and wives. Following the birth of the first child, dissatisfaction may emerge due to the demands of the infant, fatigue, frustration, and a loss of time to focus on each other. These issues are generally only compounded with the birth of subsequent children which further divides adults' time and energy. The situation usually declines rather than improves as the children age. The adolescent years are particularly stressful for parents as they try to set boundaries for children who are struggling to find their own identities. The effort spent worrying about teenage issues such as sexual activity, school achievement, and drug use leaves partners with little time or energy to tend to their marital relationship. Much of this tension is relieved when the children leave the home. Thus, a curvilinear relationship is generally proposed for marital satisfaction over time, with high points existing during the early and late years with a marked decrease throughout the years in between.

Recent research has discredited the belief that elderly couples cannot have vigorous, satisfying relationships. A number of studies have found that older spouses can have increased intimacy and relatively frequent sexual encounters. Rather than resenting growing dependence on one another due to health problems or a shrinking social network, many older people are comfortable with their high interdependence and enjoy the sense of belonging with one another.

WILL THE DEBATE END?

The debate surrounding then and now marriages and which is the best method for couples to follow is not likely to end soon. The continued high divorce rate in the United States is valid evidence that a large number of couples are not finding the satisfaction they desire in marriage. Advocates of traditional and modern marriage both feel the model of matrimony they support is a viable solution to this problem. A major argument of then proponents is that the complementary roles of father breadwinner/mother homemaker unions create clear expectations for spouses, and that contemporary couples experience conflict over role confusion. Now marriage advocates, on the other hand, believe it is the blending of marital roles that gives strength to modern couples, allowing them to share responsibilities and grow together in all aspects of their lives. Because each marriage form works for a number of couples giving strength to each proponents' claims, the controversy surrounding the merits of the models is regularly refueled.

The media play a role in this controversy. Television, movies, and other media are major sources of information about norms, expectations, and the way members of society live. From these informants people receive a variety of images that may cause confusion. For example, manly men are often portrayed by the media as the ideal. These men work 70 or more hours per week, ruthlessly strive to get ahead in their careers, protect their families against all dangers, and don't know the difference between a mop and a vacuum. Such masculine portrayals are juxtaposed with the sensitive men. These characters, sharing power and duties with their mates, are depicted as weak individuals who are not taken seriously by their wives or children.

Women are also illustrated in various ways. Some images present independent working wives as positive role models who know how to get what they want while still finding happiness at home. At the same time, these women can come to represent superwomen; individuals who are able to be everything to everyone and work tirelessly for others with little or no recognition. Finally, the media can create a view of women as subordinates, holding lower-level jobs or spending their husbands' money faster than the men can make it. With all these mixed messages, it is understandable that people would be unsure of the right type of marriage and lifestyle to attempt.

While couples receive pressure from the media, politics, religion and other influences to undertake marriage in a certain way, the ultimate choice of how to seek marital satisfaction is theirs. Contemporary couples display a multitude of forms. Rather than taking a strictly traditional or modern stance, most approach marriage in a way that combines both traditional and egalitarian ideas. For them, marital satisfaction is not a debate but a goal toward which they must work every day.

See also Adversarial and No-Fault Divorce; Benefits of Marriage; Developmental Disability and Family Stress; Divorce as Problem, Symptom, or Solution; Employed Mothers; Extramarital Sexual Relationships; Family Roles; Remarriage; Transition to Parenthood.

Further Reading: Amato, Paul R., Alan Booth, David R. Johnson, and Stacy J. Rogers. *Alone Together: How Marriage in America is Changing.* Cambridge, MA: Harvard University Press, 2007; Buri, John R. *How to Love Your Wife.* Mustang, OK: Tate Publishing and Enterprises, 2006; Chapman, Gary. *The Five Love Languages: How to Express Heartfelt Commitment to Your Mate.* Chicago: Northfield Publishing, 2004; Doherty, William J. *Take Back Your Marriage: Sticking Together in a World that Pulls Us Apart.* New York: Guilford Publications, 2001; Doyle, Laura. *The Surrendered Wife: A Practical Guide to Finding Intimacy, Passion, and Peace.* New York: Fireside, 2001; Fowers, Blaine J. *Beyond the Myth of Marital Happiness: How Embracing the Virtues of Loyalty, Generosity, Justice,* *and Courage Can Strengthen Your Relationship.* New York: Jossey-Bass, 2000; Glenn, Norval D. "With This Ring: A National Survey on Marriage in America." National Fatherhood Initiative. http://www.smartmarriages.com/nms.pdf (accessed January 2008); Gottman, John M. *What Predicts Divorce? The Relationship Between Marital Processes and Marital Outcomes.* Hillsdale, NJ: Lawrence Erlbaum Associates, Inc., 1994; Gottman, John M. and Nan Silver. *The Seven Principles for Making Marriage Work.* New York: Three Rivers Press, 1999; Markman, Howard J., Scott M. Stanley, and Susan L. Blumberg. *Fighting for Your Marriage: Positive Steps for Preventing Divorce and Preserving a Lasting Love.* New York: Jossey-Bass, 2001; McCarthy, Barry, and Emily J. McCarthy. *Getting It Right the First Time: Creating a Healthy Marriage.* New York: Brunner-Routledge, 2004; Morgan, Mabel. *The Total Woman.* New York: Pocket Books, 1990; Weiner-Davis, Michele. *The Sex-Starved Marriage: Boosting Your Libido: A Couple's Guide.* New York: Simon and Schuster, 2004.

Nicole D. Garrett

MARRIAGE PROMOTION

Marriage promotion is the introduction of social and political policies that encourage persons to marry. In particular, these policies are targeted at single-parent families and assume that marriage will help alleviate some of the challenges that these families typically face by providing for a more traditional family structure and opportunities for financial stability. A less-obvious goal of marriage promotion programs is to reduce the numbers of women and children receiving government-sponsored public assistance funds.

INTRODUCTION

Since the late 1960s, an increasing amount of attention has been given to the rise in the percentage of children who grow up in single-parent households. This attention has been driven by two main concerns: first, the recognition that, on average, children who grow up in single-parent homes are more likely to suffer negative outcomes, especially poverty, compared with children raised in two-parent homes, and second the view that the traditional family is rapidly disappearing. To address the problem of child poverty and to strengthen the family, Congress passed the Welfare Extension and Marriage Promotion Act, under the Personal Responsibility and Work Opportunity Reconciliation Act (PRWORA), popularly known as welfare reform, which emphasized marriage as critical to the well-being of children. Promoting marriage as a national agenda is quite controversial. On one side of the controversy are those who contend that promoting marriage is in the best interest of children and the family, while on the other side are those who argue that single-parent families can be beneficial for children as long these latter families receive adequate financial and social support.

SINGLE-PARENT FAMILIES

Once a rare family type, single-parent families have become a notable and permanent feature of family life in the United States. Single-parent families, at least historically, had been most often formed as a result of widowhood with many single-headed households being formed as a result of the death of the mother during childbirth or the death of the father in relation to occupational accidents or war. Although most often poor, these families were not necessarily seen as having been created by individual choice but through unforeseen misfortune. However, over the course of the twentieth century, virtually every aspect of modern society changed rapidly, as did the structure of the family. With family structure changing at such a swift rate, one growing and extremely important family structure has emerged in a variety of forms—the single-parent family.

According to the "Family and Living Arrangements: 2006" report, released by the U.S. Census Bureau in 2007, there are approximately 14 million single-parent households (10.4 million single-mother households and 2.5 million single-father households) in the United States today, and those parents provide care for approximately 21.6 million of the nation's children age 18 years and younger.

While most single-parent families were formed by marital disruption such as divorce, separation or widowhood in the 1960s and 1970s, the increase in the birth rates among unmarried women fueled the growth in single-parent families in the 1980s and beyond. In terms of female-headed households, 45.9 percent are currently divorced or separated and 30.5 percent have never been married. Of children living with one parent, 38 percent live with a divorced parent, 35 percent with a never-married parent, 19 percent with a separated parent, and 8 percent in other living arrangements.

Family structure seems to play a role in the quality of life of children. For instance, children raised in mother-headed households are five times more likely to be poor than are children reared in married-couple households. Childhood poverty translates into a host of negative child outcomes such as poor health, low educational attainment, food insecurity, and housing instability. Children of never-married mother-headed households, on average, fare far worse than any of the other single-parent type families. Of those children living with never-married parents, the U.S. Department of Commerce reports that less than two-thirds have parents who have completed high school and live in rented homes, 59 percent have unemployed mothers, and 69 percent live in poverty.

MARRIAGE PROMOTION

From an economic and social perspective, the spread of single motherhood and the persistence of childhood poverty have dominated the concern of family and child advocates, women's right advocates, policy researchers, politicians, and governmental agencies. After much debate in Congress, on August 22, 1996, President Clinton signed PRWORA into law. PRWORA completely revamped the prior welfare system, which had been attacked for decades by policy-makers, the press, and the public for increasing government spending.

Under this welfare reform legislation, Temporary Assistance to Needy Families (TANF) replaced the old welfare programs known as Aid to Families with Dependent Children (AFDC), the Job Opportunities and Basic Skills Training (JOBS) program and the Emergency Assistance (EA) program. With the creation of TANF, a new emphasis was placed on family formation, with the specific goals of providing assistance to needy families, ending dependence of needy parents on government benefits by promoting job preparation, work, marriage, preventing and reducing the incidence of out-of-wedlock pregnancies, and encouraging and supporting the formation and maintenance of two-parent families.

In line with these goals, PRWORA required welfare recipients to work within two years of receiving assistance, and it put a five-year lifetime limit on the receipt of benefits. It also ended the entitlement status of welfare benefits. In addition, the act made other, less-publicized changes to several social welfare programs, both restricting the availability of benefits (making it harder for disabled children to qualify for assistance, limiting eligibility for food stamps, and denying welfare benefits to most legal immigrants) and strengthening programs that aid children (reorganizing and increasing funding for child care, as well as toughening the enforcement of rules for child support).

In a 2001 policy speech, President Bush proclaimed that marriage promotion would be a focus of his administration.

> To encourage marriage and promote the well-being of children, I have proposed a healthy marriage initiative to help couples develop the skills and knowledge to form and sustain healthy marriages. Research has shown that, on average, children raised in households headed by married parents fare better than children who grow up in other family structures. Through education and counseling programs, faith-based, community, and government organizations promote healthy marriages and a better quality of life for children. By supporting responsible child-rearing and strong families, my Administration is seeking to ensure that every child can grow up in a safe and loving home. (http://www.acf.hhs.gov/healthymarriage/about/mission.html)

The Healthy Marriage Initiative is a centerpiece of welfare-reform reauthorization bills. The initiative targets low-income couples because, unlike more affluent couples, low-income couples either do not have the resources to purchase marriage-education services or those services are not currently available in their communities. The aim is to give low-income couples greater access to marriage-education services and thereby improve their chances of forming and sustaining healthy, stable marriages. Healthy marriage promotion activities include: (1) public advertising campaigns on the value of marriage and the skills needed to increase marital stability and health; (2) education in high schools on the value of marriage, relationship skills, and budgeting; (3) marriage education, marriage skills, and relationship skills programs, that may include parenting skills, financial management, conflict resolution, and job and career advancement, for nonmarried pregnant women and nonmarried expectant fathers; (4) premarital education and marriage skills training for engaged couples and for couples or individuals interested in marriage; (5) marriage enhancement and marriage skills training programs for married couples; (6) divorce reduction programs that teach relationship skills; and (7) marriage mentoring programs which use married couples as role models and mentors in at-risk communities.

FAMILY STRUCTURE VERSUS FAMILY PROCESS

Throughout discussions related to the changing family in the United States is a debate concerning which is the most crucial variable, family structure or family process. The former focuses on who is in the family, suggesting that family form is crucial to success and positive outcomes. The latter highlights how the family works to meet the needs of the members, regardless of who they are.

The Family Deficit Model (FDM) views the nuclear or two-parent family as the ideal family structure. According to this model, single-parent families have a negative impact on children simply because they do not have a nuclear family structure. Research using the FDM begins with the assumption that single-parenting is bad for children, and the results of these studies typically support this assumption. In fact, single-parent families have been accused of many social ills and these social ills were used to support marriage promotion.

On the other hand, in the early 1990s, the Risk and Protective Factor Model (RPFM) was developed. This model does not regard single-parent families as irregular or bad because the assumption of this model is that all family types have both strengths and weaknesses. Rather than view single-parenting as the cause of negative outcomes for children in these families, the RPFM describes family structure as one of many risk factors. Risks in this model are either background characteristics or life events that may have a negative impact on child development. Protective factors are characteristics and events that positively influence children and help limit the impact of risks. Essentially, according to this model, risks are the weakness and protective factors are the strengths of any given family.

MARRIAGE PROMOTION: STRENGTHENING MARRIAGE AND FAMILY

Marriage is a social good. An underlying view of marriage promotion supporters is that marriage is a fundamental social institution and safety net that provides important social and economic benefits for adults and children, as well as society as a whole. They argue that the erosion of the institution of marriage has had widespread negative consequences on children and adults. Supporters of marriage promotion have as a goal to defend traditional marriage, arguing that too many welfare programs undermine marriage among the poor.

Advocates highlight a host of social science research, data, and government surveys that show that being reared during the rise in single-parent families, especially never-married types, is associated with an increase in a number of social problems. For example, this body of research indicates that children born out of wedlock are much more likely to experience poverty, need public assistance, have lower academic achievement, have behavioral and emotional problems, and use drugs more often than children raised in two-parent families. In addition, never-married younger mothers are less likely to have a high school diploma and more likely to be victims of domestic violence than are married mothers. With the rise of the above problems comes high governmental program cost paid by taxpayers to deal with the short-and long-term effects of these social problems. Federal and state taxes are used to support welfare, child care subsidies, child support collection costs, costs associated with court administration, foster care, and crime-control efforts.

Advocates argue that it is reasonable for public policy to promote marriage because marriage protects children from the negative consequences associated with being raised in single-parent families. Marriages increase the economic and social well-being of the family by increasing family income. Couples who share in the economic stability of the family are able to amass more wealth and provide more resources (*e.g.*, food, clothing, shelter, security, finances, and education) for their children than are single parents, especially young never-married mothers.

In addition to the economic benefits, marriage provides social protection for both children and adults. Married couples offer social support to the family, which can help reduce the stress of everyday living. Married couples are more likely to provide social support to each other as well as to their children than are singe parents, who may or may not have a significant other on which they can rely, or who may be too stressed to give social support to their children. Moreover, married couples are able to access additional forms of social support from each other's extended family, job connections, and friends. These additional levels of social support, which the children of singe parents may not have, are beneficial to the well-being of children, giving children others who are present to help.

Finally, the children of married couples are offered social protection through parental supervision. Proponents maintain that the two-parent environment is optimal for providing parental supervision. Having two parents present in the home increases the level of supervision compared with single-parent families. The reduced level of supervision in single-parent families is associated with increased involvement in potentially life-altering behaviors, such as early initiation of sexual intercourse, teen pregnancy, violence, and drug and alcohol use.

According to advocates, increasing marriage rates in low-income neighborhoods just makes sense. Children from married-couple families have better health and are less likely to be depressed, have higher rates of educational attainment, and fewer emotional and behavioral problems. Whether the problem is abuse, neglect, poverty, or emotional and behavioral problems, proponents highlight the host of research that suggests that the best living arrangement for children is with their biological parents who are in a stable, healthy marriage.

MARRIAGE PROMOTION: MISSING THE REALITIES OF POVERTY

Critics of marriage promotion also view marriage as a social good. However, while supporters of marriage promotion view marriage as socially beneficial for low-income single mothers, critics argue that the goal of strengthening families might be best served through a combined package of social and economic policies and programs that promote the familial, educational, and employment needs that are unique to low-income communities. The Healthy Marriage

Initiative takes money away from programs that create stable families. For instance, programs such as the Earned Income Tax Credit, publicly subsidized child care, fatherhood initiatives, job training programs, and efforts to reduce pay discrimination would assist low-income community members in stabilizing the family, while offering benefits to couples interested in matrimony. Critics assert that public policy that seeks to strengthen families by promoting marriage misses a critical point; that is, low marriage rates among the poor are a symptom of poverty and not the cause. Few persons would want to start a married life together when they are already having trouble meeting basic financial needs as single people.

In addition, critics argue that marriage promotion should not be a major component of antipoverty policy. Because women in low-income communities are likely to date and marry men in their community, it is doubtful that if single mothers married the father of their child(ren) that the earnings of the fathers, which would be so low, would lift the family out of poverty. Research has consistently found that children raised in poverty, regardless of parent's marital status, suffer a host of deleterious effects, such as delinquency, poor academic achievement, emotional and behavioral problems, poorer health, and drug use.

In considering marriage as an antipoverty strategy as well as a means for strengthening low-income families, never-married mothers face many obstacles to forming and maintaining healthy marriages. Research shows that there is a substantial shortage of marriageable men for single mothers to marry. Low-income men are more likely to be unemployed or underemployed, in poorer health, use drugs, become a victim of violence, and be arrested and incarcerated than are men in higher social classes. Similarly, young single mothers who lack a high school diploma and who are not gainfully employed may not be considered marriage material for men whose social standing is higher than their own.

Finally, opponents contend that promoting marriage as public policy and specifically targeting low-income women puts governmental pressure on women's intimate decisions and places victims of domestic violence at increased risk. In addition, the idea of strengthening families by promoting marriage is in essence favoring one family over another. Critics argue that there are policy changes that would go a long way in strengthening single-parent families without promoting marriage, such as removing time limits on vocational training, full funding for child-care subsidies, and eliminating the cap on the number of families who can receive education and training activities counted as work.

See also African American Fathers; Deadbeat Parents; Family Roles; Fatherhood; Poverty and Public Assistance; Teen Pregnancy.

Further Reading: Administration for Children and Families. "Healthy Marriage Initiative." http://www.acf.hhs.gov/healthymarriage/about/factsheets_hm_matters.html; American Psychological Association. http://www.apa.org/monitor/sep04/marriage.html; Coontz, Stephanie, and Nancy Folbre. "Marriage, Poverty, and Public Policy." http://www.prospect.org/cs/articles?article=marriage_poverty_and_public_policy; The Heritage Foundation. http://www.heritage.org; Institute for Women's Policy Research. http://www.iwpr.org; Mincy, Ronald B. "Marriage, Child Poverty, and Public Policy." http://www.americanexperiment.org/uploaded/files/aeqv4n2mincy.pdf; National Association for

Social Workers. http://www.socialworkers.org; National Organization for Women. http://www.now.org;

Annice Yarber

MATE SELECTION ALTERNATIVES

Mate selection refers to choosing a marital partner. There are many different ways in which the selection of mates can proceed, some of which are very traditional and others are driven by technology. There are advantages and disadvantages to each mate selection method. In societies such as Great Britain, Australia, Canada, and the United States, young people are responsible for mate selection through dating. However, there are societies, mostly in predominantly Muslim countries, in which dating is forbidden. While dating is the most familiar method of selecting a mate in westernized countries, it is by no means the only method employed. In some cultures, marriages are primarily arranged, often based on tradition, and there is little input from young people. This may involve matchmakers, kinship driven alliances, or other procedures.

As marrying for the first time has occurred later in the lives of young people in industrialized society in recent decades, people often date for longer periods of time and have more dating experiences with more different people. As people wait longer to look for a serious relationship or as they feel less pressure to marry, they often have more difficulty finding a suitable partner when they are ready to marry. When persons are actively seeking partners, they are said to be in the so-called marriage market. As a consequence of postponing marriage, the marriage market has changed so that persons may select their partners in a number of different alternative ways. Among the options for mate selection are matchmakers, computer match services, speed dating, Internet dating, and others. Many of these services cater to daters with specific needs. For example, they may be persons dating for remarriage, dating as single parents, or dating based on a specific leisure interest.

For persons who travel extensively or who move frequently it may be difficult to find a partner in their locale. They may need an intermediary to give them a chance to encounter like-minded persons. In the case of those looking for a specific type of mate, marriage market intermediaries, who can weed out the ineligible partners quickly, can be quite helpful. Persons who desire partners of a particular social standing or ethnic affiliation may find it more expedient to seek the help of a professional rather than to chance meeting the right person.

DATING

In dating, young people gather to participate in leisure activities designed to help them meet potential partners and to get to know them better. Young people set the pace for these encounters and determine the level of involvement, both emotional and sexual, between the partners. The young people themselves determine what characteristics they would most like to see in their dating partners.

TOP SOURCES OF DATES FOR U.S. YOUNG PEOPLE

According to data published in the magazine *American Demographics,* when 1,500 young people were asked in the spring of 2001 where they met their current or most recent dating partner, several key sources of dates were mentioned. Most participants (65 percent) cited friends, coworkers, and family as good sources through which dates may be obtained. Meeting partners at work was next (36 percent), followed by in class or at school (27 percent), at a bar or coffee shop (26 percent). Bar or coffee shop tied with online (26 percent) as a source of dates. Church or religious services were mentioned by 20 percent of the young people. Places mentioned by fewer than 20 percent of the respondents were in line at the grocery store or in libraries or bookstores. Church was significantly more likely to be mentioned by black singles as a place to meet dates. Divorced persons were twice as likely as persons who had never been married to look online for partners.

The source of dates is most often friends, work associates, and chance meetings. The primary benefits to marriage that come from dating are that partners can know each other in a variety of contexts prior to making a permanent commitment to one another. Additionally, partners can terminate their relationship at any time and need never see each other again. Social pressures applied to dating couples often mean that they may introduce sexual contact as part of their dating relationship fairly early in the process.

This sexual element has been a source of concern historically and presently. To counter some of the expectations of sexual intimacy that accompany dating in the United States, some organizations, primarily those with a fundamentalist religious orientation, have proposed a return to a courtship model of mate selection where parents are largely in control. Under courtship, young people are formally introduced to each other and their contact occurs under carefully chaperoned conditions. Sexual contact is not permitted until the couple is married. Interested young men must ask permission of a young woman's father in order to court her. Courting implies that a young man would seriously contemplate marriage to the woman. Before being permitted to get to know the woman, the man must spend time getting to know her father and persons who know the suitor must vouch for his sincerity. If the father approves, and the daughter is interested in the young man, they then begin to spend time together.

Dating is filled with challenges for young people. First, one has to select a partner and have him or her agree to the date. One issue that concerns many college students is having enough money to spend on dates to sufficiently impress the partner. Often partners who have been dating for some time have difficulty coming up with new and interesting activities to share. Others point to communication problems as a factor limiting their success on dates. More serious problems that may arise in dating include physical or sexual violence and emotional exploitation. Patterns of jealousy and domestic violence that begin in dating relationships are often carried over into marriages.

In today's nontraditional dating, there is less pressure on either partner to perform a specified role. Either person may ask, pay, plan, drive, or initiate sexual contact. These patterns appear to be more common among persons who are dating after a divorce or who are not currently looking for a marital partner. The incidence of asking by women seems to be fairly high, although women do not always pay the expenses of the dates they initiate. Many women today may choose to pay their own way on a date. By going dutch (having each participant pay for his or her own expenses) they will not feel obliged to participate in sexual activities with the partner as part of the date script. Likewise, today's emphasis on group dating may shield young people from the traditional expectations of sexual intimacy on a date.

DATE RAPE

Also known as acquaintance rape, date rape involves unwanted sexual activity perpetrated by a date or acquaintance. More than one-half of college women indicate that they have experienced some form of sexual aggression while in a dating relationship. Among the factors that contribute to the likelihood of violence or date rape in a relationship include misunderstandings and arguments between the partners, feeling jealous or insecure about the relationship, experiencing rejection from the partner, and increasing power struggles in the couple. Another likely factor in date rape is brought about by women's expected role of sexual-limit-setter and flirt. He may misinterpret her flirtation as an invitation to sexual activity. Routinely included in the research as a risk factor for date rape, drugs and alcohol inhibit good decision making among daters. The prevalence of date rape drugs has led many colleges and universities to institute safe partying programs for students. Chief among the advice is never to leave one's drink unattended nor to accept a drink purchased by someone else.

ARRANGED MARRIAGES

Arranged marriages have historically been the way mates were selected around the world. The exact procedures vary by group, but most societies have some mechanism for the older, established members of society to select partners for the younger members. Arranged marriages serve several key social functions. First, they help form alliances between groups. One example from history would be the aristocracy of Europe forming alliances to prevent war and share wealth. On a smaller scale, farmers might find that marrying their children will consolidate land holdings and keep them competitive. Arranged marriages provide older members of society with influence over who joins the family. This is particularly important in traditional economies where the family is the primary source of employment. In addition to the alliances formed by marriage, marriage is a positive relationship in that it reproduces society. Persons who are married are more psychological and economically stable and contribute more readily to the smooth functioning of society. Arranged marriage, as a social pattern, is not about the love between the partners, sexual desirability, or search for a soul mate. Rather, it is about the role each partner is expected to play in maintaining the orderliness of the culture.

The bride and groom in an arranged marriage may have little or no contact with each other prior to the wedding. In most cases, once marital terms have been agreed upon, they are unlikely to be rescinded. While some societies permit young people to meet independently and the parents have the final veto power over partner choice, other societies take the opposite approach. In these cultures parents select potential mates and the young people have veto power over the marital choice. In other forms of arranged marriage, the position in the family determines with whom one will be partnered.

One of the hallmarks of arranged marriages is that partners must have many social characteristics in common. While religion and race or ethic classification are likely the same among selected mates, economic standing is a key determinant in whether a partner is likely to be included in one's field of eligible mates. Among recent immigrants to the United States who wish to maintain their marital traditions, a matchmaking service may be employed. Brokers, Internet advertisements, and magazine classified advertisements offer ways for families to identify suitable partners for their marriageable children, even if they live in a different country or part of the country from each other. This pattern is particularly common among Asian Indians. The traditional Indian caste system required that marital partners meet certain criteria.

Because arranged marriages operate largely on an economic model, they can be quite useful at consolidating holdings and potent in creating political allies. They are, however, arrangements that may not serve the best interests of young people, particularly women. In most arranged marriages, it is customary for the bride or groom or both to contribute something financial to the new household or the parental household. That which the wife provides or brings with her to the marriage, often furniture or homemaking items, is referred to as the dowry. Families who can offer a high dowry are likely to attract a higher status groom for their daughters. Dowries can be quite extensive and are usually based on the economic prospects that the future groom has. Some evidence from India suggests that women have been murdered when the dowry that they brought was too little compared to what the groom felt he deserved.

For males the economic cost is the bride price. A young man or his family would offer a certain amount of goods or money to a woman's family in exchange for the permission to marry her. The idea is that he is compensating her family for the loss of her talents and economic productivity. In some societies, the young man's family will assist him in gathering the items needed to meet the bride price. In instances where the extended kin may have financially contributed to the acquisition of the wife, they may feel entitled to her domestic skills. Often the girls are quite young when they are purchased and will marry and begin an adult life quite young. One of the consequences of such an arrangement is that girls remain very poorly educated when compared with males.

MISCELLANEOUS ALTERNATIVES

Various alternatives to the traditional mating patterns of arranged marriage and Western style dating have emerged in recent years. All are really adaptations to the changing patterns of family life in the United States. Facilitated by waiting later in life to marry, many older persons who would like to be in a partnered relationship find that it is difficult to meet dates. Others claim that they have difficulty finding a suitable partner. A common complaint in the dating world is that all the good ones are taken. This desire to be in a partnered relationship pushes many singles to try alternative ways to selecting mates. New services, often facilitated by technology, have been developed to help these persons connect. Finding a partner when the time is right is a difficult proposition for persons who attempt to navigate the dating waters. Beginning in the early 1990s, the Internet became an increasingly popular resource for daters. Estimates are that more than 5 million people regularly consult online matching sites. These sites have gained legitimacy as respected academics have endorsed them. Perfectmatch. com has partnered with relationship expert Dr. Pepper Schwartz to tout a compatibility and matching system based on scientific research.

Matchmaker versus dating service. Matchmakers are persons who attempt to find suitable partners for clients for a fee. Matchmakers are often successful because they take into account many aspects of a person's life in addition to physical attractiveness and bank account. In a match service, whether an individual matchmaker or a computerized matching service (*e.g.*, www.eharmony.com), the neutral third party does the selecting based on information provided by the clients. In a dating service the participants themselves do the selecting (*e.g.*, www.americansingles.com). Often they must weed through hundreds of profiles of potential partners, usually with photographs attached, to find those persons with whom they might like to interact. This important difference between the two means that the criteria for partner selection that is readily available differs. Because the dating service and its clients are selective in the information that gets revealed, they may hold back any negative information in an attempt to attract as many potential dates as possible. In dating services, daters reveal only what they want potential partners to know, so they may not be as honest at revealing less-than-flattering information about themselves. Thus, users may have to date many different people before finding a good match. The matchmaker, in contrast, usually has extensive information about each potential partner and may be better able to assess the compatibility of the potentials.

Personal Ads. Formerly viewed as a method of last resort and the only option available to persons who were lonely losers who could not otherwise meet partners, personal ads are much more common today because they have lost much of their earlier stigma. They are seen as an efficient way to select a partner because one indicates in the space of a few lines key qualities that are desirable in a mate, as well as ones that the advertiser can offer to potential partners. These ads are often stereotypical, however, in that traditional gender role descriptions are common and partners tend to play the stereotypical roles of passive female and aggressive male in their presentation of themselves.

The acceptance of personal ads into mainstream partner selection is undisputed today and newspapers across the country (including the New York *Times*) list personals among their classified ads. Not all personal ads are placed in the newspaper today. Many websites are devoted to the task of helping partners connect. There are even books that tell potential advertisers how to be successful in the personal ad marketplace. Shorthand and abbreviations help readers to see at a glance if an advertiser might be right for them. In addition to electronic opportunities to connect, there are several magazines that help partners to connect. One of the biggest criticisms leveled against these tactics is that they have been employed to secure mail order brides.

Speed Dating. In speed dating, persons interested in making a connection for romance are brought together and permitted a predetermined amount of time in which to introduce themselves and determine potential compatibility. Speed dating was first proposed by a rabbi concerned over the trend for Jews to marry outside the faith. The argument was that it was simply too hard for Jews in large cities to meet each other amid so many non-Jews and this would introduce them to other singles for potential dating and marriage relationships. The length of each speed date varies, but it conventionally has been under ten minutes (see www.8minutedating.com). After the time with each potential partner expires, participants rotate to meet the next eligible partner. At the conclusion of the evening, contact information can be shared between those persons with a mutual interest. Research suggests that persons can usually determine whether they are attracted to each other quite quickly (perhaps even within seconds), so there may be some utility to the efficient approach.

See also Arranged Marriage; Dating; Mail Order Brides.

Further Reading: 8 Minute Dating. http://www.8minutedating.com; *Alaska Men* (magazine); Calvo, Emily T., and Laurence Minsky. *25 Words or Less: How to Write Like a Pro to Find That Special Someone Through Personal Ads.* New York: McGraw-Hill, 1998; Deyo, Yaacov, and Sue Deyo. *Speed Dating: A Timesaving Guide to Finding Your Lifelong Love.* New York: HarperCollins Publishers, Inc., 2003; eHarmony, Inc. http://www.eharmony.com; Halbig, Marlene C. *Personal Ads: Never Be Lonely Again.* LaPuenta, CA: Baron Publishers, 1992. IndianMatchmaker.com. http://www.indianmatchmaker.com; Jeevansathi Internet Services. http://www.jeevansathi.com; Match.com, L.L.C. http://www.match.com; MatrimonialsIndia.com. http://www.matrimonialsindia.com; Perfectmatch.com. http://www.perfectmatch.com; suItablematch.com. http://www.suitablematch.com;

Kimberly P. Brackett

MIDWIFERY AND MEDICALIZATION

For a number of years questions have been asked about the care provided to pregnant and laboring mothers by midwives. Many of the questions have come from the medical establishment. This leads women to ask whether the caregiver they have selected, be it a midwife or a physician, is a skilled attendant or whether the caregiver will insist upon dangerous interventions in childbirth.

Midwives attend 8 percent of the over four million births that occur annually in the United States. Midwives, or trained childbirth assistants, have historically been the primary caretakers of childbirth, but in the United States over the course of the twentieth century they have experienced continuous opposition and faced legal suppression. Only recently have they experienced a professional resurgence that has allowed them to carve a small but tenuous niche in the childbirth industry. While some types of midwifery are legally practiced throughout the United States, many states maintain a ban on other forms of midwifery, and, even where it is legal, the regulations and practices that govern it vary greatly.

Despite the growing professionalization of natural health care and the development of consumer movements in health, midwifery remains at the nexus of a visceral debate regarding the appropriate authority over and practice of childbearing. On one side of this debate, midwives and their supporters contend that for most women, midwifery offers the ideal model of childbirth care producing healthier babies and happier mothers. On the other side of the debate, medical opponents argue that childbirth is a medical event and should be medically managed, with any practice of midwifery in child labor occurring only under medical supervision.

MIDWIFERY

The term midwife typically refers to two types of skilled birth attendants. The Certified Nurse Midwife (CNM) is trained first in an accredited nursing degree program with additional specialty training in childbirth assistance. CNMs legally practice throughout the United States, many of them working in hospitals or independent birth centers. A Direct Entry Midwife (DEM) has also received training in birth assistance, although this can be either through an accredited institution or an informal apprenticeship and is not preceded by a formal education in nursing. DEMs also practice throughout the United States although in 11 states this is explicitly prohibited, and in 17 states there is no legal, regulatory protection for practicing midwives.

Midwives differ from medical providers in their underlying philosophical orientation to birth as a normal process, the ways in which they respond to the physiological changes that occur during pregnancy and labor, and the emphasis they place on the relationships they strive to build with their clients. Most midwives serve as women's primary care attendants throughout pregnancy and labor and some also provide postpartum care. Prenatal care under a midwife focuses on building strong nutrition and overall health as well as fostering emotional empowerment and confidence in preparation for and throughout labor. Because physicians view physiological processes in terms of detecting pathology, the prenatal care they offer tends to center around identifying complications and is punctuated by a schedule of routine examinations and screening for abnormalities. Throughout the labor and birth, physicians often employ the routine use of technological interventions for monitoring and measuring the progress of the woman and the condition of the fetus. The duration of labor is also highly regulated by physicians and medically managed through the use of artificial hormones and the artificial rupturing of membranes. If dystocia, the failure of the woman to progress in labor, is diagnosed then physicians will perform a cesarean section to remove the fetus who they believe to be at risk. Midwives, especially DEMs, respond to labor pain and timing differently than physicians. Midwives offer natural remedies, nonmedical techniques to ease and tolerate contractions, and allow women to labor for longer periods of time before resorting to more serious interventions.

The midwifery model of care emphasizes the importance of developing relationships of trust between providers and clients, and primary-care midwives attend to the laboring mother throughout her entire pregnancy, offering longer prenatal visits in an effort to establish closer relationships with their clients for whom they will serve as the primary caregiver at their clients' labors. Some primary-care physicians will attend to their clients' deliveries when they are on call, but often women are attended primarily by hospital nursing staff throughout their labors and the staffed hospital physician will attend their deliveries when the labor has advanced to the final stage. DEMs attend to their clients' births at home, bringing some emergency equipment with them. Many physicians oppose this practice, arguing that homebirths are unsafe and giving birth outside of the hospital poses a serious risk to both the mother and the baby. However, the hospital as the principal locale for birth is a recent phenomenon, resulting from the rapid medicalization of birth in the United States during the twentieth century.

HISTORICAL TRANSFORMATIONS IN MATERNITY CARE

Midwives were once the dominant caretakers of childbirth in America. The practice of midwifery was a convention the colonists' brought with them to the New World. Midwives, or female birth attendants, were the community specialists in childbirth, and often each community employed a full-time midwife to care for all labors and deliveries. Many women's historians refer to the time before the mid-eighteenth century as the age of the midwife. The Japanese *samba,* French *sage-femme,* black slave's *granny,* and Jamaican *nana* were all midwives. The term midwife literally meant "with woman" in Old English and "the childbirth assisting woman," the *hameyaledet,* in Hebrew. In the Old Testament book Exodus midwives were not only mentioned but praised by God for their refusal to kill male Hebrew newborns.

Beginning in the thirteenth century the guild of barber-surgeons existed in Europe. This guild, exclusively male, had the sole right to use surgical instruments. When birth was impossible the midwife had the barber-surgeon perform an embryotomy, killing the infant, or a caesarean-like procedure, after the death of the mother. These barber-surgeons were called upon only when the death of either the mother or child was inevitable. The invention of crude forceps provided a way for a baby to be delivered alive in formerly impossible births. Barber-surgeons coveted this instrument, often using it unnecessarily. Male surgeons were often unaware and unconcerned with the basics of the birthing process.

Having rarely seen normal births, they treated all births as difficult, using tools that were unnecessary and damaging to both woman and child.

Childbirth was an entirely female matter in colonial America, and the women of the community would collectively help with preparation for the birth and care for the family and household during the labor and postpartum or lying-in period, often concluding the event with a so-called groaning party, which was a collective sharing of their own experiences in labor and motherhood. The midwife, who was commonly the primary general health care provider, was knowledgeable in natural remedies for many types of ailments and brought natural agents and techniques to aid in labor and recovery. Nevertheless, childbirth was a potentially risky event, marked by the element of unpredictability, and it was not uncommon for women or babies to die in childbirth. The midwife was therefore also respected as the guardian over the unknown and mysterious aspects of labor.

The training of midwives varied greatly from woman to woman. The usual process involved a midwife training another as an apprentice but in many cultures it was just necessary for the midwife to be postmenopausal. The witch hunts that took place from the fourteenth to seventeenth centuries were concentrated in Europe but occurred in America as well. Midwives were often accused of witchcraft due to the mystic nature of their work and the desire of some male healers to take over their coveted profession. Midwives would keep the nail of their pinkie finger long and sharp in order to cut the umbilical cord of a newborn, which led to some of the common caricatures of witches with unnaturally long fingernails that exist in contemporary society. Midwives who delivered babies with deformities or even daughters instead of desired sons feared being branded a sorcerer or witch.

In 1716, however, New York required the licensing of midwives, a step in undermining the autonomy midwives enjoyed. This licensing was more concerned with the midwives' ethics and virtue rather than competence as a doctress. In America midwives were better tolerated and respected than their English counterparts. Colonial midwives, as well as those in Europe, were not just called upon to deliver babies. They were summoned by courts to take part in a jury of matrons that determined if a woman found guilty of a crime was pregnant or if a baby was a result of fornication.

At the end of the eighteenth century, colonists who went to the mainland for medical training brought back the practice of a new male midwifery that laid the ground for the medicalization of childbirth. Professionally trained male midwives began to compete with traditional lay midwives for dominance in the new, professional sphere of childbirth care arguing that formal training and new technology made them safer providers during labor and delivery. Dr. William Shippen offered courses in human anatomy and midwifery to midwives in Philadelphia and Dr. Thomas Ewell attempted to get federal funding for a midwifery school geared toward women. Neither of these endeavors was very successful. Women were largely illiterate and did not have the time, money, or ability to participate in formal education. Many experienced midwives saw no reason to study under men who had not had their years of experience and who were relatively unfamiliar with the birthing process. Traditional lay midwives resisted the challenge and argued that as women, the skills they acquired from personal experience in giving and assisting with birth could not be attained through the study of texts or trial and error experimentation in the field. They were also skeptical about the use of the forceps (a large hinged instrument used for grasping the baby's head to pull it out of the birth canal) that often resulted in damage to the fetus when misused.

Government and philanthropic hospitals began in the eighteenth century and they were notoriously unhygienic. Fatalities of both mother and child were common and doctors remained largely ignorant of basic sanitation. In the mid-1800s hospitals began to become more aseptic and laboring middle-class women began to admit themselves into hospitals. Hospitals began to charge and it was only upper-class women that could afford better services. In 1894 the first documented caesarean was performed by using a method German doctor Max Sanger invented. Silk thread was used to suture the uterine and abdominal walls and both baby and mother survived. The lack of midwives, new drug concoctions that made labor free of most pains, and increasing prestige of doctors made hospitals more popular.

However, with the inception of the field of obstetrics and the rapid professionalization of medicine through organizations like the American Medical Association (AMA) in the late nineteenth century, the male obstetrician became the dominant provider, and scientific progress and advances in medicine offered promise to those who believed childbirth could be a safer event when managed by medical expertise and the use of new technologies.

THE MIDWIFE "PROBLEM"

At the beginning of the twentieth century, obstetricians began to encourage their clients to come to the hospital maternity ward, previously only used by research universities that served indigent women, because there physicians could treat a larger number of clients on a more regular schedule. This shift of childbirth into the hospital was followed by advancements made in technological interventions, such as the cesarean section and the introduction of drugs for relieving the pain of labor. Also by this time, the AMA had successfully campaigned to have midwifery outlawed in major urban areas, but lay midwifery was still practiced in immigrant enclaves, in rural areas, and in many regions of the segregated south. In the medical community this was perceived as a problem, even though few doctors wanted to travel long distances or across racial and ethnic divides to serve poorer clients.

Doctors argued that midwifery was problematic because it was practiced without any standardized training or regulation, and this threatened the safety of their clients and the progress of medical advancement. Midwives argued that the only threat posed to doctors by the persistence of their practice was physicians' superior vocational status. In response to the growing debate over the midwifery problem, medical authorities recommended that midwifery be regulated only until the introduction of obstetric charities would gradually eliminate the practice.

By the 1920s states began to implement laws that regulated the practice and training of midwifery. Meanwhile, another recommendation that the practice of midwifery become merged with that of nursing, as was occurring in Europe, soon developed into a new vocational training program and practice for professional nurse-midwives. Beginning with the Frontier Nursing School in rural Kentucky, several programs developed throughout the United States that trained women first in nursing and then in midwifery. During the 1950s and 1960s some nurse-midwives practiced as birth assistants under obstetrics' supervision in hospitals and others as primary childbirth providers in rural or impoverished areas with poor access to quality health care. As the use of midwives in childbirth persisted through the latter half of the century, midwifery, once a problem that many sought to eliminate, became a question of how best to standardize and regulate midwifery alongside or in assistance to the practice of medicine.

THE MIDWIFE "QUESTION"

The practice of lay midwifery was popularized during the 1970s and 1980s. This occurred in response to growing discontents with care expressed by consumer movements in health care. Additional support grew from the influence of the ideals of natural childbirth that had gained momentum in the 1960s. Women, many having worked as childbirth educators, began to study midwifery manuals on their own and develop a new practice of homebirth. These new direct-entry midwives rejected the medicalization of birth practiced in the hospital and later organized to form accredited training programs that would not require students to pass through a formal education in nursing first but to focus solely on midwifery. DEMs soon petitioned for state licensing and the right to practice privately. Some medical professionals, like those involved in the American Academy of Family Physicians (AAFP), opposed the licensing of midwives altogether and argued that childbirth is a medical event representing the best interest of quality patient care, while other organizations, like the American College of Obstetrics and Gynecology (ACOG), worked toward licensing only CNMs who would work under obstetricians' guidelines and supervision.

In 1938 about half of American women were giving birth in hospitals. Currently in the United States, 99 percent of births occur in the hospital with 1 percent of births occurring at home. This figure has remained the same for more than 20 years. While midwives do attend to a small percentage of laboring women, over 90 percent of women give birth under the care of an obstetrician and over 95 percent of women experience medicated childbirth. Although midwives work in a small and marginalized niche of the market, a contentious debate continues reflecting three distinct opinions about midwifery and medicalization: (1) some physicians feel that childbirth is a physiological process that is best cared for entirely under the auspices of medical management and that midwifery has no place in a progressive medicalized health care practice; (2) many physicians feel that midwifery may be a good option for some low-risk women and support a limited practice of midwifery under the guidance and supervision of obstetricians; and (3) midwives and midwifery advocates argue that midwifery is the optimal health care choice for most women and that medical management should be reserved for worst-case scenario emergencies. This debate centers around two principal concerns with the outcome of childbirth. The first concern is the safety of the mother and the baby, and the second is the relational care providers may offer.

MALPRACTICE POLITICS AND MEDICAL INTERVENTIONS

Parallel to the debate over the safety of routinely used medical interventions in childbirth is a discussion about the current state of professional risk in practicing obstetrics. In the 1980s, a malpractice crisis in obstetrics, and medicine more generally, marked the dawn of a new era of maternity care. The increased risk of being sued for prenatal or birth-related injury resulted in a widespread professional transition; the practice of prenatal and maternity care by the family physician became nearly obsolete and the cost of malpractice insurance for obstetricians skyrocketed. However, this period was also followed by the momentum gained in consumer movements that continued to demand greater accountability and safer outcomes in medical practice.

In the mid-1990s widespread concern over rising cesarean rates, which had tripled between 1968 and 1977 and continued to rise throughout the 1980s, was evidenced in the U.S. Health Public Health Service's 1990 objective to reduce the rate of cesarean section to 15 percent or less by the year 2000. The rate of cesarean sections did eventually lessen to 21.2 percent by 1994, as did the rates of other routine medical interventions in childbirth, but currently is climbing upwards of 30 percent and more in most U.S. hospitals. Through studies like those conducted by the World Health Organization, midwives and their advocates show that midwife-attended births yield one-third or less the standard rate of emergency operations, recommending that midwifery become the new convention for low-risk birth. While pundits on both sides of this debate point to the fear of malpractice as another form of professional risk in the childbirth industry, one that directly affects doctors' diagnoses of physiological risk for their patients, consumer advocates hold the right to litigate as critical to their own safety, and obstetricians continue to perform interventions earlier and more often.

SAFETY AND RISK IN CHILDBIRTH

ACOG's Statement on Midwifery explains that, as a professional medical organization, they are committed foremost to safety in women's health care. In the name of safety, ACOG supports the practice of midwifery only by those midwives who have passed an examination administered by the American College of Nurse Midwives (ACNM) and hold certification under ACNM's auxiliary certification board. Lay midwives or those who have not passed this certification and do not agree to adhere to the regulations specified for certified nurse-midwives are not deemed to be safe childbirth providers. Doctors who argue that unregulated practice is unsafe point to cases in which women giving birth at home or without the care of a physician have experienced poor outcomes, often regarding the health of the baby, such as oxygen loss during or immediately after the birth, or the health of the mother who may experience hemorrhaging or other postpartum complications, both of which may result in the death of the infant or the mother. While midwives routinely transfer women who experience complications during or after their deliveries to the hospital, doctors argue that by the time they arrive under medical care it may be too late.

Midwives offer several responses to accusations that midwifery is not safe. First, they argue that by accepting only women who are considered low-risk, in other words those who display a generally healthy constitution and have had no previous health problems that could affect their labor and delivery, they can avoid predictable complications. Second, midwives will refer to a physician those women who exhibit potential risks during the progression of their pregnancy, such as multiparous births (the presence of twins and multiples) and breech-positioned babies. Last, DEMs argue that by avoiding the cascade of interventions that women are routinely subject to in medical environments, midwife-attended births at home, in the birth center, or even in the hospital are safer alternatives than the medical norm. They point to statistics that show that low-risk births are as safe at home as they are in the hospital and that routine medical interventions lead to longer labors and are more likely to end in cesarean sections. They also garner legitimacy from international organizations like the World Health Organization that cites that the United States ranks twenty-eighth in infant mortality and recommends midwifery as the preferred model of childbirth for low-risk women.

In October 2006, ACOG released a statement describing homebirth as an unsafe option and prohibiting all elected officials and college staff from participating in out-of-hospital births while discouraging individual fellows from condoning or participating in out-of-hospital practices. In collaboration between ACNM and eight other national professional nursing and midwifery organizations, ACNM released a response to ACOG's homebirth statement expressing concern that the policy implicated in the statement disregards scientific studies that demonstrate the safety of homebirth. They also express worry that recent indications of potential pandemic outbreaks of influenza and exposure to other harmful bacteria in hospitals poses serious risks to birthing mothers and infants, more so if the alternatives of giving birth at home or in birth centers were eliminated.

THE MIDWIFERY MODEL OF CARE

Citizens for Midwifery, a national organization of lay advocates for the midwifery model of care, articulates this childbirth philosophy as predicated on the belief that well-being throughout pregnancy and labor is physical, psychological, and social. The Midwives Alliance of North America describes midwifery care as "uniquely nurturing, hands-on care before, during, and after birth" (www.mana.org). They explain that developing a close and trusting relationship with one's midwife is integral to achieving the holistic model of health that they profess. For many women, this holistic model of health is the most appealing selling point of midwife-providers and they embrace midwifery as the alternative to what they claim is cold, insensitive medical care where providers are little more than strangers attending a significant life event and making critical advice over a woman's most intimate health care needs.

Interestingly, this movement toward the midwifery model of care has been influenced by both traditionalists and feminists. Traditionalists, often religious midwives and their communities, believe that the intimacy of the birth act is something that should only be attended by intimate family members, other women of the community, and midwives, the female specialists in childbirth. Feminists argue that decisions over a woman's intimate physiological processes should be made by the woman herself. The provider's role, ideally a midwife, is to empower and support the woman to make her own decisions about her labor and birth and offer encouragement for the woman's innate natural ability to give birth. Midwives remind clients that they are "with women" (the meaning of the word midwife) and their job is to assist the woman in her own delivery as opposed to the obstetrician who stands "before women" (the meaning of the word obstetrics) to delivery the baby for her.

In connecting the importance of relational work to safety, midwives have also pointed out that women need to feel psychologically secure in order to have a safe and easier labor. To bolster this argument they reference studies that show that labors often slow or fail to progress upon entering the hospital environment, that anxiety and stress increases labor complications, and that the presence of a support person shortens the duration of labor and lessens complications. Midwives are adept at offering relaxation techniques and they sometimes are accompanied by doulas, a woman whose sole responsibility is to accompany a woman throughout her labor and offer encouragement and support.

In contrast, some women prefer to deliver and to have medically managed births where physical pain is not experienced, and others now elect to have cesarean sections so that vaginal delivery may be avoided altogether. While the medical model has incorporated some of the language of the new midwifery movement advertising "sensitivity" and "human touch" coupled with their technological expertise, and hospitals have adopted some of the nonmedical practices for pain and relaxation, they remain focused on the instrumental aspects of physiological care. Because the medical model is the normative safe practice for birth in the United States and because of medical organizations' political power in maintaining this image, few insurance providers allow women to elect to have a midwife as their principal provider in childbirth, and fewer still compensate for births at home, although the overall costs of this practice are minimal when compared with the costs of giving birth in a hospital. Advocates for midwifery and childbirth alternatives argue that countering the dominant medical practice will require cultural measures, such as educational reform in medical institutions and for the laity, as well as political measures, such as strengthening the legal monitoring and regulation of obstetric practices and taking political action for so-called humanized birth.

See also Breastfeeding and Formula Feeding; Childbirth Options; Cosleeping.

Further Reading: American College of Obstetrics and Gynecology. http://www.acog.org/; American College of Nurse-Midwives. http://www.acnm.org/; Citizens for Midwifery. http://cfmidwifery.org/index.aspx; Katz Rothman, Barbara, Wendy Simonds, and Beri Meltzer Norman. *Laboring On: Birth in Transition in the United States.* New York: Routledge, 2006; Midwives Alliance of North America. http://www.mana.org/; Rich, Adrienne. *Of Woman Born: Motherhood as Experience and Institution.* New York: W. W. Norton and Co., 1986; Rooks, J. P. *Midwifery and Childbirth in America.* Philadelphia: Temple University Press, 1997; Thurer, Shari L. *The Myths of Motherhood: How Culture Reinvents the Good Mother.* New York: Penguin Books, 1994.

Selina Gallo-Cruz

MOMMY TRACK

Many women today face conflicting and constraining expectations regarding work and family roles. Surveys reveal that a significant percentage of working mothers feel torn between the demands of their job and the desire to spend more time with their family. Many women report feeling guilty about not having enough time or energy to one domain or the other. Mommy track is a term, often used in a derogatory manner, to refer to jobs that permit women to spend greater amounts of time with family. The term is also used to describe the women's goals for employment as secondary to their goals for motherhood.

BACKGROUND

Today, women who choose to become mothers confront two dominant cultural scripts or images—that of a full-time mother who does not work outside the home, or that of a woman who adds employment to her primary role as a mother. Furthermore, there remains a certain amount of cultural ambivalence about mothers who choose to work outside the home. Some might say that all mothers, whether employed or not, face a no-win situation. If they remain at home, mothering full-time, they may feel unfulfilled or certainly unappreciated by those around them. They also pay a financial price in decreased retirement funds and benefits relative to employed women. On the other hand, if they work outside the home, either by choice or necessity, they may feel judged and criticized by others or believe that they are failing their children. This guilt, coupled with continuing discrimination in the workplace, can leave women questioning their decision to work.

While there is a popular cultural sentiment that women can have it all, most workplaces have not caught up with changing social expectations, gender roles, and economic realities. For the most part, the workplace is still guided by traditional assumptions—that married men are the primary providers and that married women are caretakers of the home. Furthermore, employers may operate under the assumption that married women are being provided for and that their earnings are only supplementary. Convincing women that their primary responsibility is to maintain the home and not to work outside of it may have a less obvious motive—it also ensures that many women will be willing to work for less because they believe that their earnings and professional ambitions are secondary to their husband's and peripheral to their identity. Social psychological studies routinely find that women undervalue their contributions, relative to men's, when given a group task.

The labor market is not the only area of social life that continues to be guided by traditional gender roles and family expectations. The private sphere, family life, also appears to be reluctant to change. It is estimated that American women continue to perform about 80 percent of the childcare and over two-thirds of the housework. Interestingly, recent polls find that most fathers would like to spend less time at work and more time with their families. Also, while many Americans want fathers to be more involved with their children, most disapprove of a man who chooses his family over his job or takes time off from work simply to spend more time with his kids. Thus, women may feel compelled to squelch their career aspirations in favor of supporting their husband's careers by performing traditionally female tasks.

Our cultural image and expectations of the ideal worker are of someone who works at least forty hours each week with conventional or 9-to-5 hours with, at most, two weeks of vacation each year. Based on this definition, however, only about one-third of American women are so-called ideal workers. A significant percentage of women who are mothers work for pay part-time, which severely restricts not only their earnings but also their chances for promotion if and when they should decide to reenter the labor force on a full-time basis. The particular likelihood that white women will pursue part-time work while married and raising children helps to explain why, over the course of their work lives, white women will earn less than their black female counterparts who are more likely to work full time. It has been shown, for instance, that part-time lawyers who resume full-time work, even after a short period, are likely to earn considerably less than lawyers who have always worked full-time. Furthermore, the most challenging and interesting assignments are reserved for full-time attorneys, leading some to speculate that a so-called pink collar ghetto of women lawyers, most of whom are mothers, is emerging.

Even when offered, many employees refuse a part-time employment option, fearing that it will prevent them from advancing in their fields. In a study of 188 Fortune 500 manufacturing firms, it was found that while 88 percent of the firms offered a part-time track, only 3 to 5 percent of the employees took advantage of it. Of course, it is possible too that parents fear the resentment of nonparents, who may feel that mothers and fathers are benefiting from special privileges such as flex-time.

It is also important to consider that, for the most competitive and most remunerative positions, workers are still expected to work long days, to engage in weekend work, or agree to out-of-town travel. To be sure, workers who cannot work overtime often suffer negative professional consequences. Furthermore, for a variety of reasons, the vast majority of mothers in the United States are unable to work overtime. There is considerable evidence that having children has a definite negative effect on women's lifetime earnings. Interestingly, the wage gap between working mothers and other workers has widened in recent years.

Because of the gender expectations associated with housework and childcare, working mothers are at a considerable disadvantage professionally, as compared to working fathers. It is very difficult for women to aspire to the emerging ideal of the satisfied and driven professional in a culture that continues to assign primacy to marriage and motherhood. Recent surveys indicate that about two-thirds of Americans believe it is best for women to stay home and care for family and children. While fathers are largely relieved of domestic responsibilities to pursue their primary obligation of providing, working mothers are either expected to do both or are expected to relinquish their paid work roles and devote attention to the family.

THE MOMMY TRACK

In an attempt to assist working mothers and employers to deal constructively with the competing role expectations facing women, corporate career consultant Felice Schwartz offered a proposal, which has since been labeled the mommy track. The phrase mommy track itself was actually coined when the New York Times ran an article about Schwartz's proposal. The idea is that businesses and other professions create positions that demand less time and involvement for women who wish to make their primary focus home and family life (so-called career and family women). On the other hand, women who are more career-oriented (so-called career primary women) could select positions that are very time-consuming and more demanding, with the expectation of greater upward mobility and better compensation. In this way, family-focused women could still enjoy moderately demanding careers, at mid-level, for example, but would not be expected to compete with others who are more primarily focused on professional excellence at any cost. Women who pursue this mommy track would not feel pressured to mimic the career trajectories of those around them, nor would they feel that their positions were jeopardized by their lower commitment to paid work. In addition, businesses might be attracted to the idea, arguing that they should not have to invest in workers who will interrupt or terminate their careers when family obligations become too great.

While Schwartz has been an advocate for women's equality and rights in the workplace, especially the corporate world, her proposal has garnered a certain amount of negative attention from feminists, work and family experts, and political liberals. In fact, Schwartz has been accused of being antifeminist and for proposing that employers engage in gender-discriminatory hiring practices.

The proposal is certainly appealing in some respects, but it warrants concern as well. Schwartz's research has been criticized on several grounds—that she was somewhat vague in her descriptions of the data sources, vague in her reporting of the findings, and that she failed to offer alternative explanations beyond differential treatment of mothers for women's professional outcomes.

There is a concern that the idea of two tracks for working women—a mommy track and a fast track—perpetuates the belief and expectation that it is women, and not men, who are expected to care for the family and who must decide between these competing domains. By extension, the proposal threatens to cast a negative light on all women workers by suggesting that women in general will have trouble meeting the demands of both work and family. The association of women with domesticity means that even those women who choose to pursue both domains will be assumed to be less committed to paid work, and perhaps less competent, and will be dubbed suitable for pink collar or mommy track positions only. Positions on the mommy track may be or may become dead-end. Because these jobs would not merit significant advancements in position in the company, an employer may feel no real obligation to professional development among these workers. Reserving such jobs for women perpetuates the belief that women do not care about paid work or professional advancement. Additionally, how having been on the mommy track would affect a woman after she had reared children and wished to enter a career primary track is uncertain. Employers may not be willing to invest in these women because they would likely be mid-career by that point.

The other assumption made by Schwartz is that only women would want or opt for a less-demanding career track. Some have argued for a comparable daddy track. Indeed, a 1990s survey found that 39 percent of fathers said they would quit their jobs to have more time with their children. Another found that almost three-quarters of fathers preferred a daddy track job over a fast track job. Of course, the primary concern for these fathers was how to maintain adequate incomes to support their families if they were to exercise such an option.

Perhaps the single largest concern of the proposal, to many, is that rather than tackle dominant ideologies regarding work and family (notions of the ideal worker, the conventional work day, gender roles, *etc.*), the proposal only reinforces such ideologies and perpetuates gender inequality both at work and at home. If not challenged, child-rearing and work ideologies serve to maintain the current power structure and to reinforce the subordinate status of women. Women are encouraged to subordinate their work-related aspirations to marriage and motherhood, and Schwartz's proposal would seem to assist employers in facilitating this. Should they decide to combine work and family, they are penalized and judged for emphasizing one over the other (*i.e.*, women who work too much are neglectful mothers and women who don't work enough are uncommitted workers). The dominant ideology of child rearing also benefits the capitalist class—the employers—who enjoy the uncompromised commitment of male workers who are fortunate enough to have the emotional and practical support of a spouse at home. In addition, the current ideology ensures that men in the workplace are protected from the competition of many women workers.

Work-family experts have offered a number of suggestions for how to avoid or minimize the effects of motherhood on employment. First, women planning to take maternity leave should communicate with their superiors regarding their planned dates of departure and return. Second, projects or clients should be transitioned in a timely and efficient manner. Employees should avoid missing or leaving work early to tend to child-related matters; whenever possible, the help of a family member or friend should be enlisted. Others suggest keeping family photos and phone calls to a minimum and maintaining professional dress once one returns to the workplace. Finally, while on leave, mothers should make an attempt to maintain contact with colleagues and supervisors. In addition, using email or other avenues of communication to maintain some level of professional activity helps to convey that one is not entirely disconnected from the workplace and has every intention to return.

See also Child Care Policy; Employed Mothers; Family and Medical Leave Act (FMLA); Motherhood, Opportunity Costs; Transition to Parenthood.

Further Reading: Coltrane, Scott. *Family Man: Fatherhood, Housework, and Gender Equity.* New York: Oxford University Press, 1996; Crittenden, Ann. *The Price of Motherhood: Why the Most Important Job in the World is Still the Least Valued.* New York: Henry Holt and Company, 2001; Galinsky, Ellen. *Ask the Children: The Breakthrough Study That Reveals How To Succeed At Work and Parenting.* New York: HarperCollins Publishers, 1999; Hays, Sharon. *The Cultural Contradictions of Motherhood.* New Haven, CT: Yale University Press, 1996; Hochschild, Arlie Russell, and Anne Machung. *The Second Shift.* New York: Penguin, 2003; Padavic, Irene, and Barbara Reskin. *Women and Men at Work.* Thousand Oaks, CA: Pine Forge Press, 2002; Schwartz, Felice N. "Management Women and the New Facts of Life." *Harvard Business Review* 67 (1989): 65–76; Williams, Joan. *Unbending Gender: Why Family and Work Conflict and What To Do About It.* New York: Oxford University Press, 2000.

Susan Cody-Rydzewski

MOTHERHOOD, OPPORTUNITY COSTS

While motherhood is exalted as a cultural ideal and the most fulfilling role for women, it carries with it many so-called opportunity costs, or missed opportunities. The term was originally used to refer to the economic opportunities, such as wage earning and money for investing, that parents give up when they are rearing children. Children's needs and expenses decrease a couple's standard of living significantly. In addition to the direct financial costs of raising children, which are staggering, becoming a parent also requires an enormous commitment of energy, time, and attention. As a result, many other areas of one's life, such as career, earnings, marriage, or personal time may suffer. These expected lifestyle changes are also a form of opportunity costs and they are felt more acutely by mothers than by fathers.

MOTHERING TASKS

It is widely known that mothers are more involved in direct parenting than are fathers, especially when the children are young. While fathers today are more involved with their children than were fathers in the past, most often the type of involvement between fathers and children is one of accessibility rather than direct engagement or responsibility. It is not uncommon for men to pursue activities unrelated to child-rearing while in the presence of children, and to view this type of interaction as parenting. Women are much more likely to be engaged in hands-on activities with children and to feel ultimately responsible for their entertainment, well-being, and self-esteem. Therefore, parenting is more costly for women than it is for men because women make more accommodations to their own schedules and commitments as well as experience the obligations of parenting more psychically.

Women spend more actual time with children as well as more time preparing, planning for, and anticipating their needs. In other words, in addition to performing more of the daily tasks (e.g., clothing, feeding, bathing) that are sometimes known as maintenance care, women spend more time trying to coordinate their schedules with the activities and demands of their children. It is common for fathers to describe their contribution to parenting as helping out or baby-sitting. This reference to men's parenting as baby-sitting angers some men because they feel that it denigrates the good parenting that they do. Some women are angered by the term baby-sitting because it serves as a reminder of the view that mothers are primarily responsible for parenting rather than the tasks being shared equally by both parents. Because baby-sitting is most often a paid task performed by someone outside the family with a lower investment in the developmental outcomes of the child, it can be an offense when used to discuss fathering.

Women are assigned primary responsibility for parenting, especially with infants. Some women may feel threatened by the possibility that husbands display competence at dual roles—paid work and parenting. Thus, they may discourage or criticize fathers' attempts at involvement. A common consequence of parenthood, especially for women, is loss of freedom and flexibility. While mothers may anticipate some of these changes, the societal pressures upon them to fulfill this role may come as a surprise. There is clearly a so-called leisure gap between fathers and mothers, with mothers having considerably less free time. Some organizations attempt to ameliorate the stress of mothering through programs designed to give full-time mothers a break, such as Mother's Day Out.

Culturally, there is a strong association of parenting with mothering and women are expected to curtail their other responsibilities and interests once they become parents. While it is socially acceptable for men to continue with professional, personal, or other pursuits once becoming fathers, women who attempt to maintain their preparental identities and involvements once they become mothers will likely encounter social disapproval. Career-oriented women who become mothers are in a lose-lose situation. They are discouraged from pursuing paid work on a full-time basis, unless they are working-class, even though it is paid labor that is most highly valued by society. On the other hand, should they decide to continue investing time and energy in their careers, they may confront a rather harsh social stigma for their supposed lack of commitment to motherhood. Stereotypes of employed women often relate to the negative outcomes that are supposed to befall their children. Interestingly, studies have found that children of working mothers experience certain benefits over those with stay-at-home mothers. When mothers work, their children tend to score higher on tests of verbal and mathematical ability, have higher self-esteem, view women more positively, and are generally more independent.

The role of mothers is one fraught with inconsistencies and misunderstandings. Industrialization resulted in the notion of the unproductive housewife, a disparaging view of wives and mothers and the work that they do in and around the home. Prior to the Industrial Revolution, no such view existed because all family members worked and, for the most part, all work was domestic. Although housework is typically viewed as leisurely, unstructured, unintelligent, and unproductive, feminist scholars as well as economists have found that the monetary value of unpaid domestic labor is significant. Furthermore, without this labor the nation's economy would be negatively affected. Increasingly, it is recognized that success in school and in the workplace begins with success at home—children who are reared in stable, happy homes are more likely to excel in the public domain. In fact, a majority of the Gross Domestic Product (GDP) can be traced back to the skills and capabilities of individual persons. Unfortunately, however, unpaid domestic labor remains unseen, unappreciated, and undervalued.

STRUCTURAL OPPORTUNITY COSTS

In many ways, the opportunity costs associated with motherhood are socially structured; they are not the result of individual choices but rather of social factors and institutional practices. In the United States, for example, child care is not subsidized by the government as it is in many other advanced nations. The United States is only one of five countries worldwide that does not offer paid maternity leave. In addition, until recently, few employers in the United States offered flexible scheduling. Employees, even those with young children, have had to work rigid, inflexible schedules while trying to coordinate with child care agencies, baby-sitters, schools, and other institutions. Consequently, some workers, particularly women, have opted out of the labor force, at least for a while. Termination of employment, even on a part-time basis, results in reduced or lost Social Security and pension benefits.

In addition, stay-at-home and part-time workers are not eligible for disability insurance or unemployment compensation. The loss of income experienced by women who choose to leave the labor force entirely when they have a child or for an extended period of time has been dubbed the mommy tax and is estimated to be in the millions. Unfortunately, the long-term economic and professional consequences of reduced or terminated employment are quite severe and often irreversible. Compared to their childless counterparts, and to working fathers, working mothers will very likely experience diminished opportunities for career advancement and substantial reductions in lifetime earnings. In fact, the wage gap between mothers and childless women now exceeds the gap between young men and women.

Much more so than men, women who wish to become parents must often strategically plan when to have children. Some may opt to become mothers once their careers are well-established while others may wish to start their families before career opportunities peak. Women who return to work after being home with a young child may find that they are assumed to be on a mommy track, a professional pathway involving fewer challenges, lower compensation, and fewer promotional opportunities. Social attitudes toward working mothers remain largely unsympathetic—it is assumed that women who become mothers made that choice freely and that they must live with its consequences, however dire. This has lead to an increasing support movement that seeks to educate the public and employers about the need for employment, but the inherent challenges of doing both paid employment and parenting well. One such organization, the Families and Work Institute, is a nonprofit organization that examines the changing nature of work and family life.

RELATIONSHIP OPPORTUNITY COSTS

In addition to the economic costs of parenthood, there are also a number of marital and personal costs associated with it. While children have a stabilizing effect on marriage (that is, they lower the risk for divorce), they generally have a negative effect on marital quality or happiness. In other words, while couples may stay together for the sake of the children, they may not be as happy or satisfied with their relationships as they were before they became parents. Children exact a heavy toll on marriage, financially and otherwise. Parents experience more stress, anxiety, and depression than nonparents; this is especially true for women. With children present, conflicts over work, finances, religion, education, extended family, and leisure time are much more likely to occur. Interestingly, the more children there are, the more that marital happiness declines.

Marital happiness may be affected by changes in gender roles and in the division of household labor. While some couples are able to maintain a somewhat egalitarian division of labor prior to becoming parents, very few will maintain such a balance afterwards. Men tend to invest more time in paid work while women invest less. In fact, employers may actually view fathers as more committed employees than men who do not have children. This increased financial role for fathers make them more responsible. In addition to performing most of the childcare, or arranging for it, after having children, women typically assume a greater level of responsibility for the housework more generally, even if they continue to work full-time. This additional shift of work experienced by working mothers is well-documented and is known as the second shift.

Gradually, partners may feel that they have less in common and are less able to relate to other another. The relationship may become less spontaneous and less intimate. Spouses often find that they do less together and that their sexual lives are negatively affected. Wives and younger spouses seem to be more vulnerable to the damaging effect of children. As mentioned earlier, women are more likely than men to experience dramatic life changes upon the birth of a child. Younger spouses are more likely to possess individualistic values and to believe that they can have it all. In the past, individuals placed less emphasis on personal happiness, freedom, and flexibility. Thus, younger spouses are more likely than older spouses, who were raised with more traditional and familial values, to experience a decline in marital satisfaction upon becoming parents. It may also be that younger parents have less experience working or playing with children than do older parents. A decline in family size, together with greater affluence, has resulted in less sibling care.

Despite the negative effect of children on marital happiness, most Americans have more than one child. Furthermore, most women who have children say they would do it again if given the choice. Even while new parents describe the stresses and strains associated with having children, they also describe the experience of parenthood as deeply meaningful and joyful. Many persons seem to take pride and satisfaction in fulfilling such a highly valued social role. Parenthood, more than any other life transition, confers adult status. While the romantic aspects of marriage may decrease temporarily, the companionate aspects may increase as a result of becoming parents. In other words, partners may feel that their partnership is strengthened by parenthood.

CONCLUSION

Children make for substantial additional work in a home. This work involves the physical care of the child as well as the parenting tasks of developing mentally and emotionally healthy and responsible children. These tasks exact an emotional cost on parents. However, as children age they may become more of an asset by assisting in household tasks and adding emotional value to the family. While the opportunity costs remain, they are most acutely felt in the earliest years of parenting. While society continues to suggest that the individual choices of women are the most important component in their decision to work or not while rearing children, it is increasingly a choice based on economics. Publications, such as *Working Mother* magazine help mothers define their choices in a positive light. However, this is aimed at individual women, not social policy. As the numbers of mothers who are working stays high, we need social policies that support the successful combination of work and family roles. One option, flextime, has met with some success in recent years, as has telecommuting. These trends will likely continue as a way to do hands-on parenting while limiting some of the financial opportunity costs.

See also Employed Mothers; Mommy Track; Overscheduled Children; Transition to Parenthood.

Further Reading: Blades, Joan, and Kristin Rowe-Finkbeiner. *The Motherhood Manifesto: What America's Moms Want—and What To Do About It.* New York: Nation Books, 2006; Crittenden, Ann. *The Price of Motherhood: Why the Most Important Job In the World is Still the Least Valued.* New York: Henry Holt and Company, 2001; Families and Work Institute. http://www.familiesandwork.org; Maushart, Susan. *The Mask of Motherhood: How Becoming a Mother Changes Everything and Why We Pretend It Doesn't.* New York: New Press, 1999; Peskowitz, Miriam. 2005. *The Truth Behind the "Mommy Wars": Who Decides What Makes a Good Mother?* Berkeley: Seal Press, 2005; Stark, Marg. *What No One Tells the Mom: Surviving the Early Years of Parenthood With Your Sanity, Your Sex Life and Your Sense of Humor Intact.* New York: Penguin, 2005; Steiner, Leslie Morgan. *Mommy Wars: Stay-at-Home and Career Moms Face Off on Their Choices, Their Lives, Their Families.* New York: Random House, 2007; Stone, Pamela. *Opting Out? Why Women Really Quit Careers and Head Home.* Berkeley: University of California Press, 2007; Wolf, Naomi. *Misconceptions: Truth, Lies, and the Unexpected Journey to Motherhood.* New York: Doubleday, 2001.

Susan Cody-Rydzewski

NONMARITAL COHABITATION

Nonmarital heterosexual cohabitation refers to living with a partner in a marriage-like relationship without being married. Another common name for this behavior is living together. What role does cohabitation play in society and marriage today? Currently cohabitation is viewed by researchers in two primary ways. In one view it is seen as a stage in courtship where couples cohabit as part of a dating or other romantic relationship. In this way it is a prelude to marriage. The other view suggests that some persons choose cohabitation as a life-long alternative to marriage, and never intend to marry. For these persons cohabitation is a substitute for marriage.

STATISTICS

Estimates from the U.S. Census Bureau indicate that about 4.7 million households of opposite-sex couples were cohabiting households in 2000. This is a dramatic increase from 30 years before when, in 1970, there were 523,000 such couples. This represents a nearly 900 percent increase from 1970 to 2000. This increase in nonmarital cohabitation has been occurring in most Western nations. In Canada and Western Europe, cohabitation rates are much higher than they are in the United States. In the United Kingdom, for example, cohabitation has become so commonplace that partners can gather information about options and the legal status of cohabitation through official government websites. In Sweden, for example, one in four couples are living together without being married, and virtually all Swedes cohabit prior to marriage.

More than half of the cohabitants in the United States are younger couples under the age of 35, but persons might enter into such an arrangement at any age. Nearly 22 percent of cohabitants are under the age of 25, and 36 percent are between 25 and 34 years old. According to the census bureau, 4 percent of cohabitants were over the age of 65. The reasons that each age group chooses to cohabit are likely quite different, however.

Rates of cohabitation vary by geographic region as well. More cohabiting couples are found in the West and the lowest rates of cohabitation are in the Southern states. The state with the smallest percentage of nonmarried cohabitors among its population is Alabama. The state with the highest percentage is Alaska.

Most cohabitants are persons who have never married. Fifty-eight percent of cohabiting households contain partners who have never married, and 67 percent of cohabiting households do not contain children. Cohabitation is often an option for persons after divorce. In the United States 32 percent of cohabiting partners were divorced. Among those persons who were divorced, widowed, or cohabiting apart from a marital relationship, approximately one-third of them had children residing with them.

THE EVOLUTION OF COHABITATION

Although by no means a new phenomenon, heterosexual nonmarital cohabitation has changed in scope and frequency in recent decades. Formerly, living together without being married was an adaptation among the poor. Today cohabitation is more likely among lower-income and less-educated groups, although persons of other social classes do participate. While cohabitation is primarily a behavior of young people, cohabitors are of all ages. Cohabitation might be viewed as a reasonable alternative to marriage for lower-income persons because there is not the initial economic investment that there is with marriage.

Cohabitation was formerly viewed as a wholly unacceptable lifestyle and was illegal in many states. The primary impetus for its unacceptability was the presumption that couples were engaging in sexual activities. As a consequence of this element, cohabitation has been termed living in sin or shacking up by some critics of the practice. This perception persists today among more religiously conservative Americans. The Catholic Church has been critical of the practice and parishes around the country have refused to marry couples until they spend at least some time living apart prior to the marriage. The unacceptability of cohabitation became institutionalized in many state laws in the 1800s. Several of these laws are still active today.

In the 1960s and 1970s cohabitation was favored by persons in the antiestablishment movement as another way to resist the power of governmental institutions. Additionally, cohabiting couples are more likely than married couples to be of different races and ethnicities. Perhaps this is because a marriage is less likely to be supported by the family and friends of the couple. Thus perceptions of cohabitation as a marginal status remain in today's society.

In the past 30 years, there has been a dramatic shift in behavior and attitude regarding cohabitation. There are several factors that have contributed to decreases in disapproval of the practice. Among the key elements is an increasing freedom for young people in all aspects of their lives. As young people move away from parents and live in co-ed dormitories and apartments, they make choices about what they desire as individuals. This new-found freedom permits options outside of traditional parental control. A second element is that women's roles continue to change and evolve with regard to economic independence and personal choice. As women increase their financial stability, they perceive financial and personal options beyond marriage.

Divorce has played a role in cohabitation as well. As people are less confident about the stability of marriage, they may delay marriage for fear that they will end up divorcing. This factor has lead to more couples citing testing the relationship as their motivation for living together. Other reasons that more people cohabit today relate to economic and emotional benefits from such relationships. Cohabiting partners vary in terms of their level of commitment to one another, but some couples are clearly committed and experience emotional rewards from their association. In terms of economic benefits, partners can pool resources for daily living costs by maintaining one residence rather than two.

The groups and organizations that have been most critical of cohabitation are those that place a premium on traditionally organized heterosexual marriages. Religious organizations, such as Focus on the Family, express concern over cohabitation as a factor that leads to weaker marriages and less structural support for marriage as an institution. Nonreligiously affiliated groups, such as the National Marriage Project and its cofounder David Popenoe have expressed a similar concern with cohabitation. The dominant approach of persons who would like to see lower rates of cohabitation and discourage the practice has been to cite a link between cohabitation prior to marriage and higher rates of divorce in the first few years after marriage has occurred.

Those individuals and organizations that have been more supportive of cohabiting couples have couched their support in terms that focus on function, rather than form. Organizations such as the Alternatives to Marriage Project and its cofounder Marshall Miller stress the notion that a variety of relationship forms and circumstances might be equally suited to meet the needs of differing couples. The more important issue for this viewpoint is tolerance for relationships other than traditional legal heterosexual marriage. The Council on Contemporary Families is a well-known organization from this perspective. Among researchers, Pamela Smock, Andrew Cherlin, and Stephanie Coontz have pointed out positive aspects of and rationales for choosing cohabitation.

COHABITATION AS A STAGE IN COURTSHIP

One of the primary ways that cohabitation is discussed and viewed by persons in the United States currently is as a stage in a dating relationship. When researchers suggest that cohabitation is a stage in courtship, they are indicating that cohabitation may be one more component of a dating relationship that

LIVING APART TOGETHER (LAT)

Virtually all Swedish couples cohabit before marriage, and approximately one quarter of Swedish couples are in such a relationship currently. A phenomenon that is similar to cohabitation that many Swedes engage in is described by sociologist Jan Trost as LAT (living apart together). In these situations, partners are exclusive with one another and have a marriage-like relationship, but they choose to maintain separate residences. They might spend considerable time at one another's residences, frequently staying overnight or for weekends, but each maintains his or her own space. These couples are generally viewed by themselves and others as married.

partners participate in on the way to finding the permanent mate. Courtship refers to the process whereby young people select suitable marital partners. Research suggests that living with a partner before marriage as part of a loving relationship is more common in society today. Estimates are that 60 percent of marriages begun in the 1990s were preceded by cohabitation. Most of these data can be gathered by examining the addresses couples use when they apply for a marriage license. If the address is the same, researchers assume the couple is living together. Some researchers predict that more than 70 percent of couples that marry this decade will cohabit before marrying.

One of the reasons that partners might choose to live together at higher rates now compared with the past is that partners are single for longer periods of time today, but still are likely to be in a romantic relationship. While partners may not be ready for marriage, they do want to move to the next level of commitment with the partner. Since the 1960s the age at which men and women marry for the first time in the United States has been steadily increasing. On average in society today, males are 27 years old and females are 25 to 26 years old when they marry for the first time. This means that many young people could have been dating for some time prior to committing to marry, thus giving them the opportunity to cohabit as part of dating.

Persons who are considering marriage may live together before the marriage for a variety of reasons. Among them is convenience, to test the relationship and ensure it is with the right partner, or to save for an expensive wedding. Cohabitation provides an opportunity to determine how the partner might act in a marital relationship. In essence the relationship acts as a trial marriage for the partners. It might also serve as a way to act married without all of the legal commitment to the partner that marriage entails. In this way partners might determine whether their choice of a mate is a good one and decide to proceed with or cancel any prior plans to wed. As persons in U.S. society are increasingly concerned about the experience and consequences of divorce, cohabitation may seem like a reasonable preventive measure on the pathway to marriage. Testing the relationship is one of the most popular reasons that cohabitors give for their behavior.

The length of most cohabiting unions is limited. On average, cohabiting relationships last less than one year. One of the factors in their short duration is that partners often proceed to marriage, particularly if they had plans to marry prior to cohabiting. In other cases, partners may realize that they are not well suited and end the relationship before it becomes too serious, just like they might end any other dating relationship that does not involve living together. The pressure that couples who are cohabiting receive from friends and family might also be involved in the short duration of these relationships. Despite the increase in cohabiting relationships, couples often receive pressure to make the relationship legal or to end it. These pressures are particularly salient for women.

Evidence for cohabitation as a stage in courtship also comes from the fact that most cohabiting partners are persons who have never married. Because cohabitation is a pattern entered into by younger persons, it is seen as a reasonable bridge between singlehood and marriage. It is also perceived as a stage in courtship for persons before remarriage as many divorced persons will cohabit with a partner prior to remarriage.

THE LEGALITY OF COHABITATION

While cohabitation is a common experience for U.S. couples today, the legality of cohabitation is still being debated in some states. Seven states have laws strictly forbidding cohabitation. Florida, Michigan, Mississippi, North Carolina, North Dakota, Virginia, and West Virginia have statutes making the practice illegal. In North Carolina, for example, the issue reached the courts when Debora Lynn Hobbs was given an ultimatum by her employer to marry, move out, or leave her job.

COHABITATION AS AN ALTERNATIVE TO MARRIAGE

Cohabiting as an alternative to marriage is more common among persons who have fewer financial resources and lower education levels. It is higher among African Americans, who as a group are much less likely to marry than are other ethnic groups. In these ways, cohabitation is true to its roots as a status with less support and legitimacy than marriage.

The cohabiting lifestyle may be chosen by persons who are less committed to each other or who perceive some potential problems in their relationship. This could account for data that indicate that persons who cohabit prior to marriage have higher rates of subsequent divorce than those who do not live together before the wedding. Additionally, persons who choose to cohabit are likely to see divorce as an option if the marriage does not work out. The choice of an unconventional lifestyle, cohabitation, indicates they may be liberal on relationship issues as a whole.

In addition, some cohabiting relationships proceed because they are convenient for the partners, not because there is any long-term commitment between them. These relationships are referred to as casual-convenience cohabitation. The partners are in the relationship as long as their needs are being met, but may not plan to be with the partner for the long term. It may be for sexual or for economic convenience.

Given that a significant percentage of cohabitants have been divorced, they might perceive cohabitation as the best choice to help them avoid problems that precipitated their divorce. Likewise they may be concerned about a subsequent marriage being unsuccessful and having to divorce again. While the ties between cohabiting partners may be emotionally or financially difficult to sever, cohabitants do not have legal ties to dissolve like spouses do when a marriage ends. For some divorced persons the financial ties from the previous marriage might make cohabitation more attractive than remarriage. If one owes the partner alimony or other support, taking on the complete financial obligation of a new family situation may be cost prohibitive.

The persons in the cohabiting relationships of longest duration are those who see cohabitation as a permanent alternative to marriage. These persons may reject marriage as a social institution, or remaining single could be part of their personal philosophy. Because marriage is an institution that has been demonstrated to be oppressive to women, those more staunchly supportive of feminism might choose to be coupled without the legal bonds of marriage. Persons who choose to permanently cohabit usually make it known to family and friends that they have no intention of marrying, but they are partnered. These are the cohabitants most likely to plan children together. They may be likely to seek some kind of legitimacy and legal protection for their relationship, such as registering as domestic partners.

MOTIVES FOR COHABITATION

While the reasons that persons cohabit are likely to be as varied as the persons themselves, research has uncovered a few very common reasons that partners elect to cohabit. Clearly the future relationship roles that the partners expect to play, whether they plan to marry or not, are important in their decision to cohabit.

Gender issues. Males and females cite different reasons for their decisions to cohabit. Among males the convenience of living with the partner is a dominant factor in the decision-making process. Because men are still the ones most likely to travel to see a partner and provide transportation for a date, residing with the partner decreases these tasks. Cohabitation helps partners manage the logistics of seeing each other as frequently as possible.

For women, cohabitation is often viewed as a prelude to marriage, thus subscribing to the cohabitation as a stage in courtship model. When women view cohabitation as a step toward permanence, they may be more dissatisfied than men are with the arrangement. Because the majority of cohabiting relationships do not end in the partners marrying each other, women's expectations are often unfounded. Both males and females suggest that a primary motive for cohabitation is to spend more time with the partner because of attraction and affection.

Testing. Among the primary motives for cohabitation is the testing of the relationship or evaluating the compatibility between partners. The rationale behind this motive suggests that you can only really get to know a partner when you reside together. Some research has considered this phenomenon a trial marriage. Therapists and others are recognizing that testing is a powerful motive, but they are urging their clients to tread cautiously because the data are inconclusive about any benefits or harms to their relationship that may result. For example, there are websites that warn cohabitors to make an informed choice about their lifestyle, and that suggest that the detrimental effects of cohabitation on marriage are probably small for all groups of cohabitors except serial cohabitors (those who have cohabited multiple times).

Economics. Men and women who are economically unstable are more likely to cohabit. Couples might feel that their financial standing would not provide a good start to marriage and cohabit while working for better financial circumstances. As women have increased their participation in the labor force and their economic success, they may not want to fall into the traditional expectations of wifely duties so cohabitation is a way to maintain the romantic relationship without sacrificing career for a traditional role as wife and mother.

Among persons who have no long-term commitment to each other cohabitation has practical benefits in terms of sharing expenses. This permits partners to maintain one residence rather than two and to share financial and domestic responsibilities. Cohabitants are much less likely to pool their resources than are married couples, preferring to maintain separate finances and responsibilities. This is particularly true when there is no specific commitment between the partners to marry in the future or when at least one of the partners is cohabiting after a divorce.

See also Childfree Relationships; Cohabitation, Effects on Marriage; Common Law Marriage; Domestic Partnerships; Fictive Kin.

Further Reading: Alternatives to Marriage Project. http://www.unmarried.org; Barlow, Anne, Simon Duncan, Grace James, and Alison Parks. *Cohabitation, Marriage and the Law: Social Change and Legal Reform in the 21st Century.* Oxford: Hart Publishing, 2005; Hindin, Michelle, and Arland Thornton. *The Ties That Bind: Perspectives on Marriage and Cohabitation (Social Institutions and Social Change).* Piscataway, NJ: Aldine Transaction, 2000; Smock, Pamela. "Cohabitation in the United States: An Appraisal of Research Themes, Findings, and Implications." *Annual Review of Sociology* 26 (2000): 1–20; Solot, Dorian, and Marshall Miller. *Unmarried to Each Other: The Essential Guide to Living Together as an Unmarried Couple.* New York: Marlowe and Company, 2002; Stanley, Scott M. *The Power of Commitment: A Guide to Active, Lifelong Love.* San Francisco: Jossey-Bass, 2005; Waite, Linda, and Maggie Gallagher. *The Case for Marriage: Why Married People are Happier, Healthier, and Better-off Financially.* New York: Broadway Books, 2000; Whitman, Stacy, and Wynne Whitman. *Shacking Up: The Smart Girl's Guide to Living in Sin without Getting Burned.* New York: Broadway Books, 2003; Wu, Zheng. *Cohabitation: An Alternative Form of Family Living (Studies in Canadian Population).* New York: Oxford University Press, 2001

Kimberly P. Brackett

O

ONLY CHILD

The only child is a truly unique position in the family. An only child is a child with neither biological nor adopted siblings. The influence of being an only child is controversial, with some experts suggesting that the personalities of only children are deficient as a result of their status and other family experts claiming that the benefits available to only children mediate any stereotypical negative outcomes. A considerable amount of theory exists about only children and the effects of having no siblings.

FACTORS PROMOTING ONLY CHILD FAMILIES

Only child families are becoming increasingly common in the United States. In 1972, there were between 8 and 9 million only children. In 1995 there were 13 million only children, and in 2000 there were 16 million only children. Today over 20 percent of families in the United States have only one child (Mancillas 2006). This is not the first time in the nation's history, however, when only-child families were common. Families formed during the Great Depression were quite likely to be one-child families. Some of the factors that contribute to the increase in only child families in recent years include changing marital patterns, economic concerns, and new roles for women.

The high divorce rate and couples choosing to marry later in life may contribute to shorter marriages and more only children as fewer persons spend an extended time in marriage during their most fertile reproductive years. Inflation and high unemployment rates reduce the family income and may encourage parents to have fewer children. Today families that are concerned over their ability to provide all of the things that are expected to be part of a middle-class childhood may choose to target their efforts to a smaller number of children or only one. As the costs of rearing a child to the age of 18 continue to climb, couples may consider it impossible to afford more than one. Additionally, as some women choose single motherhood, having only one child to provide for may be more attractive than multiple children.

The majority of women are now employed before they have children. The added income and involvement with work helps push women to postpone childbirth and have fewer children as they may be reluctant to leave careers, even for a limited time. Additionally, as women increasingly find fulfillment in employment, they may not feel a strong need to gain identity through motherhood.

STEREOTYPES OF ONLY CHILDREN

Negative Stereotypes

A traditional view commonly assumed that for a child to develop normally, he or she should have siblings. Without siblings, the child is expected to experience detrimental effects on adjustment, personality, and character. There is a belief that only children would be lonely, selfish, maladjusted, and deprived of opportunities to develop social skills. Only children may at times experience feeling lonely, and do compensate through fantasy play and the creation of imaginary friends. Because of this expectation of social deprivation, the parents automatically over-indulge and over-protect the only child and this produces an unhappy, maladjusted, selfish, and isolated individual. Only children are depicted as self-centered, anxious, domineering, and quarrelsome. Only children are often characterized as lacking social competence because they are deprived of the social experiences that siblings can give them. Concerns arise that only children can become difficult adults because they did not have to share with siblings or compromise for the sake of family harmony.

Only children's personalities are often categorized into two groups. The first is the spoiled, egocentric, difficult, and unsocial child. The second is the shy, sensitive, hesitant, and often excessively dependent child. The factors that cause the two groups of personalities are the lack of necessary association with other children and the receipt of too much attention from adults, mainly the parents. Often these children feel pressure to be perfect and to fit the mold that parents have for the ideal child. The only child does not receive adequate training in competing with his or her siblings and the parents are over-attentive. One area of concern beginning to appear in the literature involves parents doting on children that were conceived after a period of infertility. The negative stereotypes of only children are not exclusive to the United States, but are seen in other cultures across the world including Great Britain, Korea, the Netherlands, and China.

Positive Stereotypes

Contrary to Alfred Adler's contention that only children would experience primarily negative outcomes, Toni Falbo, a well-know researcher of only children, suggests that only children are very adaptive. They learn to be children on their own, are more dependent on themselves, and have no problem being alone. They are no more likely to be maladjusted than are children with siblings. Only children are the sole recipients of their parents' resources and attention. This can have lasting positive outcomes. One of the most practical is that financial resources do not have to be shared. The targeted finances can be used to provide additional advantages such as private schooling, academic and leisure lessons, and cultural experiences that parents may have to limit when budgeting for multiple children. It is well-documented that first-born and only children are the birth positions that earn the highest incomes on average.

Only children do not have to experience the conflict and competition that comes with having siblings. Because they do not compete with another child for their parents' attention, they may maintain high self-esteem.

Only children receive more of their socialization from adults than from peers. As a consequence, only children are believed to be more accustomed to dealing with adults than are children in other birth-order positions. Only children receive the advantage of the maximum parental attention. Because of this they are thought to have better health, safety, and security than children with siblings. The academic performance of only children is generally superior to children in larger families, due in part to parents' availability to assist with homework and other school-related tasks. Only children have better language skills and develop high verbal ability, perhaps due to the majority of their social interactions occurring with adults. Only children's personalities are often described as highly motivated, self-confident, and achievement-oriented.

Given that so many children attend organized day care today, the traditional assumption that only children wouldn't learn social skills and would experience higher levels of loneliness compared with their peers who have siblings seems unfounded. While there are not built-in playmates at home, parents of only children often make a concerted effort to expose their youngsters to other children. They learn the needed interaction skills; they just may learn them at a later age. Indeed, as adults, only children marry at approximately the same age as others and are no more likely to divorce than persons who were reared with siblings.

Consequences of the Stereotypes

It is quite reasonable that people's beliefs about the differences children demonstrate based on their birth order influence the expectations that parents have for their own children, as well as what they expect about people in general. The stereotypes that emerge may encourage only children to internalize the expectations for their group and cause a negative effect on self-esteem and self-concept. Another possible consequence of the stereotypical thinking about only children is that some parents of only children may internalize the stereotypes and push their children to behave in accordance with the expectation. This can affect the parent-child relationship and the satisfaction of both parties. An additional potential consequence of the reliance on the stereotype is that parents may be pressured into having another child to prevent the first child from being saddled with the negative labels assigned to only children.

THEORY ON THE ONLY CHILD

Research into only children has largely come from a psychological tradition. Only children have been evaluated in five main areas: personality, intelligence, achievement, sociability, and general psychological adjustment. Three will be briefly discussed here.

Adler's Theory

The concept of birth order as a device to understand children's behavior was formally developed by Alfred Adler, an Austrian psychiatrist. He concluded that a child's position in the family greatly influenced her overall development and attitude toward life. He believed that birth order would leave a permanent impression on the individual's style of life by influencing the way one dealt with friendship, love, and work. According to Adler, only children are usually pampered, create unrealistic expectations of always being the center of attention, and create an exaggerated opinion of their own importance. He also suggested that only children tended to be shy and dependent. He indicated that this derived from the parents, who by refusing to have more than one child communicated their own anxiety, neuroses, and fears to their child. Adler did emphasize that there could be an exception to the rule, and noted that even a child born several years after the firstborn could be treated like an only child and develop some of the same patterns.

Over the years, Adler's negative view of only children has been debated and disputed. Other factors may be equally as important as birth order in personality development. Some of these factors include parents' attitudes, illness and disability, gender roles, and social circumstances. Reviews of studies of only children, particularly with regard to personality traits, suggest that there is no maladjustment directly related to being an only child. It seems that only children are not that different from their peers with siblings. Only children do, however, seem to be higher in achievement motivation. Their lack of siblings also tends to enhance their performance on tests of verbal ability where only children, firstborn children, and children with only one sibling score significantly better than later-born children and those with multiple siblings.

Confluence Model

The confluence model is a theory about only children's intellectual development, based on the idea that family composition influences intelligence. The confluence model began as an explanation for the findings that I.Q. and family size are inversely related. That is, children from larger families have lower I.Q. scores on average than children from smaller families. Based on this pattern, one would expect that only children, who come from the smallest families, would have the highest I.Q. scores. At very young ages this pattern holds. However, the results of three large-scale studies of young adults, conducted in the Netherlands and the United States, are consistent in placing only children lower than the prediction. In these studies only children scored at levels comparable to

CHINA'S ONE-CHILD POLICY

China's one-child policy represents a special case of the trend toward smaller families. It is a government policy implemented in 1979 that was designed to slow population growth in the already heavily populated country. It encourages couples, particularly those in urban areas, to have only one child by offering incentives to those families who voluntarily control their fertility and punishing those who do not. Families that have only one child can expect the child will receive preferential treatment in school, in later employment, and in housing. These families also receive financial incentives while the child is living at home.

The policy has three main elements, promoted through media outlets, laws, policies, and members of the community who serve as compliance officers. The first aspect of the policy is to encourage young couples to delay marriage and subsequent childbearing. The second is the goal of fewer and healthier births across the Chinese population. The third is to strongly encourage couples to have only one child. Some exceptions to the one-child provision are available if the couples' first child is disabled, for example, or if they live in a rural area and the first child born is a girl. As a patriarchal society, land holdings are generally passed along the male line and males can contribute more to the household economy.

Families who violate the policy by having additional children are subject to a steep fine and the second or subsequent children are generally ineligible for the educational, health care, and social benefits made available to the only child. Perhaps more concerning to those outside of China is the human rights issues that have been raised. Because boys are seen as an asset and girls as a liability to Chinese families, male children are preferred. Due to the lack of recording of female births, selective abortion, abandonment, and even infanticide, there is a growing gap in the number of males and females of the same age. It is estimated that in some regions, boys outnumber girls by ten to one.

---

first-born children in families with from three to five children. This model, then, suggests that intelligence develops from a combination of factors, including how the child develops and the experiences that occur within the family. Being an only child is not a significant enough factor to predict intelligence outcomes.

Achievement Motivation

According to the achievement motivation theories, first-born and only children achieve more than their later-born siblings because they are more motivated to. There is some evidence to support this theory because only and first-born children score higher on the need for achievement than other birth-order positions. This theory provides evidence that higher achievement is due to greater pressure from parents on first-born and only children to behave in a more mature manner than later-born children. The higher educational ambitions of only and first-born children reflect this as well. When social class of parents is held constant in achievement studies, only children tend to complete more years of education and have more prestigious jobs than their counterparts with siblings.

FAMOUS ONLY CHILDREN

Some well-known only children include: Franklin Delano Roosevelt, Rudy Giuliani, Alan Greenspan, Tipper Gore, and Leonardo da Vinci. Sports figures Tiger Woods, Kareem-Abdul Jabbar, and Maria Sharapova are only children. Among the entertainers who are only-children are: Robert DeNiro, Robin Williams, Frank Sinatra, Samuel L. Jackson, and Natalie Portman.

FUTURE DIRECTIONS

Given the social trends toward smaller families in the United States and other western nations, only children will continue to be common. The reassurances from decades of psychological research on only children, demonstrating that they are generally well-adjusted members of society who are intelligent and successful, may help to assuage any guilt that parents feel for having only one child. Despite these positive outcomes there remains some stigma to this position in the family. However, as the only child becomes a more widely selected option, stereotypes regarding their selfishness and spoiled behavior seem likely to diminish.

See also Birth Control; Birth Order; Changing Fertility Patterns.

Further Reading: Adler, A. *What Life Should Mean to You.* New York: Perigee Books, 1931; Blake, J. *Family Size and Achievement.* Berkeley: University of California Press, 1989; Claxton, Reid P. "Empirical Relationships between Birth Order and Two Types of Parental Feedback." *The Psychological Record* 44 (2002): 475–500; Ernst, C. *Birth Order: Its Influence on Personality.* New York: Springer, 1983; Falbo, Toni. *The Single-Child Family.* New York: Guilford, 1984; Herrera, N. "Beliefs about Birth Rank and Their Reflection in Reality." *Journal of Personality and Social Psychology* 85 (2003): 142–150; Mancillas, A. "Challenging the Stereotypes about Only Children: A Review of the Literature and Implications for Practice." *Journal of Counseling and Development* 84 (2006): 268–275; McGrath, E. *My One and Only: The Special Experience of the Only Child.* New York: Morrow, 1989; Only Child Enterprises, Inc. http://www.onlychild.com; Sulloway, F. *Born to Rebel: Birth Order, Family Dynamics, and Creative Lives.* New York: Pantheon Books, 1996.

Virginia Rutland

OVERSCHEDULED CHILDREN

In recent years, child psychologists have become concerned over what they see as a new, and troubling, parenting trend—the tendency for parents to overschedule or rush their children through childhood. Experts warn about the negative effects of overscheduling for children, such as fatigue, irritability, and disinterest in previously enjoyed activities, which may be symptoms of depression. In addition, overscheduling burdens the entire family. Parents, many of whom are themselves trying to do it all, struggle to live up to unrealistic expectations for what kind of childhood they should provide for their children. Middle-class families experience the consequences of being overscheduled both psychologically and financially, as many children's activities today are structured and supervised, and involve significant membership fees. This does not even include the expenses associated with traveling, eating on the go, uniforms, and equipment for some sporting activities. Parents may find that quality family time is difficult to achieve as each member of the family is obligated to a different activity, often several times per week, in varying locations. Child development experts caution that children today are often deprived of opportunities to develop their imaginations, to play flexibly and spontaneously, and to cultivate family relationships.

BACKGROUND: CHILDHOOD THEN AND NOW

Images and understandings of children and childhood have changed quite dramatically over the course of history. In preindustrial America, children were economic assets, contributing in important ways to the family economic unit. As industrialization took hold and technology advanced, a new view of childhood emerged. This one emphasized the fragility and innocence of children, as well as their need for protection and for formal education. Gradually, children were prohibited from factory work and were required to attend school. It was assumed that children and adolescents required a certain amount of leisure time and freedom from adult-like responsibilities. It was during the 1900s that many advances in child development occurred—educational attainment increased, infant and child mortality decreased, and overall health improved. The advances in education, health, and life expectancy were so great that the twentieth century has been described as the century of the child.

Increasingly, however, children are dealing with adult issues such as violence, sexuality, poverty, mental illness, and troubled families. A significant proportion of children today express concerns over finances, health care, public safety, crime, war, and other mature matters. Involvement with the popular media, including the Internet, has resulted in exposure to a wide array of subject matter, prompting concern over Internet pornography and possible contact with child predators. Children today are exposed to too much and too complex information, much of which they are unable to accurately process. Body image and dieting have become significant concerns among young girls. Young children, boys and girls alike, are objectified and sexualized, especially in clothing advertisements. Kids growing up in single-parent homes often find themselves at home alone or assuming a large share of domestic responsibilities including child care for younger siblings. Millions of children are diagnosed with learning or mood disorders and are often prescribed strong, and potentially dangerous, drugs as the primary course of treatment. Substance abuse and teenage suicide rates are high. In addition, while the crime category juvenile delinquency was created in the early-twentieth century to protect child and adolescent offenders from the harsh punishments typically associated with adult crime, increasingly the public is outraged by what they see as lenient treatment of minor offenders and there is less support for rehabilitative programs. There are increasing instances of juvenile offenders being charged, tried, and convicted as adults. In many ways, the boundary line between childhood and adulthood is less clear than it was in the twentieth century. In fact, one psychologist recently coined the term kinderdult to refer to the simultaneous treatment of children as both kids and adults.

Perhaps in a less obvious way, the kinderdult phenomenon is apparent in the manner in which children's schedules are arranged. Many parents, especially those who are affluent, believe that rigid, full schedules are necessary for optimal child development. Thus, middle-and upper-middle-class children often find themselves involved in a number of scheduled, structured activities on a weekly or even daily basis. This phenomenon has led to the coining of several new expressions and syndromes, such as the overscheduled or overbooked child, hurried child syndrome, and hyper-parenting. Many writers have discussed the disappearance or erosion of childhood. Attention to the issue of overscheduled and hurried children originated out of concerns with changing school curricula, in which more advanced material was gradually required of lower grades and younger children and various forms of relaxed, spontaneous activity, such as recess, have been removed from the school day. At a minimum, unstructured recess or free play has been replaced with supervised, structured forms of physical activity.

According to those concerned with the overscheduling of children, the hurried child is clearly a modern and culturally-specific phenomenon. As with adults, there is tremendous pressure on children to be over-achievers. Americans are highly competitive and most parents believe that it is imperative that children learn to follow rules, accept an imposed structure and schedule, get along well with others, work hard, and achieve. In fact, it appears that adolescents today are encouraged by their parents to seek employment at earlier ages. Opponents of youth employment contend, however, that the types of jobs available to the typical teenager are unlikely to foster appreciation for work or for the value of money.

American public schools are largely governed by this belief system as well, emphasizing individual achievement, productivity, ambition, and competition among students. There is little emphasis on more passive forms of development, such as imagination, contemplation, or learning how to relax or keep oneself content. Time spent in such endeavors may be considered little more than idle time or leisure time, which for many Americans amounts to wasted time. Pursuits that are active, productive, and organized are highly valued. Thus, many children today find themselves with full, hectic schedules.

In one qualitative study of middle- and working-class families, it was found that while working-class parents felt that kids should be kids, and that it is normal and natural for children to have quite a bit of unscheduled, unrestricted time to themselves or with other children, middle- and upper-middle-class parents tended to believe that in order to excel, children must be encouraged to pursue a number of structured activities, chosen either by the parents or by the children. Consequently, affluent parents spent a great deal of time each week shuffling children back and forth from one activity to the next as well as centering their family time and routines around the children's schedules. In the end, parents and children were often physically and psychologically exhausted. Such families experienced little quiet time together and sibling relationships were often hostile as children competed against one another in performance aspects (i.e., athletics) and for parents' approval. On the other hand, children in working-class families spent a good deal of time playing quietly alone or with other children in unsupervised, unstructured activities. In addition, children in working-class homes were a bit calmer and less likely to experience overt conflict with siblings. They also spent more time with extended family members. Some child advocates speculate that children from affluent homes may actually experience a kind of separation anxiety because they are spending significant amounts of time away from the home in the presence of coaches, teachers, tutors, day care workers, and other strangers.

Child psychologists are increasingly concerned about the possible negative effects of overscheduling children. Overscheduled children are likely to report feeling tired, tense, or stressed. Involvement in multiple organized activities each week typically results in less quality time with immediate as well as extended family members. The formation of healthy family relationships is essential in learning how to form and maintain healthy peer, academic, and eventually intimate and professional relationships. Children who are overscheduled miss out on opportunities for self-reflection. It is vital that kids not only learn how to entertain themselves, at least temporarily, but also that they have time to reflect on who they are, what they enjoy, and the environment around them. An abundance of activities results in an abundance of actual, and psychological, noise—which makes it difficult to find time to ponder one's experiences.

THE OVERSCHEDULED CHILD: MYTH OR REALITY?

There is some debate as to whether or not childhood is threatened today. Opponents of the idea contend that this argument is based upon faulty reasoning. The argument presumes the historical existence of a golden era, in which children were coddled and protected from the harsh realities of adult life. However, most evidence would seem to suggest the contrary. Throughout most of history, children as young as toddlers were exposed to much harsher realities than they are today including severe illness, hunger, over-crowding, and death. While contemporary parents may reminisce about their lazy, carefree childhoods, one must remember that preindustrial children spent hours each day involved in very difficult and time-consuming physical chores in the home and on the farm. It is leisure, not work, that is the exception.

Proponents of the overscheduled child argument fail to acknowledge subgroup variations in the experiences of children. For instance, is the primary concern with hurried preschoolers or with adolescents? Are girls and boys rewarded similarly for early and advanced development or are they socialized to view productivity and upward mobility differently? The emphasis on overscheduled children fails to take into account class and race variations. While some children are forced into multiple, organized activities, these children are overwhelmingly middle- to upper-middle class, and it is quite possible that working-class children and parents might view their hectic schedules as a privilege rather than a burden or unnecessary obligation. A disproportionate share of African American children, especially those who reside in inner-city areas, confront much harsher realities than being overscheduled at school or in extracurricular activities. Also

CHILDREN'S SCHEDULES: ADVICE FOR PARENTS

Scheduled activities are not intrinsically bad for children and, if handled properly and done in moderation, may provide certain benefits to all family members. Involvement in sports, music, civic, or religious activities can boost self-esteem and provide a certain amount of structure that children require. Parents may want to use the following guidelines, however, to ensure that they do not over-extend their child. First, be sure that your child's weekly schedule is age appropriate. Young children grow tired more quickly and involvement in too many activities can easily lead to feelings of frustration and exhaustion. Second, help your child identify his strengths and interests and then encourage him to select no more than two structured activities per week in which to participate. Beyond this, children's and parents' schedules become too hectic and children are often unable to develop skills and self-confidence in any one area. Third, if you notice changes in your child's temperament, eating habits, or activity level, consider reducing the number of activities. Parents should discuss this with their children, being careful to explain that this is not a punishment but a way for them to spend more time doing what they really enjoy. Never mandate that a child participate in a long list of structured activities; doing so will most likely result in disinterest of the activity and a strained parent-child relationship. Most children will eventually gravitate toward at least one outside activity on their own. Finally, explain to your child that it is okay to begin something but then stop if it becomes unpleasant, stressful, or more work than fun. Kids should understand that there can be value in quitting an activity too. Finally, if it seems that your child is becoming distant from the rest of the family or that family time is clearly diminishing, a reduction in activities is most certainly in order.

concerning is that, either explicitly or implicitly, women's employment has been identified as a factor contributing to the speed-up and disappearance of childhood. The increase in women's labor force participation has been cited as a factor leading to so-called latch-key children (who are unsupervised for a portion of the day), and shortages of down time and quality family time because mothers who work are likely to be tired and frustrated at the end of the day. However, maternal employment, in and of itself, has not been found to result in any negative consequences for children. In fact, mothers' employment, when viewed positively by husbands and wives, has been found to be beneficial for the development of children. This is particularly true when it contributes substantially to the household income and when high-quality care options are available for children.

Finally, for under-privileged groups, the concerns associated with overscheduled or overburdened children are not necessarily new. Historically, black families have experienced higher rates of poverty and single-headed households; thus, domestic work, sibling care, and exposure to mature issues such as poverty, unemployment, divorce, incarceration, and addiction is not simply the byproduct of a recently sped-up society. Relaxed, unencumbered childhoods have been a luxury afforded only the most privileged classes. In addition, while early employment may be viewed as potentially problematic for the white middle class, it is unemployment and chronic underemployment that plagues much of the urban lower class.

BENEFITS OF ACTIVITY PARTICIPATION

There is no doubt that extracurricular activities can be beneficial for children. Involvement in sports, for example, has been found to improve academic performance, boost self-confidence, and lower the risk for involvement in high-risk activities, such as drugs, truancy, or sexual behavior. Kids who participate in a moderate amount of scheduled activities often experience higher levels of self-esteem and are more comfortable with competition. However, it is important to remember that activities should be scheduled in moderation. When children are overscheduled, negative consequences, such as fatigue and irritability, may override any potential benefits.

In addition, involvement in too many different activities is likely to result in an inability to fully cultivate interests and talents in any one activity. Children may begin to feel overwhelmed and pressured by their parents to excel in multiple activities, which is unrealistic at any age. While parents may believe that kids will grow up and fondly remember all of the activities they were involved in, it is just as likely that such children will grow up and remember feeling hurried and pressured.

See also Motherhood, Opportunity Costs; Parenting Styles.

Further Reading: Cooke, Barbara, and Carleton Kendrick. *Take Out Your Nose Ring, Honey, We're Going to Grandma's.* Bloomington, IN: Unlimited Publishing, 2003; Elkind, David. *The Hurried Child: Growing Up Too Fast Too Soon—25th Anniversary Edition.* Cambridge, MA: Perseus Books, 2006; Elkind, David. *The Power of Play: How Spontaneous, Imaginative Activities Lead to Happier, Healthier Children.* Cambridge, MA: Perseus Books, 2006; Galinsky, Ellen, and Judy David. *Ask the Children: What America's Children Really Think About Working Parents.* New York: William Morrow, 1999; Kotlowitz, Alex. *There Are No Children Here: The Story of Two Boys Growing Up in The Other America.* New York: Anchor Books, 1991; Lareau, Annette. *Unequal Childhoods: Class, Race, and Family Life.* Berkeley: University of California Press, 2003; Postman, Neil. *The End of Education: Redefining the Value of School.* New York: Alfred A. Knopf, 1995; Postman, Neil. *The Disappearance of Childhood.* New York: Vintage Books, 1994; Shehan, Constance L. "No Longer a Place for Innocence: The Re-Submergence of Childhood in Post-Industrial Societies." In *Through the Eyes of the Child: Revisioning Children as Active Agents of Family Life,* vol. 1, ed. Constance L. Shehan, pp. 1–17. Stamford, CT: JAI Press, Inc., 1999.

Susan Cody-Rydzewski

PARENTING STYLES

Ask any parent or parent-to-be about their biggest concerns and you will likely hear some comments about parenting correctly. Often this means parenting in a way that produces a well-adjusted, confident child. Other times it refers to following the advice of a particular expert. It is clear that different parenting personalities produce generally different outcomes for parent-child interaction. The question of whether there really is a correct way to rear a child has a lot to do with one's social class, race, and gender.

Parenting is more than likely the hardest job on the face of the Earth. What else requires more talent and determination than being an effective and efficient parent? With the advent of television, radio, the Internet, iPods, and many more technological devices that can socialize children quickly and erroneously, parenting has become even more difficult. While competing with all of the conflicting messages of the culture, it is true that parents, more than anyone else, interact with their children on a continuing basis. As a consequence, they have a crucial impact on the physical, social, and emotional development of their children. Clinging to a model of parental influence, more parents than not believe that the decisions they make as parents can either adversely or positively affect a child's life. This suggests that the child could be president or a prostitute depending on parental actions and decisions.

Although many experts have tried repeatedly to produce one, there is no manual available that accurately describes how to successfully raise a child; however, over the years teachers, sociologists, pediatricians, and other researchers have deduced that parenting, or child rearing, styles can be grouped into four basic types: authoritative, authoritarian, permissive, and negligent or uninvolved. Among the persons working in this area, Diana Baumrind was one of the first to examine the patterns of parenting that emerge in families over time.

Child rearing styles can be defined as an amalgamation of parenting behaviors and actions that occur over a variety of situations, and which creates a lasting child rearing, or parenting, environment. Several factors such as race, age, income, and educational backgrounds affect what parenting styles one chooses. There are three basic differences between the types of parenting styles: acceptance and involvement, control, and independence granting. Concerns over the types of children that each produces remain central in the work of professionals who study and counsel families, including many child psychologists. Syndicated child rearing columnist and child psychologist John Rosemond, for example, is quite critical of parents who are overly involved in micromanaging their children's lives, suggesting that such a pattern encourages dependence and sends a message that the parents don't trust the child's abilities.

AUTHORITATIVE PARENTING

Authoritative parenting can succinctly be described as the most successful approach to parenting. In authoritative parenting there is a high level of acceptance and involvement, and parents are able to discern when a child is prepared for some level of independence. Parents who engage in this type of parenting are often described as warm and attentive. They are often close to and have a stable relationship with the child. Discipline, which is an important aspect of parenting, is administered fairly and efficiently. More importantly, children with authoritative parents are well informed of expectations made of them and the reasons for those expectations. Children are often described as well adjusted and mature by teachers and other authority figures. Moreover, authoritative parents progressively engage in allowing children to make decisions, granting autonomy when the parents deem the child is ready. Throughout childhood authoritative parenting is linked to various aspects of competence in children, such as an upbeat and cheerful mood, cooperativeness, and self-control. Furthermore, into adulthood individuals with authoritative parents report higher self-esteem, moral maturity, school performance, and mood.

Often described as balanced parenting, not too tough and not too lenient, parents who follow this approach try to provide appropriate environments and stimuli for their children, often exposing them to new and different things. These parents also tend to be very attentive, although sometimes to a fault, as this approach tends to put the needs of the child above those of the parents. Additionally, parents who overly reward every positive thing that their child does may be teaching the child that she is the center of everyone's world.

Several factors can be taken into account when discerning who will more likely be an authoritative parent. For example, individuals who come from middle-class backgrounds are more likely to be authoritative parents. They often have high concern for and resources with which to provide a variety of experiences and opportunities. In addition, those individuals who come from a warm, authoritative parental environment are more likely to parent in the same authoritative way. Individuals with more education are more likely to conduct this form of parenting. The more education a parent has, the more likely he or she is to grant the child autonomy and educate the child about choices. Furthermore, individuals who wait to have children until they have at least completed two years of college are shown to be more effective disciplinarians and parents overall.

AUTHORITARIAN PARENTING

Another type of parenting is authoritarian. An authoritarian parenting style can be defined as one that is minimal in acceptance and organization, high in coercive control, and low in independence given to the child. This is sometimes referred to as autocratic discipline. Authoritarian parents focus on discipline. Furthermore, authoritarian parents are often known to yell and command, much more than authoritative parents. Moreover, authoritarian parents are more likely to use force or punishment, specifically corporal punishment (spanking). Parents who practice this parenting style do not grant as much authority or control to the child or as much autonomy as do authoritative parents. Children that hail from authoritarian homes demonstrate high levels of anger and defiance within the classroom. However, children from authoritarian parents fare better in school because they are accustomed to a submission to authority. These children are also less likely to engage in socially unacceptable behaviors, such as drinking or smoking.

Asian Americans often practice authoritarian parenting. Among Asian American parents, exhibiting control over the child helps to instill the Confucian beliefs in strict discipline, respect for elders, and socially desirable behavior, including not drinking or smoking, and so on. Furthermore, many Asians believe that frequent praise leads children to feel less fulfilled and hinders the incentive to realize one's full potential, so they are less likely to employ the high praise found in authoritative approaches. In this culture and those of Hispanics and Asian/Pacific Islanders a high level of respect for the parents, particularly the father, is expected. However, the use of authoritarian parenting in these eastern cultures does not seem to have the same negative effects as it does in western homes, were children often rebel against strict limitations. Asian American children are often well-adjusted and do not have high levels of anger and defiance, like those seen in whites parented this way; however, Asian American children do report that they are strongly expected to achieve.

Most Caucasians who practice authoritarian parenting hail from lower- or working-class families. Among whites, authoritarian parents tend to be older and come from authoritarian homes themselves. These groups who have less income and less education tend to demand discipline and submission from their children. Children often feel distant from their parents after punishments for small rules violations.

However, African American children often respond well to authoritarian parenting. Most African American parents, especially single-parent families and lower- and working-class families are authoritarian parents. Authoritarian parenting is pervasive in the black community. The single-mother phenomenon plays a substantial role in authoritarian parenting. Moreover, African Americans are more likely than their Caucasian counterparts to engage in forms of corporal punishment; furthermore, studies indicate that African Americans value discipline and control in children more than Caucasians. All of these factors play into African Americans' acceptance of authoritarian parenting.

PERMISSIVE PARENTING

Another form of parenting is permissive, sometimes known as laissez-faire. The permissive parenting child rearing style is warm and approachable; however, these parents are not involved and seem inattentive. These parents have little control over their children's behavior, and often allow children to make decisions on their own about goals, rules, and limits. Sometimes this happens when the child is not mentally prepared to do so. Permissive parents are not able to or may choose not to set limits; their children often act out, might not eat properly, or may not have an organized schedule. The children are often impulsive and disobedient. Furthermore, these children often do worse in school than children from authoritative and authoritarian homes, and they are more dependent on adults. Moreover, boys that hail from permissive homes are frequently more rebellious and nonachieving. Some parents who practice permissive parenting often believe that they are doing what is best for their children by letting the children work it out. However, many more are the parents who lack confidence in their capability to influence their child's behavior. In addition,

PARENT AND CHILD SOCIALIZATION: A TWO-WAY STREET

In the past, theories of child rearing generally made one critical assumption: that parents' act on their children who more or less adapt to the constraints, limits, and expectations that parents and the larger society put upon them. This deterministic model suggests that adults are responsible for shaping children's behavior by reinforcing what is proper and punishing what is improper. In this scenario, children are the passive recipients of their parents' life lessons and have little direct input regarding the information that the lessons contain. More recent considerations of parenting experiences, however, suggest that children are not simply passive in the process of socialization to parental and societal expectations and wholly subject to parental influence. Children can and do construct their own perspectives of the world and are active at negotiating their place in the family. Influence moves in both directions, from parents to children and children to parents. The ways in which children behave may elicit particular responses from parents that change the relationship. Children clearly manipulate parents for their own ends, such as playing one parent off the other to gain a desired outcome. Likewise, they can positively influence the parents (to eat healthier, protect the environment, etc.). The power and authority that parents have over their children is not absolute and children are not the blank slate that the child rearing experts of the last century envisioned.

many permissive parents are from upper-class families, where the parent is often gone from the household. To compensate for their lack of attention to the child, the parent often over-indulges or spoils the child. The lack of limits can be quite problematic as the child approaches the temptations of the teen years.

UNINVOLVED PARENTING

Uninvolved parenting, or negligent parenting as it was once called, can be defined as an amalgamation of low acceptance and involvement with little control and general apathy to autonomy granting. Parents that practice negligent parenting are often depressed and overwhelmed by stress. At its extreme, uninvolved parenting is a form of neglect, and falls under the heading of child abuse. Children that hail from negligent homes often have severe developmental problems, depending on when the parent became negligent. Children from negligent homes often do worse in school than children from authoritative, authoritarian, and even permissive homes; they have poor emotional self-regulation, and engage in antisocial acts at a much higher frequency than children from authoritative and authoritarian homes. Overall, uninvolved or negligent parenting is the worst form of parenting, if one can even consider it parenting, with detrimental effects to the psyche of the child and the parent. It is important to recognize that uninvolved parenting is usually a temporary phenomenon as other family members or even the state, through foster care, may step in to help guide the child's development.

DISCIPLINE

An important aspect to all models of parenting is discipline. The discipline instilled in a child is instrumental in determining a child's values. The amount of discipline given to a child varies culturally. Minorities tend to administer more discipline to their children, whether it is scolding, positive discipline, or corporal punishment. Caucasian Americans, however, use more verbal methods of discipline than do minorities. Caucasians are less likely to use corporal punishment and more likely to opt for a time-out or, in the case of older children, a lecture or privilege restriction approach. Discipline is not just punishment; discipline encompasses setting limits and boundaries so the children learn what is acceptable both in the home and in the larger society.

Positive discipline, which is most effective, encourages good behaviors and conduct, and forms a respectful bond between parent and child. Positive discipline encompasses praise for good behavior and setting examples of good behavior up-front to ideally reduce misbehavior later. In a study conducted on preschoolers, those who had more cooperative relationships with their parents demonstrated more pronounced conscience development. This was exhibited by sharing and thinking of others. Children with a specific bedtime, rules and regulations within a household, and other forms of discipline (limits) are more likely to be described as well adjusted by teachers and outside caretakers. Most child psychologists agree that children want boundaries from parents; they need discipline in their routines.

CHOOSING A STYLE

Choices also play an important role in parenting. When and where people decide to have children affects their parenting styles. People who get married earlier in life are more likely to become authoritarian parents. The stress of marriage and parenting can deeply affect younger adults who are not well established in their careers or lifestyle. Research indicates that people who choose to wait until they are at least 28 years old to have children are more likely to become authoritative parents. They are more established in their careers and life. People over the age of 28 are more likely to have a college education, a career, and a partner with whom they feel comfortable. The birth of the first child places more strain on a marriage than any other event. The decision to have more children also affects the parenting style. Most parents report parenting differences in their interactions toward the first and second child; that difference is more dramatic if the children are different sexes.

There is no mold for parenting and some parents go through a variety of parenting styles in a child's lifetime. There are several life events, however, that can result in an adjustment of parental styles. Among these changes are remarriage, the changing of occupation, the death of a spouse, and the birth of additional children. Although all of these changes often result in a shift in parental style, the biggest factor in changing of parenting style in America is divorce. This life-altering event often has negative consequences for children and parents. Family conflict often rises as parents try to settle disputes over children and possessions. Once a parent moves out, additional events threaten positive interactions between parents and children, such as remarriage or moving in with grandparents. Furthermore, mothers are often granted custody of children and this creates a drop in income for most families. This drop in income, coupled with new living arrangements, often forces authoritative parents to become more authoritarian because the mother is forced to work more. The transition from marriage to divorce typically leads to high maternal stress and anxiety. Sometimes the anxiety forces a shift to permissive or even negligent parenting. Children often report a difference in the parenting of both their mother and father after a divorce; mothers become stricter, whereas fathers become more permissive and over-indulgent. Some of the indulgent behavior of fathers may be linked to the infrequent contact they may have with children following a divorce. Divorce is a major event in the life of the child and the parent, and it requires many adjustments.

It is reasonable to suggest that parents do not choose a parenting style; it chooses them. Through socialization and intergenerational transmission, the passing on of behaviors and beliefs from one generation to the next, most parents will parent the way they were parented. If your parents were rather strict, you will tend to follow their example and be rather strict with your own children. Parents are often reminded that every child is different and they quickly find that what worked with one child might be a horrible failure with the next. Parenting is not just a one-size-fits-all endeavor. Consequently, the choices that most parents make do not fit neatly into one category or another. Often the most successful parents are the ones who can combine the best elements from the parenting styles highlighted above to meet the needs of their own families at a particular stage of development. Even the experts (such as Brazelton, Spock, Sears, and Mindell) debate the best strategies. This leaves middle- and upper-middle-class parents, who are more likely to seek the advice of experts for child rearing challenges, confused as to who has the answer that will be most effective. It often causes parents significant stress because competing suggestions are offered by persons in and outside of the family.

All of these factors taken together affect the children's lives. Children either respond well to a particular parenting style or they rebel against it. The statistics show that children from authoritative and authoritarian homes are better adjusted and go on to pursue successful lives and parenting environments. Children from negligent or permissive homes are shown to be more rebellious. They engage in socially unacceptable behaviors, such as drinking and smoking.

Parenting is the hardest job on Earth; there are no instructions on how to raise a child. Effective parenting requires the right amount of discipline, independence, and attention, however right is measured. Parenting styles can be grouped into four basic groups: authoritative, authoritarian, permissive, and negligent. Authoritative parenting is the most effective parenting style longitudinally. Authoritative parents are often described as warm and loving. They grant their children autonomy periodically throughout the child's life. Children from authoritative homes are well adjusted. Authoritarian parents require more discipline and obedience from children than their authoritative counterparts. This form of parenting is pervasive among minorities. Authoritarian parents are also warm and attentive to their children, but grant less control to their children. Children from authoritarian homes are well adjusted and do well in school. Permissive parents set no limits or boundaries for children and are overindulgent. Children from permissive homes are often rebellious and engage in socially unacceptable behavior. The worst form of parenting is negligent. Negligent parents pay no attention to their children; they are neglectful. Negligent parents are often mentally disturbed due to stress and life events. Several factors such as race, age, occupation, education, and background affect ones parenting style. Parents often go through a cycle of parental styles throughout a child's lifetime.

See also African American Fathers; Attention Deficit Hyperactivity Disorder (ADHD); Birth Order; Child Abuse; Corporal Punishment; Cosleeping; Developmental Disability and Marital Stress; Fatherhood; Homeschooling; Juvenile Delinquency; Overscheduled Children; Transition to Parenthood.

Further Reading: Baumrind, Diana. "Parental Disciplinary Patterns and Social Competence in Children." *Youth and Society* 9 (1978): 239–276; Berk, Laura E. *Infants, Children, and Adolescents*, 5th ed. Boston: Pearson, 2005; Comer, James P., and Alvin F. Poussant. *Raising Black Children*. New York: Penguin Group, 1992; Fisher, Seymour, and Rhonda Fisher. *What We Really Know About Child Rearing*. New York: Basic Books, Inc. 1976; Gosciewski, F. William. *Effective Child Rearing: The Behaviorally Aware Parent*. New York: Human Sciences Press, 1976; Stewart, K. A., and Christian P. Gruber and Linda M.

Fitzgerald. *Children at Home and in Day Care.* Hillsdale: Lawrence Erlbaum Associates Publishers, 1994.

Ruby R. Reed

PET DEATH AND THE FAMILY

The social structure of the American family is constantly changing. Recent statistics track the changes in family composition as the definitions and roles of family members have evolved. Anthropomorphic thinking encourages the inclusion of animals into the social structure, including the family. Ultimately two broad questions must be addressed. First, what is the proper place for companion animals in our families? Second, what is the proper response to the death of companion animals as they become integrated into the family structure? Because these issues are debated and companion animals increasingly are viewed as legitimate members their role in the family will become less controversial.

INTRODUCTION

The structure of the American family has undergone substantial change over the last few decades. In 1970, 45.3 percent of all families were composed of a married couple or a single person with children (Fields 2001). By 2000, the percentage of married- or single-headed households with children dropped to 32.8 percent (U.S. Census Bureau 2001). During this same time single persons living alone greatly increased. Lastly, the graying of America has increased the number of couples with grown children that have left to start their own lives and families.

The confluence of these trends has led to situations that have increased the inclusion of pets, also referred to as companion animals, as a major part of the American family structure. Because these families spend less on children they may spend more on their companion-animal "children." The American Pet Products Manufacturers' Association (APPMA) tracks the economic impact of our living with companion animals. This manufacturers' group estimates that people will spend $9.3 billion on goods and medicines alone, and $38.4 billion overall on pet-related expenses.

The fact that Americans are buying more dog toys and catnip does not lead to the conclusion that companion animals are becoming a vital part of the family. The willingness to provide extensive medical treatments and day care for our companion animals are stronger indicators. Just as we would not deny our human children quality day care and medical care, a growing number of people are providing these services to companion animals. In an American Animal Hospital Association (2004) survey 53 percent of the respondents said that they are spending more on their pets today than just three years ago. The proliferation of online pharmaceutical companies and sophisticated medical treatments (for example, MRIs and chemotherapy) for animals is also a strong indicator that we are seeing companion animals as more than just pets. The willingness to spend money on pet death care may be the strongest evidence of the changing, and somewhat controversial, attitude concerning the place for companion animals in the American family.

ANTHROPOMORPHISM

Anthropomorphism is the interpretation of what is not human in terms of human characteristics. The belief that our companion animals share characteristics similar to humans is what some refer to as the irresistible taboo. As such, these pet owners run the risk of being categorized as irrational and possibly mentally unstable.

From 50 to 75 percent of people define their companion animals as people (Hoyt 2002). Many more refer to pets as human members of their family. Sociologists have understood the importance of language and definitions for some time. The Thomas Theorem states, "If men define situations as real, they are real in their consequences" (Thomas and Thomas 1928). This theory helps us to understand the way that personhood is placed onto companion animals. As people define their companion animals as children or babies through language and interaction, they actually become children and babies.

Anthropomorphic thinking is generally divided into two broad types. The first is what can be classified as explicit anthropomorphism. This line of reasoning argues that animals do have cognition and behavior just as humans do. The second type is what can be referred to as mock anthropomorphism. This type of anthropomorphism views human cognition as analogous to animal behavior. Mock anthropomorphism is a short-hand way of understanding animal behavior in a way that makes it understandable in human terms. Mock anthropomorphism is not to be taken seriously. This position views animal behavior as human, not that it is human.

René Descartes' declaration that animals did not have a soul and therefore were dumb machines is often cited as the start of the debate. The orthodox Christian position is one that views animals as soulless because humans were given domain over the animal kingdom. Other religious doctrine (such as Jainism) believed animals were to be respected. It is not the place of this work to make a definitive conclusion on this issue. For background it is only important to understand that many people do view their companion animals at some level as equals. This position will ultimately lead to the inclusion of their companion animals as vital members of their family.

The intimacy that people share is the foundation of a family. A deep level of intimacy is the key characteristic of a primary group. As such, family members enjoy a type of love reserved only for those that would be included in their definition of family. To be sure, the term love is used so broadly in vernacular English that it is very difficult to define. Attunement is that level of intimacy in which the participants share a common viewpoint. This shared perspective is an important ingredient for any meaningful interaction to be maintained.

Genuine love is when attunement is combined with attachment. This level of intimacy is characterized by the sense that one misses the other when he or she is not present and experiences a sense of comfort when they return. Twenty-one percent of the respondents in one survey said that they thought of their pet all the time that they were away, while 54 percent thought of them at least a few times a day (AAHA 2004).

It is this point in the human and animal relationship that we can equate to that found in human and human relationships. Anyone, or anything, that is loved will enjoy similar treatment in the event of the death that a human would receive. When linked to anthropomorphism, this mix of intimacy is what will motivate the behavior that can be witnessed in the event of a death. Said another way, love is the reason we act as we do when a loved one dies.

EUPHEMISMS

Attitudes are expressed through language. Some linguistic determinists have argued that there is a systematic relationship between how people speak (language) and what they do (behavior). All meaningful expressions flow through language directly into our interactions with others, both human and nonhuman. Euphemisms are the use of indirect or vague words or phrases to soften the impact of an event.

Death educators debate the usefulness of euphemisms. As a linguistic aid to the grieving process euphemisms may be of value. Euphemisms allow us to avoid the use of words such as death or dead. In the absence of more direct and accurate language, euphemisms become a short hand for discussing uncomfortable events and experiences.

For example, when we use euphemisms to understand death, they may not be as useful as a direct, frank discussion. Euphemisms can be especially confusing for children. In one case, a family told their young son that they had lost grandpa last night. A few days after the funeral they noticed that their son was wandering around the house, looking behind doors and under beds. When the son was asked what he was doing, he replied, "You said we lost grandpa, I'm just looking for him." Many people also utilize euphemisms to talk about the death of companion animals.

TEACHABLE MOMENTS

One of the earliest experiences with death for children is the death of a family companion animal. These early memories may impact the way that people respond to death throughout their lives. It is for this reason that these teachable moments must be constructive. Teachable moments open the door to conversations about uncomfortable topics. Everyday life brings many opportunities to learn; the death of a companion animal can be one of the strongest and longest lasting impacts on a child's concept of death.

The same family rituals used in the death of a human family member are often utilized in the death of a family pet. The fish gets a burial at sea and the hamster is provided a traditional funeral complete with a shoe-box casket. Emotions displayed at these animal funerals often are as intense as for human family members.

There is a great deal of inconsistency with how this issue is interpreted. Social attitudes concerning the death of a companion animal are changing, yet many still view these deaths as unimportant. Statements such as, "it's only a dog" or "you can always get another kitten" are often freely expressed. You would never hear expressions such as, "it's only a sister," or "you can always get a new son" in regards to the death of a human family member. For someone who feels that their companion animal is a part of their family, both sets of remarks are equally hurtful. It is at these times that we can clearly see that this issue is still very controversial. Ultimately, how a child sees adults treat the death of the family animals will form the foundation for their future death attitudes. Adults need to be aware of what messages are sent to younger members of the family.

PET HEALTH CARE

Spending large sums of money on companion animals may be viewed as an unwise choice to many, yet this number is shrinking. Just as Americans spend more on pet products, the amount spent yearly on animal health care is also on the rise. One strong indicator of this trend is the growth of pet medical health insurance to help cover medical expenses. One of the largest pet health insurers, Veterinary Pet Insurance (VPI), has paid out more than $300,000 in claims. Americans spent a total of $24.5 billion on animal health care in 2006 (American Veterinary Medical Association 2007). When asked which they visit more often, their own physician or their pet's veterinarian, 58 percent answered their pet's veterinarian (American Animal Hospital Association 2004).

This increased attention to the health of companion animals creates a situation in which animals are living longer. Just as we see a strong causation with living longer and the increase in age-related illnesses in humans, we are starting to see a similar trend with companion animals. The number of dementia and cancer cases in animals is on the increase.

PET CEMETERIES AND CREMATION

Early in the history of sociology Emile Durkheim argued that cemeteries are collective representations that demonstrate a collective attitude concerning the death of its members. To be sure, Durkheim was referring to human community members. It is anthropomorphic thinking that extends Durkheim's line of thought to the nonhuman world.

Social conventions govern how people handle the deaths of other humans. Funerals and other rituals are completed almost without thought. As the ideas concerning who deserves the attention of our time and ritual are altered we can see the resulting behavioral change. Sociologists have long studied these rituals with the funeral being the clearest example. We refer to this aspect of our economy as the death care industry because we care.

Ultimately, funerals are for the survivors. They demonstrate the concern we have for the loss and serve to relocate the deceased into a new social position. None of this argument is controversial, until it is applied to animals. The strongest indicator that companion animals are increasingly being included into our families at a very deep level is demonstrated by our reactions when they die. It is only as animals gain legitimate social position other than as mere pets that society will see a need to provide companion animals with funeral rituals.

We should be reminded that, as with all losses, the bond between persons and pets should be acknowledged and respected. Emotional reactions to socially unrecognized deaths are called disenfranchised grief. This type of grief is experienced at the loss of any person to which one is not supposed to have such reactions. Examples of disenfranchised grief include: death of a coworker, a secret lover, and, very often, companion animals. Individuals must be encouraged to mourn in ways that are meaningful. The ways in which we react to the death of a companion animal, especially in our interactions with our children, speak loudly about how we think of these deaths. Pet cemeteries are helping us re-enfranchise pet grief.

The Hartsdale Pet Cemetery and Crematory is the oldest pet cemetery in America. Located in Hartsdale, New York, this pet cemetery is the final resting place for more than 70,000 animals. In 1896, as a favor to a friend, a local owner of an orchard allowed a dog to be buried among the apple trees. As people heard of this compassionate gesture requests for other burials followed. This was the beginning of the Hartsdale Pet Cemetery.

As word about the Hartsdale Pet Cemetery grew, other pet cemeteries started to offer burials for companion animals. In 1946, Earl Taylor started the first pet cemetery on the West Coast in response to requests to bury pets in human plots. The San Diego Pet Memorial Park was established on specially zoned land in 1962, stimulating a steady increase in pet cemetery openings throughout the state. The International Association of Pet Cemeteries and Crematories (IAPCC) was organized in 1971 and serves as the professional organization that provides guidance for pet cemeterians. In 1972 there were 96 pet cemeteries in America; today there are about seven hundred. September 9 is National Pet Memorial day.

A few pet cemeteries are offering full funeral services for companion animals. Pet Angel Memorial Center in Carmel, Indiana, may be the first full-time pet funeral home in America. Coleen Ellis used to work at a traditional, human funeral home before starting her pet funeral service in 2004. Ellis offers animal funeral services from her 1,200 square foot facility with prices starting at $230. Demand for her services has grown to the point that she soon plans to start franchising her funeral home nationally.

CONCLUSION

Social institutions are very resistant to change. The taken-for-granted nature of social life directs members to do today what was done yesterday. Many people are very comfortable with the predictability that social structures offer. The members of a social group are always reluctant to modify the status quo in any great measure. Having said this, we also know that social change does occur.

Social change does not often come without a struggle. Some of the changes in how we view companion animals have occurred with a marginal level of disruption. Other changes are more difficult to accept and therefore are more controversial. These changes when applied to the death of companion animals can be categorized into one of two larger questions.

The first asks just what role is proper for companion animals in the family. I have only touched on a few of the shifting positions that all members of families, as well as companion animals, are experiencing in contemporary American families. As just one example, many who have studied how we house our families have clearly found that we are sheltering in larger and larger homes. Spatial realities of larger homes have transformed the relationship dynamics within the American family. The average home now has a bathroom and Internet connection in every room. Family members routinely occupy selected spots in the home that contain all that is needed, rarely having to see another member of the family. Likewise, many new homes have specially designed areas for pets just as they do for other family members. Built-in dog washes and doggie doors to outside runs are just two examples.

The question of just where companion animals are in our family structure will continue to be controversial. Yet, as with all social change, the level of controversy will lessen as time passes. Today's controversies tend to become tomorrow's status quo. As our anthropomorphic thinking continues, regardless of whether it is explicit or mock, the place for companion animals will continue to evolve in ways that will generate further discussion. There is little doubt that this trend is toward more inclusion of companion animals as legitimate family members.

Second, how should we acknowledge the death of a companion animal? Our reactions to a death are a strong indicator of the importance of the death. Deaths can be categorized as high- or low-value deaths. Examples of high-value deaths are children, high-status members of a community, and close family members. Low-value deaths are those that are more distant from us, such as the deaths of nonfamily members.

Until recently, the death of a pet would have been more likely considered a low-value death. Early research on the subject showed that those that viewed their companion animals as human substitutes experienced greater signs of grief as compared with those who view pets in a less personal manner. The stronger the attachment to a companion animal the more intense the emotional and physical reaction experienced when the animal died.

Social reaction to the disruption of any relationship can be very strong. As with any death, the breaking of the bonds we experience with companion animals can elicit strong rituals to demonstrate the importance of the death. What we view as affective responses to pet death will continue to evolve. Just as there is not one proper way to mourn the death of a human, it is also true that there is no one proper way to mourn for companion animals. As pets become more central to our family structure, the death rituals that demonstrate the importance of human deaths will no doubt be increasingly applied at the time of pets' deaths.

Pets are said to give humans unconditional love. In return they ask very little. It is this bond, as well as the changes in how we see animals, that will continue to motivate their changing status in our families. Anthropomorphism is at the core of this way of seeing companion animals. Some may find the anthropomorphic question to be a nonissue. This group would say it is just a matter of economics. They may point to our increased disposable income as one reason for the changes in how we treat the death of our pets rather than some anthropomorphic thinking.

There is little doubt that companion animals will become more accepted as socially legitimate members as the American family structure continues to evolve. To be sure, continued change in the family will be slow as each generation re-addresses these controversies. The application of human death rituals to companion animals will accelerate the transition of this issue to one that will eventually become a part of the status quo. As time passes the controversies involved in the treatment of a pet death will lessen as we see companion animals as so-called people in disguise.

See also Children as Caregivers; Fictive Kin.

Further Reading: American Animal Hospital Association. "2004 Pet Owner Survey." http://www.aahanet.org (accessed 2004); American Pet Products Manufactures' Association. "Industry Trends and Statistics." http://www.appma.org/press_industrytrends.asp (accessed 2007); American Veterinary Medical Association. "U.S. Pet Ownership and Demographics Sourcebook." http://www.avma.org (accessed 2007); Cain, A. O. "Pets as Family Members." *Marriage and Family Review* 8 (1985): 5–10; Congalton, David, and C. Alexander. *When Your Pet Outlives You: Protecting Animal Companions After You Die.* Troutdale, OR: New Sage Press, 2002; Cowles, K. V. "The Death of a Pet: Human Responses to the Breaking of the Bond." In *Pets and Family.* ed. M. B. Sussman. New York: Haworth Press, 1985; Daston, Lorraine, and Gregg Mitman. *Thinking with Animals: New Perspectives on Anthropomorphism.* New York: Columbia University Press, 2005; Descartes, René. "Animals are Machines." In *Animal Rights and Human Obligations,* ed. T. Regan and P. Singer. Upper Saddle River, NJ: Prentice Hall, 1976; Durkheim, Emile. *The Elementary Forms of Religious Life,* trans. from French by Joseph Ward Swain. New York: Free Press, 1965; Fields, Jason, and Lynne M. Casper. "America's Families and Living Arrangements: 2000." *Current Population Reports* P20–537 (2001): Figure 1. http://www.census.gov/prod/2001pubs/p20-537.pdf; Fogle, B., and A. Edney. *Interrelations between People and Pets.* Chicago: Charles C. Thomas, 1981; Gadberry, James H. "Pet Cemeteries Help Recognize Pet Bereavement." *Mortuary Management* 86 (September 2000): 18–19; Grier, Katherine. *Pets in America: A History.* Chapel Hill: University of North Carolina Press, 2006; Hirschman, E. C. "Consumers and Their Companion Animals." *Journal of Consumer Research* 20 (1994): 616–632; Hoyt, Peggy R. *All My Children Wear Fur Coats: How to Leave a Legacy for your Pet.* West Conshohocken, PA: Infinity Publishing, 2002; International Association of Pet Cemeteries and Crematories. http://www.iaopc.com; Katcher, A. H., and A. M. Beck. *New Perspectives on our Lives with Companion Animals.* Philadelphia: University of Pennsylvania Press, 1983; Kay, W., H. A. Nieburg, A. H. Kutscher, R. M. Grey, and C. E. Fudin. *Pet Loss and Human Bereavement.* Ames: Iowa State University, 1984; Kennedy, John S. *The New Anthropomorphism.* New York: Cambridge University Press, 1992; Lanci-Altomare, Michele. *Good-Bye My Friend: Pet Cemeteries, Memorials, and Other Ways to Remember.* Irvine, CA: Bowtie Press, 2000; Ross, Cheri Barton, and J. Baron-Sorenson, J. *Pet Loss and human Emotion: a Guide to Recovery,* 2nd ed. London: Brunner-Routledge, 2007; Serpell, J. "People in Disguise: Anthropomorphism and the Human-Pet Relationship." In *Thinking with Animals: New Perspectives on Anthropomorphism,* ed. Daston, L. and G. Mitman. New York: Columbia

University Press, 2005; Thomas, W. I., and D. S. Thomas. *The Child in America: Behavior Problems and Programs.* New York: Knopf, 1928; U.S. Census Bureau. "Census 2000, Table DP-1," *Profile of General Demographic Characteristics,* 2001.

James H. Gadberry

PLURAL MARRIAGE

Plural marriage is the term applied to the situation of an individual married to more than one spouse at a time. Only the first marriage is recognized by convention and law in the United States. The second and subsequent marriages are not legally recognized, but are generally performed by a religious leader and are frequently referred to as spiritual marriages. Sometimes additional wives are called concubines.

In anthropological and sociological research into marital form plural marriage is also known as polygamy, which literally means many marriages. A term that is sometimes included in a discussion of plural marriage is bigamy. Bigamy is a legal term used when someone is married to two or more persons. The latter marriages are contracted under false pretenses of being single at the time of the marriage and therefore constitute fraud. Researchers prefer to use polygamy because it is a more inclusive term.

Plural marriage is a concept that is difficult to comprehend for the majority of Americans, who live their lives following the marital pattern of monogamy, one marriage to one person. The issue of plural marriage, or polygamy, is a polarizing topic in today's society. Most Americans have a strong opinion either in favor of or in opposition to this practice. Most recently, polygamy has been in the news because of the criminal convictions of Warren Jeffs, a fundamentalist Mormon leader, and his cohorts for numerous crimes against women and children.

Polygamy is practiced in different parts of the world, in different cultures, and for a variety of reasons. To begin to understand plural marriage, we must first define polygamy and also examine the biblical and historical roots of this practice. Following this brief introduction, we will focus on the nineteenth century Church of Latter-day Saints' (LDS) practice of plural marriage, discuss polygamy today, and note the social and legal implications for the individuals who practice this lifestyle.

TYPES OF POLYGAMY

Polygamy is a broad term that refers to multiple simultaneous marriages. Polygamy and monogamy often coexist in societies. Given the sex ratio (the number of males for every 100 females) in most cultures, there would not be enough women for every man to be married to more than one. The two types of polygamy that have received the most attention are polyandry and polygyny. The former pattern is one woman married to several men, while the latter is used when one man has several wives.

Polyandry

While only a few societies today are know to practice polyandry, historically the pattern was more common. Globally, the most common type of polyandry is fraternal polyandry, the simultaneous marriage of a woman to all of the brothers in a family. Such arrangements can be beneficial in maintaining land holdings or other capital within a family, rather than dividing it among the sons and thereby diluting the wealth. Additionally, the fatherhood of children is less of an issue when biologically related men had the opportunity to be the father.

When women are in short supply, the practice of multiple husbands also occurs. If the resources are such that a man would have great difficulty supporting a woman on his own, polyandry may ensue. Patterns of social life might encourage polyandry. If men are gone from the home for extended periods of time (to hunt, fight, etc.) having another man at home helps maintain the safety and stability of the household.

Sometimes polyandry is accompanied by polygyny were the husbands may take wives to bring into the household. This forms sort of an extended network of married persons residing together. Some cultures that have practiced polyandry are found in Tibet, the Himalayas, areas of Southwest India, Nigeria, and Sri Lanka.

Polygyny

Far more common than polyandry, polygyny, the social pattern permitting men to take more than one wife, is estimated to have been the preferred marriage pattern in over three-fourths of the world's traditional cultures. While most persons in the United States consider this marriage pattern to be untenable, it remains popular today in parts of Africa, the Middle East, Indonesia, Thailand, and India. Historically polygyny was found among ancient Hebrews and in traditional Chinese society. In some polygynous variations the cowives are sisters, while in others they are unrelated. In a few cases men are obliged to marry their brothers' widows.

Many factors relate to the ability of a man to have multiple wives. Certainly the sex ratio plays a role, so that many later wives are significantly younger than their husbands. Also the wealth of the man and his family can limit his ability to pay the bride price (compensation to the wife's family). The desire or need for additional children might influence the decision, though one must be wealthy enough to support these wives and children. It is important to recognize that even in societies where polygyny is encouraged, monogamy remains the norm due to these social factors.

In the United States polygyny has largely entered the public consciousness through the religious denomination of the Church of Jesus Christ of Latter-day Saints (LDS), also known as the Mormons. A fundamentalist sect of the group has retained its polygamist origins despite the objection of the church and the violation of civil law.

TIMELINE OF PLURAL MARRIAGE IN THE UNITED STATES

EARLY 1830s: Joseph Smith, founder of the Church of Jesus Christ of Latter-day Saints, the Mormon Church, confides to church elders about his thoughts on plural marriage.

1843: Smith notifies the rest of the church population, as well as his wife, on his views of plural marriage

1862: The first U.S. federal law is passed outlawing polygamy.

1885: Polygamists move to Mexico and Alberta, Canada.

1890: Wilford Woodruff, LDS church leader, fears that polygamy casts a negative light on Utah and may affect it gaining statehood. He then issues an "Official Declaration," also known as "The Manifesto," to halt polygamy. As a result, a splinter group is formed in Colorado City, Arizona.

1928: The first splinter-group of polygamists moves to Short Creek, Arizona. They choose Short Creek due to its isolation.

1924: The United Effort Plan is formally established to manage properties and affairs for the fundamentalists.

1944: Federal agents raid Short Creek. Similar raids are conducted in Utah, Idaho and other Arizona sites.

1953: On July 26, Arizona police conduct a raid at Short Creek and arrest 31 men and nine women practicing polygamy. Two hundred and sixty-three women and children are taken into state custody. After negative publicity, the governments in Utah and Arizona have misgivings about another raid.

LATE 1950s: Polygamists living in British Columbia combine forces with fundamentalists in Short Creek.

1986: Rulon T. Jeffs is named president of the Fundamentalist Church of Jesus Christ of Latter-day Saints (FLDS).

1990: A number of women who fled from polygamy demand an investigation into polygamous practices at Bountiful, UT. The Creston RCMP launches an investigation.

2007: Warren Jeffs, leader of the FLDS is convicted of felony child rape.

2008: Texas Child Protective Services seize more than 400 children from the Yearning for Zion Ranch, a polygamist property in western Texas.

BRIEF HISTORY OF U.S. POLYGAMY

People first began speaking of polygamy in the United States somewhere between 1830 and the early 1840s. This practice was isolated in people of the Mormon faith in Utah and California. However, the first official declaration came from the faith's founder Joseph Smith in 1843, only one year before his death, in a very thorough document on marriage, and specifically eternal marriage. In addition to speaking of eternal marriage, it most famously stated that in certain circumstances a man may be allowed to have more than one wife. This brought the concept of plural marriage to the United States. This sacred stance on polygamy was allegedly revealed to Joseph Smith in connection with his study of the Bible, possibly around 1831, a decade before it was first committed to paper on July 12, 1843. However, Joseph Smith's teachings were not shared with the public-at-large until five years later. LDS reports that passages from the Joseph Smith Translation of the Bible indicate that his thorough study of the Bible and of the patriarchs of the Old Testament who had more than one wife prompted Joseph Smith to pray to ask the Lord about plural marriage. Reportedly, Joseph Smith learned that when the Lord commanded plural marriage, it would not be considered a sin if a man chose to marry another woman while his first wife is or was still living.

Historians have not come to a consensus on why Joseph Smith decided to practice polygamy. The primary argument used by Mormon spokesmen was the fact that men mentioned in the Old Testament practiced polygamy. This is a true historical fact as numerous men in the Bible, for example, Abraham, Jacob, David, and Solomon, were known polygamists.

Joseph Smith, personally, did not want to practice plural marriage, but believed that he was being commanded to do so by God. Joseph Smith reportedly agreed to a life of plural marriage so that he was obedient to God. However, according to the LDS, he did so with trepidation but reportedly had more than 30 wives. Interestingly, when he told his revelations to his wife, she reportedly burned the writings in the fireplace. However, Joseph Smith anticipated such an occurrence and had another copy already printed.

After God revealed the doctrine of plural marriage to Joseph Smith and commanded him to live it, Smith began teaching some of his close friends and other leaders in the Church about this practice. After a period of time during the beginning years of the Church, he and a limited number of Church leaders entered into plural marriages. Scholars at Brigham Young University, a Mormon institution, report that it was difficult for the members who practiced polygamy to do so, and they suffered through a trial of faith.

Increasing numbers of Latter-day Saints entered into plural marriages at the same time that they moved west under the direction of Brigham Young. Beginning in 1862, the United States Congress adopted several laws against polygamy. In 1862 the Republicans had full control of the Congress and the White House. They began their term by issuing the Morrill Anti-Bigamy Act. This piece of legislation made it clear that polygamy was illegal in all U.S. territories. However, LDS believed that the practice of polygamy was protected by the personal freedoms guaranteed by the U.S. Constitution. In 1879, the Supreme Court declared that polygamy was not protected by the Constitution. This was based on the legal principle that states' laws are designed to help govern the actions of individuals. Although laws cannot be made that interfere with religious opinions or beliefs, they may limit some religious practices. This move toward antipolygamy legislation was due in part to rumors about polygamy that were beginning to grow. By the 1880s many Latter-day Saints men who practiced polygamy were either living in secrecy or had been imprisoned.

In 1889, then-Church president Wilford Woodruff decided to make a statement about polygamy as a result of the threats received by members from those outside of the church. He penned a document that officially ended the sanctioning of plural marriage by the Church. This document was simply called the "Manifesto." It was then published in the "Doctrine and Covenants" and was accepted at the general conference in 1890. Although the Manifesto was published and accepted, a small number of plural marriages were still being performed. However, in 1904, then-president Joseph F. Smith called for a vote abolishing all post-Manifesto plural marriages. Many LDS members viewed the turn against polygamy as a form of religious treason. Splinter groups were created in direct response to this document. The Fundamentalist Latter-day Saints (FLDS) was created as a result. This group is the most well-known polygamous group in the United States today.

PLURAL MARRIAGE TODAY

LDS church has publicly denounced polygamy and has the policy of excommunicating any member who practices this type of lifestyle. In 1998, Church president Gordon B. Hinckley made the following statement about the Church's position on plural marriage:

> This Church has nothing whatever to do with those practicing polygamy. They are not members of this Church . . . If any of our members are found to be practicing plural marriage, they are excommunicated, the most serious penalty the Church can impose. Not only are those so involved in direct violation of the civil law, they are in violation of the law of this Church. (lds.org)

Much still remains unknown about the practice of plural marriage today. The culture remains shrouded in secrecy. However, it is estimated that approximately 40,000 fundamentalist people practice polygamy across the region of the Intermountain West, although the number could be higher. They are concentrated in the western United States and Canada. Many of these individuals live in the polygamous communities of Hildale, Utah and Colorado City, Arizona. The FLDS is the most widely known polygamous group in the United States and has approximately 10,000 members. These members are located in communities in Utah, Arizona, Colorado, Texas, and British Columbia. Polygamy is at the very center of life in a FLDS compound. Members of the FLDS sect believe that for a man to reach the highest stage of heaven, he must have at least three wives. They also believe that the only way for a woman to enter heaven is if her husband takes her with him. Although polygamy remains illegal in all 50 states, most polygamists today circumvent the law by only legally marrying their first wife and then spiritually marrying their subsequent wives. However, fundamentalist polygamists have only rarely been prosecuted by the government.

Two of the most notorious polygamists who were in fact prosecuted by the U.S. government are Tom Green and Warren Jeffs. Tom Green is husband to five wives and father to 29 children. In May of 2001, Green was charged and convicted of bigamy and failure to pay child support. On June 24, 2002, he was convicted of child rape for sex with a 13-year-old who later became his legal wife. He was sentenced to five years to life in prison. Green was released from prison on parole on August 7, 2007.

Warren Jeffs is the leader (prophet) of the FLDS whose personal headquarters was in Colorado City, Arizona. Jeffs' father, Rulon Jeffs, was the former leader of this sect, but gave full control to his son after suffering a stroke in 2002. Warren Jeffs is said to have arranged unknown numbers of marriages between underage men and women, and it was this practice that led the authorities to arrest him. He was one of the FBI's "Ten Most Wanted" and was a fugitive for numerous months. After being arrested by Nevada police, he was tried and convicted in September 2007 of accomplice to rape for arranging a marriage between a 14-year-old girl and her 19-year-old cousin. He was convicted and sentenced to two consecutive five-years-to-life terms. He is awaiting trial after being indicted in Texas and Arizona on additional similar charges. As of September 2008, no trial date had been set.

NEGATIVE ASPECTS OF PLURAL MARRIAGES

For most of mainstream America, polygamy is seen as unnatural and for many, immoral. However, there are some who believe that this lifestyle is an essential aspect of living a life obedient to the commandments of God. Those groups, such as the FLDS, receive a great deal of social pressure to give up the practice of plural marriage and conform to the dictates of monogamy. This pressure comes from legal avenues and society in general. Sometimes, even family members will stress that the changes in Mormon doctrine should be upheld.

Polygamy was only practiced in the Mormon Church for a relatively brief period of time over a century ago, but it has become a defining characteristic of society's viewpoint of the Mormon faith and culture. It has also caused individuals who are not Mormons to view all Mormons and their beliefs more negatively. Additionally, it has had a profound impact on LDS members' self-definition, furthering the belief that Mormons are a people apart from the dominant culture.

According to LDS, the family is ordained by God and marriage between a man and a woman is a vital part of God's plan. Their Church web site (lds.org) indicates that although they abhor the practice of polygamy today, at certain times and through His prophets God has directed the practice of plural marriage. LDS reports that in their obedience to direction from God, Latter-day Saints followed this practice for about 50 years during the 1800s but officially ceased the practice of such marriages after the Manifesto was issued by president Woodruff. Since that time, plural marriage has not been approved of by the Church of Jesus Christ of Latter-day Saints and any member doing so is subject to losing his or her membership in the Church.

Polygamy has been viewed in a negative light since its introduction into American society for a variety of reasons. For most Americans, polygamy is foreign to their everyday lives. There have been numerous documentaries and now a popular cable television program ("Big Love") depicting individuals who practice this type of lifestyle, but much remains unknown by society at large about this practice. This is due in large part to the fact that in the United States polygamy is illegal. Individuals who practice this way of life must do so in private for fear of criminal prosecution. Additionally, they fear public scorn and possibly losing their livelihood. They are not able to live openly in society and in many instances, live in isolation. Secrecy is necessary to protect these individuals from serving prison time.

Much of the negative attention directed at plural marriage comes from the assumption that it is a system that subordinates women. It exploits their domestic and sexual labor, without providing a legal status for any wives beyond the first. Because many of these marriages occur between younger girls and older men, there is the exploitation of her fertility and sexuality. It is this gray area between legal age of consent and rape that has colored the current debate about plural marriage in the United States.

Other negative aspects include how the children are reared; they are often homeschooled and cared for communally. Questions have arisen as to how this impacts the children's bonds with their father as well as their mother, who is the primary caregiver. Jealousy is another issue that enters the debate. The anthropological record suggests that jealousy is not uncommon, but is usually an attempt by cowives to secure maximum resources for their children and themselves, rather than a battle over sexual rights.

POSITIVE ASPECTS OF PLURAL MARRIAGES

There is a good deal of literature dealing with the negative aspects of polygamous life. However, there are many women living in polygamous households that are not only content, but are happy regarding their life choice. Cowives can experience a fair amount of autonomy in their daily lives, including freedom to pursue activities that are of interest to them. Some benefits that wives accrue include help with daily domestic and economic tasks, absence of constant supervision by the husband, and reduced pressure for sexual activity by the husband.

Because of the secretive nature of these arrangements, women may feel comfortable only commenting on their situations in anonymous ways. One outlet is on a pro-polygamy web site—principlevoices.org. On the site women speak of the joys of an intimate bond with their sister-wife and the convenience of having another woman in the house to assist with the daily household chores and child care. For many that comment, jealousy is not as serious an issue as one outside of this lifestyle would think.

When jealousy does occur, it is often mediated by the senior wife, who is often responsible for ensuring fairness in the relationship with the husband and subsequent wives. These women do not feel victimized or exploited, but rather revered as important members in their family.

FUTURE OF U.S. POLYGAMY

As knowledge of polygamous groups in the United States becomes more widespread, additional challenges will likely emerge. Not only is there increased curiosity from those who practice monogamy, but there is increased contact with government entities. More women, some via the technology of the Internet, have revealed their participation in polygamy.

A polygamist group gaining some attention from the media and researchers are Muslim polygamists. Some estimates place the number of Muslim polygamist families in the United States at nearly 50,000. Islam permits husbands to have up to four wives, although a husband cannot favor one over the others with a greater share of his love or money. This practice is most common in conservative, poorly educated Muslim immigrants from African countries. The women in these unions are vulnerable to exploitation. Under civil law the husband can only be married to one woman; the first wife. The other wives, in spiritual marriages, are legally invisible and live in fear of deportation. Because a husband can only sponsor one wife, his green card or citizenship can only protect the one. This is an area to watch as debates over immigration cross paths with religious and personal freedom.

Although plural marriage has numerous detractors, there are others who defend this lifestyle and lobby for the de-criminalization of the practice. These individuals seek to live the principle and simply to follow the tenets of their religion. In August of 2006 at a rally at the Salt Lake City Hall, over 250 youth, most living in plural families, came to make a stand against the criminalization of plural marriage, professing that they support this type of lifestyle and their parents. With the introduction of the legalization of homosexual marriage in Massachusetts, some polygamists believe that the time will come when they too can live their lives openly.

See also Extramarital Sexual Relationships; Fictive Kin; Religion and Families.

Further Reading: Bennion, Janet. *Women of Principle: Female Networking in Contemporary Mormon Polygyny*. New York: Oxford University Press, 1998; Bistine, Benjamin. *Colorado City Polygamists: An Inside Look for the Outsider*. Scottsdale, AZ: Agreka Books, 2004; Brigham Young University. http://www.ldsfaq.byu.edu; Evans, Richard C. and Elder Joseph P. Smith, Jr. *Blood Atonement and the Origin of Plural Marriage: Church of Jesus Christ of Latter Day Saints*. Whitefish, MT: Kessinger Publishing, 2007; Gibbs, Nancy, Hylton, Hilary, and Peta Owens-Liston. "Polygamy Paradox." *Time*, October 7, 2007, 48–50; Gordon, Sara Barringer. *The Mormon Question: Polygamy and Constitutional Conflict in Nineteenth Century America*. Chapel Hill: The University of North Carolina Press, 2002; Hales, Brian C. *Mormon Polygamy and Mormon Fundamentalism: The Generation After the Manifesto*. Draper, UT: Greg Kofford Books, 2007; Krakauer, Jon. *Under the Banner of Heaven*. London: Pan Books, 2004; Mormonism Research Ministry. http://www.mrm.org; Solomon, Dorothy Allred. *Daughter of Saints: Growing Up in Polygamy*. New York: W. W. Norton and Company, 2004.

Hayley Cofer

POVERTY AND PUBLIC ASSISTANCE

Public assistance programs are meant to relieve the hardships impoverished families experience as well as prevent families from remaining impoverished in the future or into the following generation. Over 12 percent of Americans—nearly 37 million people—are currently living below the poverty line. Even more Americans have income above the poverty line, but still experience difficulties making ends meet. The poverty level for a family of four is just over $20,000 per year; this is roughly the equivalent of two parents each working a full-time, minimum-wage job 5 days a week for 52 weeks. Before discussing the policies that seek to help impoverished families, we should understand the characteristics of the Americans most likely to be impoverished today.

Families and persons most likely to be impoverished or affected by poverty are the elderly, minorities (especially African American and Latino), children, women, single mothers, young parents, people living in the South, the poorly educated, the unemployed, and those who live in very urban or very rural areas. Particular attention has been paid to the elderly poor in America, and programs such as Social Security and Medicare have alleviated a great deal of elderly poverty since their inception. Minorities face numerous challenges to employment and have less access to high-paying jobs, making them more likely to be impoverished than whites. It is important to note, however, that there is a greater absolute number of poor whites than there are poor minorities in the United States; it is a common misconception that most poor families are African American or Latino. Children make up a large percentage of impoverished Americans because they have no source of personal income, and are largely dependent on their parents for support. Women, similar to racial and ethnic minorities, face employment challenges and still make less money dollar-for-dollar than do men in comparable jobs. As the primary caregivers of their families, single mothers face even more difficulties in the workforce because they have to manage work, child care, and parenting duties without the help of a partner. For these reasons, single mothers are also more likely to be impoverished as compared to two-parent families.

Young parents, such as those who begin to have children while in their teens, face a greater likelihood of poverty than parents who postpone childbearing until later ages; this is due to their having little time to establish a career or finish higher education. Families living in the South or in urban or rural areas are at higher risk for poverty as well. Although poverty used to be a solely urban phenomenon, rural residents have become increasingly impoverished through the decline of small, family-owned farms and now face the same limited access to low-paying jobs as urban residents. Additionally, rural residents lack public transportation resources and often cannot retain a job because they have no reliable means of getting there. Urban residents and families living in the South lost good jobs that included benefits and a decent wage as industry moved out of these areas into lower-cost parts of the country (like the suburbs), or to other parts of the world. Individuals with low educational achievement or those who are unemployed are also more likely to be impoverished than individuals who have high levels of education or who hold jobs.

Poverty can result in a number of complications for families, including low educational achievement due to living in neighborhoods with poorly funded schools and over-filled classrooms. Two of the most visible effects of poverty are poor health and sub-par access to preventative health care. Families living in poverty often cannot afford health insurance without public assistance, and therefore forgo preventative care such as yearly checkups, immunizations, prenatal visits, and cancer screenings, which results in allowing serious diseases to proceed or worsen undiagnosed. Families without health insurance often rely on hospital emergency care when necessary, which is a less-efficient and more-expensive option than visiting a family doctor or other primary care provider. Impoverished families also tend to neglect dental care; untreated dental problems have future implications for general health and access to employment. Fathers of impoverished families are the most likely family members to neglect health care, followed by mothers and then children.

Living in poverty can also cause poor nutrition, and several programs have tried to provide the resources for adequate nutrition, appropriate caloric intake, and access to nutritious foods. Homelessness and access to sub-standard housing also occur as a result of poverty because families often cannot afford to pay market-priced rent, let alone purchase a home. Several assistance programs are in place exclusively to prevent families from being without a place to live, as well as to regulate the standards of housing available. Sub-standard housing has been held accountable for compromising children's health. Old lead paint on cracking banisters can cause lead poisoning, and mice, cockroaches, or other vermin have been cited as causing children's asthma.

PUBLIC ASSISTANCE PROGRAMS

Antipoverty programs remain among the most highly criticized of all government programs in the United States. Much of this can be explained by the misperceptions that average Americans have of persons who are in poverty and who receive public assistance. There is a long-standing stereotype that persons receiving public assistance are attempting to work the system or are cheating to qualify for additional benefits. However, all public assistance and antipoverty programs in the United States are means-tested programs, meaning a family's income has to fall below a specific guideline in order for that family to qualify for services. Public assistance programs are funded in part by the federal government and in part by state and local governments. The federal government sets guidelines for how families can qualify for programs as well as for how much funding each state must also contribute to the programs. Also referred to as the welfare system, public assistance is comprised of five major programs: Temporary Assistance to Needy Families (TANF); the food stamp program; the Special Supplemental Nutrition Program for Women, Infants, and Children (WIC); Medicaid; and Subsidized Housing Programs.

The United States did not have any comprehensive public assistance programs until President Franklin D. Roosevelt mandated that the government provide employment through public spending during the Great Depression. Public assistance continued to provide services to impoverished Americans until President Lyndon B. Johnson's War on Poverty attracted attention and, subsequently, scrutiny. Following the War on Poverty, the number of people accessing public assistance services grew rapidly. The enrollment for Aid to Families with Dependent Children (AFDC, a program that preceded TANF) increased by 270 percent, and enrollment for Medicaid (a program introduced in the 1960s) skyrocketed. The American public continued to scrutinize the welfare system throughout the 1970s and 1980s, and all federally funded public assistance programs were eventually overhauled during the 1996 period of welfare reform under President Bill Clinton. The Personal Responsibility and Work Opportunity Reconciliation Act of 1996 (PRWORA), commonly known as welfare reform, was hotly contested by advocates for the poor, but did not end the debate over welfare. Although the number of people accessing social services has greatly declined since the 1996 Reform (by as much as two-thirds), public assistance programs continue to undergo constant evaluations of their effectiveness.

TEMPORARY ASSISTANCE FOR NEEDY FAMILIES

Temporary Assistance for Needy Families (TANF), is also referred to as cash assistance namely because it provides qualifying families with a monthly stipend of cash based on the number of persons present in a household and proportionate to the cost of living in their state. In order to qualify for TANF, recipients must generally have an income below the federal poverty level for their household size and must care for one or more dependent infants or children. Because mothers, rather than fathers, are often more likely to have custody of their children, the vast majority of TANF recipients are women and their dependent children. Single persons not taking care of dependent children generally do not qualify for TANF.

Prior to the 1996 reform, TANF (then called AFDC) did not impose a time limit on recipient families, meaning that families could receive AFDC cash assistance indefinitely as long as they continued to meet the eligibility criteria. Opponents and critics of AFDC argued that the lack of time limits was not providing impoverished families with any incentive to get off assistance and go to work, and so post-1996 TANF instituted a federal standard of a 60-month lifetime limit per recipient. The second notable change of the reform called for stricter work requirements for its recipients, meaning a mother with children has to spend 10 to 40 hours per week participating in some kind of job training, job search, or educational program in order to remain eligible for TANF benefits.

Despite imposing time limits and work requirements, the 1996 reform also offered states some autonomy with respect to TANF. Individual states must follow the federal guidelines of the program, but are allowed to amend the qualifying requirements if they so choose, meaning a family in one state might be permitted to have up to $2000 in savings and still qualify for cash assistance, whereas another state might require families to have almost no assets in order to qualify. The lifetime limit for TANF can also be extended by individual states through the use of additional state funds, although some states have elected to make the 60-month-limit noncontinuous (meaning a person can only be on TANF for 24 continuous months, and then must leave welfare for at least a month before exhausting the rest of the time limit). States were also granted the ability to waive or change work requirements for recipients as part of various state-sponsored trial projects; this flexibility allowed states to experiment with TANF requirements in order to arrive at the best and most-efficient way to move individuals from welfare receipt to employment.

The effectiveness of the change from AFDC to TANF is notable, as the number of individuals seeking cash assistance has declined by two-thirds. TANF is still not without controversy, however, as the program has been criticized for not significantly improving the lives of those who seek its assistance. Families that leave welfare often do not make a clean break from the program and get caught in an on-again, off-again cycle until they've exhausted their lifetime limit. Because families sometimes remain impoverished even after their TANF receipt, many argue that the program's role as a transition from poverty to nonpoverty and employment has not been fulfilled. The emphasis on work requirements for welfare recipients has been very well received, as critics of TANF and AFDC were opposed to the idea that one could qualify for cash assistance without making a concerted effort to find employment. The success of these work requirements is limited, however, because requirements restrict the time a mother has to spend with her children and can put a strain on child care arrangements. Often, work programs offer child care assistance and other benefits, such as help with resume writing or transportation assistance, but these are not universally granted to all of those enrolled. Work programs are also criticized by recipients as being useless or as not teaching them anything, and the employment they find is often that of the minimum-wage, service-sector variety and offers no health insurance. One major challenge TANF faces in the future is to assist families in eventually achieving permanent, gainful employment in order to make a successful permanent transition out of poverty.

FOOD STAMPS

The food stamp program began in 1961 in response to physicians and army recruiters who noticed the pervasiveness of malnutrition within urban and rural populations. Created in order to provide a better opportunity for families to meet their basic nutritional needs, the food stamp program follows federal guidelines for qualification that are more lenient than those for TANF, meaning families who do not qualify for TANF may at least receive some food stamp assistance. If a family is already receiving TANF, they are automatically eligible for food stamps. If not receiving TANF, a family must have a gross income of less than 130 percent of the federal poverty level and less than $2,000 in assets (excluding the worth of their home and one car worth less than $4,500) to qualify. Food stamps may be used to purchase any type of food item except hot, prepared foods intended for immediate consumption. The amount of food stamps a family receives is based on the family size as well as the state's cost of living. An average family of three (one adult, two kids) receives $200 per month in food stamps. Families must re-qualify for food stamps every six months to one year, but are not required to report changes in income in between re-qualification periods.

The effectiveness of the food stamp program has been criticized because food stamp participants are still more likely to have poor nutrition than are nonfood stamp participants. The 1996 National Food Stamp Survey found 50 percent of respondents still experience times without adequate food, and many households do not get enough folic acid or iron in their diets. Food stamps are not restricted only for the purchase of healthy foods, which leads some researchers to believe they have not improved impoverished families' nutrition and overall health. Food stamp participants are more likely to be obese, which could be due to families' choosing to purchase high-fat foods. However, families that receive food stamps tend to spend more on food than they would otherwise, and food stamp participants showed increased consumption of protein, vitamins A, B6, and C, and other important minerals.

Food stamp fraud presents another point of concern for the food stamp program because food stamp recipients sometimes sell food stamps for cash as opposed to using them to buy food. The going rate for food stamp resale is between 50 and 65 percent of face value, meaning $100 of food stamps is worth only about $50 on the street. Studies have suggested, however, that the people selling food stamps also buy stamps. This indicates that families might be so strapped for cash that they prefer to sell stamps when they need cash, but then later buy their stamps back to purchase food. Scholars have proposed that the food stamp program can circumvent this issue by distributing stamps throughout the month rather than in a once-per-month lump sum.

WIC

Like the food stamp program, the Special Supplemental Nutrition Program for Women, Infants, and Children (WIC) was formed to provide nursing or pregnant mothers and children under 5 years old with better nutritional resources. WIC provides participants with certificates redeemable at participating markets for food items such as milk, cheese, cereal, beans, baby formula, and peanut butter in an amount equivalent to roughly $40 per month. These food items are sources of iron, vitamins A and C, calcium, and protein. WIC also provides participants with a nutritional education session each month when they come to get their WIC coupons, and monitors the development of infants and children under five years old. Children are no longer eligible for WIC benefits after their fifth birthday and mothers must be nursing or pregnant to qualify.

Participants must have incomes under 185 percent of the federal poverty level, although mothers or children under five years old automatically qualify if they are also receiving Medicaid. The more generous income guidelines have come under fire because this allows more people to qualify for WIC, and raises the cost of the program, although participation rates for WIC are much lower than they would be if every eligible individual participated. However, this under-enrollment raises questions as to whether or not WIC is truly serving the families who might need it the most. WIC, compared to the Food Stamp Program, loses very little money to fraud, probably due to the food-item-specific nature of the program. The food coupons have very little resale value because they are restricted to certain food items and, furthermore, specific product sizes and brands.

Because WIC is the most-studied federal nutrition program, there is less controversy over whether or not WIC is effective than compared to the Food Stamp Program or the National School Lunch Program. WIC participation has reduced the incidence of low and very low birth-weight babies, meaning public money spent on WIC saves on medical expenditures in the long run. Studies of WIC have also found positive health outcomes for toddlers, although not to the same extent as the outcomes for infants. Some have criticized the WIC program because it offers nursing mothers free formula and subsequently provides a disincentive to breastfeed. The health portion of the WIC program has begun to encourage mothers to breastfeed, but WIC mothers are still less likely to breastfeed when compared to mothers not in the program. This program continues to cause controversy among health professionals and scholars who believe breastfeeding to be an important part of developing infants' immunity, the mothers' health, and the mother-child bond.

MEDICAID

The Medicaid program seeks to provide federally and state-funded health insurance to qualifying low-income women and children. The Medicaid program also offers public health insurance to disabled (Disability Insurance) and elderly persons (Medicare). About half of all Medicaid recipients are low-income children and one-fifth are low-income women. Medicaid is the most expensive public service program, spending about $280 billion annually, with most of the costs going toward the health care and treatment of the elderly. The $47 billion that goes toward impoverished women's and children's health care is still very costly, especially when compared to the annual cost of TANF ($16 billion) or the Food Stamp Program ($24 billion). Despite the program's vast spending, each year over the past decade roughly 12 percent of all children in the United States have gone without health insurance.

Access to health insurance and preventative care is important for impoverished families' well-being, and Medicaid insurance provides very low-cost health care to families who qualify. As of the change implemented by the Deficit Reduction Act of 1984, any families who qualify for TANF are automatically eligible for Medicaid benefits as well. The Medicaid income cut-offs continued to become more generous, and more federal funding was set aside in order to guarantee more children's access to health care. Medicaid benefits became available to pregnant women, two-parent families, and to teenage mothers living with their parents, as long as the incomes of these various types of households fell within the qualifying income guidelines. By the 1990s, families with incomes at 130 percent of the federal poverty line or below became eligible for Medicaid, with some states choosing to raise eligibility guidelines further, up to 185 percent of the poverty level. By October of 1997, 41 of 50 states were using their own funds to raise the income guidelines for women and children.

Having Medicaid does not necessarily translate into having access to health services, as providers often restrict their practice to allowing only a certain percentage of Medicaid patients, or refuse to see these patients at all. Additionally, the length of Medicaid doctor visits is, on average, shorter than the average non-Medicaid visit, which may indicate a lower quality of care for Medicaid patients. Medical institutions often cite Medicaid's slow reimbursement and excessive paperwork as a reason to prefer privately insured patients. Despite Medicaid's controversial position with practitioners, public health remains an important service that, at the very least, makes preventative and routine health care available and affordable to low-income women and their children.

HOUSING PROGRAMS

Although there are multiple kinds of housing programs, only two will be discussed here. Housing programs began in general with the passing of the Housing Act of 1949, which called for an end to unsafe, sub-standard housing. Some housing programs operate by offering incentives to contractors to construct low-income housing. In contrast, the programs discussed here provide low-cost housing to families at lower-than-market rent. Public housing developments are perhaps the most visible of these programs. These developments offer available units to families with income below the poverty level for rent proportionate to one-third of their monthly income.

Although public housing must meet a certain standard of cleanliness and construction, some housing developments have not uniformly met these guidelines. Public housing is often referred to as the projects, and generally gets a bad reputation regardless of its quality or location. Families must also often sign up for housing years in advance, due to the long waiting lists that exist for these units. In cities such as New York, over 100,000 families are on a housing waiting list. In contrast, the availability of public housing units in central Pennsylvania has motivated families to move to the area just to have access to housing.

The Section 8 program operates along the same income and benefit guidelines as public housing developments, except Section 8 allows families to select the housing of their choice. After a family gets past a waiting list longer than that for most public housing, Section 8 grants the family with a voucher and the family must find private-sector housing that meets the quality standards of public housing. If a family is able to do this, the voucher pays for a portion of the family's rent. This amount is typically proportionate to two-thirds of the market-rate rental price. As with public housing developments, the family ends up paying for only one-third of the total rental amount.

Public housing is exceedingly helpful for the families who are able to get through the waiting lists, although a great deal of controversy remains over whether or not public housing developments are actually good and safe environments for children. The main issue public housing faces is providing all of those families in need with affordable housing options. As waiting lists indicate, this goal has not been met.

ENDING POINT

Poverty is clearly a problematic circumstance for families, and although antipoverty programs have had success in reducing the number of families in poverty, public assistance programs face various controversies of their own. Perhaps one of the most important issues with public assistance programs is their uniform neglect of fathers. Fathers cannot qualify for cash assistance unless they have full custody of their dependents, and fathers do not qualify for food stamps for the same reason. WIC is aimed only toward women and their children under five years old, and public housing does not typically provide housing services to men without families. In cases where the father is not married to the mother of his children, the father's presence in a public housing unit is actually illegal and may cause a mother and children to lose their housing subsidy.

In light of recent programs that promote marriage among low-income, unmarried parents (such as the Healthy Marriage Initiative), public assistance programs should consider expanding the eligibility requirements to men rather than restrict services to women and children only. Marriage programs do not cooperate with public assistance programs in a way that is productive for creating stable families; the fact that a mother can lose access to public housing if her partner lives with her is an indication of this. In order to successfully continue to provide impoverished families with much-needed resources, perhaps even a resident father's income, and encourage unity among families, public assistance will have to consider changing its policies in the future.

See also Child Support and Parental Responsibility; Culture of Poverty; Deadbeat Parents; Foster Care; Marriage Promotion; Teen Pregnancy.

Further Reading: Almanac of Policy Issues. http://www.policyalmanac.org; Blank, Rebecca and Ron Hoskins. *The New World of Welfare.* Washington, DC: The Brookings Institution, 2001; Currie, Janet M. *The Invisible Safety Net.* Princeton, NJ: Princeton University Press, 2006; Dossin, Steven C. "Coming Together: A Proposal for Social Progress in Welfare and Tax Reform." http://www.comingtogether.info; Grogger, Jeffrey and Lynn A. Karoly. *Welfare Reform: Effects of a Decade of Change.* Cambridge: Harvard University Press, 2005; Urban Institute. http://www.urban.org.

Lane Destro

PREMARITAL SEXUAL RELATIONSHIPS

The term premarital sexual relations refers to the sexual activities, particularly vaginal-penile penetration, of adolescents and young adults before committing to marriage. The term often assumes heterosexuality, and it privileges sexuality within a marital context. Certainly sexual expressions exist among same-sex persons, and among persons (heterosexual and others) who will not marry. However, conventional use of this language in academia and the larger culture follows the above definition. Most of the scholarly research on premarital sexual relations focuses on the first sexual intercourse, especially the age at which it first happens.

IS ORAL SEX REALLY SEX?

Some argue any sexual behavior, particularly to the point of orgasm (such as genital touching, oral sex, and anal sex) counts as having sex, while others argue only vaginal-penile penetration counts as having sex. Debates also include the difference between giving and receiving oral sex, and the difference between cunnilingus (oral sex performed on a woman) and fellatio (oral sex performed on a man). Some research suggests that there is no consensus from health educators about whether or not oral sex constitutes abstinent behavior.

For heterosexual couples, oral sex is often viewed as part of the sexual script before sexual intercourse. (Sexuality often follows a "script" or pattern, such as hand-holding, then mouth kissing, then touching or caressing of breasts, genitals, *etc*.). Whether or not oral sex counts as sex is further complicated for gay and lesbian couples, who may have different sexual scripts than heterosexuals.

Regardless of how it is defined, research shows that adolescents are engaging in oral sex more now than ever before. It should be noted that this may in part be a factor of adolescents willingly admitting to behaviors that no longer carry a negative connotation compared with the recent past when these behaviors were not discussed. In other research it was found that more than half of 15 to 19 year olds interviewed reported engaging in oral sex and that an equal number of girls and boys reported receiving oral sex. The increased acceptance of oral sex is often attributed to former President Bill Clinton and the Monica Lewinsky scandal. In 1998, Clinton remarked, "I did not have sexual relations with that woman, Miss Lewinsky." He later admitted to an improper physical relationship with her, including receiving oral sex from her and allegedly inserting a cigar in her genitals. These events led to a national debate about the meaning of oral sex, and to the finding that many teenagers were indeed having oral sex and not defining it as sex.

Adolescents may be engaging in oral sex and other genital touching, sometimes colloquially referred to as outercourse or sortacourse, because it is more socially acceptable and entering into mainstream media conversation. Teens also have the misperception that it is safer than vaginal-penile intercourse. Adolescents often view oral sex as less significant and less intimate because it reduces the chances of becoming pregnant or getting a sexually transmitted infection. Teens often report that engaging in oral sex compared with intercourse lessened the chances of jeopardizing their reputation, and lessened any feelings of guilt. Oral sex is usually not taught or discussed in sex education classes, and parents are much less likely to cover the topic of oral sex with their teens, leaving them to learn about oral sex through the media and peers. Adolescents are largely uninformed of the risks of unprotected oral sex (without a barrier such as condom or dental dam), such as transmission of herpes, chlamydia, gonorrhea, and other sexually transmitted infections (STIs).

FIRST SEXUAL INTERCOURSE

Traditionally, premarital sexual relations, especially when a person loses their virginity, have meant engaging in vaginal-penile penetration. However, younger individuals are much more likely to view virginity loss as including a range of sexual activities. Engaging in first intercourse is often not the same as first sexual activity. Many young people who have not engaged in intercourse have engaged in other genital sexual activities with a partner such as genital touching or oral sex.

AGE OF FIRST SEXUAL INTERCOURSE

The average age of first intercourse is between 15 to 18 years old. It is reported that more than 80 percent of 20-year-olds in the United States have engaged in intercourse, and they argue that teenage sexual experiences tend to be episodic and less frequent compared with adult sexuality.

From the 1970s to the 1990s, the average age of first sexual intercourse declined, and although the decline in age is well documented, there is less consensus regarding as to why this is so. Explanations often include historical changes (such as the 1960s sexual revolution), an increase in the age of first marriage, and less parental supervision due to an increase in parental divorce, and both parents working outside of the home, particularly in the after-school hours. Adolescents with divorced parents are likely to engage in sexual relationships at an earlier age compared with those with married parents. This is explained in part because children of single parents may have less available supervision than that in two-parent families, and they may see the role modeling of parents engaging in nonmarital sexual relations. Many divorced parents choose to cohabit rather than remarry, which likely influences adolescents' attitudes about sexuality and marriage.

In addition to examining the role of the family, scholarly research has examined the impact of religiosity in premarital sexual relations. Religious youths are more likely to wait to engage in first intercourse and to be less sexually active compared to youths who are less religious. When they are sexually active, religious youths are less likely to use effective contraception.

Certain scholars have found that at the beginning of the twenty-first century, teens are slightly more sexually conservative, and, particularly for boys, may be delaying their first sexual intercourse. The decline in sexual activity may be attributed to successful sex education programs (abstinence-based or comprehensive-based), cultural backlash against the sexual revolution, and greater fear of disease. Unlike older generations, young people today have grown up with cultural messages of safe sex, especially protection from HIV/AIDS. However, being sexually active and unmarried is the norm for young people in our culture. The vast majority of 20-year-olds are sexually active, yet not married. The trend is for teens, both boys and girls, to have sexual relations within relationships as opposed to casual sex. However, relationships may be broadly defined by teenagers as including a couple together for two weeks; adults typically view two weeks as too short a time to constitute a meaningful relationship.

Race, ethnicity, social class, and gender are some of the more powerful factors that consistently differentiate early from later debuts of sexual intercourse. Studies consistently find that African Americans, compared with whites or Latinos, and persons from lower social classes, compared with those from higher income brackets, are more likely to engage in sexual intercourse at a younger age.

Regarding gender, males tend to report a younger age of first sexual intercourse than females; however, in the last decade, the gender gap is closing with boys' decreasing sexual activity.

CONTEXT OF FIRST SEXUAL INTERCOURSE

The context of the first sexual intercourse typically occurs within a dating relationship and is described as a spontaneous event. Sexual debut, for men and especially women, tends not to be a very satisfying emotional or physical experience. Both men and women report experiencing anxiety at the first sexual event. Compared with men, women tend to be much less likely to report having an orgasm, more likely to report feeling guilty (especially if a dating relationship is not established), and more likely to say retrospectively that they wish that they had waited. Females experience less pleasant reactions to first coitus than do males. For example, females are more likely to be nervous, in pain, worried about pregnancy, and worried about possible negative outcomes of having intercourse. Women who were in late adolescence or young adulthood when they lost their virginity reported less negative reactions compared with those who were younger. The age of the first sexual partner also impacts women's reactions because sex with someone younger or the same age is often reported as more pleasurable than first-ever sex with an older partner. As for why people engage in first intercourse when they do, women are more likely to report that they engaged in first sex to strengthen a relationship, while men are more likely to cite physical pleasure as the reason for engaging in first sex.

An increasing number of adolescents use contraception, with the condom reported as the most common method at first intercourse. The Allan Guttmacher Institute reports that contraception use has doubled since the 1970s, with nearly 80 percent of adolescents today using contraception at the first intercourse.

A later age of first sexual intercourse is correlated with women indicating that they wanted the sex to occur. About one-quarter of women report that their first intercourse was voluntary, but not wanted. Wanting to engage in first intercourse is significant for quality of life factors; the meaning of sexuality in our society is that it is a pleasurable event, and not a chore, that people choose to engage in. Additionally, women who want the first sexual intercourse to take place are more likely to report using contraception.

IMPLICATIONS

Adolescent sexual behavior, especially for women, often carries a negative connotation. Researchers and policymakers often make the connection between a younger age of first sexual intercourse and increased risks of social problems such as unwanted teen pregnancy rates (often resulting in abortion or single-teen motherhood), increased risk of STIs, including HIV/AIDS, and juvenile delinquency. Early sexual debut is also associated with ineffective sex education programs, a harsher reputation to especially young women, and poor decision making by ignoring potential risks.

Research has found that persons who have sex at a younger age tend to have more nonvoluntary sex partners, to have more sex partners, to have more frequent intercourse, to be less likely to use effective contraception, and to be more likely to cite that they were too young to have sex. Many of these consequences are as a result of having more opportunities for risk-producing behaviors (such as more chances of unwanted pregnancy). Several studies note that young teenagers are less likely to use contraception, not out of lack of knowledge, but out of greater perceived costs (economic, social stigma) as opposed to rewards (less likely to get a disease or pregnant). This may be because the costs are immediate, and the rewards may be delayed. Because adolescent sexuality is often viewed as a negative health risk, policymakers have tried to utilize various strategies, often argued to be ineffective, to delay teenagers' first sexual event. Tactics include relying on abstinence-based sex education programs or encouraging adolescents to sign virginity pledges.

Strategies to Delay Sex Are Ideal

Despite strong social pressures to be sexual, and a culture that glamorizes adolescent sexuality, many young persons are proudly proclaiming their virginity as a choice, and not a source of embarrassment. This attitude shift of the meaning of virginity may demonstrate the malleability of the term virgin as many debate what counts as having sex. Virginity pledges, or written vows to remain (or become) celibate, often until marriage, offers the hope that young people will delay intercourse.

Some scholars point to the effectiveness of virginity pledges to delay the onset of sexual behavior, especially within the right context. For example, too many adolescents pledging within one context tends to decrease the effectiveness. Some parochial schools mandate that students sign virginity pledges, and these forced pledges tend to be ineffective in delaying sexual behaviors. Virginity pledges and campaigns such as True Love Waits create a moral community where young people have support and a social context of sharing the sacred meaning of sexuality. For example, young people who commit to the True Love Waits campaign, sign: "Believing that true love waits, I make a commitment to God, myself, my family, my friends, my future mate, and my future children to a lifetime of purity including sexual abstinence from this day until the day I enter a biblical marriage relationship." Such pledges emphasize the special and sacred meaning of sexuality within the correct context, often a loving, heterosexual, committed relationship, as opposed to casual sexual relationships or behaviors which satisfy physical urges (such as masturbating to pornography).

Many groups, especially conservative Christian groups, celebrate what is known as a purity ball, or more specifically a Father-Daughter Purity Ball. At these events, young women in a wedding-like ceremony pledge their virginities to their fathers, promising to save their sexuality for their future husbands. The emphasis is often on family unity, especially to strengthen father-daughter relationships, with the goal of decreasing social problems such as teen pregnancy, divorce, and domestic violence. Morality and purity are highlighted, not only in sexual relationships, but also in mind, spirit, and behavior.

Research has found that religious behavior was a main factor in postponing sexual activity for unmarried adolescents, and others agree that religious reasons for virginity were strongly associated with a positive reaction for young people. Many cite that strategies to delay adolescent sexuality are ideal not only for religious and moral reasons, but other reasons as well. Adolescents may be ill-equipped to deal with adult decisions and consequences that can come from sexual relationships, such as unwanted pregnancy, diseases, and even emotional reactions to having sex. Sexual expressions, especially vaginal-penile penetration, constitute a deeper symbolic meaning in our culture, one that teens may not be prepared to handle.

Strategies to Delay Sex Are Ineffective

Some scholars take issue with the goal to stop or delay adolescent sexuality because such messages tend to reiterate a sexual double standard. Often it is women's sexuality that is emphasized, as women bear the consequences of unintended pregnancy. Women are sexually objectified, and serve as the sexual gatekeepers in our society, who often control the pace of sexual expression and are judged much more harshly than men for being sexual. Instead of delaying teen sexuality, some argue that the goal should be responsible and informed sexuality. Many scholars argue that delay strategies like virginity pledges, purity balls, and abstinence-based sex education programs are not only ineffective, but produce sexually risky adolescents who are misinformed or guilt-ridden.

Researchers found that virginity pledges do not have much effect in delaying sexual intercourse. Most break their pledge within the year. Critics suggest that as many as 88 percent of girls who take purity pledges break them within four years, often times engaging in unprotected sex with many partners. Girls who come from highly religious families may be shamed by their families if they are caught. It has been estimated that of those who do keep the oath, about half regularly engaged in oral sex thinking that it does not count. When young people do decide to have sex, they are often not prepared to do it safely. In addition to not keeping their virginity pledges, researchers have found that teens often misreport their sexual history, or deny ever pledging their virginity. Misreporting sexual history can have dire consequences if risky behaviors are not reported to medical doctors and future sexual partners.

Purity balls have also been critiqued by feminist scholars and in the popular media as being creepy. Donned in formal attire and their ballroom best, fathers put purity rings or chastity bracelets on their daughters, who are usually early grade school through college aged, that the girls are supposed to give to their husbands on their wedding nights. Some in the popular media suggest these ceremonies resemble incestuous weddings. Also troublesome is how the purity balls maintain patriarchy. Young women's sexuality is controlled first by her father, then by her husband. Young girls may internalize the message that they need to be protected, or controlled, by a man as the mothers are often largely absent from such ceremonies.

CONCLUSION

Engaging in premarital sexual relations marks important life experiences for most youths. For good or bad, especially the first sexual intercourse is an event that most will remember throughout their lives. Examining the experience of adolescent sexuality provides insights into how it impacts other behaviors and risks, and how it influences future relationships. The debate continues over the role that young people's sexuality should play in the lives prior to marriage.

See also Abortion; Birth Control; Dating; Teen Pregnancy.

Further Reading: Bearman, Peter S., and Hannah Bruckner. "After the Promise: The STD Consequence of Adolescent Virginity Pledges." *Journal of Adolescent Health* 36 (2005): 271–278; Carpenter, Laura. *Virginity Lost: An Intimate Portrait of First Sexual Experiences.* New York: New York University Press, 2005; Houts, Leslie A. "But Was It Wanted? Young Women's First Voluntary Sexual Intercourse." *Journal of Family Issues* 26 (2005): 1082–1102; Remez, Lisa. "Oral Sex Among Adolescents: Is It Sex or Is It Abstinence?" *Family Planning Perspectives* 32 (2000): 298–304; Risman, Barbara, and Pepper Schwartz. "After the Sexual Revolution: Gender Politics in Teen Dating." *Contexts* 1 (2002): 16–24; Sprecher, Susan, Anita Barbee, and Pepper Schwartz. "'Was it Good For You, Too?': Gender Differences in First Sexual Intercourse Experiences." *Journal of Sex Research* 32 (1995): 3–15; Sprecher, Susan and Pamela C. Regan. "College Virgins: How Men and Women Perceive Their Sexual Status." *The Journal of Sex Research* 33 (1996): 3–15.

Leslie Houts Picca

PRENUPTIAL AGREEMENTS

A prenuptial agreement is an agreement that a couple makes before they marry that defines how their assets will be divided in the event that the marriage is unsuccessful. It specifies who brought what to the marriage and to what each person is entitled in the event of divorce. It might also indicate what the property rights of each person are during the marriage. While many persons suggest that prenuptial agreements are a recent phenomenon developed in response to rising divorce rates and increasing material wealth in the United States, prenuptial agreements have a long history among royalty and landed aristocracy. Anyone who might stand to lose a great deal if a marriage were to be terminated can perceive the benefits of a prenuptial agreement. Often prenuptial agreements make news when a famous person loses a significant amount in a divorce and persons wonder why there was no prenuptial agreement between the couple. Costly celebrity settlements that did not include prenuptial agreements were the divorces of Rosanne Barr and Tom Arnold and that of Paul McCartney and Heather Mills.

Prenuptial agreements have caused many controversies throughout history, and were even the source of jokes in British theater in the late 1600s and early

1700s. Many people view a premarital contract as a precursor for divorce, which leads people to find this matter quite offensive to discuss. In addition, this topic is closely regarded by individuals as a matter that is normally taken on by the wealthy or those who are simply greedy, placing more importance on their assets than their partners. However, there has been an obvious increase in the use of this type of contract over the last few decades. Many lawyers specializing in family law suggest that prenuptial agreements have been given a bad reputation as the tactic of untrustworthy spouses, but there are many instances in which they can be beneficial for both parties. Here we will discuss both the legal and cultural aspects of premarital agreements along with the debates.

BACKGROUND

Prenuptial agreements, also known as marital contracts or ante-nuptial agreements, have been around since the sixteenth century in Anglo-American tradition. There are some accounts, however, that suggest they were not unknown in ancient Egypt. Marital contracts first took place in Anglo-Saxon society when a groom was purchasing a wife. It seems likely that parents initially negotiated these contracts on behalf of the couple. Upon the formation of the marital bond, a groom and the family of his wife often had a private contract negotiating a bride price, which entailed the exchange of property so that the wife would have some financial stability in the case where her husband was to die before her. Due to constant problems that arose from the difficulty of guaranteeing that the wife received the agreed-upon property upon the death of her husband, efforts were made to more strongly enforce prenuptial contracts over the next couple of centuries. By the middle of the seventeenth century these contracts had become so important that they were required by Parliament to be in writing.

Prior to 1970 in the United States, prenuptial agreements were virtually unenforceable if they indicated how the assets were to be divided in the event of divorce because they were seen as encouraging divorce. They were treated with skepticism because they almost always involved the waiver of financial and legal benefits by the less wealthy spouse. The legal principle of fairness was not upheld in most early marital contracts. Today, however, all states permit them and when they have been deemed fair to both parties they are generally upheld if contested. California has been a leader in legislation and precedent related to prenuptial agreements.

PURPOSES OF PRENUPTIAL AGREEMENTS

Surprisingly there are many purposes for prenuptial agreements. Consistent with the historic goals of such contracts, one of the main purposes for most individuals having this contract is to specify and maintain money and property assets. One of the important reasons for having this contract is to guarantee that family businesses and other inherited properties will be protected from the claims of the former spouse if the marriage is terminated. In addition, some couples may require the use of prenuptial contracts in order to ensure that their children's assets will be protected in the case where a parent dies or the partners divorce. This is especially relevant if the child is the offspring of a previous marriage. Also, because these contracts deal with the distribution of assets, they can be used to specify which assets or estates are considered personal or marital property during a divorce. Furthermore, these premarital agreements are also used to specify simple details of a couple's daily life. For example, a couple may put into their agreement how much money they will spend each week or what they will spend it on. Though the latter use for these contracts has increased, it is far less likely to be enforced by the courts. Specifically, it is seen as improper for the courts to intervene in married couples' daily affairs.

Another area in which prenuptial agreements can be useful is in determining how a couple would like their property dealt with when their wishes differ from the standard distribution under state law. If there is no overriding agreement, state laws can determine who owns the property acquired during the marriage and what happens to that property at a divorce or death. Specifications regarding assets after death are critical when a partner dies intestate (with no valid will) because the state regulation determines how much of the assets are available to the partner and what portion goes to the state. Because the regulations for asset distribution, probate, and survivor benefits vary by state, couples with a prenuptial agreement can ensure that their plans are carried out even if they move from one state to another that has different regulations. A prenuptial agreement can supersede any automatic rights to ownership granted by the marriage license. For example, in those states known as community property states, all property acquired during the marriage is to be divided equally at divorce without regard to who earned the assets. Community property statutes currently apply in Arizona, California, Idaho, Louisiana, Nevada, New Mexico, Texas, Washington, and Wisconsin.

Such written agreements can also get persons out of assumed responsibility for their partner's debts. For couples entering a second or subsequent marriage, this lack of accountability for the partner's debts and other obligations may be particularly attractive. For some couples, who may not realize the utility of such arrangements until later, a contract is established after the marriage has begun. These postnuptial or marriage contracts work similarly to prenuptial agreements and specify how the couple wishes their assets be divided.

Over the last few decades prenuptial agreements have become increasingly popular. In just a single year approximately 5 percent of marrying couples sign such an agreement in the hopes of salvaging arguments and property during a divorce or death of their partner. Some spectators say that this increase in the utilization of premarital contracts is due to people remarrying, some multiple times. In fact, persons who are divorcing after remarriage account for the highest percentages of divorces in the United States. Prenuptial agreements are particularly recommended for remarrying couples.

In addition, people are also getting married at older ages; this means that they perhaps have accomplished a lot on their own prior to the marriage. For instance, these people already have their own finances and may already have property outside of their marriage. As a result, they need to be sure that their particular assets are protected in case of a divorce or the death of a spouse. Another reason for this increasingly popular contract is women's prominence in the work force. This has allowed for women to have a substantial amount of income going into a marriage, so that the conventional wisdom of husbands supporting their wives does not always apply. Finally, due to constant cases revolving around the distribution of property upon dissolution of a marriage, courts are more willing to abide by and enforce prenuptial agreements.

COSTS OF PRENUPTIAL AGREEMENTS

Prenuptial agreements can cost anywhere from $1000 to $40,000. This wide-ranging estimate is a testament to the variety of issues that couples include in the contracts. The accuracy of this cost estimate depends on how much detail is put into the contract, how difficult it is for the attorney to have the premarital contract written up, and how many billable hours in attorney fees are involved. Because they are not as common as other types of contracts, one may have to find the right attorney to assist with the task. These contracts can be quite difficult to write and subsequently enact because if there is a flaw of any sort found in the contract then the contract itself can be thrown out of court. When there is a very detailed agreement that is properly written, a judge is more likely to enforce the provisions of the agreement.

BIZARRE PRENUPTIAL CLAUSES

One of the components of prenuptial agreements that many find distasteful are what are called lifestyle clauses. These are statements about how the partner will behave in certain circumstances. There are many different areas of daily life that couples have sought to control and codify. For example, partners might include provisions about how to divide pets upon divorce. One of the most interesting reports suggested a clause in the prenuptial agreement about who got the domestic staff should the couple divorce. Other unusual stipulations included how many football games a husband could watch on Sundays, fines for a husband if he was excessively rude to his mother-in-law, and stipulations of how long one would visit with relatives. Particularly offensive to some are clauses about a partner's physical appearance, most notably specifying a partner's weight was not to exceed a certain amount. Actors Catherine Zeta Jones and Michael Douglas are rumored to have an infidelity clause where he pays her a specified amount if he strays. Other areas couples have attempted to control are random drug testing, child rearing plans (particularly plans to remain childfree), and sexual relations frequency.

Persons employing these lifestyle clauses would probably be better off with a separate document that focuses on daily coupled life, such as a marriage contract. Judges reserve the right to invalidate the whole premarital agreement if the spousal behavior guidelines are too odd or unenforceable.

DEBATES SURROUNDING PREMARITAL CONTRACTS

Despite the increasing discussions about and prevalence of such prenuptial contracts, they remain controversial. There have been several attempts to mandate them as fairer than traditional asset distribution in some states. Because couples establish and agree to the terms themselves, the assumption is they would be more likely to abide by them if a marriage dissolved. While opposition remains, the support for these contracts continues to grow, particularly among those who say they are realistic about relationships today.

The Opposition

On the personal level, requests for a prenuptial agreement can be viewed as insulting, particularly if it seems like you don't trust each other or love each other enough. Those who romanticize marriage and relationships tend to assume that they do not need them because they will stay together forever. This false optimism, where people do not believe divorce can happen to them, leads partners to say that it is just not romantic to sign a premarital agreement. A Harris Interactive poll conducted in 2002 for lawyers.com found that 19 percent of respondents agreed that when two people love each other there is never a need for a prenuptial agreement. While the stereotypical portrayal of the prenuptial agreement is something sprung on the partner at the rehearsal dinner with the stipulation of calling off the wedding if the document is not signed, legally such contracts must be signed at least 30 days prior to the wedding.

Although prenuptial agreements are becoming very common in society there are still individuals that find this practice, or even the thought of having this contract, offensive. Some spectators believe that some of the objection to having a premarital contract is that it can be considered as a preliminary for a bad marriage or even a premonition that a divorce will occur. It sends out a so-called bad vibe about the marriage if one is thinking about divorce before a marriage has even been contracted. Fifteen percent of respondents in the Harris poll felt a prenuptial agreement doomed a marriage from the start. In addition, this contract may also show that the distribution of money and assets are becoming more important to a couple than the marriage itself. Another attack against prenuptial agreements is that the wealthier party may be in control of the terms of the contract. This alone can cause the other spouse to be hurt during the divorce procedure. Thus some oppose these contracts because it will cause women to be put into poverty and have to depend on the state for stability after a divorce if they are no longer entitled to their former spouse's assets.

Furthermore, some commentators are against this agreement due to the fact that a divorce is a very touchy subject and if the contract is not upheld, then the lawyer who drafted the contract may get sued. Other objections include the thought that it is unethical for an outside person (a lawyer) to have to know so much detail about a couple's personal life in order to make any kind of contract. However, some lawyers would even suggest that in the majority of cases state laws have been adequate to meet the clients' needs. This is particularly true if the partners favor community property outcomes. The time may not be right for some people to need a premarital agreement. A couple with few or no assets would likely opt out of such an agreement because it would not be presently relevant.

Finally, one of the main attacks on prenuptial agreements is one of religion. Some religions believe that people should put more emphases on the five Cs of marriage. Jonathan P. Decker suggests a focus on communication, commitment, conflict resolution, children, and church would lead to successful marriages and no need for prenuptial agreements. By not following the above terms of marriage society has forgotten that you have to work in anything that you do in life, including marriage.

The Supporters

Supporters, many from the field of family law, posit that having a premarital agreement is a very practical thing to do and can be a way to show that you love the partner and are concerned with providing for him or her. In order to construct a binding prenuptial agreement, partners have to put their financial cards on the table and cannot remain secretive about their assets. Having a premarital agreement may show that they do have faith in the relationship because they are showing that they have nothing to hide from their mate.

In that same vein, legal experts argue that the work of establishing a prenuptial agreement strengthens the relationship. It supports good communication and discussion of issues, something that might benefit the couple later in their marriage. Premarital contracts can also be used to help couples establish rules for how they will deal with other issues that will arise in the future. Jewish law and leaders support this approach because religious marital contracts have been around for centuries. In them, husbands in particular specify how they will support their wives. Islamic marriage contracts serve a similar function by specifying basic aspects of family and religious life.

In the event that a couple does divorce, a sound prenuptial agreement can reduce conflicts leading up to and at the time of the divorce. Additionally, it will likely save couples money in legal fees and court costs. The New York-based, nonprofit supporter of prenuptial agreements, the Equality in Marriage Institute, stresses these aspects of the contracts and provides legal advice for couples considering a premarital contract. The financial benefits of doing so can not be overlooked. Indeed, in the 2002 Harris poll for lawyers.com, 28 percent of Americans agreed that prenuptial agreements made good financial sense for anyone who was getting married. That number increased to 49 percent among persons who had been divorced. However, one-quarter of the respondents thought prenuptials only made sense for the rich and famous, not the average person.

Having this contract might actually save a marriage. Many people that have divorced have done so because there were constant disagreements in the marriage. If a couple can negotiate a prenuptial agreement before marriage, then there will be a smaller chance of continuous disagreement during the marriage itself.

Prenuptial agreements might actually be more beneficial for persons of more modest means. With few resources, a loss of assets could have very serious consequences for stability. Also, these contracts have been found to be helpful for those that have had children in previous marriages because they do not have to worry about their children's inheritance or assets being withheld. A final reason that it is good to have these contracts is because it may make a person that has been married before feel more secure and actually consider getting married again.

STATES' INTERESTS IN PREMARITAL AGREEMENTS

One of the main interests that the state may have with prenuptial agreements is to avoid putting a spouse on public assistance as result of divorce. As a result of not fully knowing or understanding the terms of the agreement, some people may waive their rights to property and some assets that they may need in order to survive. When this happens the court may intervene in the terms of the contract to ensure that a spouse will not end up on welfare as a result of the contract. Given that society will then have to pay, the contract would be a violation of public policy.

A second concern for the state is that a prenuptial contract or divorce can influence child rearing functions and questions. The state has an interest due to the potential that the child's living standards change after a divorce when the custodial parent's income decreases. Children may be affected negatively by a divorce and can have psychological problems that will have to be treated. If this occurs and the parent is not financially stable enough to tend to the child's needs then their child rearing abilities can and will be questioned. Courts, in an attempt to avoid harming children, have consistently ruled that child support awards are not a component of prenuptial agreements.

A third state interest in premarital agreements is that the terms of the contract may provide a greater incentive to divorce than to stay married. For example, some people's contracts will entitle them to receive more money upon a divorce than they are receiving or have access to while they are married. If a judge feels that this is the reason for the divorce, then the court will probably void the entire contract because it undermines one of the main purposes of getting married, and the state has a vested interest in the stability that marriage provides.

CULTURAL ASPECTS OF PREMARITAL CONTRACTS

In many non-Western cultures marriage is not looked at as a romantic relationship, instead it is viewed in terms of money and power. This can be seen through the common practice of bride wealth or bride price. This involves some kind of transfer of money or goods between the families of the bride and groom. Most commonly, the transfer is from the husband's family to the wife's family. Many who marry in these societies often have an arranged marriage and therefore love is not a big concern. Consequently, a premarital contract is not seen as a personal affront. In contrast, Americans value love and other romantic sentiments when it comes to that special someone. Americans' emphasis on romance may be the main reason why there are so many divorces in the United States. It also may be the reason that so many individuals in western society have been reluctant to construct prenuptial agreements.

See also Arranged Marriage; Divorce, as Problem, Symptom, or Solution; Preparation for Marriage; White Wedding Industry.

Further Reading: Equality in Marriage Institute. http://www.equalityinmarriage.org; Marston, Allison. "Planning for Love: The Politics of Prenuptial Agreements." *Stanford Law Review* 49 (1997): 887–916; McLellan, David. "Contract Marriage: The Way Forward or Dead End?" *Journal of Law and Society* 23 (1996): 234–246; Prenuptial Agreements.org. http://www.prenuptialagreements.org; Smith, Lona. *Help! He Wants Me to Sign a Prenup.* Miami Beach, FL: Help Publishing, Inc., 2007; Stark, Barbara. "Marriage Proposals: From One-Size-Fits-All to Post-modern Marriage Law." *California Law Review* 89 (2001): 1479–1548; Stoner, Katherine E., and Shae Irving. *Prenuptial Agreements: How to Write a Fair and Lasting Contract.* Berkeley, CA: Nolo, 2005.

Shaquona Malone

PREPARATION FOR MARRIAGE

The American familial landscape was radically altered during the twentieth century due to major social, political, and cultural changes that took place in the nation. One correlation of these various transformations was a rise in the divorce rate. As the government, media, and public grew anxious over increasing divorce, clergy, lawmakers, and other social practitioners began to develop methods aimed at its prevention. Of the methods proposed and attempted, many consider formal premarital preparation the most hopeful. The major goal of premarital preparation is to give couples skills, tools, and resources to help them stay married. A secondary goal of preventing unhealthy or incompatible partners from wedding has become more publicized in recent years. These skills, tools, and resources often focus on communicating effectively, managing conflict, managing finances, handling sexual issues, and parenting. Practitioners today hope premarital preparation will help couples learn enough about one another to make informed decisions regarding the commitment of marriage, take marriage seriously, and make every effort to stay together for the rest of their lives if they decide that marriage is right for them.

Those who believe in the value of premarital preparation often praise these efforts as effective divorce prevention techniques. But others are skeptical, finding fault with research that has been done, or feeling premarital preparation's impact on marriage stability is more a result of selection effects than any direct benefit of the training. In general, both sides are likely to agree that the area of premarital preparation and its ability to prevent divorce still needs much study.

BACKGROUND

Though Ernest Groves is credited with holding the first recorded premarital intervention in 1924, formal professional relationship counseling did not become popular until the 1970s, at a time when divorce laws were becoming more lenient and an increasing number of couples were choosing to divorce. Prior to mid-century, relationship advice was generally provided by family members and community elders. A number of causes led to the emergence of prescribed marriage preparation, including the increased mobility of American society, which often physically separates people from more traditional counseling and support networks. This generally occurs as people seek the measures of success valued by American culture by moving far from extended family in pursuit of educational or career opportunities. This moving for work or school results in a situation in which young people are often making relationship decisions independently or with only the advice of the peer group.

Another factor that influenced the public to turn to formal counseling services was society's increased faith in educated and particularized experts compared with purveyors of traditional folk wisdom. In the specialized nature of American society, diplomas and certificates are highly valued symbols of knowledge, separating those qualified to lead others in specific areas from those who are not. Thus, the general population began to place more trust in professionals trained to guide them in all realms of life, including marriage.

In addition to the nation's anxiety over the seeming loss of marriage longevity, new research areas of the 1960s and 1970s also encouraged the creation of premarital preparation programs. Researchers empirically determined relationship factors that were especially hazardous to marital stability, including contempt, criticism, defensiveness, and stonewalling (refusing to engage in communication with or listen to one's partner). The identification of these factors gave counselors a base around which to structure courses. The discovery of emotional intelligence as a measurable component of the psyche also encouraged premarital program development. Scientific discovery of links between areas of the brain handling emotions and those dealing with rationality gave rise to the notion that emotional skills could be learned. Therefore, practitioners began to argue that, through professional guidance, spouses could be taught how to better relate to one another emotionally.

Premarital preparation today generally comes in three varieties: educational programs, enrichment workshops, and counseling. Examples of educational programs and enrichment workshops include Engaged Encounter and the Prevention and Relationship Enhancement Program (PREP), the most popular and widely studied premarital programs to date. Such programs are offered in various forms: individual couple sessions with a counselor, group session involving many couples, weekly sessions, monthly sessions, and weekend or week-long intensive retreats. Some workshops may only meet once while other programs spread out over a year. Sometimes partners are asked to engage in skills-based activities, perhaps with other couples, or to complete homework assignments addressing tough issues, such as sexuality.

All three types of premarital preparation often incorporate inventory instruments into their methods. Common inventories include the Personal Assessment of Intimacy in Relationships (PAIR), Premarital Inventory Profile (PMIP), Facilitating Open Couple Communication, Understanding and Study (FOCCUS), and Premarital Personal and Relationship Evaluation (PREPARE). Of these instruments, PREPARE is the most prevalent and extensively researched. These instruments are generally completed by both partners separately after which their answers are compared and scored by using various methods to determine such things as compatibility or relationship strengths and weaknesses.

Three different types of professionals dominate the premarital preparation field: clergy, mental health workers or counselors, and physicians. Of these, clergy by far interact with the majority of couples, due in large part to the requirement by many religious sects of marriage training for couples who wed in their houses of worship. These requirements range from a single informal meeting of the officiant and couple to specific courses sanctioned by an entire faith, such as the Catholic Church's Pre-Cana Program. However, the number of secular counselors and social workers in the field is growing. In light of this, many colleges and universities today offer graduate programs that specifically train marriage and family therapists. A minority of practitioners in this field are physicians whose premarital preparation generally revolves around a physical examination and blood test.

PREMARITAL PREPARATION: A PREREQUISITE FOR MARRIAGE?

A number of states have passed bills that, while not outright requiring premarital preparation before receiving a marriage license, provide incentives to couples who voluntarily participate in courses or counseling. For example, Georgia waives a couple's marriage license fee if they provide proof of completion of counseling or premarital education. Florida takes such incentives a step further: couples who attend a premarital program conducted by a provider registered with the state receive a discount on their marriage license plus a waiver for the three-day waiting period to receive their license.

THE ARGUMENT FOR PREMARITAL PREPARATION

Advocates of premarital preparation, such as Scott M. Stanley and Robert F. Stahmann, are optimistic about the value of the guidance that programs and counseling can offer couples, and the positive effects that they can have on marital satisfaction and stability. Supporters claim a benefit of premarital preparation is that it encourages partners to address complex issues that they have either avoided or have yet to consider. The majority of engaged couples spend weeks or months planning their wedding ceremony. They have lengthy discussions about the location, food, and honeymoon. But research has shown that little time is spent talking about crucial topics such as values, finances, parenting, labor division in the home, or conflict management. Many counseling and educational sessions focus on knowledge and skills-based training, emphasizing effective communication, conflict management, compatibility assessments, and addressing possible future problem areas. The goal is to provide engaged pairs with resources and techniques to manage the ups and downs of married life.

Scott M. Stanley identified four benefits of premarital education in general. First, it fosters deliberation and gets couples thinking about tough issues. Second, it sends the message that marriage matters. Third, it exposes couples to potential options, such as further counseling, if they need help later. Finally, premarital education has been shown by limited research to decrease the likelihood of marital discord and breakup.

Other proponents have noted less-obvious possible benefits of premarital preparation. One is the prevention of unstable relationships from continuing on to marriage. Although the main goal of enrichment and other counseling or programs is to help two people grow stronger together, sometimes it helps them identify irreconcilable incompatibilities prior to taking their vows. This is evidenced by studies showing that a significant percentage of couples using preparation techniques, such as PREPARE, break up before marrying. Another benefit, supporters argue, is that even if they do not last the entire lifespan of the marriage, positive skills learned in premarital preparation help couples make it through the tough early years during which the majority of divorces have been reported to occur. In conjunction is the documented result that couples who attend sessions before their wedding are more likely to seek further professional assistance following it. The experience of helpful premarital intervention has been found to make a number of couples more open to attending counseling or enrichment later when difficulties surface. Therefore premarital preparation directly affects the satisfaction and stability of the early years of marriage, and then, when its direct effects wane, indirectly influences spouses to try more counseling before abandoning the relationship through divorce.

Some of the strongest evidence of the value of premarital preparation has come from surveys and evaluations given to participants following these sessions. Many couples who complete workshops, counseling, and other preparation options self-report satisfaction with the experience and a willingness to recommend it to others. National polling has also found that couples who had undergone premarital counseling reported considering divorce less than did those who had not attended counseling.

A Closer Look at Two Specific Techniques

In addition to the support of premarital preparation in general, there are positive findings on specific programs and instruments. Two popular premarital preparation components which have been widely evaluated with positive results are the PREP program and the PREPARE inventory.

PREVENTION AND RELATIONSHIP ENHANCEMENT PROGRAM (PREP)

Markman, Blumberg, and Stanley's PREP builds on research indicating the characteristics and skills of happy, healthy couples and tries to teach these skills to other couples before their wedding dates. Participants can attend an intensive weekend retreat or six once-weekly sessions.

The University of Denver conducted a ten year study of PREP outcomes. The researchers found that eight percent of PREP couples divorced within the first decade versus 16 percent of control couples. A similar study put the figures at 12 percent separation for PREP couples versus 36 percent for control couples after five years. Finally, a study by Markman with three, four, and five-year follow-ups found higher levels of marital satisfaction, positive interaction, and communication, and lower levels of aggression and instability in those who had attended PREP.

PREMARITAL PERSONAL AND RELATIONSHIP EVALUATION (PREPARE)

Olson, Fournier, and Druckman's PREPARE instrument contains 125 items targeting a couple's areas of strength and weakness. Categories addressed are realistic expectations, personality issues, communication, conflict resolution, financial management, leisure activities, sexual relationships, children and parenting, family and friends, equalitarian roles, and religious orientation.

The predictive ability of this instrument has been tested and shown to foretell with 80 to 90 percent accuracy the couples that would separate or divorce and those that would remain married. The validity of the measure has been judged by following couples and recording the outcomes of their marriages after they took the inventory. Couples who were dissatisfied or who later ended their marriages consistently scored lower than those who remained satisfied and together.

THE SKEPTICAL ARGUMENT

Though premarital preparation has its advocates, many other people are skeptical that it offers any real benefit to couples. One issue they propose is that engaged partners are often too starry-eyed to see the possible troubles that lay ahead. This phenomenon has been called the honeymoon effect. Those couples who reported being dissatisfied with their premarital preparation experiences tended to overlook the program's intention to help them plan for the future. Most indicated that they assumed it was to address their relationship as it was at the time. This has given evidence to the argument that engaged couples are not ready to properly learn the skills necessary to stabilize their marriage across the lifespan. Therefore, some say, these techniques are better learned in interventions following the wedding ceremony.

In addition to the honeymoon effect, skeptics have some other areas of concern regarding premarital preparation and the research that has been conducted on it. These areas involve the selection effects hypothesis and inadequate research.

The Selection Effects Hypothesis

Those who question the usefulness of premarital preparation point out a problem with the type of clients it most often includes. Researchers, including

Sullivan and Bradbury, have found that couples at low risk for disharmony and divorce are much more likely to attend premarital education, enrichment, or counseling than are high-risk couples. This factor relates to the selection effects hypothesis which posits that happier, better adjusted, more stable individuals are more likely to get and stay married than are those who are less happy, adjusted, or stable. Applied to premarital preparation, the hypothesis claims that more committed and healthy couples are likely to go to premarital preparation, to try to get the most out of the experience, and to actively attempt to employ things learned therein throughout their marriages than are less-committed persons and those in unhealthy partnerships.

Inadequate Research

Many premarital preparation critics take issue with the research that has been conducted in the area and the positive results that have been found. One problem, they contend, is the general lack of investigation addressing the verifiable benefits couples receive from premarital preparation. As the trend toward formal premarital counseling and education has taken hold, researchers have not kept pace in their study of its effects. Some extensive exploration has been given to specific techniques, such as PREP and PREPARE, but premarital preparation overall has received limited attention compared with other marriage research areas.

Some critics also find fault with the design of the limited studies that have been done. First, they point out that research on this subject has been designed as short-term rather than longitudinal studies. Although premarital preparation has been gaining popularity since the middle of last century, the longest studies of participating partners have only been 10 or 12 years. Despite the positive results these investigations have reported, some people argue that they only prove premarital preparation results in delayed divorce, not a true prevention of it.

Another criticism applies to the voluntary basis of most studies. Many critics contend that because premarital preparation is largely a voluntary activity, couples who choose to go are qualitatively different than those who do not attend. Skeptics argue that these couples are concerned with their relationship in general and are willing to put in extra effort to make their union successful. Essentially, they are more committed to the institution of marriage and would work harder on their relationships because they may not perceive divorce as a viable option. By attending premarital preparation, they are taking measures upfront, prior to wedding, that they feel will give them a better chance of staying together and not divorcing. Thus, current research is subject to volunteer bias because it does not include anyone who did not elect to attend sessions. Even partners who participate due to religious requirements have the option of not doing so and choosing to hold their ceremony outside their place of worship.

A final disparagement often noted is that the majority of research has only included white, middle-class respondents. Critics claim that the use of such nonrepresentative couples taints findings and precludes their ability to generalize to more diverse populations. This is a valid criticism because certain minority groups have higher divorce rates compared with the white population.

MARRIAGE SAVERS

Mike McManus and his Marriage Savers are on a crusade to stop divorce. His group has spread to hundreds of cities, gaining support from clergy of all denominations and laypeople alike. Marriage Savers puts into effect a Community Marriage Policy® in any community willing to participate. This policy sets uniform minimum premarital preparation requirements for couples before they can wed in any church, synagogue, and occasionally, courthouse. The Marriage Savers program utilizes the Facilitating Open Couple Communication, Understanding and Study (FOCCUS) premarital inventory and a mentoring system in which couples who have completed the program mentor couples currently involved in it.

PREMARITAL PREPARATION: TO GO OR NOT TO GO

Some experts say premarital preparation has no direct correlation with a decreased chance of divorce. Others claim that it provides engaged pairs with crucial skills, tools, and techniques for navigating marital waters and staying together. With such divergent information, at this point there is no conclusive evidence either to encourage partners to or to discourage them from investing time, money, and energy into formal premarital preparation. Perhaps that will change in time if premarital preparation is given the research attention both supporters and critics would likely agree it needs and deserves. Regardless of the outcomes, unless participation in premarital preparation becomes a national prerequisite for marriage, the decision to engage in premarital education, enrichment, or counseling is one couples will continue to have to make for themselves.

See also Adversarial and No-Fault Divorce; Dating; Family Roles; Prenuptial Agreements; Wedding and Eloping; White Weddings Industry

Further Reading: Carroll, Jason S., and William J. Doherty. "Evaluating the Effectiveness of Premarital Prevention Programs: A Meta-analytic Review of Outcome Research." *Family Relations* 52, no. 2 (2003): 105–118; Coalition for Marriage, Family, and Couples Education. "Smart Marriages." http:// www.smartmarriages.com/index.html; Gottman, John. *Why Marriages Succeed or Fail and How You Can Make Yours Last.* New York: Fireside, 1994; Renick, Mari Jo, Susan L. Blumberg, and Howard J. Markman. "The Prevention and Relationship Enhancement Program (PREP): An Empirically Based Preventive Intervention Program for Couples." *Family Relations* 41, no. 2 (1992): 141–147; Simring, Steven S., Sue Klavans Simring, and Gene Busnar. *Making Marriage Work for Dummies.* New York: Hungry Minds, Inc., 1999; Stahmann, Robert F., and William J. Hiebert. *Premarital and Remarital Counseling: The Professional's Handbook.* San Francisco: Jossey-Bass, Inc., 1997; Stanley, Scott M. "Making a Case for Premarital Education." *Family Relations* 50, no. 3 (2001): 272–280; Stanley, Scott M., Paul R. Amato, Christine A. Johnson, and Howard J. Markman. "Premarital Education, Marital Quality, and Marital Stability: Findings from a Large, Random Household Survey." *Journal of Family Psychology* 20, no. 1 (2006): 117–126.

Nicole D. Garrett

R

RELIGION AND FAMILIES

Family and religion are both considered to be critical institutions in American society. They do, however, have a strong history of impinging upon each other. For example, marriage is a social contract that couples form after gaining legal permission from the state. It is overwhelmingly the case, however, that the partners are bound through a ceremony performed by a religious officiate. Thus, family and religion are supportive of one another. In other instances, the relationship between religion and family is a less harmonious one. For example, couples that cohabit may find little encouragement from religious officials for their unconventional lifestyle choice. Religion and family may work toward similar outcomes or may have conflicting purposes.

RELIGION

Most people, when asked to define religion, refer first to a belief system concerned with matters related to a higher power, deity, or what many call god. There are religions, however, in which adherents are not expected to believe in the supernatural. Buddhism, for example, does not require belief in any supernatural entity or phenomenon. Religion has also been defined as a system of shared symbols, much like specialized language, in which those who are fluent may communicate with one another and with the higher power. Regardless of the specific supernatural-oriented content of any religion, however, all religions are concerned with moral order in society. The terms religion and spirituality are sometimes used interchangeably, but for social scientists spirituality refers to an individual orientation toward transcendent reality, while religion is a group orientation toward morality. In addition to being a symbol system and a group orientation to the supernatural, religion is also an organized method by which previous societies tell current societies how to distinguish proper from improper behavior, and that encourages people to make good choices. Religious collectivities of all sorts unite around this shared sense of moral order, and this is the primary function of religion whether the believers worship Vishnu or Allah.

THE RELIGIOUS LANDSCAPE

In the United States most residents believe in God and most of these believers profess Christianity. Of all Christian denominations, Catholicism is the most common, though if the various denominations of Protestantism are considered together, they outnumber Catholics by roughly two to one. In addition to its many Christians, the U.S. population is also composed of the nonreligious, Jews, Muslims, Unitarian Universalists, agnostics, and Buddhists, as well as many others. The U.S. is more religious than other industrialized nations, with a populace more likely than those in any other wealthy nation to report belief that religion is very important.

This is likely one source of the popularity of religious spokespeople in the United States. While from various denominations, these leaders are primarily Christian, and among the most well known are the more conservative leaders. They have been particularly vocal in matters concerning the American family. Religious leaders may advise us in the most intimate details of our lives, such as with whom, how, and when we may have sexual intercourse, while in the public sphere it is often religious sentiments that direct political leaders to argue in favor of or against legislation affecting families.

RELIGION AND FAMILY MATTERS

Social scientists observe that religion is the method by which a society reproduces ideology. Because it is a patterned way of behaving, religion is considered an institution, much as the economy (a patterned way of producing, distributing, and consuming goods and services) is. But institutions overlap in their areas of interest, and in few places is this more apparent than the connection between religion and the family. The family is the institution in which most of us learn the religious values regarding our families. Many children attend religious training classes long before their entry into the public school system. It is the earliest systematic moral and value education many Americans receive.

What do religions claim constitutes a so-called good family, and what constitutes a bad one? While the particular religions may vary in some specifics, religions generally promote a particular family structure and give adults direction in how to manage their households, including rules about intercourse, childrearing, and conflict management. Some social science research has found that people tend to choose religious organizations based on how comfortable they feel with the other congregants, rather than on the specific doctrinal stance of the religious group

Although the diversity of religion in the United States means that almost any family issue imaginable will be subject to attempts at regulation by at least one religious group, some issues stand out more clearly than others. The most well-known religiously controversial family issues in the United States include reproduction, family structure, childrearing, and marital dissolution.

REPRODUCTION

Religious debate on the family is perhaps nowhere more intense than that of reproduction. Whether or not couples should attempt to prevent conception during intercourse is a controversy that continues even today.

The Catholic Church currently opposes modern birth control methods, arguing that human reproduction is mandated by God, and that unless intercourse is conducted in order to reproduce humans should not engage in it. While the official Catholic Church position is that any form of birth control other than the rhythm method is forbidden, other Christian denominations vary widely in what is and is not permissible, with some evangelical Protestants now beginning to use the current Catholic reasoning in their opposition to modern birth control.

In addition to the Catholic opposition to birth control, some religious organizations in the U.S. currently oppose abortion in any instance, and some have actively participated in attempts to make it illegal again. When there are religious motivations for an anti-abortion position, the argument is that abortion amounts to murdering innocent children because there is no question that the fetus is human, alive, and unable, while in its mother's womb, to do wrong. Religious supporters of the right for women to abort unwanted pregnancies argue that although the fetus is human, and consists of living tissue, no one can decide when human personhood begins. They oppose attempts to restrict abortion rights on the grounds that such restrictions violate norms of social justice and would negate the women's rights to make their own moral judgments about a very personal issue. Social scientists do not attempt to answer the question of when personhood begins, but are apt to take on matters such as the demographic variables associated with the choice to continue the pregnancy (and either make the baby available for adoption or keep the baby) or to abort the pregnancy. Judging from the opposition to abortion by many religious groups we might expect to find lower rates of abortion among the religious, however at least one study has found that religiosity was positively correlated with the decision to have an abortion among adolescents. It is also interesting what while more than 82 percent of the population professes Christianity, only 17 percent (in 2004) strongly favor making abortion more difficult in the U.S. The religious category that is the most likely to strongly favor imposing more restrictions on abortion is white evangelical Protestant.

Judaism and Islam are the two largest organized religions after Christianity. Judaism supports the woman's right to decide for herself whether to have an abortion and Islam generally supports some restrictions on abortion. Even among Christians there is still debate, with the Catholic Church at one extreme, arguing that abortion is always wrong, and groups such as the Religious Coalition for Reproductive Choice, which has many Christian members, that promotes both reproductive choice and religious freedom. Some studies by social scientists include examinations of the groups seeking to restrict abortion rights and those seeking to protect those rights.

Same-sex marriage is also a reproductive issue because the heart of the religious complaint points to the children of such unions, and what harm they may suffer. While the U.S. populace opposes gay adoption, we are closely divided, with 46 percent favoring and 48 percent opposing. Religious opponents to gay marriage cite research that has found that child abuse is the least likely in homes where both biological parents are present and there is little conflict. For this reason, many who oppose gay adoption also oppose conception by either member of lesbian couples because only one of them can be the biological parent.

Unmarried women who bear children have also garnered the attention of some religious leaders. Although the media and popular culture suggest that the U.S. is currently suffering from an epidemic of births to unmarried teens, these numbers actually have been steadily declining since the 1960s. What has increased, however, is the rate of births to the unmarried. This change in family structure concerns many religious and political leaders, but is an additional concern for those interested in social problems and to those who study the resources required to rear children and the additional stresses that single parenting can place on families. Married couples also face stressors and conflicts related to family structure.

FAMILY STRUCTURE

Families, like other social groups, have rules about decision making. Although many religious groups advocate egalitarian, progressive, or liberal ideology that promotes egalitarian decision making, many others promote the dominance of the husband over the wife. Social science research, however, has found that even among religious people who argue in favor of the subordination of women to men, the couples may have interpreted these arguments to mean something more like cooperation. Current research on women's place in conservatively religious marriages suggests that women wield more power at home than their ideology would indicate. Yet some believe that the promotion of male dominance in families is at least partially responsible for the high rates of domestic violence in the U.S.

Some American feminists, for example, blame religion for the unequal treatment of women in U.S. society, including interpersonal violence against women. Yet there are Christian, Muslim, and Jewish feminists who have in common the complaint that their sacred texts have historically been read and interpreted by men alone. They argue that their religions seem to favor men over women, and the reasons that women have been encouraged to stay in abusive marriages by religious leaders is that self-serving or misdirected interpretations of their scriptures have been made exclusively by men. Some also argue that secular feminists have misinterpreted their sacred texts by adopting the same lens that the exclusively male religious leaders have used, and suggest that there may be other paradigms for the understanding and interpretation of these texts.

Despite the stereotype that religions mandate the submission of women to their husbands, some studies of conservative religious groups have suggested that even among women who support the idea that men should be in charge of the family, in practice these men and women make joint decisions even on important family questions, such as children's schools and large purchases.

The issue of male dominance only arises around heterosexual unions and most religious organizations, evangelical Christians in particular, believe that marriage should be reserved for the union of one man with one woman. In addition to the concern with the effects of gay or lesbian parenting on the sexuality and well-being of the children, these groups also worry that gay marriage will accelerate the general decline of morality in society today. This is an especially potent political issue, as it has the power to polarize large numbers of the population. Social scientists do not have a consensus on the relative decline of morality in society, but tend to view changes in statistical trends in family matters, such as divorce and single parenting, as indicators of larger societal phenomena such as industrialization, economic change, and the organization of the workplace.

Cohabitation among heterosexuals, which is still illegal in some states, is also an issue for many religious people today. Cohabitors are more likely to choose partners of other religious faiths than are married couples, and at least one study found that cohabiting females were almost four times more likely to report atheism or agnosticism than were married females. Some religious groups deny full religious participation to cohabitants, or to the divorced, yet many express tolerance of, or at least the desire to help, people in this situation.

As divorce has become more and more common in the U.S., many religious leaders have reacted with alarm. Some research has indicated that the relationship between divorce and religion may depend on the particular religion. Yet while James Dobson, a well-known conservative Christian leader, argues that religiosity can help marriages, one study shows that the divorce rates among conservative Christians is higher than for any other religious group studied, including atheists and agnostics. The research by The Barna Group, which aims "to partner with Christian ministries and individuals to be a catalyst in moral and spiritual transformation in the United States," also reports that people with college educations and people living in the northeastern U.S. are less likely to divorce than other Americans. This is in spite of the common media stereotype that associates liberals with libertinism. While sociologists generally view agenda-driven research with skepticism, these results are particularly compelling because they were produced by a conservative research organization

CHILDREARING

A comprehensive review of recent social science research reports that religion is positively correlated with adolescent health, education, community involvement, and family well-being and is negatively correlated with negative behaviors such as the use of alcohol and other drugs. Religious involvement is also associated with lower rates of sexual activity among adolescents. Some of the positive effects of religious involvement, however, may be influenced more by the religious adolescents' peer group than by his or her religious family.

It is also important to note that adolescents who have consistently been the subjects of corporal punishment are more likely to exhibit delinquent behaviors than are those whose parents did not use, or who used less, corporal punishment. Parents with more conservative religious ideology (*i.e.*, those most likely to report a belief that the Bible is literally true and that it has the answer to all problems) are more likely to use corporal punishment with their children, and they are more likely to approve of such use. Conservative religious leaders are also partially responsible for recent headlines in public education because they have attempted to control the content of some science classes for adolescents in public schools. In particular, some have called for the prohibition of instruction in evolution or as an alternative, the requirement that students receive additional instruction in creation science. Indeed, anxiety about the content and the quality of public schools has influenced the increasing frequency by which parents decide to school their children at home. It is not only evolution, but also sex education to which religious conservatives may object and wish to have greater involvement in their children's education. Because religion is a group behavior, the findings by Wilcox showing that higher paternal religiosity is correlated to higher involvement with children is not surprising. Religion doesn't just tell us right from wrong—religion binds us.

Regardless of the religion being studied or its specific ideological content, social scientists tend to agree that religion is often associated with many positive life phenomena because of the social support that it renders. In other words, when people attend religious services they join others who will help them in times of trouble. Whether it is delivering food at a death or baby-sitting while the parents go for counseling, religious participation offers the adherent a ready-made group of people who are more likely to volunteer their aid when requested. This aid can be a powerful resource for stressful situations, and may contribute to the beneficial effects of religion on family life.

See also Abortion; Covenant Marriage; Divorce, as Problem, Symptom or Solution; Family Roles; Plural Marriage; Religion, Women, and Domestic Violence; Remarriage.

Further Reading: Adherents.com. http://www.adherents.com/; The Barna Group, Ltd. http://www.barna.org/; Catholic Answers Forums. http://www.catholic.com/; Focus on the Family. http://www.family.org/; Henze, Lura, and John Hudson. "Personal and Family Characteristics of Cohabiting and Non-Cohabiting College Students." *Journal of Marriage and the Family* 36, no. 4 (1974): 722–727; Ontario Consultants on Religious Tolerance. http://www.religioustolerance.org/; Ortiz, C. G., and Ena Vasquez-Nuttal. "Adolescent Pregnancy: Effects of Family Support, Education, and Religion on the Decision to Carry or Terminate among Puerto Rican Teenagers." *Adolescence* 22 (1987): 897–917; Regnerus, Mark. 2003. "Religion and Positive Adolescent Outcomes: A Review of Research and Theory." *Review of Religious Research* 44, no. 4 (2003): 394–313; Religion and Ethics Newsweekly. http://www.pbs.org/wnet/religionandethics/index_flash.

html; Religious Coalition for Reproductive Choice. http://www.rcrc.org/about/index.cfm; Schoen, Robert, and Robin Weinick. "Partner Choice in Marriages and Cohabitors." *Journal of Marriage and the Family* 55, no. 2 (1993): 408–414; Thomas, Darwin, and Marie Cornwall. "Religion and Family in the 1980s: Discovery and Development." *Journal of Marriage and the Family* 52, no. 4 (1990): 983–992; Turner, Bryan S. *Islam: Critical Concepts in Sociology. Volume III. Islam, gender, and the family.* New York: Routledge, 2003; Wilcox, Bradford. "Good Dads: Religion, Civic Engagement, and Paternal Involvement in Low-Income Communities. CRRUCS Report." Manhattan Institute for Policy Research, 2001. http://www.manhattan-institute.org.

Carolyn F. Pevey

RELIGION, WOMEN, AND DOMESTIC VIOLENCE

Among the misconceptions that Americans hold about domestic violence is the idea that highly religious partners would never participate in abuse. Questions remain as to the relationship between religion and domestic violence. Some experts suggest that conservative religious beliefs support domestic violence and prevent victims from seeking help. Other research suggests that conservative religious wives are no more likely to be abused than women from other religious traditions. One of the lingering concerns is over the view that the victims themselves have of the abuse.

INTRODUCTION

Although domestic violence has been a social problem for perhaps centuries, many Christian clergy emerged from seminaries ill-trained, unprepared and, in some cases, resistant to respond to domestic violence within their congregation or abused religious women's needs. Not helping the situation was the belief that such problems happen to those outside their churches or congregations. As Adams and Fortune recall, "Episcopalians could believe that it is a Methodist problem, the Methodists could believe that it is a Baptist problem, and they all could believe that it is a Roman Catholic problem" (Adams and Fortune 1995). Broad-based attention toward abused religious women seems to have occurred during the late 1970s, as clergywomen found themselves in pastoral care and crisis intervention with victims or survivors of incest, rape, and battery. Clergywomen were far more likely to be involved in this sort of pastoral role than were men.

As social scientists developed an interest in the links between religion and domestic violence, much of their research focused on denominational worldviews and the incidence of violence among intimate partners. The exact conceptual nature of conservative Protestantism (*i.e.,* evangelical Christians, fundamentalist Christians) is debatable but is often said to favor marital permanence and a male-headed or patriarchal family and social order. As such, some observers of religion and violence among intimates may ask if conservative Protestant males are more likely to commit acts of intimate partner violence as a result of the emphasis on male authority in the family. Indeed, the role of patriarchy in the etiology of abuse has been a site of contention among researchers. Feminist sociologists, for instance, perceive violence as part of a broad-based system of male control. Family researchers and sociologists from other substantive areas, however, argue that patriarchy is just one of many variables that promote violence.

Empirical research has yet to show clear evidence that conservative Protestants are more inclined to abuse their partners than are the affiliates of other denominations. In fact, findings link religious involvement to reduced levels of domestic violence, suggesting that religious attendance has, in some situations, a protective effect. Weekly religious attendance among men, for example, is inversely associated with intimate partner violence perpetration. Men who often attend religious services have significantly lower rates of victimization due to domestic violence than those who infrequently attend religious services. Moreover, a number of conservative Protestant couples are more equality-minded than often presumed. While they may affirm male headship as a group, many couples are just as receptive to marriages in which decision-making is pragmatic and negotiated between both partners.

Succinctly put, not every religious spouse having patriarchal power abuses his role or, for that matter, is abusive to women. But while violence does not appear inherent in hierarchal, Christian family life, it can develop as a by-product in some religious families. Once violated, certain doctrinal teachings and expectations of gender, power, and control in marriage may limit a religious woman's choices, options, and safety in an abusive relationship.

RELIGIOUS WOMEN'S RESPONSES TO DOMESTIC VIOLENCE

Religious or not, many women feel obligated to maintain family cohesion and want to succeed in their roles of wives or mothers. However, doctrinal interpretations that rigidly require marital permanence, husband headship, and wifely submission may promote or worsen problems at the onset of abuse. Such beliefs are a core of fundamentalist teachings. Believing that she is not submissive or religious enough, for example, a religious woman may blame herself for her own violation. Despite abuse and fear of injury, she may uncover no clear scriptural basis to leave the relationship, but find biblical support for wifely submission. What is more, abusers may rationalize or tighten control by misusing religious codes aligned with gender and behavior. The abuser is then using religious teaching as a justification for his abusive behavior.

Advice from family, friends, and clergy might inadvertently lead to potentially hazardous compromises for the victim of abuse. Those invested in keeping the family together may exert pressure on the wife to forgive her abuser and continue the relationship before true reconciliation and reliable safety conditions are met. She may be encouraged to stay and pray that God miraculously changes the perpetrator or intervenes in the abuse. Invariably, these strategies displace the perpetrator's role or accountability in abuse. What is more, there is little evidence suggesting that any of these approaches will end the cycle of violence but, in fact, may prolong endangerment for the victim. Still, in her search for meaning and answers, an abused religious woman's coping may reflect these very influences.

In one coping strategy, the glorification of suffering, a victim may believe that, like Christ, her suffering will spiritually benefit herself or her abuser. Perceiving the violation as a test of faith in God is another problematic means of making sense of mistreatment. As one psychologist points out, it is "not at all unusual" for women to align violation with the account in 1 Peter 1:7 of being "tried with fire" (Burnett 1996). Altogether, the result may be that many abused religious women experience a unique sense of despair or entrapment. At times, working against her is a type of dual identity—one as a violated woman and the other as a committed woman of faith. From this perspective, she may delay any actions toward removing the violation (such as divorcing, removing herself or the abuser from the home, confronting the spousal mistreatment, *etc.*) for fear of dishonoring the religious worldviews and behaviors she has been socialized to accept. As disturbing as they are, passive coping strategies like these may be the best an abused woman can do given her conceptions of abuse and religion, access to support systems, and fear of retaliation, which is a paramount concern.

Although receptive to a religious approach, abused religious women also employ practical options toward survival and safety. Research suggests they are as likely, if not more so, than those who are less religious to report the abuse to a friend, lawyer, shelter, crisis line, police officer, or physician. Some have credited empowerment to an evolving, more flexible religious orientation, having uncovered more equality-centered biblical interpretations of spousal conduct in the Christian marriage. In short, abused religious women employ an array of subversive acts that are crucial to their survival.

INSTITUTIONAL RESPONSES TO RELIGIOUS WOMEN AND DOMESTIC VIOLENCE

The possible tolerance of abuse based on doctrinal interpretation has provoked little outcry or explanation from religious institutional settings or authorities. Among the many media presentations on the traditional family or the fear of its demise, few address the issue of violence against wives. One reason for this omission may be that strong churches are dependent upon on intact, nuclear families and, thus are inclined to avoid those topics that undermine the imagery of a happy, contented Christian life. Additionally, the way faith contexts understand or present wife abuse may explain some institutional inaction. Some churches, for example, perceive congregational family violence as spiritual dysfunction or scriptural misapplication and not a broad-based social problem with secular origins.

At the same time, religious clergy offer rich opportunities in the aid and intervention of abused women of faith. Unlike those persons in other helping professions, a pastor or minister may have an ongoing relationship with a victim and the professional privilege to interpret acceptable or nonacceptable family behavior. Even so, tensions between the sanctity of marriage and the possible benefit of ending the relationship in cases of domestic violence may hinder effective counsel.

Research on the clergy's response to domestic violence suggests some level of dissatisfaction with ministerial help options. Research has uncovered mainly problematic assistance from clergy with regard to domestic violence. Women were encouraged to forgive their abusers, seek a marriage counselor, return home out of respect for their duties as wives, or only given religious advice. Abused women in one study complained most about clergy who denied the problem existed or were reluctant to listen. Several were told they could not leave the relationship or that leaving was equivalent to sin. In a Canadian study, there was no evidence that clergy members deliberately or directly dismissed battered women's needs. However, researchers note that clergy were reluctant to support the dissolution of even a violent marriage, preferring a temporary separation followed by counseling and reconciliation.

An apparent distrust between the secular and the religious intervention milieus can perhaps deepen a woman's confusion. Some clergy have misgivings about secular help entities, as if domestic violence shelters might motivate women to leave their abusers and church communities. Conversely, mainstream or secular professionals are concerned that clergy will advise women to return to their abusers.

MERGING RESOURCES FOR THE ABUSED CHRISTIAN WOMAN

For a successful relationship between the Christian church and domestic violence community, sociologists, such as Nason-Clark, suggest that violence be approached and condemned through language having religious and practical significance in abused religious women's lives. Perhaps the most established attempts are from feminist theologians and clergywomen. Similar to writings of equality-minded religious conservatives, feminist theology locates and recasts biblical traditions believed to obstruct women's power in social, religious, and family life. Invariably, its scholarship unites historical, political, or linguistic scrutiny with other interpretive tools to unearth egalitarian threads in patriarchal passages of early church authors. By this, they offer a means with which to biblically substantiate nonviolence in relationships and reassess potentially harmful religious convictions.

A growing number of religious writers have confronted interpretations of a unilateral or wifely submission through competing scriptures. By emphasizing a mutual spousal regard—mutual submission—as biblically sound, they recast the practice as a benevolent, safer mandate requiring spiritual and developmental reciprocation between spouses. In so doing, these scholars scripturally challenge the misuse of submission and condemn abuse as separate from religious principles.

Not all religious affiliates find that mutual submission in the Christian marriage is an appropriate arrangement. Such a stance should not be interpreted as permitting abuse or the mistreatment of wives. Rather, women and men from certain Protestant Christian denominations find that wifely submission to her husband's headship is a biblical mandate and, thus, important to the continuance of the traditional, Christian family.

CONCLUSION

For many embattled by war, poverty, loss, mortality, and other adversities, religious beliefs, rituals, and contexts impose meaning and offer a sense of control over events that threaten assumptions of resilience and justice. As such, when abused or threatened by her spouse or intimate partner, a woman may seek religious guidance for solace, hope, and a sense of protection. However, researchers, help professionals, and some theologians caution against the kinds of messages she may import into that meaning-making and how they might channel her responses.

Traditional or hierarchical family life does not unequivocally translate into an abusive home or violence against women. On the other hand, fear of divorce or injury to the family unit along with rigid interpretations of gender and power in marriage may entrap some women once they have been abused. As a result, prioritizing both safety and the sacred can aggravate an already complex and painful experience. An abused religious woman may believe that actions that she takes against the violation will compromise her religious beliefs and identity. Meanwhile, religious authorities may feel more obligated to uphold traditional marital arrangements, despite abuse, that to help individual victims escape the abuse.

Feminist theologians and more equality-minded religious conservatives advocate, in essence, a middle ground. They suggest that abuse be repudiated through a language having both sacred and practical utility. Given this option, they argue, abused religious women need not believe that their convictions force them to tolerate mistreatment.

See also Battered Woman Syndrome; Domestic Violence Behaviors and Causes; Domestic Violence Interventions; Mandatory Arrest Laws; Religion and Families.

Further Reading: Adams, Carol, and Marie Fortune. *Violence against Women and Children: A Christian Theological Sourcebook*. New York: Continuum, 1995; Alsdurf, James, and Phyllis Alsdurf, P. *Battered into Submission: The Tragedy of Wife Abuse in the Christian Home*. Downers Grove, IL: Intervarsity Press, 1989; Alwani, Zainab, and Salma Abugideiri. *What Islam Says about Domestic Violence: A Guide for Helping Muslim Families*. Herndon, VA: Foundation for Appropriate and Immediate Temporary Help, 2003; Bartkowski, John. *Remaking the Godly Marriage: Gender Negotiation in Evangelical Families*. New Brunswick, NJ: Rutgers University Press, 2001; Beaman-Hall, Lori, and Nancy Nason-Clark. "Translating Spiritual Commitment into Service: The Responses of Evangelical Women to Wife Abuse." *Canadian Women's Studies/Les Cahiers De La Femme* 17 (1997): 58–61; Brinkerhoff, Merlin, Elaine Grandin, and Eugene Lupri. "Religious Involvement and Spousal Violence: The Canadian Case." *Journal of the Scientific Study of Religion* 31 (1992): 15–31; Burnett, Myrna. "Suffering and Sanctification: The Religious Context of Battered Woman's Syndrome." *Pastoral Psychology* 44 (1996):

145–149; Cunradi, Carol, Raul Caetano, and John Schafer. "Religious Affiliation, Denominational Hegemony, and Intimate Partner Violence among U.S. Couples." *Journal for the Scientific Study of Religion* 41 (2002): 139–152; Ellison, Christopher, and Kristin Anderson. "Religious Involvement and Domestic Violence among U.S. Couples." *Journal for the Scientific Study of Religion* 40 (2001): 260–286; Ellison, Christopher, John Bartkowski, and Kristin Anderson. "Are There Religious Variations in Domestic Violence?" *Journal of Family Issues* 20 (1999): 87–113; Ellison, Christopher, Jenny Trinitapoli, Kristin L. Anderson, and Byron Johnson. "Race/Ethnicity, Religious Involvement, and Domestic Violence." *Violence against Women* 13 (2007): 1094–1112; FaithTrust Institute. "Working Together to End Sexual and Domestic Violence." http://www.faithtrustinstitute.org/ (accessed January 2008); Fiorenza, E. Schussler. *Bread not Stone: The Challenge of Biblical Feminist Interpretation.* New York: Beacon Press, 1995; Horton, Anne, and Judith Williamson. *Abuse and Religion: When Praying Isn't Enough.* Lexington, MA: D. C. Heath and Company, 1988; Kaufman, Carole. *Sins of Omission: The Jewish Community's Reaction to Domestic Violence.* Boulder, CO: Westview Press, 2003; Knickmeyer, Nicole, Heidi Levitt, Sharon Horne, and Gary Bayer. "Responding to Mixed Messages and Double Binds: Religious Oriented Coping Strategies of Christian Battered Women." *Journal of Religion and Abuse* 5 (2003): 29–54; Kroeger, Catherine, and James Beck. *Healing the Hurting: Giving Hope and Help to Abused Women.* Grand Rapids, MI: Baker Books, 1998; Kroeger, Catherine, and Nancy Nason-Clark. *No Place for Abuse: Biblical and Practical Resources to Counteract Domestic Violence.* Downers Grove, IL: Intervarsity Press, 2001; Nason-Clark, Nancy. *The Battered Wife: How Christians Confront Family Violence.* Louisville, KY: Westminster John Knox Press, 1997; Nason-Clark, Nancy. "When Terror Strikes at Home: The Interface between Religion and Domestic Violence." *Journal for the Scientific Study of Religion* 42 (2004): 303–310; Pagelow, Mildred. "Secondary Battering and Alternatives of Female Victims of Spouse Abuse." In *Women and crime in America*, ed. Lee Bowker. New York: MacMillan, 1981; Pargament, Kenneth. *The Psychology of Religion and Coping: Theory, Research, and Practice.* New York: Guilford Press, 1997; Poling, James, and Christie Neuger. *Men's Work in Preventing Violence against Women.* Binghamton, NY: The Haworth Press, 2003; Shannon-Lewy, Colleen, and Valerie Dull. "The Response of Christian Clergy to Domestic Violence: Help or Hindrance?" *Aggression and Violent Behavior* 10 (2005): 647–659; West, Traci. *Wounds of the Spirit: Black Women, Violence, and Resistance Ethics.* New York: New York University Press, 1999.

Shondrah Tarrezz Nash

REMARRIAGE

Remarriage is a legal marriage in which one or both partners are marrying again, either following widowhood or divorce. In the United States, the majority of those who remarry do so following a divorce. Only 10 percent of remarriages are accounted for by those marrying after widowhood. A divorce is the legal ending of a marriage through the decree of a court. Not everyone views the phenomena of divorce and remarriage in the same ways. Those who believe the value of marriage in the United States is on the decline, such as the Family Research Council, see divorce and subsequent remarriage as further evidence of the casual attitude held toward marriage today. On the other side, for those who see divorce as proof that Americans view marriage seriously, remarriage is confirmation that Americans believe in the institution of marriage regardless of negative past experiences. Americans do have the highest remarriage rates in the world. There are several areas of particular interest to persons who study remarriage. They include comparisons between first marriages and subsequent marriages, individual consequences of remarriage, the role of religion, and the creation of stepfamilies. Briefly examining some statistics about divorce can help us understand the issue of remarriage more completely.

INTRODUCTION

Divorce is very common within U.S. society. Based on life experiences and circumstances, divorce can mean different things to different people. Some see divorce as a legality required to end a relationship that didn't work, while others regard it very seriously and take any measures necessary to save the marriage and avoid divorce. Some estimates suggest that about half of all first marriages begun today in the United States will end in divorce. With such high rates of divorce, critics of divorce charge that Americans are devaluing the institution of marriage. As further evidence of this devaluing of marriage, critics site the pattern of so-called serial marriage. This occurs when a person divorces and remarries several times.

One of the largest consequences of such serial marriages is likely the issue of custody and visitation with children that were the product of the consecutive unions. For men, there is often a pattern of serial parenting. That is, parenting the children that are currently residing in the home, particularly their biological children, rather than making consistent efforts to parent children from prior relationships. This results in de facto single-parent families where mothers are the primary custodial parent.

Persons who view divorce and remarriage more favorably are likely to say that the unwillingness of partners to remain in a marriage that is no longer satisfactory is evidence of the high value placed on fulfilling marital relationships. We demand a lot of our relationships and want to find the one that will last a lifetime. Persons who enter a remarriage relationship demonstrate the optimism that a so-called Mr. or Ms. Right has been selected. The issue of remarriage can be used to support both of these opposing arguments.

While it may seem logical that individuals who have been divorced would be unlikely to marry again as a result of the doctrine of once bitten, twice shy, studies show the opposite to be true; roughly 75 percent of people in the United States who have been divorced will remarry. In the early 2000s, nearly half of the marriages contracted in the United States consisted of at least one spouse who was remarrying. In the past, remarriage most often followed the death of a spouse; however, beginning in the 1970s, divorce became the primary cause for remarriage. Researchers took notice of this change and began to study remarriage and stepfamilies. However, most research on remarriage and stepfamilies was not conducted until the 1990s. There were three times more studies on remarriage and stepfamilies published within the decade of the 1990s than there had been in all previous years combined, a good indication of the changing patterns of personal relationships and increasing questions about the consequences of such changes. Since the 1990s, remarriage and stepfamilies have continued to be popular research topics as more and more Americans have experiences with these family relationships.

FACTORS AFFECTING RATES OF REMARRIAGE

Data collected by the U.S. Census Bureau indicates that rates of remarriage vary by age, race, sex, socioeconomic status, geographic location, and the presence and number of children. The age at first marriage, age at first divorce, and age at remarriage are common factors discussed in remarriage research. Age at first marriage can act as a predictor for both divorce and remarriage. The younger a couple is a the time of the first marriage, the more likely they are to divorce, and the younger they are at the time of their first divorce, the more likely they are to remarry. Each of these variables seems to influence women's likelihood of divorce more than men's. For women, divorce rates peak among those who marry between the ages of 15 and 19 and decline with increasing age. In regard to remarriage, younger women are significantly more likely to remarry so that the older a woman is the less likely she is to remarry. Thirty-one percent of women who divorce in their 30s remarry; less than 1 percent of women who divorce in their 50s are likely to remarry. Men's age has little effect on their likelihood to remarry because men are more likely to remarry than women are at any age. Forty-two percent of men who divorce in their 30s remarry, while 41 percent of those who divorce in their 50s do.

Divorce and remarriage rates also vary by race. White women are more likely to remarry, and remarry sooner, than are African American or Hispanic women. According to a vital statistics and health report released by the Department of Health and Human Services in 2002, marriage and cohabitation relationships of black women are not as stable as those of white women. These differences are believed to be related to characteristics of the women themselves, as well as the communities in which they live. The fact that the black women's marriages are not as stable as white women's gives insight into why they are less likely to remarry. The decreased likelihood of remarriage for black women has also been explained by what is known as the marriage squeeze that is experienced by black women as a result of a limited pool of eligible black men from which to choose. As a result of high mortality and incarceration rates, as well as high levels of unemployment of black males at the likely ages for remarriage, the number of eligible males is smaller than the number of eligible females. This uneven sex ratio significantly impacts black women's chances of remarrying. Black men who choose to marry non-black women also play a role in the marriage squeeze. According to the 2000 U.S. Census, black men marry non-black women more often than black women marry non-black men. This increases black men's pool of potential spouses, while it simultaneously limits the pool for black women.

A person's sex, male or female, is another factor contributing to the likelihood of remarriage. In the United States, approximately two-thirds of women and three-fourths of men who have been divorced will remarry. These gender differences continue to vary across the life cycle. As stated previously, as women age, they are less likely to remarry, especially when compared to their male counterparts. The differences in remarriage rates for men and women can be caused by the greater number of women in the population, which leads to a shortage of potential marriage partners for women. The tendency of women to marry older men further limits eligible partners, especially for older women who often live longer than men.

Socioeconomic status has been found to affect remarriage rates as well. Women with higher socioeconomic status and income levels, who can support themselves after a divorce, are less likely to remarry. The opposite is true for men; men with higher socioeconomic status are more likely to remarry, probably because they are more attractive partners on the marriage market. In general, however, due to the greater likelihood of divorce among persons of lower socioeconomic levels, persons who remarry have less positive finances than persons who remain in first marriages.

An individual's geographic location can also play a part in the instance of remarriage. This assertion is based on areas with high divorce rates, such as the West and South. Persons in these areas have a greater likelihood of remarriage because they are more likely to have been married before. Additionally, in areas where marriage at young ages is more common, such as in the South, the higher risk of divorce among this group again contributes of a greater chance for remarriage following divorce because the divorced persons are relatively young. One of the most interesting elements of marriage and divorce in the South is the influence of conservative religious views. Despite religious doctrinal pressures to remain married, some of the highest divorce rates are found among members of conservative southern religious groups.

Whether or not a divorced individual has children, and the number of children, can have an impact on the choice and chance to remarry. The issue of children from a previous relationship has the greatest effect on women. Women who have children are less likely to remarry than those who do not. The trends indicate that the more children a woman has, the less likely she is to remarry. Men's choice to remarry is not affected by whether and how many children they have. However, the woman they choose as their remarriage partner is: men with no children are likely to marry a woman who has never been married, and men who have children are likely to marry a woman who has also been previously married.

DIFFERENCES BETWEEN FIRST MARRIAGES AND REMARRIAGES

As a result of the differing trends discussed above there are both quantitative and qualitative difference between first marriages and remarriages. One issue that has been publicized frequently about remarriage is the greater propensity for partners to divorce. After 10 years, 33 percent of first marriages can be expected to have ended in divorce. For remarriages, the expected percentage ending in divorce is 39. For black couples specifically, the number is even higher at 48 percent. Additionally, when divorce happens in a remarriage it occurs earlier in the relationship. The reasons for these differences are not entirely clear, but there are some reasonable suggestions.

The decision to remarry is usually made earlier in a relationship. Partners might more quickly determine that they should marry than do those dating for first marriage. Perhaps this speedy decision results from learning more about what they desire in a partner, having learned from previous mistakes, or simply growing into a better judge of character. Partners in remarriage are older and presumably more mature so the decision to marry quickly may not be questioned by those outside the relationship.

It seems clear from studies of remarriage, however, that there are some important personal characteristics that relate to a greater chance of divorce due to decreased marital satisfaction. First, remarriages tend to involve more heterogamous couples. This occurs when the partners are of different ages, races, or religions, which are all characteristics that can lead to increased relationship instability. Remarried partners tend to be less integrated into each other's extended families. This means that the bonds between parents and in-laws that would normally be supportive of marriage may be weaker. Remarriage partners express a greater acceptance toward divorce and indicate that they are more willing to leave the marriage if necessary. Also these partners are of lower social class, a risk factor for divorce.

One critical element that distinguishes remarriages from first marriages is the greater likelihood that a remarriage relationship involves children. This can result in a ready-made family, rather than providing an opportunity for the partners to relate as spouses first and then parents, and has been shown to make the relationship tenser. Not only are children an intrusion on the marriage, but they may be a source of conflict, particularly when a mother and stepfather clash over the role that he should play in the lives of residential children. Childrearing and discipline issues are most often a source of conflict. Not only do children impact the remarriage, but the intrusive presence of the previous partner can have an impact on the current relationship. This is particularly true if there are joint-custody decisions that must be made, or if issues remain from the previous marriage.

One fact about remarriage compared to first marriage cannot be overlooked: first marriages have a tremendous amount of social support and there are clear norms that guide how partners are supposed to relate to each other and the tasks that each is supposed to fulfill. For remarriage, however, these norms are much less clear and may even be absent. This has lead many family researchers to describe stepfamilies as a normless norm. This recognizes that remarriages and the resulting stepfamilies are very common, but they are complicated by vague and often confusing roles and expectations that leave the participants unsure of how to relate to each other and their extended kin.

STARTER MARRIAGES

In real estate terms, one's first home is often referred to as a starter home. This implies it is a good house for the present time, but the purchasers will likely trade up to an even better house as their needs change. Based on the idea that one moves up to better circumstances, some researchers have suggested there is a new trend in marriage in the United States today, the so-called starter marriage. Starter marriage refers to marriages that last for less than five years and do not include children. The probability that the marriage of a white couple with no children will end within five years is 30 percent. This supports the belief that there are at least some persons who enter marriages today thinking that they are a temporary situation to enhance personal growth. When and if marriage does not fulfill their expectations, they will end the relationship and look for a new partner that might better meet their needs.

CONSEQUENCES OF REMARRIAGE

The differences between first marriages and remarriages lead to differing patterns of interaction and likely consequences, both negative and positive. These consequences are for individuals and their families, but they extend beyond a given couple to society as a whole.

Negatives

Many couples who are considering remarriage will ask themselves or will be asked whether it is too soon to get back into a relationship. There is a fear of rebound, where partners are simply using each other to get over the breakup. A large rebound phenomenon, while common in postdivorce self-help literature, does not seem to be supported in the academic literature as having an effect on remarriage stability. A fear of another divorce, however, may be a legitimate concern for many contemplating remarriage. This prospect leads some to cohabit instead of remarrying. In fact, among singles over the age of 55 who are dating, remarrying and cohabiting are almost equally preferred.

The evidence is clear that persons in remarriages are more likely to divorce. Some of this may be the result of a selection bias. Persons who have divorced may perceive divorce as more of an option if things do not work out with the new partner. There is some evidence to suggest that the differences in divorce rates for first marriages compared with remarriages are converging. This might mean that remarriages are becoming more stable as couples seek resources to help them succeed. On the other hand, it might imply that first marriages are becoming less stable.

Remarried couples are more prone to disagreements. Some of these are over finances. For example, a new wife may resent that her husband has child or spousal support obligations that must be paid to the former family every month. This leaves less money to support the current family, particularly distressing if the remarried couple have children together. Given the difficulty of separating financial ties in the event of divorce, remarried couples are less likely to pool their incomes and are more likely to maintain separate bank accounts. While this is helpful in the event of a divorce it does not necessarily demonstrate an unbreakable commitment to the relationship and implicit trust of the partner. While couples might disagree over money, the biggest source of conflict is over stepchildren. This issue will be addressed below.

Positives

The news is not all negative for persons who enter remarriage. In the best of circumstances, the end result is more happily married partners. Because most persons' mental health improves if they remarry following divorce, the personal benefits are strong. Researchers indicate that there are lower rates of psychological distress in remarried persons compared with divorced persons who are living singly.

Remarriage can provide one more chance for a person to get marriage right. Perhaps it was the case that one was just married to the wrong partner the first time around. This optimism helps partners handle challenges that might arise early in their marriage. Ideally, partners who are remarried would have sought counseling for issues that arose in the first marriage and be better prepared to handle those same sorts of things in the remarriage. Marrying to a different, more supportive partner, however, can actually help persons heal from the hurt of their unsuccessful marriages.

Despite the potential of having to pay child support or even spousal support following a divorce, the finances of persons who remarry can be better than the first time around. This is because partners are older at the time of remarriage and theoretically have advanced in their careers. It is true that persons who are in a remarriage, particularly women, experience lower rates of economic distress compared with divorced persons who have not remarried.

Religious

One of the consequences of increasing divorce and remarriage rates is that many religious websites about Christian remarriage are devoted exclusively to this issue. For many Christian denominations the answer is simple; marriage is a sacrament and indissoluble in the eyes of God and the church. In this instance the only acceptable remarriage follows the death of one's spouse. This stance has served the Roman Catholic Church for many years, but has necessitated a great deal of specificity regarding religious annulment. For some other Christian denominations, the answer is not clearly articulated and has been a source of concern for both religious leaders and the faithful. As more parishioners have asked about the biblical bases for divorce and remarriage, church leaders have developed platforms that represent their interpretations of scripture.

There are at least four competing views on the issue. The first says that there should be absolutely no divorce and no remarriage for any reason. This approach argues that marriage is a commitment before God and one who breaks the commitment will be cast out of the fold. The second approach suggests that once a person has been divorced, there is neither provision nor need for remarriage. The person must atone for the divorce, because in the eyes of God he or she is still married. A third approach specifies that remarriage is permitted only when the divorce has been obtained because of the adultery or desertion of the spouse. In this case the victim in the divorce would not be faulted and would be free to try again to maintain a lifetime marriage commitment. Most conservative churches stress that it is preferable for the offended partner to forgive the other and attempt reconciliation. Some groups even ask the faithful spouse to consider why the indiscretion may have occurred and consider their role in it. The fourth approach, which is a bit more liberal, suggests that there could be various other reasons to permit remarriage after divorce. Often these relate to the psychological state of the partners. A common reason would be if the believer divorced a nonbeliever.

Among those religious leaders who take a more liberal approach to divorce and remarriage, one way to view these behaviors is that they can be forgiven because they occurred before the individual had been saved. Another approach suggests that while neither is desirable, they are not the ultimate sin and God will forgive those who divorce and remarry if they seek forgiveness. Nearly all religious leaders stress that the ideal situation is when one chooses a suitable partner initially, thereby decreasing the chances of subsequent divorce.

REMARRIAGE AND STEPFAMILIES

Research that began in the 1990s focused on the complexities of remarriage and stepfamily relationships that had previously been inadequately researched. The remarriage relationship is fundamental because it is the legal contract that forms a stepfamily. There are certainly additional concerns in a remarriage based on the presence of children, both biological and step. The level of structural complexity within a remarriage and stepfamily relationship varies based on the individuals involved. A remarriage relationship can consist of one partner who was previously married and one who has never been married; both partners could have been previously married; both or one could have been previously married and divorced several times, and so on. The more previous marriages each remarried spouse has been involved in, the more complex the relationship can become. Each subsequent remarriage also contributes to the likelihood that the relationship will end in divorce.

Children from previous marriages for one or both of the spouses also add a new dimension to the remarriage, which is then commonly termed a stepfamily. It is also known as a remarried family, reconstituted family, blended family, or binuclear family. Stepfamilies consist of a biological parent, that person's children, and the biological parent's spouse. According to the U.S. Census Bureau, in 2000 there were more than 4.4 million stepchildren in the United States. The issues incumbent with stepfamilies are too numerous to mention here; however, there are several factors that relate directly to the remarried couple's relationship that will be mentioned.

One important issue is that the children have a biological parent living elsewhere. Thus there may be different rules with that parent that complicate how the residential parent and stepparent monitor and rear the children. While one common assumption suggests that having an additional parent as a result of remarriage would help alleviate some of the difficulties experienced by children reared in a single-parent home following divorce, it does not seem to be the case. Particularly among adolescents, children in stepfamilies show more adjustment difficulties than children from intact two-parent families and about the same amount as children in single-parent families. One way to decrease negative outcomes is for the couple to cohabit prior to the marriage. In this way, perhaps cohabitation provides a period of transition to incorporate all members of the family into the new routine.

Another important consideration is that the parent-child relationship predates the marriage. This sets up a situation in which the child may feel replaced by the emphasis on the new spouse. Because living with only one parent increases the power that children have over that parent, the dynamics must be realigned. It seems that when remarriage occurs sooner after divorce, the transition to a stepparent in the home is less disrupting. With this pattern there is less time for children to get used to living in a single parent household.

The question of boundaries can make remarriage and stepparenting difficult tasks. It is sometimes not clear who is a member of the new family, and even less clear what obligations each participant has to the others. What are the expected roles for stepmothers and stepfathers? How do grandparents relate to the stepchildren? Even though there is a legal relationship that binds the remarried partners to one another, the relationship of stepparent to stepchildren is socially and personally defined, but not legally binding, calling into question the appropriate behaviors and interactions.

FUTURE DIRECTIONS

While remarriage remains popular following divorce, there is a significant contingent of persons favoring cohabitation over remarriage. This is particularly true among black women. As persons delay the age at first marriage, this may have direct consequences for whether they will choose to remarry if the first marriage ends in divorce. Because these couples are more likely to have cohabited prior to wedding for the first time, will they return to cohabitation if marriage is unsuccessful? Whether these behaviors replace remarriage will be an interesting topic for future scholars to monitor.

See also Adversarial and No-Fault Divorce; Divorce, as Problem, Symptom, or Solution; Marital Satisfaction; Religion and Families.

Further Reading: Blackstone-Ford, Jann, and Sharyl Jupe. *Ex-Etiquette for Weddings: The Blended Families' Guide to Tying the Knot.* Chicago: Chicago Review Press, Inc., 2007; Coleman, Marilyn, Mark Fine, and Lawrence Ganong. "Reinvestigating Remarriage: Another Decade of Progress." *Journal of Marriage and Family* 62, no. 4 (2000): 1288–1307; Coleman, Marilyn, and Lawrence H. Ganong. *Stepfamily Relationships: Development,*

Dynamics, and Interventions. New York: Kluwer Academic/Plenum Publishers, 2004; Department of Health and Human Services. *Vital and Health Statistics* 23, no. 22. "Cohabitation, Marriage, Divorce, and Remarriage in the United States." Hyattsville, MD. http://www.cdc.gov/nchs/data/series/sr_23/sr23_022.pdf; Fisher, Bruce, and Robert E. Alberti. *Rebuilding: When Your Relationship Ends,* 3rd ed. Atascadero, CA: Impact Publishers, Inc., 2006; Hetherington, E. Mavis, and John Kelly. *For Better or For Worse: Divorce Reconsidered.* New York: W. W. Norton and Co., 2003; Parrott, Les, and Leslie Parrot. *Saving Your Second Marriage Before It Starts.* Grand Rapids, MI: Zondervan, 2001; U.S. Census Bureau. "Adopted Children and Stepchildren: 2000." http://www.census.gov/population/www/socdemo/ms-la.html; U.S. Census Bureau. "Marital Status: 2000." http://www.census.gov/population/www/socdemo/marr-div.html; Wenham, Gordon, William A. Heth, Craig S. Keener, and Mark L. Strauss. *Remarriage After Divorce in Today's Church: 3 Views.* Grand Rapids, MI: Zondervan, 2006.

Kimberly P. Brackett

SAME-SEX MARRIAGE

Same-sex marriage refers to the concept of individuals of the same-sex applying for license to marry in hopes of receiving the same treatment and benefits afforded to married opposite-sex couples. Marriage has been defined as "the union of a man and a woman." However, due to changes in the social environment, as well as the emergence of nontraditional family models, this definition has been widely questioned by the gay and lesbian populations of the United States and other countries.

BACKGROUND

Marriage has been previously defined as the union of a male and female in the hopes of creating a family and ultimately propagating the human race. In recent decades that idea has been challenged in a number of ways, ranging from the nontraditional family, in which there may be a couple living in cohabitation, with or without children, to the more controversial idea of same-sex marriage. The goal is to give the same acknowledgment, benefits, and rights to homosexual couples that their heterosexual married counterparts enjoy. Examples of such challenges have arisen across the United States (and the globe) from Hawaii to The Netherlands and practically everywhere in between. With changes in the social environment, as well as in the political arena, changes in the idea of what constitutes a marriage have followed. Same-sex marriage has been debated on every possible level of society, from the personal to the political to the religious and moral levels. What some consider a battle for personal rights the opposition views as a breakdown of the moral fibers of society and the legal system. This polarity between interest groups—personal and emotional versus religious and moral—has been the driving force for the argument regarding this recent change in the family model of American society. With celebrities like Rosie O'Donnell, Melissa Etheridge, Elton John, and Ellen DeGeneres bringing the idea of same-sex marriage equality to the forefront of popular culture and the likes of Bill Clinton, George W. Bush, and numerous legislative officials backing the opposition, this battle will likely rage on, spurring debates about what constitutes a so-called proper marriage in America.

MARRIAGE AND FAMILY LAW

Marriage rights constitute a complicated and incredibly detailed area of the legal system. The general consensus is that there are some 1,400 to 2,000 laws, rights, and benefits interwoven into the idea of marriage. When one considers that idea for a moment, the fight for marriage equality makes sense. Marriage has been considered the very core of society, regardless of the place of religion within that society. However, it is that intersection of church and state that spurs a great many debates regarding the topic of same-sex marriage. The proponents feel that the state has overstepped its boundaries by dictating who can and cannot marry on the basis of sexual orientation, and yet the opposition has a generalized argument that marriage is a sacred union between a man and a woman and has been so throughout history; altering that now would be disastrous to the present and future of society.

HISTORIC FIRSTS AND PROMINENT CASES

Over the last decade, there have been numerous instances of subtle uprisings within individual states regarding the issue of same-sex marriage. These instances have ranged from lawsuits filed by various same-sex couples to entire counties standing in defiance of state government by issuing same-sex couples a marriage license after being told to cease doing so. The following is a brief overview of some of these instances.

Minnesota

In 1971, two African American lesbian residents of Minneapolis sought marital rights at the local city hall. This eventually led them to federal court, in which they were ultimately unsuccessful in their attempts at equality. Also in 1971, the Minnesota Supreme Court ruled in the case of Jack Baker and Mike McConnell, two men who wanted to marry one another. The couple utilized the argument that because there was no mention of a law banning gay marriage on the Minnesota law books, the legislature must have intended on recognizing same-sex marriages. However, they too were denied, and the court found that the institution of marriage was a heterosexual arrangement. The court noted that marriage as a union of man and woman, particularly given the involvement in the procreation and rearing of children within a family, could be traced to biblical traditions as old as the book of Genesis.

Arizona

In 1975, a county clerk in Phoenix, Arizona, granted two men a marriage license. However, citing the same biblical instance as the Minnesota court, the Arizona Supreme Court invalidated their marriage and subsequently the state legislature followed this decision with a bill specifically prohibiting gay marriage.

Colorado

In 1975, Boulder County clerk Clela Rorex allowed six gay couples to marry, after receiving no word that the Colorado state law held any opposition to her doing so. However, this action received little nationwide publicity because there was minor interest in the legality of the issue at the time.

District of Columbia

In 1987, the American Civil Liberties Union (ACLU) issued a statement in which it said that their intention was to break down the barriers of legality regarding gay marriage, while 2,000 gay couples held a mass mock wedding in the Internal Revenue Service (IRS) building.

It is clear that gay marriage was quickly gaining its place among the political agenda of the late twentieth (and eventually the twenty-first) century. However, it wasn't until 1990 that these early activists saw a success in their fight for equality.

Hawaii

A Honolulu couple, Genora Dancel and Ninia Baehr were denied a marriage license, just as other couples had been denied across the country. Despite the recent proclamation by the national ACLU, the group's local sector offered no legal help for the couple. However, Dancel and Baehr, along with fellow gay and lesbian couples, took their fight to a higher power—the Hawaii Supreme Court. In 1993 the court ruled in favor of the couple's right to marry, based on the state's equal protection clause. The court, however, did specify that the ruling was not on the basis of gay rights but rather on the basis of gender rights. Regardless of the reasoning, a success is a success, and so began the counterattack on same-sex marriage.

DEFENSE OF MARRIAGE ACT (1996)

Passed by the U.S. Congress in 1996, the Defense of Marriage Act (DOMA) defined marriage as existing only between a man and a woman, specifically when in reference to federal laws, affecting taxes, pensions, Social Security, and other federal benefits. DOMA also gave the states the individual freedom to refuse to recognize gay marriages performed in other states. This meant that regardless of where the marriage had been performed, there was a strong likelihood that it would not be recognized at all anywhere in the United States. Because marriages are certified at the state, rather than the federal, level this act gave states permission to ignore the common practice of reciprocity with regard to homosexual couples. For heterosexual couples, reciprocity (the recognition that a marriage is legal in other states regardless of the state in which it was performed) still applied. However this federal legislation did not dampen the spirits of the same-sex marriage proponents. If anything, it likely fueled the fire to a new level of frenzy.

The passing of DOMA likely resulted in the drafting and implementation of a Federal Marriage Amendment (FMA) which first saw activation in Colorado in 2002 and again in 2003. The FMA was an attempt to squash objections that DOMA had overstepped its constitutional authority by allowing states to disregard legal agreements (contracts) that other states had considered valid and binding. Supporters of an FMA felt that this constitutional amendment would clarify any gray areas regarding marriage, defining it solely as a male-female union, as well as including a clause that stated that no state constitution or other body of law was to be construed as being forced to allow and recognize same-sex marriages. By the early twenty-first century, nearly four-fifths of all states had already passed laws or even amended their own constitutions to ban same-sex marriages from within their borders. The action that could be considered the biggest in magnitude regarding opposition of same-sex marriage was taken by George W. Bush in 2004, as he announced his support for a constitutional amendment prohibiting gay marriage. As with the creation and enactment of DOMA, Bush's support of a constitutional ban on gay marriage likely did nothing but temporarily boost his image and fuel the fire for gay-rights equality in the marriage arena.

SUPPORTERS OF SAME-SEX MARRIAGE

Advocacy groups in support of same-sex marriage have utilized the ever-changing social environment to their advantage, ultimately giving support to their position that a just society translates as one that accepts the practice of same-sex marriage as one of simple fairness, full and complete citizenship, and equal rights. While many involved in the battle over same-sex marriage approach it from a religious standpoint, those that are religiously-affiliated but do not attack the issue on a negative level, such as the Unitarian Universalist Association, have called for fully legalized same-sex marriage. In 2005, the United Church of Christ (with some 1.3 million estimated adult members) became the first Christian denomination endorsing the right of homosexual marriage, concluding that "in the Gospel we find ground for a definition of marriage and family relationships based on affirmation of the full humanity of each partner, lived out in mutual care and respect for one another" (www.ucc.org). Some churches have not come to grips with a full decision regarding the topic. The Episcopal Church (with its three million adult members) has not sanctioned full marriage rights, specifically in terms of actually enacting legal documentation. However, in 2003, the leaders of the Episcopal denomination in the United States approved a resolution at their annual convention that states that under the pretenses of "local faith communities operating within the bounds of our common life as they explore and experience the celebration of and blessing of same-sex unions" (Sheridan and Thrall 2003). In a roundabout way, the Episcopal Church has thrown in a pro-vote without necessarily donning a rainbow banner in the middle of the sanctuary.

Stepping back onto the secular side of the pro-argument, the biggest players on this team are advocacy groups. Examples of these groups include the ACLU, the Human Rights Campaign (HRC), the National Gay and Lesbian Task Force, as well as numerous others. Their ability to create change through lobbying, campaigning, fundraising, and numerous other tactics depends on a number of factors, specifically environmental conditions, as well as policies favored strongly by the public. However, that last factor, public policy, is not strong enough to stand on its own as a deciding factor. It must be approached from the right angle at the right point in time for the advocacy groups to pull through as effective promoters of change. To obtain substantial legislative change, these groups must start at the ground level and work their way up, persuading everyone in their path to their reasoning of the argument in order to cut a path of agreeable successes from the starting line to the finish. One thing that must be kept in mind when considering the groups advocating same-sex marriage is that they are much smaller in number, poorer in financial resources, and more deeply polarized in political ideology than their opposition counterparts.

GROUPS OPPOSING SAME-SEX MARRIAGE

Like their counterparts who support same-sex marriage, interest groups opposing same-sex marriage have their work cut out for them. With the ever-changing social environment and the turbulent political waters surrounding the issue, the battle has certainly been a heated one and will likely continue as such. Examples of interest groups in opposition of same-sex marriage include the Family Research Council, Focus on the Family (brought to the headlines of politics by its founder Dr. James Dobson), the Christian Coalition (with figures such as Pat Robertson at the helm), and many others. These groups have substantial advantages over the proponents of same-sex marriage in a number of areas. The first is that these groups need only keep things in their favor or keep the status quo. This specifically applies to legislation that these groups do not have to advance. Rather, they must simply block the pro-same-sex marriage groups from advancing their own legislative measures. Their second and perhaps largest advantage is that a large majority of these groups are religiously-affiliated, thus they are interconnected with a number of networks of individuals with various resources readily available for opposition mobilization, ready for attack at any sign of progressive successes. While blocking policy change is a deep advantage for the opposition, as a group they have not been pleased with their successes in this area. These same groups are also responsible for enacting laws and legislation at various levels that will ultimately define marriage in all finality as being defined as the union of a man and a woman.

An example of one of these groups' arguments was found posted in an essay on the Family Research Council's web site that specifically states that they oppose same-sex marriage "not because homosexuality is a greater sin than any other. It's not because we want to deprive homosexuals of their fundamental human rights. It's not because we are afraid to be near homosexuals, and it's not because we hate homosexuals. On the contrary, I desire the very best for them. And desiring the best for someone, and acting to bring that about, is the essence of love" (Sprigg 2004). One aspect of same-sex marriage that the opposition has recently chosen to utilize is the prominence, presence, and well-being of the children involved in these proceedings.

RECENT ACCOMPLISHMENTS AND FUTURE DIRECTIONS

Same-sex marriage has once again found itself at the fore of issues in American politics. While the issue was formerly a hot topic in Massachusetts, the first state to legalize gay marriage, more recent controversies have arisen in none other than gay-haven extraordinaire, California. Known for its prominent gay population (an estimated 92,000 gay couples reside there), California has held a reputation over recent decades for being in general a rather liberal-minded and forward-thinking state. Family legislation and other social policies that begin in California often make their way to other states; such was the case with no-fault divorce in the 1970s. The state took its liberal reputation leaps forward in 2008 when the California court system announced that until further notice, the State of California would recognize gay marriages within its borders. Within days of this announcement, thousands of gay couples throughout the state flocked to their respective courthouses and city halls, applying for licenses and preparing for their wedding ceremonies. However, like any success in gay marriage history, the opposition was not far behind. There is talk of a stay being issued on this decision that would ultimately halt progress until the official ballot is cast in the state's upcoming elections.

Same-sex marriage has polarized not only religious communities and political communities across the country but also nearly every state individually. Whether in support, opposition, or indecision, there is definitely a growing interest in and importance placed on the issue of same-sex marriage and gay-rights equality regarding the subject of marriage within the United States. New faces, new figures, and new challenges within the gay rights arena are likely to continue.

See also Domestic Partnerships; Gay Parent Adoption.

Further Reading: American Civil Liberties Union http://www.aclu.org; Bull, Chris, and John Gallagher. *Perfect Enemies: The Battle between the Religious Right and the Gay Movement*, updated ed. Lanham, MD: Madison Books, 1996; Christian Coalition. http://www.cc.org; DOMA Watch. http://www.domawatch.org; Focus on the Family. http://www.focusonthefamily.com; Human Rights Campaign. http://www.hrc.org; Gay and Lesbian Association Against Defamation. http://www.glaad.org; Jost, Kenneth. *Gay Marriage. Issues for Debate in American Public Policy*, 5th ed. Washington, D.C.: CQ Press, 2004; Koppelman, Andrew. *The Gay Rights Question in Contemporary American Law*. Chicago: The University of Chicago Press, 2002; Kranz, Rachel, and Tim Cusick. *Gay Rights*. Library in a Book, rev ed. New York: Facts on File, Inc., 2005; National Gay and Lesbian Task Force. http://www.thetaskforce.org; Partners Task Force for Gay and Lesbian Couples. http://www.buddybuddy.com/partners.html; Rimmerman, Craig A., and

Clyde Wilcox. *The Politics of Same-Sex Marriage.* Chicago: The University of Chicago Press, 2007; Same-Sex Marriage in California. http://pewforum.org/events/?EventID=138; Sheridan, Sharon, and James Thrall. "Deputies Approve Compromise Resolution on Same-Sex Unions," *Episcopal News Service*, August 8, 2003. http://www.episcopalchurch.org/3577_18576_ENG_HTM.htm; Sprigg, Peter. "Homosexualty: The Threat to the Family and the Attack on Marriage," March 29, 2004. http://www.frc.org/get.cfm?i=PD04F01; United Church of Christ. http.//www.ucc.org.

Jeffery Jones

SIBLING VIOLENCE AND ABUSE

Sibling violence and abuse is a significant social problem, impacting a large number of families each year. This form of family violence is considered to be the most common of all violent family interactions and children are thought to be the most violent members of our society. Researchers have identified that the largest predictor of childhood aggression is the presence of a sibling. According to a recent national survey, as much as 75.5 percent of children between the ages of 3 and 17 reported having been victimized by a sibling at some point during the previous year. Furthermore, as much as 78 percent of siblings experience psychological abuse at some point in their lives (Keslica and Morril-Richards 2007). Sibling abuse is clearly concerning, but historically has been often viewed and excused as a normal part of childhood relationships.

Outcomes associated with being victimized by a sibling include: difficulty with interpersonal relationships, repeating the victim role in other relationships, over-sensitivity, self-blame, feelings of anger toward the sibling perpetrator, development of eating disorders, substance abuse problems, depression, and posttraumatic stress disorder. In addition to the negative outcomes of being the victim, there are also negative ramifications associated with perpetration. Such outcomes include habit or conduct disorders, the presence of neurotic traits, developmental lags, and suicidal behaviors. In relation to sibling abuse, Tremblay and colleagues stated: "Not only is childhood physical aggression a precursor to the physical and mental health problems that will be visited upon victims, but also aggressive children themselves are at higher risk of alcohol use, drug use, accidents, violent crimes, depression, suicide attempts, spousal abuse, and neglectful or abusive parenting habits" (Tremblay et al. 2004).

The limited amount of research concerning violence and abuse between siblings has classified the behaviors into three forms, much the same way that other forms of family violence have been categorized: physical, emotional and sexual abuse.

PHYSICAL ABUSE

Physical abuse among siblings includes behaviors such as: punching, kicking, choking, striking with an object or weapon, or can involve any additional behavior acted out with the intent of causing physical harm. Physical violence is typically the most visible form of sibling abuse, and is more likely to receive public attention than other forms. Between 63 and 68 percent of all siblings engage in violent behaviors against each other (Gelles 1990). Additionally, 85 percent of males and 95 percent of females have been physically victimized by a sibling (Barnett, Miller-Perrin, and Perrin 2005). Not only does sibling violence often result in physical harm, but the lack of recognition of this abuse often can result in the victim not receiving needed help.

EMOTIONAL ABUSE

Emotional, or psychological, abuse includes behaviors such as: excessive teasing, degrading, threatening, exacerbating a fear, or destroying personal property. It is the most-pervasive, and the least-recognized, form of abuse among siblings. However, as is the case with many other forms of abuse, little attention is paid to emotional abuse in sibling relationships. This is due to the difficulty of detecting psychological abuse; perhaps as a result of the normalization of this form of abuse, inappropriate parental response, or its co-occurrence with other, more visible forms of abuse. Scholars report that the outcomes associated with psychological abuse victimization among siblings has had impacts similar to psychological abuse in other types of relationships (such as in domestic violence or parent-child abuse). However, due to its lack of recognition, it is highly unlikely that intervention will take place. Therefore, there is a substantial risk that children who are victimized by a sibling will internalize the destructive messages they receive in the home, and will carry this trauma into adult relationships.

SEXUAL ABUSE

Behaviors associated with sexual abuse include: fondling, touching, intercourse (rape or sodomy), exploitation, exposing to materials of a pornographic or sexual nature, or sexual activities that exceed the child's developmental level. Behaviors that are characterized as nontransitory or not motivated by curiosity can also be considered as problematic. Finally, if the child is too young or developmentally unable to provide informed consent, the behavior is typically considered abusive.

Outcomes associated with sibling sexual abuse victimization can include feelings of fear, shame, anxiety, trouble establishing interpersonal boundaries, as well as sexual behavior problems (e.g., avoidance of sexual contact, sexual compulsiveness, promiscuity, or sexual response difficulties). In relation to sexual behaviors, scholars also report that children who have been sexually abused by a sibling often have trouble separating feelings of pleasure from feelings of pain, and separating fear from desire in later adult sexual relationships.

PROBLEMS IN RECOGNIZING AND RESPONDING TO SIBLING MALTREATMENT

Despite the potentially devastating outcomes associated with sibling violence and abuse, this form of maltreatment receives little research attention, and is highly unlikely to be detected and reported within the family unit. This is in part due to the pervasive failure to recognize maltreatment in the context of sibling relationships as problematic behavior. This can further traumatize a victim because it becomes nearly impossible to receive the validation that is essential for survivors of family-related trauma.

To begin with, many scholars and practitioners have reported that having poor parental supervision is among the most pervasive characteristics observed where sibling violence and abuse is present. A case study that interviewed adults who had been victimized by a sibling during childhood found that participants commonly reported that the abuse occurred while the parents were not at home. In association with a lack of parental supervision comes the common practice of leaving older siblings in the care of younger siblings. This increases the risk of abuse, especially in situations where a child is placed with responsibilities over their younger siblings that may exceed their own developmental capabilities.

Even in situations where parents are able to identify abuse between their children, inappropriate responses to such behaviors can often exacerbate the problematic behaviors. Common dysfunctional parental strategies include: minimizing abuse, ignoring abuse altogether, not believing the victim, blaming the victim, striking out at the perpetrating sibling, and in some situations engaging in the abuse themselves.

Often, parents will assume that abusive conflict is a normative part of child development. Common words and phrases used in our culture also lend to the normalization of abusive behaviors. Phrases such as rough-and-tumble play, boys will be boys, and sibling rivalry identify behaviors that may be abusive and conceptualize them as normal, healthy aspects of childhood. In fact, studies have shown that some parents actually encourage their children to engage in conflict situations because they believe it will teach them to stand up for themselves or to successfully handle conflict situations. Expressions of aggressive behavior between siblings may even be encouraged by social norms. In general, aggressive behavior among siblings is attributed to normal sibling rivalry. Thus it is treated as something that children will presumably outgrow and adults will inevitably forget. This reflects a perception that many have that sibling abuse is a normative aspect of child development, and that it is to be expected. However, distinctions have been made between behaviors that comprise rivalry and those that constitute assault.

Rivalry between siblings is characterized by conflict that involves possession of something the other also wants. It can lead to a strengthening of the relationship as well as balanced comparisons between siblings. Assault, in contrast, involves patterns of repeated physical aggression with the goal of harming, humiliating, or defeating the sibling. It is also part of an escalating pattern of sibling aggression and retaliation. The behaviors continue even after parental intervention and serve to solidify the roles of victim and offender between siblings.

Such norms and values regarding sibling abuse are further perpetuated by the belief of many professionals and parents that sibling conflict is healthy and necessary for the development of conflict resolution skills, decreasing the likelihood of recognition and appropriate response when sibling violence does occur. Parents might actually encourage this behavior for siblings to release their anger at each other and work out their disagreement. Unfortunately, this usually has the effect of promoting aggression in the child rather than easing hostility. This is not to say that all conflict that occurs between siblings is abusive because much of the time this behavior is harmless. However, assuming that all violent interaction is normative can be problematic because it can cause parents and practitioners to overlook this form of child victimization.

In relation to the concept of minimizing sibling abuse, some parents may be aware of the behavior and ignore it altogether. Because it is common for abuse to occur when parents and caregivers are not around, sibling violence and abuse can be easily overlooked. Even in situations where the abuse occurs in the presence of a parent, they may divert their attention elsewhere. For example, parents often report that they become sick and tired of their children's rivalry, and learn to simply tune it out. Others believe that interfering in sibling disputes will prevent them from working out the conflict, and that it is best to leave them to their own devices.

Another maladaptive reaction that parents may have in relation to sibling violence and abuse is to not believe the victim. This may occur especially in situations where sexual abuse is present because even if the victim is able to disclose the abuse, the parent may have trouble accepting it. This not only ties into the common perception in our society that children are asexual, but many parents believe that their children are not capable of the accused behaviors. For example, parents are more likely to be unaware of sexual abuse than they are of other forms of maltreatment within the sibling dyad. This is understandable because it can be very difficult for a parent to consider one of their children as a perpetrator. Also, because of the taboo nature of incest, parents may be very uncomfortable accepting that such activities could occur in their families at all. Such a reaction can be very difficult for victims because they are not only invalidated, but it is rare for this type of behavior to stop without professional counseling.

Blaming the victim for abuse is a common theme across all types of family violence, and is no exception in sibling abuse. In some circumstances, parents may be aware that abuse is occurring, but will blame the victim for such activities. It is common that parents respond to sibling abuse by claiming that the victim must have done something to anger the abuser, and therefore deserved it. This is extremely hazardous to the physical and mental health outcomes of a victim, who is more likely to internalize the message that they deserve the abuse. They may also be more likely to transfer their role of victim into other domains, such as into dating relationships.

In some cases, parents may respond to violence and abuse in such a way that traumatizes the perpetrator. That is, one child may be abused by the parents because of abusive behavior with a sibling. This is not only harmful to the child, but also sends a message that violence is a legitimate method of conflict resolution. In addition, parents who react to their children's behavior in violent and maladaptive ways increase the likelihood that similar behaviors will be expressed in sibling relationships, both in the presence and absence of parental supervision. Practitioners recommend that parents model healthy, nonviolent conflict resolution strategies to their children because many abusive behaviors may be attributed to family dynamics.

A final strategy, and perhaps the most devastating, occurs when parents choose to engage in abuse themselves. One type of family dynamic that is especially vulnerable to this form of abuse applies to situations where violence and abuse cascades throughout the family unit. The cascade effect is used to describe family relations that are characterized by coercion, power, and control, and in which older, more powerful members often exhibit their dominance over younger or weaker members. Often, when domestic abuse and parent-child abuse are present, abused children will attempt to gain feelings of control by exhibiting their dominance on those in positions of lower power, such as a younger sibling or an animal. Another family dynamic that may be conducive to parental engagement in sibling abuse pertains to family situations where a target child is present. A target child is often a specific member of the family that, for a variety of reasons, has been singled out as the target for ridicule and abuse. Reasons for the targeting of a specific child can range from parental factors such as mental illness or negative associations with the child to child factors such as having a physical, behavioral, emotional, or cognitive disability.

SUGGESTED INTERVENTION STRATEGIES

Several intervention strategies have been suggested for families where sibling abuse is present. Vernon Wiehe, a sibling abuse scholar, has developed the SAFE model. In this approach parents can take the following steps to address violence between siblings: (S) stop the behavior immediately, (A) access the situation and identify what is actually going on, (F) find out how to avoid the dysfunction, and (E) evaluate the situation again in a couple of days to be sure the behavior has subsided. Wiehe goes on to list some common indicators of sibling violence and abuse for parents to recognize, such as conflict high in frequency and intensity, conflict where there one sibling is clearly being victimized, behaviors that are not appropriate for a child's age, and behaviors that intend to control, dominate or belittle. In relation to other forms of suggested intervention or parenting education programs that focus on sibling violence and abuse, sources are limited, and little information is available for parents who may face this problem with their own children.

CONCLUSION

Sibling violence and abuse is considered the most pervasive form of family violence in our society. However, empirical attention has been lacking in this area. The research that does exist indicates that although this has been among the least-recognized forms of family violence, the outcomes can be devastating and long lasting. Few intervention programs exist to address the problem of sibling violence and abuse. This may be due, in part, to a failure on behalf of researchers and practitioners to recognize maladaptive sibling conflict as problematic. There are great strides to be made in the research field relating to sibling violence and abuse. Increasing research, refining methodological techniques, increasing public and professional awareness, and designing intervention strategies are all needed to address the problem of abuse in sibling relationships. With such increases in attention, we can make strides to prevent this form of abuse, as well as the negative outcomes associated with both perpetration and victimization for children and families.

See also Child Abuse; Domestic Violence Interventions; Juvenile Delinquency.

Further Reading: Ammerman, R., and M. Hersen. *Case Studies in Family Violence.* New York: Plenum Press, 1991; Barnett, O., Miller-Perrin, C. L., and R. D. Perrin. *Family Violence Across the Lifespan: An Introduction,* 2nd ed. Thousand Oaks, CA: Sage Publications, 2005; Caffaro, J., and A. Conn-Caffaro. *Sibling Abuse Trauma.* New York: Haworth Maltreatment and Trauma Press, 1998; Cooke, P., and P. J. Standen. "Abuse and Disabled Children: Hidden Needs?" *Child Abuse Review* 11 (2002): 1–18; Eriksen, S., and V. Jensen. "All in the Family? Family Environment Factors in Sibling Violence." *Journal of Family Violence* 21 (2006): 497–507; Feshbach, S. "The Function of Aggression and the Regulation of Aggressive Drive." *Psychological Review* 71 (1964): 257–272; Gelles, R. J., and C. P. Cornell. *Intimate Violence in Families,* 2nd ed. Thousand Oaks, CA: Sage, 1990; Gelles, R. J. "Violence in the Family: A Review of Research in the Seventies." *Journal of Marriage and the Family* 42, no. 4 (1980): 873–885; Haskins, C. "Treating Sibling Incest Using a Family Systems Approach." *Journal of Mental Health Counseling* 25, no. 4 (2003): 337–351; Hoffman, K. L., and J. N. Edwards. "An Integrated Theoretical Model of Sibling Violence and Abuse." *Journal of Family Violence* 19, no. 3 (2004):185–200; Kettrey, H., and B. Emery. "The Discourse of Sibling Violence." *Journal of Family Violence* 22 (2007): 769; Kiselica, A., and M. Morril-Richards. "Sibling Maltreatment: The Forgotten Abuse." *Journal of Counseling and Development* 85 (2007): 146–160; Linares, L. O. "An Understudied form of Intra-family Violence: Sibling-to-sibling Aggression among Foster Children." *Aggression and Violent Behavior* 11 (2006): 95–109; Straus, M. A. "Forward." In *The Violent Home: A Study of Physical Aggression Between Husbands and Wives,* ed. R. J. Gelles. Thousand Oaks, CA: Sage Publications, 1974; Tremblay, R. E., D. S. Nagin, J. R. Séguin, M. Zoccolillo, P. D. Zelazo, M. Boivin, D. Pérusse, and C. Japel. "Physical Aggression During Early Childhood: Trajectories and Predictors." *Pediatrics* 114, no. 1 (2004): 43–50; Wiehe, V. R. *Sibling Abuse: Hidden Physical, Emotional, and Sexual Trauma.* Thousand Oaks, CA: Sage Publications, 1997; Wiehe, V. R. *What Parents Need to Know About Sibling Abuse.* Springville, UT: Bonneville Books, 2002.

Rachel Birmingham

STAY AT HOME DADS

The numbers of families choosing alternative parenting strategies have increased over time. A style of childrearing that has been subject to both celebration and denigration is the stay at home dad (SAHD). A stay at home father is a man who assumes full-time childrearing duties such as those traditionally assigned to a housewife. While men who elect to stay home while their wives work may find tremendous satisfaction in the arrangement, they often face questions from those who assume that the rightful place for men is in the world of paid employment rather than in the home.

INTRODUCTION

In previous generations it was seen as the mother's duty to stay home to rear the children. The father, on the other hand, was expected to work and to provide financially for his family. Today, this is no longer the case. Because many mothers work outside of the home (some earning high incomes) fathers have had to take a more active role in parenting. As parenting has evolved into a more equally shared job among couples, mom is no longer expected to sacrifice her personal goals to raise the children. Because times have changed, fathers are now willing to postpone their careers to stay home and raise the children while mothers continue to work and provide for the family.

This change in the family has led to a relatively new group of men known as stay at home dads. Because SAHDs do go against the cultural norm, they experience challenges and obstacles as they redefine fatherhood. At times, SAHDs are revered by society for their active participation in their children's live. Other times, they are looked down upon for their deviant behavior. Overall, SAHDs are rejected and misunderstood by the culture because of their decision to opt out of a more powerful role in society and take on a task traditionally associated with women.

BACKGROUND

As SAHDs increase in number, researchers have begun to take a closer look at this growing phenomenon. The U.S. Census Bureau indicates that the count of SAHDs has tripled in the past 10 years. They estimate that for the year 2006 there were between 150,000 to 200,000 full-time fathers in the United States caring for children under the age of 15. However, researchers studying the phenomenon estimate that the actual participation may be 10 times that number because the census eliminates a great deal of SAHDs on technicalities (Hartlaub 2006), such as the men working from home part-time while caring for children. These SAHDs were caring for approximately 283,000 children. Research also indicates that the majority of SAHDs are white males with an average age of 37. A large majority of these men also have a bachelor's degree or higher and are employed prior to becoming full-time fathers. Forty percent of this group was estimated to have annual family incomes of at least $50,000.

There are many reasons behind the increasing number of SAHDs. Not surprisingly, many men decide to stay home with their children because it is the most economically beneficial decision for the family. Unlike the common stereotypical ideas, men do not stay home because they are unemployed or feminine. With 25 percent of all women earning more than their husbands, it seems logical that dad would opt to stay home over mom. Among the changes in the labor market over the past 30 years has been the tendency for employed women with children to be increasing as a percentage of all workers. Men's employment data suggest that male employment rates fluctuate as a result of changes in the economy and calls to military service; however, men have decreased as a percentage of all workers. While some of this is accounted for by the younger ages at which men enter retirement today and the evolving service economy, men who voluntarily leave the labor force to rear children are also a part of the changing trends.

An additional explanation as to why more fathers are staying home is that many mothers and fathers do not want to put their children in day care. These parents value the idea of a parent being the primary caregiver for their child. Also, some fathers' personalities are better suited for raising children than are the mothers' personalities. Probably the single most important factor for a dad deciding to stay home is that many mothers now work outside of the home, contributing significantly to the overall economic status of the family; therefore, parenting has moved from the mother's role to the parent's role. In sum, the research indicates that fathers usually decide to stay home because it is what is most practical for the family at the time.

CHALLENGES FOR STAY AT HOME DADS

Once these fathers have made their decision to stay home, they certainly do not experience ready acceptance or support from the culture. Many SAHDs report feeling lonely and isolated from society. In fact, 63 percent of them experience isolation or some form of depression (Nordstrom 1998). As many fathers exit the corporate world, they give up friends and acquaintances to establish their new identities. Because there are such low numbers of SAHDs and father groups, isolation and loneliness are sad realities for these men. Dads who do not allow loneliness or isolation to become a dominating factor can take the initiative to get out and find play groups, which can allow them the opportunity to socialize and meet other parents.

There are also many people who feel that SAHDs are not beneficial to society, furthering the isolation that these fathers experience. Stay at home mother groups have been unwelcoming to full-time fathers and often mistake these men for perverts at the park rather than involved parents. Some SAHDs have found close friends among stay-at-home mothers that welcome them; however, this arrangement is not comfortable for all. This arrangement is very difficult for African Americans, who may go years without ever meeting another African American male in their same occupation. Most shocking is that some religious groups oppose full-time fathers and its break-down of the traditional family. Organizations such as Promise Keepers argue that men should be the head of the household and being a SAHD does not fulfill this role. Particularly there is concern that boys would suffer when fathers stay home because a SAHD is not a powerful role model for them.

Family and friends make it difficult for fathers as well. Many fathers feel that their roles are stigmatized and their performances as fathers are put under the microscope. Because full-time fathers are taking on work commonly assumed by women, the culture too often questions their masculinity. Research indicates that society is not ready to let go of traditional gender roles and accept men in atypical positions. Those who research full-time fathering report that many fathers in this role experience odd looks and rude comments in public. This problematic situation continues to occur as the culture's definition of fatherhood is being challenged by more involved dads. Even wives of SAHDs are sanctioned for their family's deviant behavior. Although the rejection is disheartening, research indicates that SAHDs can overcome this and prevail nonetheless.

Unfortunately, the media has not helped create a more positive image of SAHDs. From Michael Keaton in the 1983 movie *Mr. Mom* to Adam Sandler in *Big Daddy* (1999) and Eddie Murphy in *Daddy Day Care* (2003), Hollywood has taken every opportunity possible to make full-time fathers appear comical. Movies and many television shows portray fathers as haphazard, domesticated idiots. Even commercials exhibit a harsh portrayal of fathers and their abilities to effectively parent. These stereotypes definitely make it harder for full-time fathers to be accepted and taken seriously by society. These negative depictions are always a good indicator of what the culture is not fully ready to accept.

Another challenge full-time fathers endure is being mistaken as feminine. As fathers deal with their masculinity being challenged, research shows that fathers who can disassociate themselves from such negativity are much happier fathers. Dr. Aaron Rochlen believes that this whole idea of masculinity can be bad for full-time fathers and their children. This is because masculinity is associated with work-related success, competition, power, prestige, superiority, and restricting emotions and parents are those that can be expressive, patient, emotional, and not money oriented. It is evident how negative masculinity can be for fathers and how important it is for the culture to let this notion of masculinity subside.

Although many of the challenges full-time fathers face are similar to those of full-time mothers, they differ in many ways. Whereas both mothers and fathers experience isolation as stay at home parents, mothers experience much more acceptance than fathers as primary caregivers. Also, mothers and fathers parent differently. Full-time fathers generally describe their method of parenting by saying that a full-time father is fathering and not mothering.

Full-time fathers also have to deal with changes in their marriages. Marriage contentment has much to do with why the couple chooses this arrangement and how they delegate power and responsibility when one spouse decides to remain home. Most married couples experience difficulties initially as they adjust to changes and establish their new identities apart from cultural expectations. When parents are comfortable in this arrangement, it can be much less stressful and even beneficial for the relationship. It allows parents to focus on their children and not worry about childcare. It also frees couples from the challenge of deciding who will miss work when the children are sick. Unfortunately, if this arrangement is not a joint decision or is fallen into by default, marriages can experience many problems. Overall, couples can benefit their marriages and their children from this arrangement.

BENEFITS TO STAY AT HOME DADS

Although research may lead one to think that SAHDs are constantly fighting their critics to remain in the role, there are actually many benefits that full-time fathers and their families receive from such an arrangement. Today, as these full-time fathers challenge old definitions of masculinity and redefine themselves and their role as a parent, they have found a tool that helps them deal with uncomfortable situations and a lack of social acceptance. Many SAHDs have turned to the Internet for help. The Internet provides fathers with an opportunity to connect with other SAHDs, affirm their new identity, and deal with loneliness. This support is particularly useful when fathers are first transitioning into the role of primary caregiver.

This is the perfect tool for communication for men who do not naturally reach out for support. Through the use of websites such as athomedad.org or rebeldad.com, many SAHDs have found help and support from other fathers like themselves. Most of these sites offer advice for full-time fathers and encouragement through the struggles that they face. Some websites have local meetings for fathers and their children. SAHD groups have been most successful in the Pacific Northwest and Mountain states where the numbers of SAHDs are higher.

Research has shown that today's fathers, whether they stay at home to rear their children or not, put much more focus on nurturing and caring for their children than did fathers of the past. Children of at-home-father families tend to have a strong father and mother influence and both parents are important in the child's life. This is somewhat different from the at-home-mother family, in which a child experiences high contact with the mother and a more detached relationship with the father. When children spend more alone time with fathers early in life, it forges bonds that result in fathers remaining active parents throughout the ensuing years.

Research also indicates that full-time fathers tend to have more independent children. These children who experience increased time with their fathers usually earn higher grades in school, have greater ambition, have fewer anxiety disorders, and have a reduced risk of delinquency or teen pregnancy. It gives daughters an opportunity to see their mothers be successful and experience a nurturing father figure. Boys benefit from this arrangement by observing an involved male figure. Although there is anecdotal concern that boys will grow up to be feminine, research has yet to find this to be true and it represents one of the unfounded assumptions about SAHDs.

Most stay at home fathers report that they are happy with their new identities, however, it was difficult to adjust to because they had to view their accomplishments differently and measure them with a different yard stick. Support is crucial for their contentment as full-time fathers. Aaron Rochlen found in a survey of SAHDs that support was a critical element in the psychological well-being of stay at home fathers. Additionally, the increased emphasis on what fathers can contribute, outside of finances, leads many of them to gain greater confidence in their parenting abilities. There is no need to defer to mothers on childrearing issues (a traditional pattern) because they can trust their own instincts. They have additional opportunities to develop their fathering skills and do so in a way that differs from the skills that mothers bring to parenting. Men tend to be more relaxed and flexible parents, encouraging their children to be more independent and trust their own judgments.

FUTURE OF STAY AT HOME DADS

Increasingly, full-time fathers create new identities and accept role reversals because it is what is practical for them and their families and not because they are feminine. Support is particularly important for SAHDs because they are moving from a world in which identities are based on achievements and paychecks to one in which accomplishments are measured by children's success and growth. The Internet plays a large role in offering support to these fathers by helping them to forge a like community when one may be physically absent.

A critical point that has emerged in early research on men's choice to be SAHDs is that these fathers are not fully accepted nor understood by society and they experience a great deal of rejection. As more men enter this role, the stereotypes will likely become clearer and the strengths of fathers more apparent. Stereotypes that fathers are lazy and just do not want to work can make them question their decision. Mixed reactions from others about their decision to stay home can become tiresome. Full-time fathers say that the culture just does not understand why they choose to remain home with their children, but as the practice becomes more accepted these concerns should decrease.

A likely outcome of the increasing questions about SAHDs is an intellectual interest in fathering. While fathers and their roles in children's lives have been more extensively researched since 1990 the explorations are in their infancy. The phenomenon of SAHDs should encourage greater interests in the qualitatively different styles that mothers and fathers bring to their interactions with children. Ideally we will learn precisely what constitutes fathering. Given that some fathers are particularly uncomfortable that their parenting be compared to mothering, special skills of both parents will likely be made clearer. While these fathers assume predominately female work, they parent much differently than their female counterparts. They do not completely end all masculine chores, but they add feminine work to their traditional responsibilities.

There are practical outcomes to the increases in SAHDs. As society grows and changes, there will eventually be greater acceptance of these men and their families. However, advancements need to be made in the work arena to allow more fathers paternity leave. While leave may be guaranteed for some fathers under the Family and Medical Leave Act (FMLA) most have been reluctant to take it because of how they might be viewed by employers and colleagues. One way to help integrate fathers into the lives of their children is to have more opportunities for them to volunteer at schools and child care facilities. Lastly, more local support for fathers, whether through religious groups or through local full-time fathers' groups, can affirm the positive influence that fathers can have in the lives of their children. These changes will definitely impact the future of full-time fatherhood and would benefit these men greatly.

See also Employed Mothers; Family Roles; Fatherhood; Housework Allocation.

Further Reading: AtHomeDad.org: The Stay at Home Dad Oasis. http://www.athomedad.org; Cullen, L. T., and L Grossman. "Fatherhood 2.0." *Time*, October 4, 2007. http://www.time.com; Fisher, S. W. "The Stay At Home Dad: Why Some Christian Couples Are Choosing to Reverse Roles and How it Affects Their Marriage." *Marriage Partnership*

17 (2000): 24; Hartlaub, P. (July 23, 2006). *Full-time Dad and Fine With It.* http://www.sfgate.com; Nordstrom, N. "When Dad Stays Home." *Jugglezine* June 12, 1998. Herman Miller, Inc. http://www.hermanmiller.com; Owen, S. "Numbers of Stay-at-Home-Fathers Are Rising." http://www.thenothwestern.com (accessed March 5, 2008); Randall, K. "University of Texas Stay-at-Home Father Survey Results." Austin, TX: University of Texas Department of Educational Psychology. http://www.utexas.edu; Rebeldad, "A Father Puts the Stay-at-Home Dad Trend Under the Microscope." http://www.rebeldad.com; Stritof, S., and B. Stritof. "Full Time Dads and Marriage." http://marriage.about.com; Shaver, K. "Stay at Home Dads Forge New Identities, Roles." *Washington Post,* June 17, 2007; Tucker, P. "Stay at Home Dads: At-Home Dads Can Benefit Children and Mothers." *Futurist.* http://www.allbusiness.com (accessed June 15, 2008); U.S. Census Bureau. March 2006. *America's Families and Living Arrangements, 2006.* Current Population Survey and Report.

Victoria Adams

SURROGACY

Surrogacy is a form of reproductive assistance in which one woman bears a child for another woman to rear. While it sounds like a simple proposition, something a woman might do for another out of the goodness of her heart, it is far more complex than it initially sounds. Likewise the ethical, moral, and legal controversies surrounding surrogacy continue to be revealed.

SURROGACY: A BRIEF U.S. HISTORY

Surrogacy, as scientific assistance for pregnancy and birth, became a part of public discourse around the mid-1970s, despite its having been mentioned in the Bible in Genesis. The first documented instance in the United States comes from an anonymous advertisement in the mid-1970s requesting the help of a surrogate mother. According to the advertisement, the surrogate would receive a total of from $7,000 to $10,000 for her services and $3,000 for medical expenses. The amount established in the 1970s has been the accepted minimum form of assistance for all commercial surrogacy cases. It is important to note that the fees given to surrogate mothers today are not necessarily payments for a child. Most states have made it illegal to pay a woman for a child, so the payments given to a surrogate are couched in phrases like medical assistance, food, and shelter. This is done to eliminate the stigma of baby selling.

The first time a surrogacy case went to court was in 1981. Unlike the more widely known cases like Baby M and *Johnson v. Calvert,* this particular case was about payment. The case was a challenge to Michigan laws that would not allow a payment in exchange for relinquishing parental rights. Leading this case was the so-called Father of Surrogate Motherhood, Noel Keane. He challenged Michigan laws regarding payment to surrogate mothers, but the trial did not go in his favor and the state upheld their law against fees being paid for a child. In fact, Michigan was so staunchly opposed to surrogacy that they tried to ban surrogacy contracts outright in 1988 and was the first state in the nation to take a stand on surrogacy.

As the 1980s progressed, surrogacy became a more prevalent form of assisted reproductive technology, but it also became more entrenched in legal battles. The law was unable to keep up with the emerging technologies, and before anyone could reconfigure concepts of parenthood, cases like Baby M and *Johnson v. Calvert* took the national stage. When the Baby M case hit the New Jersey courts in 1986, both the United Kingdom and the United States had had their first successful in vitro fertilizations, and surrogacy had taken on new dimensions. The jargon surrounding surrogacy shifted, creating four different categories of cases:

1. Traditional Surrogacy: a case in which a couple decides to have a child through a surrogate mother, and the husband provides the sperm and the surrogate provides the ovum. In this case, the surrogate mother is the genetic and gestational mother.
2. Gestational Surrogacy: a case in which a couple decides to have a child through a surrogate, and the husband and wife provide the necessary gametes. In this case, the surrogate is not genetically linked to the child. Also, gestational surrogacy can occur with the use of anonymously donated sperm and ova, thus creating some potentially difficult legal issues (see *Jaycee B. v. the Superior Court of Orange County* 1996 and *In re Marriage of John A.B. and Luanne H.B.* 1998).
3. Commercial Surrogacy: a case in which a couple pursues surrogacy usually through an agency, paying for the agency services as well as providing financial assistance to the surrogate mother.
4. Noncommercial Surrogacy: a case in which a couple pursues surrogacy, usually through a private agreement, in which no fees are exchanged between the couple and the surrogate mother.

Although there are four types of surrogacy, they are not mutually exclusive. A surrogacy cannot be traditional and gestational at the same time nor commercial and noncommercial concurrently. However, it can be a traditional, commercial surrogacy or even a traditional, noncommercial surrogacy. Depending on the combination of labels, the moral, ethical, and legal ramifications of each surrogacy case increases. While there have been several legal cases involving surrogacy, three have received the most media attention: *In re the Matter of Baby M*, *Johnson v. Calvert*, and *In re Marriage of John H.B. and Luanne A.B.* The three cases have set the precedents for all surrogacy cases and have brought various issues into the national discourse.

The Case of Baby M

When the New Jersey Supreme Court ruled on *In re the Matter of Baby M* in 1988, the case had received an enormous amount of national attention. The case was the first of its kind, with the surrogate mother demanding that the court acknowledge her parental rights. The case of Baby M was a traditional, commercial surrogacy.

William and Elizabeth Stern, the intended parents, had contracted an agreement with Mary Beth Whitehead as the surrogate mother. According to the contract, Ms. Whitehead would undergo artificial insemination with Mr. Stern's sperm, carry the child to term, and upon the child's birth would relinquish her parental rights to the Sterns. In exchange for fulfilling the contract, Ms. Whitehead would receive $10,000.

As the pregnancy advanced, Ms. Whitehead had reservations about giving up the child and decided that she wanted to keep it. Upon the birth of Baby M, Ms. Whitehead fled to Florida against court orders. When the case went before the Superior Court, the judge upheld the legality of the surrogacy contract and demanded that Ms. Whitehead return the child to the Sterns.

Upon appeal, the case went before the New Jersey Supreme Court where it garnered national media attention. The court, without precedents for surrogacy cases, treated the arrangement between the Sterns' and Ms. Whitehead as they would a custody battle between divorced parents. Because Elizabeth Stern had no apparent claim to the child, the court did not consider her intent in having a child. The court reversed the Superior Court's decision on the basis that the contract between the Sterns and Ms. Whitehead was illegal. Because the contract outlined payment for a child and the relinquishment of parental rights rather than payment for medical expenses, the contract violated New Jersey public policy and was null and void.

The court, having dismissed the surrogacy contract, then dealt with the issue of custody and the child's best interests. In the hearing, it was decided that the Sterns could provide the best possible environment for Baby M, so they were awarded custody. Unlike the Sterns, Ms. Whitehead had recently divorced and was struggling financially—two things the court considered while deciding the best interests of Baby M. However, because she was deemed the biological mother, the court granted her visitation rights.

Baby M was the first case that addressed the lack of a legal framework for dealing with surrogacy issues. Without laws specifically governing surrogacy, the court had to treat traditional surrogacy as they would a custody battle between separated parties. As a result of the media attention, however, nearly every state considered laws to allow, ban, or regulate surrogacy. The Baby M case marks the beginning of public legal and ethical discussions of surrogacy issues. In the middle of the trial, a 1987 poll from the *New York Times* found that a majority of people believed that surrogacy contracts should be upheld—even if the courts seemed to rule otherwise.

The Case of Johnson v. Calvert

Six years after the New Jersey Supreme Court handed down its decision regarding traditional surrogacy in the Baby M case, the California Supreme Court handed down a decision that would inform the general consensus toward gestational surrogacy: *Johnson v. Calvert*. In this case, Mark and Crispina Calvert sought to have a child through a surrogate mother, Anna Johnson.

Anna Johnson offered to be the surrogate mother for the Calverts. Unlike the case of Baby M, where the surrogate also supplied the ovum, Ms. Johnson provided the necessary gestation for the child and Mrs. Calvert provided the ovum. By using in vitro fertilization, Ms. Johnson carried the Calvert's genetic child. Under the contractual agreement between the two parties, Ms. Johnson would receive $10,000 in installments to help finance medical expenses and basic needs. The Calverts would also insure her life with a $200,000 life insurance policy. In return, Ms. Johnson would carry the child to term and recognize the sole parental rights of the Calverts. However, the Calverts and Ms. Johnson had a falling out, and both parties filed custody suits.

According to California law (under the Uniform Parentage Act), both Crispina Calvert and Anna Johnson had equal claims to the child because the law acknowledged the role of genetic and gestational mothers as legal mothers. However, the court decided in favor of Mrs. Calvert based on a consent-intent definition, a definition that has subsequently affected all gestational surrogacy cases. By a consent-intent argument, the legal parents are the people who consented to the procedure with the intention of taking on parental responsibility. The court argued that any woman could have gestated the resulting child, but only Mrs. Calvert could have provided the ovum. As a result, Mrs. Calvert was the legal mother.

The Case of Jaycee B.

Like the two previous cases, the trials involving Jaycee B. took the national stage, as once again the law struggled to deal with issues that arise from surrogacy. However, unlike Baby M and *Johnson v. Calvert,* Jaycee B. was not a surrogacy case; in fact, the trials surrounding this child were more about child support and deciding the legal parents. The trials were labeled as a surrogacy case gone awry because Jaycee B. was the result of a rather unusual surrogacy. This case involved a gestational surrogacy in which the genetic material (the sperm and ovum) used to create the child belonged to neither of the intended parents. The intended parents had used anonymous donor sperm and ova, and under California law, donors are not acknowledged as legal parents.

When the intended parents of Jaycee B., John and Luanne, divorced one month prior to the birth of the child, questions of parentage arose. When John filed for divorce, he listed no children from the marriage and refused to pay child support for Jaycee B. In the media, reports labeled the child as legally parentless because the genetic parents were anonymous donors and the surrogate mother had filed for custody, only to take her petition back when Luanne assured her that Jaycee would be fine. As the divorce trial continued, John refused to acknowledge the child as his own because he was not the biological father. He argued that because he was not genetically linked to the child, he should not have to pay child support.

The first trial in the matter of Jaycee B. concluded in 1996, *Jaycee B. v. Superior Court of Orange County.* The first trial was meant to decide whether John should pay child support. The Appellate Court declared that because he had signed the surrogacy contract as an intended parent, he owed child support until such time as a court officially labeled him as other than the father of the child. In 1997 the case became more complicated when a higher court decided that John had no support obligations, that the surrogacy contract was unenforceable, and that Luanne would have to officially adopt the child.

The second trial in the matter of Jaycee B. concluded in 1998, *In re Marriage of John A.B. and Luanne H.B.* This specific trial dealt with the issue of parentage. The court decided that the intended parents of a child of donor gestation are the legal parents. John had argued that because he had only signed the surrogacy contract and no other legal paperwork, he could not be considered the legal father, and thus was not responsible for child support. The 1998 court decision upheld the consent-intent definition of parenthood established by *Johnson v. Calvert,* even in the absence of complete legal written documentation, but with John's full awareness of the situation. Regardless of the lack of a genetic link between John and Jaycee, he was, by intent, her father. The trials involving Jaycee B. were not necessarily surrogacy cases; no surrogate mother was protesting her parental rights, but the trials illustrate what can happen when American laws do not account for the special needs of surrogacy cases.

DOES SURROGACY AID INFERTILE COUPLES OR EXPLOIT WOMEN?

The biggest praise that surrogacy receives is that it enables infertile couples to have children that are genetically linked to at least one parent, if not both. In 1999, a study found that 2 to 3 million couples were infertile. Infertility data, combined with the fewer numbers of children readily available for adoptions, suggest that fewer couples would ever experience their desired parenthood. Surrogacy, when compared with the costs of legal adoption, may be an economically competitive form of having children.

The process can be expensive, with a surrogacy costing a couple anywhere from $10,000 to $60,000 depending on whether the surrogacy is commercial or noncommercial, traditional or gestational. Average domestic adoption costs are $9,000, and the expense increases with a foreign adoption. Both adoption and surrogacy carry a weighty cost for agency and legal fees. In an adoption the birth mother is not paid anything to compensate her for her pregnancy and childbirth. However, because the intended parents may pay money to the surrogate mother, many critics view surrogacy as exploitation.

The Case of Baby M caused an explosion of moral and ethical debates regarding surrogacy. Because the contract between the Sterns and Ms. Whitehead outlined that she would be paid upon the birth of the child and her filing to relinquish her parental rights, the courts viewed this as baby selling. Under contract, Ms. Whitehead would receive money for additional medical needs, but the $10,000 from the contract was to be given to her upon the birth of Baby M and not before and not in the case of an abortion. Radical feminist critics lashed out about surrogacy, claiming that the act exploited women and children, and that it undermined the basic mother-child bond. The stigma of baby selling continues in the dialogue about surrogacy. Even today, where it is widely recognized that surrogacy contracts cannot outline payment for children or the relinquishing of parental rights, critics argue that labeling the payments as something for medical expenses, food, or clothing is a façade. Women are being paid to have children and give them to the purchaser.

The issue of women being paid for pregnancy and childbirth brings up more controversial topics like exploitation of women and children and the commoditization of human capital. Because surrogacy is such an expensive procedure, the process favors the privileged classes, while harming lower-class women; rich couples can exploit lower-class women with the promise of money that they might not otherwise be able to earn. Because lower-class women may need the money, they would be more willing than other women to act as surrogates, and because the current system under which surrogacy operates has little follow-up for surrogates, critics argue that these women are seen as persons of use rather than persons worthy of respect.

Because a monetary figure is attached to a woman's body and the resulting child, critics contend that we have created a market for human capital; we are buying and selling people. Studies question the possible negative effects on a surrogate mother, such as the labels that society places on her and the consequences of separating a mother and child. Others wonder at the outcome for a child who learns that she or he is the result of a surrogacy arrangement. Very few studies follow up on these questions.

However, when we discuss surrogacy and exploitation, we must consider the varying definitions of exploitation. Because harm is a subjective feeling, different surrogate mothers may relate different experiences. A first possible definition of exploitive surrogacy is that the intended parents gain while the surrogate mother is harmed. In this case, the intended parents gain from hurting someone else. Because the intended parents have the economic power, they can demand whatever they wish from the surrogate, and in return, she is left to acquiesce. A second possible definition of exploitative surrogacy is that both the intended parents and the surrogate gain from the experience, but the intended parents gain more. In this case, the intended parents gain a child and the surrogate gains some kind of monetary compensation. However, because society places a high value on a child's life, but not one that is necessarily monetary, the exchange for a child and $10,000 for expenses is not a fair arrangement. A third possible definition of exploitive surrogacy is that the intended parents gain from an immoral practice. Because surrogacy violates an inherent social norm or religious viewpoint, it has to be exploitive.

The difficulty in assessing accurate data on the exploitative nature of surrogacy is the fact that harm is subjective. Undoubtedly, Ms. Whitehead and Ms. Johnson might recount similar feelings from their surrogacy experiences, but the unnamed surrogate from the Jaycee B. case might relate a different experience. While they might make the news headlines, in fact less than 1 percent of surrogate mothers change their minds and want to keep the children. Most espouse a more altruistic motive to becoming surrogate mothers. Able to have children, they decided to give a gift to another couple. The *Johnson v. Calvert* case judges cited that a majority of surrogate mothers made between $15,000 and $30,000 per year in income separate from any possible assistance from the surrogacy. Less than 13 percent made below $15,000 per year.

It has been suggested that the primary motive for women to serve as surrogates is the money that they can earn doing so. Money may not be the driving factor for surrogate mothers that some critics of the practice may like to suggest. Early studies of the practice also found women's enjoyment of pregnancy, guilt over a past abortion, or giving a child up for adoption as potential motives in addition to financial compensation. Defenders of surrogacy argue that a woman who chooses to be a surrogate mother solely for some kind of payment would actually make less for the time she invested than if she worked at a low-paying job. Because these women choose to be surrogates, a 24-hour, nine month job for a minimum of $10,000 of assistance, there has to be some other motivation. If these women choose to be surrogates, the issue of exploitation seems irrelevant. It does not make sense that a woman would commoditize her body, as critics claim, for $1.54 per hour. This figure is derived from the following information: an average pregnancy lasts 270 days for 24 hours each day, totaling 6480 hours. If a surrogate mother receives the minimum $10,000 of assistance, she makes $1.54 per hour. If she receives $20,000 in assistance, it comes out to $3.09 per hour.

Of course, to consider raising the minimum accepted assistance given for medical and basic needs might also lead to more women choosing to be surrogate mothers because of the money, rather than for more charitable motives. Ultimately, surrogacy cannot exist without surrogate mothers. We have yet to find a means of fertilizing an ovum and sperm and gestating the embryo without a gestational mother. The question is: does surrogacy help more than it hurts?

GIVING BIRTH TO ONES GRANDCHILDREN

In 1991, in one of the most pleasant and well-publicized surrogacy arrangements, a South Dakota woman gave birth to her granddaughter and grandson. Arlette Schweitzer, 43 at the time of the birth, underwent in vitro fertilization by using the eggs from her daughter, Christa, and sperm from her son-in-law, Kevin, the first documented arrangement of this type in the United States. Christa (22 at the time of the birth) had been born with functioning ovaries, but without a uterus. Upon learning of this Mrs. Schweitzer volunteered to gestate her own grandchildren. This gestational surrogacy gained publicity through a TV movie in 1993, "Labor of Love: The Arlette Schweitzer Story." In 2004 Arlette Schweitzer recounted her surrogacy experience in the book *Whatever It Takes*.

GENETICS OR GESTATION: WHO BECOMES THE LEGAL MOTHER?

In spite of the scientific developments with artificial reproductive technologies, the law has not moved fast enough to consider surrogacy cases. The federal government has been unable to provide a general law for surrogacy like the equivalent in the United Kingdom, the Surrogacy Act of 1985. The only time federal legislation for surrogacy was introduced was in 1989 when Representative

Thomas A. Luken (D-Ohio) and Representative Robert K. Dornan (R-California) introduced two different bills.

Representative Luken presented the Surrogacy Arrangement Bill that criminalized commercial surrogacy. Anyone who willingly made commercial arrangements—intended parents, surrogate mothers, and agencies—would be subject to legal action. Representative Dornan introduced the Anti-Surrogate Mother bill that criminalized all activities relating to surrogacy. The bill would have also made all current surrogacy contracts, commercial and noncommercial, null and void. No one has been able to create a federal surrogacy law, and as a result the laws vary from state to state.

The Baby M case began the legal discussions of surrogacy, and prompted debate in law reviews regarding the legal definitions of surrogacy between 1988 and 1990. The New Jersey Supreme Court's decision to treat Ms. Whitehead as the legal mother of Baby M was the first case of its kind to decide that legal motherhood is defined by genetics. Because Mrs. Stern had no role in the creation of Baby M, apart from her intent to be a mother, the court did not consider her in the case until they tried to decide the best interests of the child. With a legal vacuum for dealing with surrogacy, the court had to treat the case as a custody battle and treated the surrogacy contract as an adoption contract. However, within a few years, most states had considered some laws dealing with the issues that originated with Baby M.

By the time *Johnson v. Calvert* received national attention, California had already begun a legal dialogue for deciding parentage, The Uniform Parentage Act. According to this act, legal mothers could be determined by either genetics or gestation. This posed a problem with *Johnson V. Calvert* because according to this definition, both Ms. Johnson and Mrs. Calvert had legal claims to the resulting child. The court decided the case based on a consent-intent definition, which claimed that without the intentions of the Calverts there would have been no child. The case also solidified the role of genetics in determining legal motherhood. In fact, many people at the time argued that a genetic definition of motherhood would be the best for surrogacy cases. The genetic argument eliminates any potential inconsistencies in surrogacy law, and it is the one contribution to a child that no one else could supply. In the instance that genetics and gestation were bound in the same woman, legal motherhood would be indisputable.

But, again, because surrogacy laws change from state to state, there are no consistent laws for the process. California is the one state that has stayed the most up-to-date by considering various laws and standards for determining legal motherhood. Currently, there are three different tests for legal motherhood that courts use when deciding cases: intent-based, genetic contribution, and gestation. As previously mentioned, the intent-based definition of legal motherhood originated with *Johnson v. Calvert*. Because there would be no child without the intent of the intended parents, the intended mother is the legal mother. The genetic contribution test is the most foolproof method for determining legal motherhood because it is the contribution that only the biological donor parent provides. The gestation test is a common law assumption that the birth mother is the legal mother because she devoted time to gestating the child.

The fact that there are three tests for determining legal motherhood, and that each of these tests contradicts the other in some places, suggests a need for more uniform law regarding surrogacy. However, in considering federal laws that would regulate surrogacy at the state level, legislators would have to decide exactly what defines a parent. With only one law to govern surrogacy, there may not be room to consider the special circumstances that can arise from surrogacy cases that do not begin as surrogacy cases, like the trials involving Jaycee B.

SURROGACY AS DEVIANT TO NOTIONS OF MOTHERHOOD

Today, it is impossible to discuss surrogacy apart from issues that range from artificial insemination and donor egg transplantation, the controversy over same-sex couples, and American concepts of motherhood. When discussing the moral, ethical, and legal questions surrounding surrogacy, most people get more than agitated. For some, surrogacy is immoral based on religious convictions. For others, surrogacy exploits women and children, making people commodities much in the way that the eighteenth and nineteenth century slave trade made people commodities. And yet for others, surrogacy is one of the only chances that they will ever have to have a child.

Surrogacy has enabled couples who may not have been able to have biological children to finally have children. This includes infertile couples as well as same-sex couples. With the rise of same-sex marriage controversies in the early part of the twenty-first century, surrogacy can become enmeshed as well. Religious zealots against homosexuality may lump surrogacy, despite its ability to give children to heterosexual couples, into a category of immoral behavior. Because surrogacy can provide children for same-sex partners, and because same-sex relationships are labeled morally wrong by these groups, surrogacy must also be morally wrong.

But if we strip down surrogacy to its basic components—that a woman might decide prior to conception to choose to gestate a child for someone else to raise—then we may find that the notions of American motherhood are compromised. If American culture heralds a natural mother-child bond and maternal instinct, then what does surrogacy challenge about our notions of motherhood? If a woman willingly decides to gestate a baby for another couple, what does that say about the notions that mother knows best?

On the one hand, surrogacy does perpetuate the idea that women should become mothers. By allowing infertile couples to have children in ways other than adoption or fostering, more women can become the mothers that society expects them to become. For most people, the act of gestation alone might make a woman a mother. But what kind of mother is she if she does not keep the child? Is a surrogate mother worse than a woman who gives up a child for adoption if the surrogate mother decides before she is pregnant that she will not keep the child?

Some of the same stigmas and stereotypes of adoption are repeated in surrogacy. Over the last 30 years, there has been considerable research into both adoption and surrogacy, but very little into the women who give up the children. Arguably, it is because surrogate mothers are deviant mothers. They do not conform to American concepts of motherhood, and so have been left out of mainstream research. Surrogate mothers do not reinforce ideas like the naturalness of mothering and the maternal instinct. Despite the fact that the surrogacy cases that have received the most media attention—Baby M and *Johnson v. Calvert*—were those cases that seemed to argue that women do have an instinctual desire to be mothers, fewer than one percent of surrogate mothers have ever contested for any parental rights.

Surrogacy, despite increased popularity as a form of assisted reproductive technology, is still on the outskirts of the American legal framework. Apart from California, most state governments do not have laws guaranteeing the security of either the intended parents or the surrogate mother. Our legal system does not make it possible for a child to have two moms and one dad, or even just two dads (excepting California in a decision from 2005 that changed the Uniform Parentage Act). Because of these limitations, the jargon associated with surrogacy cases is divided, allowing for separations between normal motherhood and deviant motherhood. Surrogacy is either traditional or gestational. It can either be commercial or noncommercial. The language of surrogacy reinforces inherent American notions of good mothers, and a surrogate mother does not fit that role.

See also Biological Privilege; Infertility.

Further Reading: American Surrogacy Center, Inc. http://www.surrogacy.com; Anderson, Elizabeth. "Is Women's Labor a Commodity?" *Philosophy and Public Affairs* 19, no. 1 (1990): 71–92; Andrews, Lori. "Beyond Doctrinal Boundaries: A Legal Framework for Surrogate Motherhood." *Virginia Law Review* 81, no. 8 (1995): 2343–2375; Behm, Lisa. "Legal, Moral, and International Perspectives on Surrogate Motherhood: The Call for a Uniform Regulatory Scheme in the United States." *DePaul Journal of Health Care Law* 2, no. 2 (1999): 557–603; Blankenship, Kim, Suzanne Onorato, Beth Rushing, and Kelly White. "Reproductive Technologies and the U.S. Courts." *Gender and Society* 7, no. 1 (1993): 8–31; Coleman, Malna. "Gestation, Intent, and the Seed: Defining Motherhood in the Era of Assisted Human Reproduction." *Cardoza Law Review* 17, no. 1 (1996): 497–530; Houston Women's Center. http://www.intendedparents.com; Laufer-Ukeles, Pamela. "Gestation: Work for Hire or the Essence of Motherhood? A Comparative Legal Analysis." *Duke Journal of Gender Law and Policy* 9, no. 3 (2002), 91–134; Place, Jeffery. "Gestational Surrogacy and the Meaning of 'Mother': Johnson v. Calvert." *Harvard Journal of Law and Public Policy* 9, no. 3 (1994): 907–918; Schuck, Peter. "COLLOQUY: Some Reflections on the Baby M Case." *Georgetown Law Review* 76 (1998): 1793–1810; Schweitzer, Arlette. *Whatever It Takes*. Mandan, ND: Crain Grosinger Publishing, 2004; Shalev, Carmel. *Birth Power: The Case for Surrogacy*. New Haven, CT: Yale University Press, 1989; Surrogate Mothers Online. http://www.surromomsonline.com; Surrogacy UK. http://www.surrogacyuk.org; Wertheimer, Alan. "Two Questions about Surrogacy and Exploitation." *Philosophy and Public Policy* 21, no. 3 (1992): 211–239.

Sarah Fish

TEEN PREGNANCY

The United States has the highest rates of pregnancy, abortion, and childbirth among teenagers in industrialized nations, a fact that results in considerable social anxiety and controversy. Teen pregnancy is defined as pregnancy among girls age 19 years and younger. A term that is used to draw attention to the problems of this behavior is "children having children." Teen pregnancy leads to adolescents raising children before they are emotionally or financially ready to do so. The rate of teen pregnancy has steadily decreased since reaching an all-time high in the 1990s. The rates have fallen because teenagers today have shown an increased use of long-acting birth control and slight decreases in sexual activity.

Today fewer American young people get married as teens, compared with young people 50 years ago. They don't, however, avoid sexual relationships until marriage. Because they are involved in premarital sexual relations, often with little planning for pregnancy and sexually transmitted disease (STD) prevention, teens become parents early. This has been a factor in the increase in single-mother families. There are different reasons why teenage girls become pregnant. Teenage girls are likely to become pregnant if they were sexually abused at a young age, in need of someone to love them, or planned for motherhood. Other pregnancies were unintended, because most teens tend to be poorly prepared with contraception and tend to underestimate their chances of conceiving.

BACKGROUND

Twenty-nine million adolescents are sexually active in the nation and the number is increasing each year. More than 850,000 teenage girls will become pregnant each year and 500,000 of them will give birth. Estimates are that three-fourths of these pregnancies are unintended. About 90 to 95 percent of teens who carry the pregnancy to term will keep their babies. Surprisingly, the nation's highest teen birth rate occurred in 1957, with 96.3 births per 1000 teenage girls, compared to 41.2 births per 1000 teenage girls in 2004. These numbers seem to suggest that teen parenting was more of a problem in the past. That is misleading, however. Most of the births from the 1950s and 1960s were to older teens who were married to their partners. These teens, who married young and had high fertility rates, were the parents of the baby boom generation. Economic instability, a hallmark of teen parenting today, was ameliorated in the 1950s by a strong economy and the likelihood of finding a family-wage job with only a high school education. Because so-called good jobs were available to those with only a high school education, young marriage and childbearing was encouraged by the social circumstances. Also, there was a strong propaganda machine extolling the virtues of stay-at-home mothers. There was a stigma on girls who were out-of-wedlock mothers, so much so that many pregnant teens were sent to live with relatives until the birth when the infant was then placed for adoption. The alternative was a so-called shotgun wedding in which the couple was persuaded to marry before the pregnancy began to show. In the 1950s and 1960s more than half of the women who conceived while single married before the child was born.

Today, the story is a very different one. The overwhelming majority of teen pregnancies are among unmarried teens. Eighty percent of teenage births occur outside of a marital relationship, and most of the girls have no intention of marrying the father of the child. As the social stigma of teen pregnancy has decreased dramatically over the last 30 years, so has the pressure to marry in order to legitimize a birth. Pregnant teens attend school alongside nonpregnant teens. This is quite a contrast from the days when they were forced to drop out or were sent to the reform school for students with behavior problems so that they would not corrupt the nonpregnant females. The financial circumstances of today's teen mothers are often quite desperate and many end up seeking public assistance funds. Education beyond high school has become essential for constructing a middle-class life, but many teen mothers experience a truncated educational history, quite unlike what those teen mothers of 50 to 60 years ago experienced when their husbands had high-paying jobs.

A brief discussion of the trends in teen birth in the last 20 years can help us to understand why teen pregnancy has been described as such a problem. In 1986, the birth rate among 15- to 19-year-old women was 50 births per 1000, but by 1991 that rate had climbed 24 percent to 62 per 1000. However, over the next five years the rate fell to 54 births per 1000 women ages 15 to 19 (Darroch and Singh 1999). In 2005, the teen birth rate in the United States was 40 births per 1000 teenage girls. Most data are concerned with the 15- to 19-year-old group because they have higher rates and constitute a much larger proportion of the births to teen mothers. Today research shows that pregnancies among young girls age 10 to 14 years old have fallen to their lowest level in the past decade. Thus, in the late 1980s and early 1990s politicians, families, religious leaders, and educators began to worry about the increases in teenage births and asked what solutions would help turn the trends around.

Race and Ethnicity

Racial and ethnic groups in the United States do not all have the same teen pregnancy and birth rates. Fertility rates among American women are different because of religion, age, and socioeconomic status. During the 1970s and 1980s, African American women had the highest fertility rate, Hispanics had the second highest, and white women had the lowest. Today, however, it is Hispanic women with the highest rate, followed by African Americans, and whites. The rate of teen births among blacks has dropped more dramatically than the rates of any other ethnic group. According to the Centers for Disease Control and Prevention, in 2005 the birth rate for Hispanic teens was 82 births per 1000 girls age 15 to 19. Comparable data for black and non-Hispanic whites were 61 per 1000 and 26 per 1000 respectively. The group with the lowest teen birth rate was Asian and Pacific Islander teens at 17 per 1000.

The reasons that birth rates among races differ are because of socioeconomic factors, family structure, and perceived future options. Risk factors for teen pregnancy include living in rural areas and inner cities, where many minority groups are clustered. White adolescent girls are less likely to carry their pregnancies to term than are black or Hispanic girls. Because of their economic status and parental pressure, many will end their pregnancies through abortion. Often minority women, particularly those on public assistance, cannot afford abortion and legislation has changed so that government funds will not cover elective abortion.

Likewise, education and religion can play a role in teen births. Girls who perceive few educational or employment opportunities (usually minority girls) may be more interested in becoming mothers. Pregnancy and mothering may be a way to avoid going to work in low-paying, dead-end jobs. At least they can have control in one aspect of their lives. This is more likely to be the case for black girls. One study in Alabama found more than 20 percent of black teens between 14 and 18 wished that they were pregnant. For Hispanics socioeconomic status is also important. However, Roman Catholicism, which disapproves of both birth control and abortion, also plays a role. Hispanic culture places a high value on children, particularly in their ability to contribute to the family group.

Intervention

With the changing patterns of teen pregnancy described above and concerns over the long-term consequences for society from children being reared by teen parents or single parents, calls for intervention have increased. Specifically, prior to the welfare reform of 1996, there was increasing concern over public funds supporting these families and frequent unsubstantiated charges that teens, and other poor single mothers, were having more babies just to increase their welfare benefits. In 1992, the U.S. government realized the importance of considering the experiences of teenage mothers and began pregnancy prevention programs in earnest. These programs, which largely target girls under the age of 16, were designed not only to discourage sexual activity but to educate young people about safer sexual practices. They generally worked off the assumption that all teen pregnancies were unwanted or unintended pregnancies. While that does seem to be the majority experience, it does not fully describe teen childbearing.

Optimists predicted that these types of programs would reduce the numbers of teen pregnancies by half and increase the provision of sex education and contraceptive services for young people. It did, however, become an issue with parents as well as religiously conservative groups. While there are no definitive data, there is a concern that sex education will encourage teenagers to have sex by making them think more sexual thoughts or providing the sense that adults condone teenage sexual experimentation. Some school districts were concerned about parental reaction should they institute the federal program. Education proponents argued that if teenagers are not educated about sex they will not know how to protect themselves and the result will be pregnancy or STD. Teenagers are curious and they are going to experiment whether they have had sex education or not. Proponents argued that another reason why teenagers have sex is peer pressure, and comprehensive sexuality education could help counter that.

Beginning with the George H. W. Bush administration these education programs focused heavily on teaching young people about abstaining from sexual behavior until marriage. While this drew praise from conservative religious and political groups, it was not well received by those who work directly with teens, suggesting that it was too naïve of an approach given the saturation of American media with sexual images. Critical of the emphasis on abstinence of most government programs, sexuality researcher Ira Reiss has said on many occasions that vows of abstinence break far more easily than do condoms.

The government has not been the only organization working on the issue of teen pregnancy. In 1996 The National Campaign to Prevent Teen and Unplanned Pregnancy, a nonprofit private nonpartisan organization, was founded with the sole goal of reducing teen pregnancy rates by 30 percent in ten years. Through grassroots work and media influence they have been largely successful. Despite the decreases in teen pregnancy in recent years, the problems that teen mothers and their children face are daunting.

PROBLEMS WITH TEEN PREGNANCY

Politicians, educators, clergy, and the general public debate whether teen pregnancy is a serious problem in the United States. The negative consequences of teen pregnancy and parenting have been well documented by public and private agencies, including the well-regarded Annie E. Casey Foundation. The areas of concern include the children, the mothers, and society as a whole. Advocates stress that teen pregnancy is a serious problem because teen pregnancy is linked to many negative circumstances for both teen parents and their children.

Health. Early childbearing puts teen girls at risk for health problems, both mentally and physically. Teens are at higher risk of death than older women during delivery; two to four times higher by some estimates. Young girls are faced with medical problems such as anemia, hemorrhage, and high blood pressure. These complications are particularly likely in the 10- to 14-year-old age group. Sexually active teens also have high rates of STD transmission, some of which can be passed on to their infants at birth. Infection during pregnancy can cause not only health problems with the fetus, but can cause a miscarriage.

Primarily due to inadequate nutrition, adolescents are three times more likely to have a baby with low birth weight or to be delivered prematurely. Infants born to teenage mothers, then, are at greater risk for developmental and physical problems that require special medical care. The younger the teen is the higher the chance that her baby will die in the first year of life.

Most teenage girls do not admit to being sexually active. When a young girl becomes pregnant she may not tell anyone because she is in denial or is scared. When a teen does not reveal that she is pregnant she puts herself and the fetus in serious danger. Teens are less likely to receive prenatal care when they hide their pregnancies from their family. Early and adequate prenatal care, preferably through a program that specializes in teenage pregnancies, ensures a healthier baby. The mother's health and that of the baby can depend on how mature the young woman is about keeping her doctor appointments and eating healthy. Sometimes, due to insurance limits or government policies, unmarried teens can be denied funding from the government or insurers, making safe pregnancies and deliveries difficult.

Adolescent mothers are more prone to smoke, use drugs, or consume alcohol during pregnancies than are older mothers. Their children are at increased risk of growth delay and dependence on chemical substances from the drug use. Adolescents' children are often in need of speech therapy because they are behind in development. Teen mothers are less prepared for the tasks of childrearing, know less about child development, and are more likely to be depressed than other mothers.

Adolescent mothers and their children are faced with the same effects as most single-mother families. Single-mother families are one parent raising the children and taking on the role of mother and father. Coupled with teen mothers' greater chances of living in poverty and having a special-needs child, the tasks of parenting can seem overwhelming. This leads to high levels of stress. Additionally, studies indicate that these women can have difficulty forming stable intimate relationships later. These concerns are compounded when the teen has inadequate social support.

Economy. One of the largest concerns regarding teen pregnancy is the poverty status of the teens and babies. Pregnancy reduces the likelihood of completing one's education, which, because the less educated a person is the harder it is to have a good job with benefits, leads to poverty. Around 40 percent of teen mothers receive their high school diplomas. Low academic achievement is both a cause and consequence of teen pregnancy. Estimates suggest that about one-half of all teen moms will receive welfare payments within five years of the birth of their first child. This percentage increases to three-quarters when only unmarried teen mothers are considered.

Teenage childbearing places both the teen mother and her child at risk for low educational attainment. Her children will look at her for a role model and if she got pregnant early and dropped out of school they may feel they should too. Women who grow up in poor families are more likely to have been the offspring of a teen pregnancy. The children of teen mothers are more likely to be living in poor neighborhoods where schools may be under-funded, are unsafe, or are of low quality, thus not preparing them for the future. The children of teen mothers, perhaps due to diminished opportunities, can suffer from depression and low self-esteem.

Social Support. The support of family and friends is very helpful and much needed in the circumstance of teen pregnancy. Family and friends might make it possible for the teen to stay in school and continue her education. They can encourage adequate nutrition and prenatal healthcare. It is clear that there are substantial societal costs from teen pregnancies in the form of lost human capital and public welfare outlays, but support for the teen can assist her in positive parenting and active economic participation.

Teenagers may become sexually active for a number of reasons. Depending on how mature their bodies are, whether they are spending time around sexually active people, or how much television viewing and magazine reading they do, they may develop attitudes consistent with the group. This is why it is not uncommon for friends to both become teen mothers, or for sisters to have similar early pregnancy experiences. The social network is important in the outcomes. Teens are more at risk of becoming pregnant if they grow up in poverty, use alcohol or drugs, have no support from their family, have fewer numbers of friends, and have little interest or involvement in school activities.

There are differences in how families respond to the pregnancy of a teen daughter. More white girls live independently with their child after the birth, suggesting that their parents may be less accepting of such an outcome. Unfortunately, the children of teens are disproportionately represented among the ranks of children who are abused and neglected, particularly when compared with the children of single mothers in their 20s. The children of teen mothers have a greater chance of themselves becoming teen parents, participating in delinquent acts, or being incarcerated.

CROSS-CULTURAL COMPARISONS OF TEENAGE PREGNANCY

Data are consistently clear: teenagers in the United States are significantly more likely than comparable women in other developed countries to become pregnant. The Netherlands, Norway, Sweden, Iceland, France, Australia, New Zealand, Great Britain, and Canada are among the countries that have significantly lower rates than those of the United States. This leads those who work with teens to hypothesize about what is different for U.S. teens. There are several proposed factors. One is access to contraceptives and other family planning services. Many other nations have national health care systems that significantly reduce the costs of such services, making them easily accessible to all persons. Additional suggestions include American teen's ambivalence toward sexuality. Even though the media are saturated with sexual themes, they rarely communicate responsible attitudes toward sexuality. High risk-taking and an alienation of some groups from what are considered middle-class values have also been considered.

POSITIVES OF TEEN PREGNANCY

While it seems that all of the news is bad regarding teen parenting and that more problems are created than solved, some positives can be found in the experiences of teens. Some teens might actually benefit from early childbearing. A small amount of teens planned to have their children. These teens are not likely to abuse or neglect their children. They usually finish school and go on to successfully support themselves and their families. These are the teens that are most likely to be married, either before or after the birth, to the father of the child.

General stereotypes of teen mothers describe them as single, poor heads of families, but most teen mothers age 15 to 19 are not living independently with their children. The vast majority lives with relatives, including parents and, sometimes, husbands. By ethnicity, it is whites who are most likely to be living independently and with husbands. African American and Mexican American teens are most likely to be living with family members. This co-residence can provide significant support, both emotionally and financially. Through child care and other family-provided services, young mothers may still be able to finish school and gain solid employment. In this way, pregnancy and mothering may only delay, not deny, their pursuit of successful adult lives. Some economists have indicated that black teens gain less of an economic advantage by waiting to have children than do white teens. The common stereotype of irresponsible teens who behave irrationally by becoming pregnant may need to be reconsidered when it is a response to deficient and discriminatory opportunities.

In some cases teen pregnancy can be a way out of a troubled home life. Teens suggest that the true benefits of child bearing are having someone to love and someone that loves them. Sometimes the birth of a child can help them to heal scars from their own childhood. Some teens have suggested that they have used pregnancy as a way to leave an abusive home.

CONTROVERSIES OF TEEN PREGNANCY

Is Teen Pregnancy a Problem?

While the rates of teen pregnancies reached a historic low in 2004, it does not take the focus away from the situation because there are still teenage girls getting pregnant. Politicians, columnists, educators, researchers, and communities continue to argue that it is a serious problem. Almost every bad situation in society is blamed on teen pregnancies. Single parenting, poverty, delinquent children, school failure, drug abuse, child abuse, and crime have all pointed to teen pregnancy and birth as contributing factors. It seems that politicians use these data to raise the alarm in society and draw the public to their campaigns, often with the suggestion that ending poverty will be possible if teen pregnancies stop. Teen pregnancy can contribute to a given young person's chances of being poor, but it does not cause poverty. Many of these girls were living in poverty before getting pregnant. Consequently, teen pregnancy may just be the scapegoat for other social problems.

Sociologist Kristin Luker argues that adolescent girls are placed in the middle of a conflict between political factions that debate the issue of abstinence-only sex education compared with more comprehensive approaches. She argues that the phenomenon of teen pregnancy has been misidentified. Specifically, she indicates that teen pregnancies do not only occur in the United States. While our rates might be higher, the problem is not uniquely ours. However, the racial and social class distribution of teen births causes many in the United States to see them as a problem. Significantly the rates have been declining and are not out of control largely due to improved contraceptive use, particularly of long-acting contraception that does not require daily administration. Given that rates of sexual activity have increased over the same period that teen birth rates have declined, the pregnancy rates could be significantly higher than they are. Young people are physically mature at early ages today, the consequence of better nutrition and overall health, and development of their sexuality accompanies that. Luker also reminds us that the teen birth rate is not new; the mothers of the baby boom often began their childrearing in their late teens.

One of the interesting co-issues of teen pregnancy is why teen mothers are treated so much worse than are teen fathers. Females face many more negative attributions than do males. The message to young females seems to be that we are okay with you exploring your sexuality, just don't get pregnant while doing so. Given that it takes both partners for conception, one wonders when the fathers will receive comparable scrutiny.

Should Pregnant Teens Marry the Fathers of their Babies?

A popular suggestion for decreasing the negative effects of adolescent childbearing is for teens to marry the fathers of their children. They already receive pressure to declare the father's identity in order to receive state child support payments through public assistance. In the past, teens were more likely to marry before the birth. Today, however, only about 20 percent of teens marry the child's father before the birth.

When teens are encouraged to and actually get married their children have a better prospect for success later in life simply because they will have a two-parent family. The two-parent family has many documented advantages over single-parent families. Greater financial stability and more complete socialization of children are cited as reasons why teens should marry. Teens might even hear the suggestion that they have already made one mistake by becoming pregnant, they don't want to make another by failing to provide legitimacy for the child. Teen marriages are actually more stable when children are present, but on the whole teen marriages are particularly prone to end in divorce.

Marrying, then, might be the bigger mistake. Most teenage girls do not get pregnant by a teenage boy but by an older male. Data indicate that more than 50 percent of the fathers of teen mothers' babies are between the ages of 20 and 24, around 30 percent of the fathers are adolescents themselves, and 15 percent are 25 or older. When teen mothers do marry they tend to become pregnant again very quickly.

The suggestion that teens should marry the fathers of their babies fails to consider the long-term issues. The higher rates of dissolution were mentioned above. In both the United States and abroad, premarital pregnancy is correlated with a higher rate of divorce. When men are at least five years older or younger than their wives they are more likely to divorce. There are also maturity and readiness factors to consider. Lack of coping skills, inadequate preparation for marriage, and fewer life experiences contribute to marital dissatisfaction. There might also be less support from the couple's friends and family for the marriage, which decreases the social pressure for the couple to stay together.

Is Adoption the Answer?

In the current climate of decreased negativity toward nonmarital childbearing, it seems unlikely that large numbers of teens will surrender their babies for adoption. With the stigma of teen parenting significantly decreased, they may face more negativity for giving the child up for someone else to rear. It has always been the case that more white girls than black girls placed their children for adoption, and that pattern holds today. However, the rapid decline in numbers of healthy white infants available via adoption has changed the adoption industry and pushed more families to adopt internationally.

Adoption may be the answer in that it permits the teen to get on with her life and allows her child the opportunity to have a two-parent family. Those teens that place their infants for adoption tend to be older, white, have higher educational goals, and are more likely to complete additional job training. They are more likely than teens that rear their children themselves to delay marriage and to live in higher-income households. Certainly there is initial sorrow and regret over the decision to relinquish a child, but these tend to be short-term experiences.

CONCLUSION

Teenage mothers and their children are at risk of difficulty in the areas of social environment, education, and economics. The major focus on teen parents is on the socioeconomic outcomes of the mother. Literature on teenage mothers continues to show negative long term consequences for early childbearing, including consistently low levels of education and a greater dependency on welfare. In some cases people tend to see teen parents as uneducated, intolerant, impatient, insensitive, irritable, and prone to use both verbal and physical punishment. There is evidence that they are more likely than other parents to abuse their children. Economic success greatly depends on continuing school and not having more children. Older literature describes teen mothers as neglectful and unintelligent, but as research is updated there are more positive effects of teenage parenting for the women and children involved.

See also Abortion; Birth Control; Marriage Promotion; Poverty and Public Assistance; Premarital Sexual Relations.

Further Reading: Annie E. Casey Foundation. http://www.aecf.org; Darrock, J. E., and S. Singh. "Why is Teenage Pregnancy Declining? The Roles of Abstinence, Sexual Activity, and Contraceptive Use." In *Occasional Report*, no. 1. New York: The Alan Guttmacher Institute,

1999; Davis, Deborah. *You Look Too Young to be a Mom: Teen Mothers on Love, Learning, and Success.* New York: Perigee, 2004; Gottfried, Ted. *Teen Fathers Today.* Brookfield, CT: Twenty-First Century Books, 2001; Luker, Kristin. *Dubious Conceptions: The Politics of Teenage Pregnancy.* Cambridge, MA: Harvard University Press, 1996; National Campaign to Prevent Teen and Unplanned Pregnancy. http://www.thenationalcampaign.org; Planned Parenthood Federation of America, Inc. http://www.plannedparenthood.org; Williams-Wheeler, Dorrie. *The Unplanned Pregnancy Book for Teens and College Students.* Virginia Beach, VA: Sparkledoll Productions Publishing, 2004.

Santarica Buford

TRANSITION TO PARENTHOOD

Although there has been an increase in the number of childfree couples, the vast majority of Americans will, eventually, have at least one child. While most people are aware that children are economic liabilities, most still wish to become parents and the desire seems to be quite strong among both women and men. The reasons why individuals choose to become parents are multiple and complex. Many couples feel that they are not really a family without children. Some have a desire to carry on their family name and traditions or to solidify their relationship. Others may wish to see themselves or their partner in a child or may feel that a child gives them a sense of immortality. Still others may feel that becoming a parent is the ultimate expression of selflessness and the best way to give something back to the next generation. Taken together, these issues of timing of children and how parents adjust to the presence of their children are examined as the transition to parenthood.

With advances in technology, having a child today is largely a matter of choice. Increasingly, couples decide whether or not, how many, and when to have children, with the current trend being delayed parenthood. However, social and cultural factors exert a great deal of pressure on married couples to make this choice. Most religious traditions emphasize the importance of childbearing; some require it. Government and economic policies also provide incentives to have children. Newly married couples are often encouraged by family members and friends to have children. Popular culture, such as women's magazines and programming aimed at women, idealizes parenthood, especially mothering. The idea that all women should become mothers is known as compulsory motherhood. Popular images portray babies as cute, fun, and easily managed. Furthermore, many assume that parenting comes naturally and that no formal training is needed. Collectively, religious, socio-cultural, and economic pressures to have children may be thought of as a cultural press for childrearing.

RELATIONSHIP ISSUES

The birth of a child results in a number of significant and often unanticipated life changes. Unfortunately, as children, most Americans are quite sheltered and shielded from adult-like responsibility, including child- or sibling-care and therefore have very little actual experience in this regard. Studies find that having children may impact a relationship positively or negatively. Many first-time parents experience identity changes upon the birth of a child. More than any other experience, becoming a parent seems to confer adult status. New parents may also feel that their social ties are expanded, particularly those to extended family and to other parents. Having children increases one's social network in a variety of ways, especially through establishing connections to outside institutions, such as religion and education. Many parents report that having children brings joy and novelty to their lives while others feel that it gives them a sense of immortality. Children may also provide a purpose to one's life; this is especially true for those whose jobs or careers are not intrinsically meaningful.

While children provide some emotional and social rewards to couples, social scientists have paid more attention to the negative effects of having children; some have even described the transition to parenthood as a crisis. The reasons for this description are multiple: parenthood is not a role or life choice that can be reversed; most first-time parents have had very little or no experience in child rearing; becoming a parent necessitates a number of other life changes, such as those in the marital or professional realm; and finally, the transition to parenthood is not gradual, but abrupt. In addition, parenting is probably the best example of a one-sided relationship—parents give and children take. In one study of several expectant first-time mothers and fathers, it was found that almost all of the fathers and a majority of the mothers expressed worry or concern about becoming parents. Furthermore, babies are born with different temperaments—some easy, others difficult. Parents who are fortunate enough to have an easy baby may begin to feel confident and competent in their parenting abilities, while those with more difficult babies may develop feelings of inadequacy and disappointment with the parenting experience.

A consistent finding is that parenthood results in a decline in marital satisfaction. While marital satisfaction drops for both men and women, the decline appears to be sharper for women. Adjustment difficulties may occur if and when preparental expectations are incongruent with experiences. Persons who have inaccurate or unrealistic expectations are likely to experience strain and disappointment. In general, individuals whose expectations for parenthood are violated experience parenthood more negatively. Violated expectations for how housework and child care responsibilities will be allocated also have a negative impact on the parenting experience. It is estimated that mothers spend double or even the triple the time fathers do in daily care activities, such as bathing, clothing, feeding, and looking after young children. In addition to the hands-on work associated with parenting, women are more likely to attend to children's emotional needs. Because of social pressure and cultural expectations, mothers may possess more of a parental consciousness, a constant state of psychological awareness and concern for their children. Collectively, these may be some of the reasons why marital satisfaction following the birth of a child drops more significantly for women than for men.

Although less has been written on the subject, attention is now being given to the matter of fathers' adjustment to parenthood. During pregnancy, men may feel left out and jealous of their wives. Because men receive very little formal or even informal training for parenthood, they may also feel inadequate holding, bathing, or caring for their new baby. Unfortunately, new mothers (or members of the extended family, such as grandmothers) often reinforce these feelings by discouraging or even denying men the opportunity to participate in infant care. Some men may feel that their partners pay more attention to the baby than to them, which could result in feelings of jealousy or resentment. In addition, because men are taught that successful fathering is demonstrated through successful providing, new fathers may experience a great deal of stress as they try to meet the economic demands of an expanding family, often while their wives or partners are decreasing their contribution to household income.

EMPLOYMENT ISSUES

Most women who become mothers today work throughout the majority of their pregnancies or take only a short leave of absence when they give birth. In the United States, managing the demands of work and family is considered a private matter. As a result, few employers in the United States offer paid maternity leave. Consequently, women typically work as late into their pregnancies as they can and return to work soon after the birth. The United States is unique in this regard; most northern European countries offer at least some amount of paid leave to mothers, and many offer leave to fathers as well. In Sweden, for example, employees receive 80 to 100 percent of their salary for about a year so that they can be on leave to care for their child.

In the late 1990s, over two-thirds of women worked during their pregnancies; in the 1960s, just over 40 percent did. In the 1960s, only about 14 percent of mothers returned to work within six months of the birth of their child, whereas in the 1990s, about 57 percent did so. To complicate matters more, very few employers in the United States offer paid maternity leave, expecting employees to use vacation leave, sick leave, or some sort of disability compensation to pay them while they recover from the birth. Therefore, today, women who choose to become parents and to work outside of the home (which most do) face the possibility of role conflict, overload, and exhaustion. The changes and difficulties associated with the transition to parenthood result in postpartum depression in about 10 percent of mothers. Interestingly, contrary to conventional wisdom, women without children are not more likely to be depressed or anxious. In fact, there is evidence to suggest that childfree women (that is, women who have chosen not to have children) experience higher levels of psychological well-being than women with children.

PREGNANCY ISSUES

While pregnancy, labor, and delivery are physical experiences, they are also influenced by socio-cultural factors. The popular media tends to highlight the beauty, mystery, and femininity of the pregnancy experience (especially among the Hollywood elite) without giving adequate attention to the physical and emotional challenges associated with carrying a child to term. Generally, pregnancy is depicted or described along the lines of one extreme or the other. In some instances, pregnancy is romanticized and exalted as the most fulfilling experience of a woman's life. Religious groups and traditional women's literature (*e.g.*, magazines) tend to portray pregnancy as an experience that every woman desires and should have. On the other hand, movies may also depict pregnancy and other functions specific to women's physiology as painful, dangerous, or dirty. Of course, the reality is that most women's pregnancy experiences fall somewhere between these two extremes. In one study, about one-third of mothers described the time of their pregnancies as emotionally and physically satisfying. The majority of women, however, described pregnancy in less ideal terms. Many talked about the physical discomfort of pregnancy and the feeling of being out of control. Others talked about the limitations pregnancy posed to their normal, daily routines.

COMMUNICATION ISSUES

In addition to unrealistic or violated expectations, another factor affecting relationship quality during the transition to parenthood is couples' communication and other couple dynamics. Often, the birth of a child results in less or different types of communication between partners. Spouses may find that they either have little time to converse with each other or that their conversations rarely involve topics other than children. Couples may also find that the division of household labor, as well as the division of paid labor, becomes more traditional or segregated once children are present. Even couples who maintained a fairly egalitarian division of labor prior to the birth will often find that this balance is difficult to maintain afterwards. Once children arrive, men tend to spend more time and invest more energy in paid work, while women tend to spend more time and invest more energy in unpaid work. This type of role segregation can result in resentments and misunderstandings; partners may find it more difficult to empathize with one another. Women, more so than men, are likely to report feeling distracted or less productive at work once becoming a parent.

Of course, prebirth patterns are predictive of postbirth patterns. Couples with effective communication skills before the birth, whose relationships were characterized by warmth and support, and those with effective conflict resolution strategies will tend to fare better after the birth of a child. In fact, their levels of marital satisfaction may not decline and may even improve. One longitudinal study found that couples who wanted and actively planned for the birth of a child did not experience a drop in marital satisfaction. It has been found that delaying the transition to parenthood may offset some of the strains experienced by early first-time mothers and fathers. Couples whose relationships are strained, who engage in negative or critical communication of one another, or who have poor conflict resolution skills, are likely to find that the quality of their relationship declines even further once a child is born. Having a baby does not improve troubled or devitalized marriages; it tends to increase levels of strain and exaggerate preexisting problems.

POSTPARTUM DEPRESSION

Perhaps 70 to 80 percent of new mothers experience some degree of the so-called baby blues after giving birth. This typically involves a combination of emotions such as depression, anxiety, loneliness, and guilt. Normally, these feelings subside within a few days or a couple of weeks. However, about 10 percent of women experience postpartum depression, a much more serious condition which requires medical intervention. Postpartum depression is thought to result from a number of factors, some physical and others that are related to lifestyle. It is true that women experience severe hormonal fluctuations after giving birth, and such changes may result in sharp and unpredictable changes in mood. In addition to physiological changes, however, the birth of a child results in significant lifestyle changes, such as loss of sleep, lack of flexibility and spontaneity, increased domestic work and more time spent at home, modifications to one's career, as well as marital or relationship changes. All of these changes occur very abruptly. Women are almost always the primary caretakers of infants; therefore, the transition to parenthood affects them in more direct, more numerous, and more significant ways than it does men. In addition to these life changes, most women are taught to believe that motherhood will be the most fulfilling experience of their lives. There is very little preparation for parenthood and almost no attention given to the difficult and problematic changes that it often brings—financial, professional, marital, and personal. Thus, many women find that they are not only unprepared for motherhood but also less satisfied and fulfilled by it than they expected. Depression may result as women try to cope with feelings of parental inadequacy. New mothers are especially susceptible to feelings of shame and guilt if they do not bond with or attach to their infants. Because many women and men believe in the existence of a maternal instinct even though there is no empirical evidence to support such an instinct in humans, most mothers expect to bond instantly with their newborns. When this does not occur, women may feel that they are unfit or undeserving of the motherhood role. Furthermore, many women are uncomfortable sharing their feelings with others because they believe they are supposed to be happy during this time.

Women who find that they are experiencing feelings associated with postpartum depression should talk with their spouse or partner, friends, or other family members and they will most likely want to consult with their primary care physician, obstetrician, midwife, or counselor. There are several strategies for working through this type of depression, including talk therapy, medicinal therapy, or involvement with support groups, especially those designed for new mothers. Women are urged to take care of themselves, eat properly, get enough rest, and pursue hobbies or activities that are enjoyable and relaxing. In addition, new mothers should be careful not to spend too much time alone or in the home. Contacts with others and outside activities can help to alleviate some of the symptoms associated with postpartum depression.

FINANCIAL ISSUES

The transition to parenthood is also experienced financially. Each year, the United States Department of Agriculture estimates the cost of rearing a child through the age of 17. A child born in the year 1997 will cost between $220,000 and $440,000. This amount varies by social class with higher-income families spending considerably more on each child. This may be one reason why couples with higher incomes and levels of education are more likely to limit their childbearing. Interestingly, economic considerations do not factor into the decision for most prospective parents, especially for the first two children. Child care is one of the greatest expenses facing most new parents. Child care arrangements are affected by family income, marital status, and women's work schedules. With a weak economy and more people, both men and women, of all ages having to work outside of the home, fewer members of the family, such as aunts or grandmothers, are available to provide informal child care.

Having children is associated with a number of opportunity costs as well. These may not be experienced as direct financial costs, but they often carry long-term or indirect financial implications. Having a child typically results in a lower investment in paid work, especially for mothers. Women who take time off from paid work when they have a child experience lower lifetime earnings and fewer promotional opportunities. Workers who appear to prioritize family obligations over work are often judged as less committed and less reliable employees. Thus, employers are not as likely to invest in them.

SHARED PARENTING

In order to cope with some of the anticipated changes and threats to relationship quality that parenthood often brings, some couples may opt to engage in what is known as shared parenting. Shared parenting involves not only an overlap of roles but also of identities. Couples who adopt the shared parenting approach assume that both mothers and fathers are primary parents, rather than the more conventional approach that assumes that fathers parent on a supplementary or part-time basis and that mothers are the primary psychological and practical parent. Several factors influence whether or not a couple may opt for shared parenting. Studies indicate that family members or families who embrace shared parenting (1) consider themselves feminists or were influenced positively by the feminist movement; (2) typically involve partners who both have steady, secure employment; or (3) involve fathers who hold nontraditional or child-oriented careers, such as those in child development or child psychology. Interestingly, recent research indicates that fathers, as well as mothers, have had varied experiences historically. Rigid, stereotypical beliefs regarding the roles of men and women as parents may be less accurate than many believe. On a positive note, shared parenting appears to increase partners' feelings of parental competence as well as relationship quality. It also seems to decrease behavior problems in children. One negative consequence of shared parenting may be a reduction in couples' time alone.

See also Birth Control; Birth Order; Breast Feeding and Formula Feeding; Childbirth Options; Childfree Relationships; Cosleeping; Infertility; Marital Satisfaction; Mommy Track; Motherhood Opportunity Costs; Parenting Styles.

Further Reading: Belsky, Jay, and John Kelly. *The Transition to Parenthood: How a First Child Changes a Marriage; Why Some Couples Grow Closer and Others Apart.* New York: Delacorte

Press, 1995; Coltrane, Scott, and Michele Adams. *Gender and Families*. Lanham, MD: Rowman and Littlefield Publishers, 2008; Coltrane, Scott. *Family Man: Fatherhood, Housework, and Gender Equity*. New York: Oxford University Press, 1996; Crittenden, Ann. *The Price of Motherhood: Why the Most Important Job in the World is Still the Least Valued*. New York: Henry Holt and Company, 2002; Crittenden, Ann. *If You've Raised Kids, You Can Manage Anything: Leadership Begins at Home*. New York: Gotham Press, 2005; Ehrensaft, Diane. *Parenting Together: Men and Women Sharing the Care of Their Children*. Champaign: University of Illinois Press, 1990; Gottman, John. *And Baby Makes Three: The Six-Step Plan for Preserving Marital Intimacy and Rekindling Romance After Baby Arrives*. New York: Three Rivers Press, 2008; Hass, Aaron. *The Gift of Fatherhood: How Men's Lives are Transformed By Their Children*. New York: Fireside Publications, 1994; Marsiglio, William, and Sally Hutchinson. *Sex, Men, and Babies: Stories of Awareness and Responsibility*. New York: New York University Press, 2004; Taylor, Verta. *Rock-a-by Baby: Feminism, Self-Help, and Postpartum Depression*. New York: Routledge, 1996.

Susan Cody-Rydzewski

TRANSRACIAL ADOPTION

Transracial or interracial adoptions have been debated since the 1950s and 1960s when black children started to be included regularly on adoption agency lists. During that time, Asian children were also entering the United States in adoption arrangements. Transracial adoption is when a family of one race legally adopts a child from a different race. The first transracial adoption on record was in 1948 in Minnesota when Caucasian parents adopted an African American child. The most common form of transracial adoption in the United States is the adoption of a black child by white parents. There are several reasons that influence a couple's choice to adopt transracially, such as limited numbers of white children, some people feeling a connection to a different race, and some people just wanting to adopt a child, regardless of their race. Many advocates of transracial adoption feel that a loving family of any race is essential for a child, yet there are many others that firmly believe that children should be placed within their own race.

BACKGROUND

In the post–World War II era, adoption was institutionalized to cater to the white middle class. At this time, the societal ideal was to marry and start a family, but some couples were unable to have biological children. These couples turned to adoption as a way to fulfill their family goals. These families were perfect for agencies to adopt white infants into because they were economically stable. In addition to economic stability, adoption agencies required families to provide a suitable home where the child would have his or her own bedroom and a full-time mother. These rules prevented most black families from being eligible to adopt a child. Through the 1970s adoption agencies were run by white social workers who could place white healthy babies or so-called blue-ribbon babies more easily than they could place black babies. The rules were so rigorous that black couples had difficulty complying and therefore withdrew their applications from consideration. Many black pregnant women were denied the option to put their children up for adoption. These women were sent to the welfare agencies instead because black babies as well as children with disabilities were categorized as unadoptable.

Transracial adoptions gained popularity in the 1950s and peaked through the 1960s and 1970s. With fewer healthy white infants available for adoption, adoption agencies began to consider placing a child of color into the home of a white family. The main reasons for the increase in transracial adoptions were long adoption waiting periods and a decreased number of white babies available due to advances in birth control, abortion, and societal acceptance of single mothers. The Civil Rights Movement has also been credited as a cause of the increases in transracial adoptions.

The National Health Interview Survey found that 8 percent of adoptions were transracial in 1987. In the year 1998, the estimate of transracial or transcultural adoptions was 15 percent of the 36,000 foster children that were adopted. In 2004, 1.6 million children were adopted in the United States. Out of the 1.6 million adopted, 17 percent were interracial adoptions and 13 percent were foreign born, according to the U.S. Census Bureau.

THE DEBATE

The numbers of transracial adoptions have increased, sparking controversy between those who do not believe that a white family can raise an African American child and those who believe that children are entitled to a loving home, no matter what racial barriers there are. The largest adversary of transracial adoptions historically and currently is the National Association of Black Social Workers (NABSW). Native Americans also oppose transracial adoptions, claiming that this practice is cultural genocide.

ARGUMENTS AGAINST TRANSRACIAL ADOPTION

One of the main arguments against transracial adoption is that white parents will not be able to give a black child a cultural identity and survival skills in a racially diverse society. NABSW says that child socialization begins at birth, but the needs of black children differ from those of white children. Black children need to learn coping mechanisms to function in a society where racism is prevalent. Black families are capable of teaching these mechanisms in everyday life without having to seek out special projects or activities. They live their lives in a white-dominated society and their children learn by daily interactions. Even when white adoptive families actively seek out interactions and activities with black families, they put an emphasis on the differences within their family.

Cultural support can be especially difficult to give if there is limited understanding of the cultural differences of family members. Caucasians are ill-equipped in their understanding of African American culture to adequately prepare a child for life in an ethnic group other than that of the adoptive parents. Despite the best intentions, Caucasians can not fully understand life from a minority perspective because they only experience it vicariously. The unique experiences of African Americans since their arrival on American soil means that parenting strategies and coping mechanisms have been developed to help deflect hostility from the dominant members of society. Additionally, racial barriers exist in many different aspects of social life.

Over time, there has been a decline in the availability of white children to adopt. NABSW feels that white families adopt a black child so they do not have to wait for long periods of time to become parents. Adoption agencies cater to white middle class prospective adoptive parents and because white children are not as available the agencies try to persuade these families to adopt black children.

NABSW supports adoption agencies finding black families to adopt black children. They suggest that agencies should change adoption requirements so that black families wanting to adopt are not quickly eliminated from the process. They also would like to see adoption agencies work harder to find extended family members who want to adopt and keep the child within the family. Financial help should also be available for these families so adopted children have the opportunity to grow, develop, and socialize within the black community. In fact, NABSW has argued that the so-called genocide that results from the adoption of black children by white families could never promote the interests and well-being of black children.

In 1971, William T. Merritt, then president of NABSW, stated that black children that are in foster care or are adopted should only be in the home of a black family. His position paper the following year reiterated his perspective and as a consequence of the advocacy of NABSW national adoption guidelines were changed to favor or promote race-matching. In 1973, transracial placements decreased by 39 percent. In 1985, Merritt claimed that black children raised in white homes could not learn skills to function as a black person in society. He adamantly spoke out against transracial adoptions. Morris Jeff Jr., another past president of NABSW, called transracial adoption "the ultimate insult to black heritage."

Children who are adopted can sometimes face certain concerns regardless of the adoptive parents' ethnicity. These problems, however, can become more intense when also dealing with racial barriers. Children placed for adoption have usually come from homes where abuse was common. They may be of an age to remember their biological parents and have unresolved conflicts because they were, in their minds, unwanted by their biological families. They often have to learn new ways of family life. In addition to adjustment issues, children who are adopted often have mental, physical, or emotional handicaps. Because adoption itself may require the child to make adjustments, the presence of racial identity questions just enhances the difficulty of transitions.

Adoption comes with a certain stigma and children who are adopted may face identity issues. Even though they accept their adoptive parents and families and appreciate being a part of the family, adopted children often have an intense desire to know their biological parents. Research shows that both adoptive parents and adult adoptees experience feelings of being stigmatized by others who question the strength of their ties with their adoptive families. This stigma can be heightened when the adoptee's ethnicity is different from that of the adoptive family.

Along with the cultural barriers and stigma of adoption, many opposed to transracial adoption say that there are enough black families interested in adoption to eliminate the placement of black children with white families. The National Urban League identified at least three million black families in the year 2000 who were interested in adoption. Adoption agencies have been faulted for contributing to the low numbers of available black adoptive families compared with white adoptive families. Critics say that many agencies do not have enough black social workers who are competent to make assessments of black families. Black families seeking to adopt may not receive equal treatment with their white counterparts, a situation that could be improved through the employment of more black social workers in adoption agencies.

ARGUMENTS FOR TRANSRACIAL ADOPTION

Legislation has stepped in to terminate discrimination in the adoption process and eliminate race as the sole factor when determining the placement of a child for adoption. The Multi Ethnic Placement Act in 1994 was created to prohibit those agencies or entities that receive money from the federal government from using race, color, or national origin as the critical criteria in the adoptive or foster parent or child decisions. While the Multi Ethnic Placement Act made improvements to the process of transracial adoptions, it still allowed for agencies to take into consideration whether prospective parents could adequately care for a child from a different race. The passage of the Adoption and Safe Families Act (1996) eliminated the use of any form of discriminatory tactics that would not allow prospective parents to transracially adopt. Any states that broke the laws would face reductions in their quarterly federal funds.

Those favoring transracial adoptions say that the statistics alone should be reason enough to disregard race as the determining factor in placement. In the year 2000, according to the U.S. Department of Health and Human Services, there were 118,000 children awaiting adoption in the U.S. and 40 percent of those were black children. In addition to the disproportionate number of black children compared with white children who are waiting to be adopted, the average black child waits more than four years before a permanent placement is obtained. Some of these inequities may be relieved if more transracial placements occurred.

The argument that suggests that harm will come to transracial adoptees because of the obviousness of the adoption and the constant reminder of being adopted may be interpreted positively. A child who is of a different race will learn sooner that he or she is adopted and being forced to recognize this will make the adoption easier to talk about, thus making for a more open relationship with the parents. It has been suggested that there are direct benefits to the child in

ADVICE FOR RACIALLY MIXED FAMILIES

The National Adoption Clearinghouse provides specific advice for families going through transracial adoptions to help with the adjustment and growth process. The following are among the suggestions offered to parents by the experts.

Become an intensely invested parent by being hands-on with parenting. Understanding the difficulties transracially adopted children experience and helping them create cultural identities is part of parenting.

Do not tolerate any racially or ethnically biased remarks. If someone makes an unacceptable remark about race, ethnic diversity, gender, or anything else tell them that they should not say things like that in front of children. Allow them to take back their negative remarks without starting an argument. Fighting never solves anything. Standing up for your beliefs shows your child that disagreements can be solved rationally.

Take advantage of the support of family and friends. Every family thrives when they give each other support. It is beneficial to also find other transracial families and families of your child's same race or culture. This allows your family to interact with others who have similar experiences.

Celebrate all cultures. This is a key way to experience and accept diversity in our communities. Finding festivals or other events that celebrate your child's culture helps him or her to develop an identity. Experiencing other cultures also enhances your and your child's understanding of others. You and your child can discuss similarities and differences between all cultures.

Communicate openly about race and culture. Open communication allows adopted children to know they can talk to their parents about both positive and negative issues. Children need to know their parents will support them and stand up for them when they need help. Parents can get advice on how to handle racial issues from friends of the same race or culture as their child.

Help your child experience a variety of activities to build self-esteem. Many people have negative feelings toward differences in families, so finding activities that your child thrives in helps to build self-esteem. Encouragement and praise lets children know that you are proud of them.

Visit places that have people predominantly from your child's race or ethnic group. This permits the child to gain exposure to their culture and lets parents experience the feeling of being the minority in the group. Parents will have a better understanding of what their children encounter daily.

---

learning early about the adoption. They include a greater openness about the adoption, a positive self-identification with the adoptive status as well as racial identity, and recognition that there is no shared biology between the parents and child. Additionally, there is a positive affirmation for the child that he or she was chosen and wanted. Given that adoptive families are often open about the adoption and encourage their other-race children to get involved with the children's heritage, black children adopted by white parents are more likely to refer to themselves as black than are black children adopted within race. As a consequence of having to learn about more than one culture, studies suggest that these children have a greater tolerance for others different from themselves and are more accepting of cultural differences.

Because the adopted child knows that he or she was wanted by the family, there is also recognition that race is not a factor in how much the child will be loved. This visible reminder that the child was chosen to be a part of the family can help to increase the child's self-esteem. The visible differences can also help to remind the child that he or she does not share biology with the parents, but psychologically this can help the child realize that differences with the parents are expected and are not frowned upon. Any genetic expectations would be decreased as well so the child might feel less pressure to develop the same interests or talents as the parent.

Other concerns regarding the psychological health of transracially adopted persons have also been disputed. Many studies have refuted the claim that white parents are ill equipped to raise socially adapted African American children with high levels of self-esteem. While this is a classic debate used by those opposed to transracial adoption, research data suggest that there are no significant differences in adjustment between transracially adopted children and those adopted within race. The most important factor influencing how the child adjusted to society is the age of the child at the time of adoption. Likewise, studies have not found a correlation between a child's adjustment and racial identity. It seems that the older a child is when adopted the more problems there are with adjustment issues. However, this seemed to be the outcome whether the child was adopted by same-race or other-race parents.

The Simon-Altstein Longitudinal Study of adoption was a classic study that examined several aspects of transracial adoption. The study began in 1972, had three phases, and involved 204 families with non-white adopted children. The first phase of interviews asked the children about their racial identity by using the Kenneth Clark doll test. This phase concluded that the study children, non-white and white, had no racial biases to either a black or white color doll. All knew their racial identities. Parents indicated that they used several means to introduce the racial culture of the adopted non-white children in the family.

The second phase of the study, conducted in 1983, measured self-esteem. The results of black, non-white, white adopted children, and white biological children were separated and compared. All groups had statistically equal levels of self-esteem. The transracially adopted children were asked about their relationships with their parents and white siblings. Most said that their relationship with their parents was better now in young adulthood than it had been when they were adolescents. Interestingly, this relationship finding was the same between biological children and parents. Racial differences had no impact in most of the relationships between the transracially adopted children and their siblings that were the biological children of their shared parents. Transracially adopted children and biological children were almost equal in choosing a parent or sibling as the ones to whom they would go if they needed help, at 46.8 percent and 45 percent, respectively.

The third phase of this study, conducted in 1991, asked again to whom they would go if they needed help. The results showed that the adopted children would still turn to their parents or siblings for help. The study's overall findings provided strong evidence that white parents are capable of raising children of another race to have high self-esteem, positive identities, and close family ties.

LOOKING AHEAD

There are several issues that families must consider before committing to transracial adoption. The most important thing to consider is the potential parents' own racial views. Another thing to consider is that the family will be in the minority after transracially adopting. Of concern may be how the parent and other members of the family will deal with opinions expressed by those outside of the family. Prospective parents could think about adopting siblings so that each child will have a familiar face to help with the transition.

Colorblind is a term frequently used by those who promote transracial adoptions. This refers to the ideal that everyone is seen equally and is not discriminated against due to race. Colorblind is used in adoption discussions because it is illegal for adoption agencies to discriminate because of someone's skin color. In matching parents and children for adoption, the United States will probably never be a society that is totally colorblind. Colorblindness helps to promote fairness with regard to race, a difficult but necessary task. On the other hand, critics of the concept of colorblind contend that it erases a person's heritage and culture. Being colorblind does not erase the questions that arise about visual differences within families and communities. Ignoring differences can cause hurt and resentment. Because race and culture are so heavily linked, to be colorblind to someone's race is to ignore his or her culture. Experts contend that children have a right to learn about their culture so that they can pass it down to the next generation.

Transracial adoption is not only a black and white issue; children are also adopted from foreign countries, although there is very little research to date on the adjustment experiences of these parents and children. Places like China and Russia are popular when families decide to adopt because the high birth rates and poor economic conditions in these locales mean that there are often children readily available. There is not as much debate about the adoption of these children as there is over black children being adopted by white families because adoption is seen as helping these children. The idea of saving a child is an idea that supporters of transracial adoption believe can happen right here in the United States by decreasing the numbers of children of all races awaiting placement with a permanent family.

See also Biological Privilege; Fictive Kin; Gay Parent Adoption; Infertility; International Adoption.

Further Reading: Adoption History: National Association of Black Social Workers. "Position Statement on Trans-Racial Adoption." September 1972. http://darkwing.uroegon.edu/~adoption/archive/NabswTRA.htm; Adoption Media. http://www.adoption.com;

Campbell, Suzanne B. "Taking Race out of the Equation: Transracial Adoption in 2000." *Southern Methodist University Law Review* 53 (2000): 1599; Children's Home Society of Washington. http://www.chswpirc.org; Child Welfare Information Gateway. http://www.childwelfare.gov; Fogg-Davis, Hawley. *The Ethics of Transracial Adoption.* New York: Cornell University Press, 2002; John, Jaiya. *Black Baby, White Hands: A View from the Crib.* Silver Spring, MD: Soul Water Rising, 2005; Patton, Sandra. *BirthMarks: Transracial Adoption in Contemporary America.* New York: New York University Press, 2000; Quiroz, Pamela Ann. *Adoption in a Color-Blind Society.* Lanham, MD: Rowman and Littlefield, 2007; Simon, Rita J., and Rhonda M. Roorda. *In Their Own Voices Transracial Adoptees Tell Their Stories.* New York: Columbia University Press, 2000; Simon, Rita J., and Rhonda M. Roorda. *In Their Parents' Voices: Reflections on Raising Transracial Adoptees.* New York: Columbia University Press, 2007; Swize, Jennifer. "Transracial Adoption and the Unblinkable Difference: Racial Dissimilarity Serving the Interests of Adopted Children." *Virginia Law Review* 88, no. 5 (2002): 1079–1118; Transracial Adoption Research and Consultation. http://www.transracialadoption.net; United States Department of Health and Human Services. http://www.hhs.gov.

Taralyn Watson

W

WEDDING AND ELOPING

From a very early age, girls dream of getting married to that special guy. Getting the guy seems to be the challenge, but they soon find out that the planning of the wedding surpasses that hurdle. Weddings require lots of time and attention to detail. With the elaborate nature that ceremonial weddings have taken on in this day and age, more and more people are considering eloping instead. Weddings are public ceremonies that involve huge amounts of planning by all who are involved. The average American engagement is 16 months long with the average age of the bride being 25.3 years old. The groom averages 26.9 years of age. On the other hand, elopements are very private affairs with few people in attendance and require less planning than the average wedding. There are substantive differences between the two choices, but each has in common a legally binding contract and both mark the beginning of a couple's life together.

POSITIVES OF A WEDDING

Weddings are a tradition that are as old as time. They have changed with the times and have evolved into events for the ages. But when it is your wedding, it can be done your way. The choices are endless. A wedding is a ceremony that signifies the beginning of a marriage or a union between two people. They also often signify a rite of passage for the couple, a movement from the status of single to the status of married. Accompanying the shift in classification is a shift in responsibilities and loyalties. This rite of passage is one that not only unites the couple but also unites the two families. Weddings allow the community to know that two have now become one and allow for the community to come and show their support for the newly united couple.

Most women dream of the big wedding, with the big cake and a specially designed dress. With 2.4 million weddings being performed every year, it is not surprising that the wedding industry is a $50 billion-a-year industry. However, at their heart weddings are essentially the celebration by family and friends of the union of two people. A wedding allows a bride to be in the spotlight while also showcasing the couple's love for one another. It is a time for the families to meet and greet one another for they are merging together just as the bride and the groom have united on this day. This is seen in the notion of in-laws who now have at least cursory obligations to each other. All of the couples' friends and families can share in their happiness and in the love that they have found in one another.

Weddings also allow for a social transition for the couple. They are no longer each their own but rather one, which gives them a position to be looked upon for advice and even mimicked by others. It marks a rite of passage for the newlyweds, for they are journeying down the path that their friends and other family members have walked previously. They are entering the adult world. Weddings can also symbolize the leaving of the nest in some cases and making one's own household. It becomes no longer the responsibility of a parent or parents to take care of the individuals, but the responsibility of the individuals to take care of one another. A wedding officially changes a person's status from individual to that of legal husband or wife and showcases that change to the community. In recognition of their new status in the community, couples can look forward to the gifts to assist them in setting up housekeeping and planning a future together. Estimates are that an average of $19 billion a year is spent on wedding gifts in the United States.

NEGATIVES OF A WEDDING

The change in a person's status can be positive, but making that change through a wedding can come at a price, like the cost of weddings in today's society. Weddings on average today cost $20,000 to $25,000. Traditionally, the father of the bride would pay for the wedding costs. Today, 30 percent of couples end up paying for their own weddings, which sufficiently depletes the couple's money to start their lives together. Some people spend so much on their weddings that they end up in debt and are near financial ruin by the end of the event. This does not make the couple happy, and leads to additional stress that they will experience as they create their married life together. Given that money (how much there is and how it should be spent) is a significant factor in why some couples eventually divorce, beginning with a heavy debt load does couples no favors.

Planning a wedding takes months and sometimes even years. On average, brides take from 7 to 12 months to plan a wedding for an average number of guests, 175, and a wedding party of 12. This planning can also be hindered by the soaring costs of the event, something of which young persons may be initially unaware. Brides can find it very stressful and time-consuming to pick out and plan every little detail of the wedding. The bride generally picks the color scheme, the bridesmaid dresses, the flowers, their arrangement, the church or place for the ceremony and reception, all of the decorations for the marriage location, the reception food and décor, the music, the tuxedos (although the groom may help here), and her dress. An average of $800 is spent for a standard wedding gown, and $2000 has likely already been spent on the average engagement ring.

All those decisions would drive anyone insane. The stress of planning and the social pressure to have the right kind of wedding leave many engaged couples wondering if it is worth the work to marry in a formal ceremony. Stereotypes over wedding stressors are routinely the story line in cable shows such as *Bridezilla* and *A Wedding Story*. Stress can also come from family members. While they might mean well and would like to help, they can end up adding to the stress with suggestions about the wedding, questions about future plans, and lack of support for plans that have already been made.

There is also less time, when planning a wedding, for the development of the coupled relationship from dating to marriage. Traditionally, engagement was the time in which couples were to make sure that the partner they had selected was the most appropriate person. Parents tended to give engaged couples, because of their specific commitment to marry, more latitude in their behavior with each other including more private time. Historically, engagements lasted longer than they do today because couples committed quickly so that they would then be permitted the freedom to get to know each other more completely. Today engagement is for a shorter period of time because couples have considerable freedoms while dating. Most persons try to know the partner very well before making the marital promise, but engagement still serves an important function of moving the couple from two persons to one partnership.

Social networking and obligations can contribute to the challenges of moving to a married state. This may be the reason why couples generally are postponing marriage these days. Couples have to "marry" their property, families, children, and sometimes social statuses. These decisions can be very taxing; for instance families may not like one another. If one's family does not approve of the partner, or even approve of marriage, it can make this decision process that much harder to complete.

Another source of contention is the choosing of the bridesmaids and groomsmen, and coordinating their schedules for the fittings, social engagements, and activities that are expected in conjunction with a formal ceremony. Coupled with this is the social pressure to conform your wedding to the model of a perfect wedding. Family members and friends may have strong opinions about what should and shouldn't take place, who should and shouldn't be chosen for the wedding party, and even who should be invited to sit at their table in a formal wedding. It is possible that bad feelings could result if certain people are not chosen to take part or if certain items or traditions are not observed. These issues must be dealt with. This is especially true about the positions of the honor attendants for both the bride and groom (maid or matron of honor and best man). The couple begins to feel the social pressure to have their perfect wedding in the standard that socially is acceptable.

POSITIVES OF ELOPING

Elopement is the act of running away to get married. Unlike weddings, eloping is a much more private affair. When they elope, most people cannot, or choose not to, invite anyone other than the required witnesses to the nuptials. Eloping is much more common today than in years past, when it was more common among the lower class because of the high costs associated with weddings. It offers people an alternative to having a traditional wedding and allows for unconventional methods to legalize their bond. Included in this is simplicity and convenience.

Some couples may find that there is little support for them to marry among their family and friends. Perhaps they are of different social classes, different ages, dissimilar races or ethnicities. Because most marriages are endogamous (couples are from the same social class, racial or ethnic category, and of similar age), couples who differ on these social traits may find that there is little support for their union. In order to avoid some of the direct criticism of their relationship, they may elope. It is even reasonable in today's society that partners are not of the same religious background. This can create challenges for couples as families may wish for one to convert to the other's religion. It may even be a requirement of some clergy prior to performing the ceremony. Eloping makes this a nonissue because the person performing the ceremony is doing so in a legal, rather than religious, capacity and being of the same religion is not a prerequisite for marriage. Sometimes, very young couples choose to elope. Despite being of legal age to marry, their parents may attempt to prohibit them from doing so by withholding financial assistance for a wedding.

Eloping offers a significant reduction in the price of the nuptials. In Las Vegas, one can have a wedding for about $200, far lower than the average price of a traditional wedding. Every year on average 120,000 weddings are performed in Las Vegas and in many other destinations like Jamaica and The Bahamas. A couple saves substantial money on the ceremonial expenses like the guest attendance and the cost of a venue for the event and the reception. Lifestyle advisor Martha Stewart, who has noticed the trend, says that instead of paying runaway prices, people are running away. People like Elvis Presley, Frank Sinatra, Bruce Willis (with Demi Moore), Kelly Ripa (with Mark Consuelos), Michael Jordan, Wayne Newton, Eddie Murphy and, Britney Spears have all eloped.

Elopement may be less stressful than planning for and putting on a wedding. Some popular places to which people elope have inclusive packages that offer certain services such as hotel accommodations, the cake, pictures, and so on for a set fee. For couples who feel that the wedding is just for them and maybe a few select guests this may be the perfect solution. Some couples are very private and wish to keep their relationship that way. They would suggest that the marriage is about them, so the legal ceremony should be as well. The joining of the partners need not be a huge, dramatic affair to lead to long-term happiness and stability. Couples who elope may want privacy, intimacy, fun, excitement, and romance that could be lost in all the little details of planning and executing a wedding.

Elopements also save time. Eloping allows for a shorter time period to put together a ceremony as well as no specific date to have it. Eloping is quick and easy with all the proper documents and witnesses in place. There has been some negative stigma attached to couples who elope. Historically this was because of the presumption that the only reason one would elope was to legitimize a premarital pregnancy as early as possible in gestation. Some couples, however, just know they should be together and see no point in waiting to start their lives together.

Finally, eloping may be a popular choice for second or subsequent marriages. Not only have many of these partners experienced a public wedding in the past, but they may come from religious traditions that frown on divorce or remarriage, making elopement more attractive. Persons who are remarrying are far more likely than persons who are marrying for the first time to have parenting and financial obligations that make a large wedding untenable. While the stigma on remarriage has lessened over time, most persons do not plan a second wedding with as much fanfare as the first.

NEGATIVES OF ELOPING

The stress that seems endemic with planning a wedding can also come with elopements. The stress when a couple decides to elope can take many shapes and forms. It can take the form of a family's disappointment with the couple's decision to elope. Families generally want to share in the big events of other family members' lives and an elopement takes that privilege away. Not only is it an opportunity to wish the couple well, but it may help to cement ties in the community or one's employment through a successful social event. The couple that elopes will not have the opportunity to be the center of attention and will likely miss out, at least to some extent, on one of the perks of the wedding: presents. Friends of the couple may not know whether it is appropriate to bestow a gift when one elopes.

It is possible that the couple will be disappointed in having eloped, especially when it means that they were not able to share this special day with those closest to them. Because people elope for various reasons, it is not always an easy decision to leave family and friends out of the special day. Given that marriage is supposed to last a lifetime, the couple will in theory never have another opportunity for their wedding. The couple also has to continuously answer the question, "Why did you elope?" Given that a wedding with guests in attendance is still the norm, couples who do something different are called to account for their decisions. In many cases observers will assume that there was a negative motive for the elopement. Commonly assumed negative motives include premarital pregnancy, parental disapproval, and financial difficulties. These factors could make a person regret eloping.

Another issue that these couples must answer is how to tell others that they have eloped and gotten married. To go along with that concern is the question of whether an apology should be included in whatever way you choose to tell others about eloping. Some people may be hurt to know they were not included in your special day, so these issues are pertinent in making some kind of amends. Because the wedding marks the time when people start to see the couple as married, not witnessing the ceremony may make it harder for some to accept that the couple is married.

CONCLUSION

Elopements and weddings accomplish the same objective; uniting a couple in marital bonds. But they do so through radically different means. Whereas weddings are public affairs that require advanced planning, multiple guests, and often great expenditures, marriage through eloping is fairly easy and economical to attain and occurs in only the presence of a select few witnesses. Therefore, it can be said to be private. This rite of passage still legally binds the couple together and the day still marks the beginning of their lives together. There are many choices in weddings, with as many options for protocol as couples care to attempt. Options for eloping are fewer, but they are increasing as more couples seek what are called destination weddings, which combine elements of a traditional wedding ceremony and eloping to an exotic location. Weddings are so ritualized and prescribed that people who will not be held to the tradition standard are pushed into eloping. This opens them up to the ridicule of choosing a way to get married that is perceived by others as less desirable.

See also Preparation for Marriage; White Wedding Industry

Further Reading: Baker, Amanda. "Eloping: An Overview Taking a Look at the Basics of Eloping." http://www.associatedcontent.com/article/48647/eloping_an_overview.html (accessed 2006); Bialik, Carl. "Calculating the Cost of Weddings." *Wall Street Journal* http://blogs.wsj.com/numbersguy/calculating-the-cost-of-weddings-175/ (accessed 2007); Dahlstrom, Kendra. "The Pros and Cons of Eloping in Las Vegas." http://www.associatedcontent.com/article/175922/the_pros_and_cons_of_elopingg_in_las.html (accessed 2007); Drake, Jennifer. "Pro's and Con's of Eloping versus Planning a Wedding Ceremony." http://www.associatedcontent.com/article/185413/the_pros_and_cons_of_elopingg_versus.html (accessed 2007); Faria, Alison. "When to Consider Eloping." http://www.happynews.com/living/eventtips/consider-eloping.htm (accessed 2005); Fisher, Laurel. "Eloping vs. a Family Wedding." http://www.happynews.com/living/eventtips/eloping-vs-family.htm (accessed 2005); Higuera, V. C. "Modern Weddings: Planning a Marriage Elopement." http://www.associatedcontent.com/article/36493/modern_weddings_planning_a_marriage.html (accessed 2006); Isabella, Kalee. "Elope." http://weddings.lovetoknow.com/wiki/Elope (accessed 2006); Mayntz, Melissa. "Places to Elope." http://weddings.lovetoknow.com/wiki/Places_to_Elope (accessed 2007); Tabb, Lisa and Sam Silverstein. *Beyond Vegas: 25 Exotic Wedding and Elopement Destinations Around the World.* Chicago: Contemporary Books, 2000; Tabb, Lisa and Susan Breslow Sardone. "Top Five Reasons to Elope" http://honeymoons.about.com/cs/toppicks/a/letselope_2.htm (accessed 2008).

Maria J. Patterson

WHITE WEDDING INDUSTRY

What could be controversial about white weddings, those wonderfully romantic events featuring beautiful brides in long, white dresses, exotic flowers, abundant candles, and elaborate parties for friends and families? Most Americans have attended—or will attend—many such weddings throughout their lifetimes. Weddings fulfill important personal, couple, family, and societal functions and are among the most widely anticipated events in families and communities.

They provide opportunities for bringing families together and getting outsiders invested in the success of the newly wed couple. They also serve as important rites of passage (*i.e.,* events that signify that individuals are moving from one important life state to another). They include numerous rituals that demonstrate to the couple themselves and to all bystanders that the relationship is important and meant to last a lifetime. In this essay, we will examine the increasing financial costs associated with white weddings in an attempt to understand the relationship between private commitment and societal and global forces and influences. Do the rites and rituals associated with weddings require such elaborate productions, with their associated emotional and financial costs, and the wide-reaching harmful effects on workers around the globe? Do they truly reflect tradition and have a personal meaning to the newlyweds or ensure that their marriages will be unique? Or, are they, as some scholars and observers suggest, the result of a very effective and extensive marketing campaign?

THE WHITE WEDDING INDUSTRY

In recent years, the number of weddings has decreased in the United States, yet the gross revenue of the U.S. wedding industry has increased dramatically as the financial costs associated with individual white weddings have increased substantially. The wedding industry (*i.e.,* the production of all the goods and services associated with the planning of weddings and all of the associated social events that occur before, during, and after the ceremonies) is estimated to contribute over $160 billion dollars to the U.S. economy each year.

Wedding goods and services. Included in the wedding industry are products such as bridal gowns and accessories, engagement and wedding rings, honeymoon travel and apparel, destination weddings (*i.e.,* guests travel to a vacation locale to celebrate the wedding with the couple), and household equipment (typically in the form of gifts to the couple). Also included are invitations and other paper products, flowers and other decorations, photos and videos, weddings cakes and other food and liquor for receptions, gifts for members of the wedding party, and wedding accessories such as ring pillows and candles. Many of the goods consumed in the course of staging a wedding in this country are actually produced outside the United States, a point to which we will return shortly. Professionals whose services are purchased for weddings and associated social events include wedding planners, photographers, caterers, hair stylists and makeup artists, chauffeurs, bar tenders, musicians, and others. About half of the economic costs associated with weddings fall into this service category. White weddings are clearly big business in the United States today.

Financial costs of weddings to families. Over the past 15 years, wedding costs in this country have increased by 40 percent and are expected to continue to increase into the near future. Representatives of the wedding industry estimate that at the end of the first decade of the twenty-first century, the average white wedding in the United States will cost approximately $28,000. There are regional variations in this figure, ranging from a low of just under $19,000 in the South, to $25,000 on the West Coast, and to nearly $39,000 in the New York metropolitan

574 | White Wedding Industry

Table W.1 Common Wedding Rituals, their Symbolic Meanings, and Likely Origins

Ritual Element	Meaning	Likely Origins
Children in wedding party	Fertility	Ancient Rome: altar boy presenting wheat cakes to god Jupiter
Candles	Presence of God; enduring flame of marriage	Torches used to light pathway as wedding procession made its way through dark streets
Flowers	Bride's virtue; abundance	Began as garlands of olive and myrtle worn by bride as headpiece; also guests scattered flowers along the road from the bride's home to the church
Bridal veil	Protects bride against malicious spirits (i.e., "the evil eye"); shows the bride's purity/virture has been protected; when veil is pulled back at end of ceremony, indicates that she has assumed a new role/status	Ancient cultures, veils (not always white) used to ward off evil spirits; Ancient Romans used red veils
Cutting the wedding cake; throwing rice	Fertility; abundance	Brides in some ancient cultures wore ears of corn around their necks to entice god of fertility; breaking or cutting cake facilitated breaking the bride's hymen (i.e., "maidenhead") and aided in the birth of first child; cake broken over bride's head, later cake crumbs sprinkled on bride's head
Giving the bride away; carrying bride over the threshold of the new marital home	Father owned daughter until her marriage; at the wedding, father publicly transferred ownership of bride to her new husband	

region. Variation by region can be linked to cost of living in these areas, as well as median family income in those locations. Of course, we are all quite familiar with the over-the-top wedding extravaganzas thrown by celebrities that can exceed two million dollars.

Wedding debt. When average wedding expenses are compared with the average annual income of American families, it is clear that many couples and often their parents are spending beyond their means and going into significant debt to host weddings. To illustrate, the cost of the average white wedding represents over 60 percent of the average annual earnings of white families in the United States and over 90 percent of the average earnings of black and Latino families. For the 40 percent of Americans who earn less than $25,000 per year, the average cost of a white wedding approximates or even exceeds their annual income. The emotional costs associated with wedding debt frequently become the source of ongoing conflict between the newly married or soon to be married couples and may push them to see a marital or financial counselor to find a way out of the stresses their wedding debts have produced. The increasing likelihood of couples going into debt to wed may be behind recent revisions in wedding etiquette that suggest the responsibility for the largest wedding expenses are no longer to be shouldered by the bride's family, but the entire expenses could be shared equally by the bride's and groom's families.

Another way to put the average cost of white weddings into perspective is to consider other important things that $28,000 could buy. In terms of education, this amount of money could pay for one year at a private college or university or, on the other hand, cover the entire four year cost of attending a public university. Alternatively, $28,000 could buy a new mid-priced car or constitute a down payment on an average priced home.

Global exploitation of workers in the wedding industry. In many parts of the world where products for American weddings are produced, $28,000 would buy basic necessities of life; for example, food for 3,000 people in South Africa; medicine for 10,000 children in Africa for one year; or 12 wells to provide clean water for people in southeast Asia, Africa, and Latin America. Another way to look at the global impact of the large and growing white wedding industry in the United States is to consider that seamstresses in China who make wedding gowns for American brides earn about 12 cents per hour under deplorable working conditions. The $28,000 spent for the average white wedding could pay 111 workers for one year. As in many other U.S. owned companies, production is being sent out of the country in order to find cheaper labor and to reduce the overall costs of production.

WHITE WEDDINGS AS RITUALS

Weddings may actually be one of the most ritualized events of the family life cycle. Wedding ceremonies are highly structured affairs that have a number of symbolic gestures such as giving the bride away, asking those in attendance if there are any objections to the marriage, various actions that involve fertility—throwing rice, or more recently, bird seed, serving wedding cake, and including children in the ceremony. The specific symbols that are involved vary from one culture to another and evolve over time. The purposes of rituals may include complying with religious obligations or ideals, satisfying spiritual or emotional needs of the participants, strengthening social bonds between families, demonstrating respect or submission, or, sometimes, just for the pleasure of the ritual itself. As we will see below, however, some critical observers of the contemporary wedding industry argue that manufacturers and distributors or sellers of wedding services and products are changing wedding rituals and even inventing new ones simply to increase their profits.

The origin of many common wedding rituals is known. Others, however, are less well understood by scholars as well as brides- and grooms-to-be. The oldest and perhaps most universal wedding symbol is the ring. A number of the aspects of engagement and wedding rings we take for granted today actually have evolved over long periods of time. For instance, why are wedding rings typically worn on the left hand? Some historians believe that this is because the left hand has been considered inferior and that is symbolizes submission and obedience. Thus, wearing a ring on the left hand to signify marriage is appropriate in that it reflects the roles and responsibilities of spouses. Why, then, is the ring worn on the fourth finger? This custom has actually evolved over time. In many earlier cultures, wedding rings were worn on the first finger. The move to the fourth and so-called ring finger may rest on the belief that there is a small artery leading from that finger directly to the heart. Today precious metals are used in wedding rings. However, in the past, these metals were not widely available so common folks used reeds or other plant materials to craft rings. Later, iron was used.

Engagement rings, which have assumed a major role in the wedding economy today, were once worn by men because they symbolized power and authority. When they came to symbolize bondage and obedience, men stopped wearing them and provided them to their intended brides instead. Today, American grooms-to-be purchase diamond rings to symbolize engagement. Manufacturers of diamond engagement rings encourage grooms to spend at least two-months salary on them as a token of how special the intended partner is to them. However, in Puritan America, diamonds—which many believed were useful in protecting against Satan—were shunned precisely because of their association with evil forces.

WHITE WEDDINGS AS IDEOLOGY

Some scholars who study weddings argue that they are more than rituals. They are part of an ideological complex (*i.e.,* a set of beliefs that cross-cut many social institutions) that is created and perpetuated by the mass media and other powerful segments of a society to justify existing sexist, heterosexist, and classist arrangements and to sell numerous wedding products and services. The depiction of the romantic, extravagant white weddings in films, television shows, and print media encourages couples to spend far more money than they can afford on weddings. The media also reproduce the idea that women are more interested in romance and relationships than are men; that weddings—and perhaps relationships themselves—are women's work and that it is unimaginable to have feelings of love and desire for commitment without investing in marriage and the expensive white wedding. Images of middle-class, middle American traditional family values are at the center of films that feature weddings and are presented as the normal standards for all to follow. Some scholars believe that the current cultural emphasis on weddings has the effect of centering women's life expectations on success on just one day—their wedding day. The emphasis on this one event in women's lives makes all other events pale in comparison and transfers energy and effort away from preparing for marriage itself.

SUMMARY

In considering this important issue in contemporary American families, the important question to ask pertains to the purpose, or meaning, of weddings. Is the wedding ceremony, and its associated social events, meant to signify the love and commitment felt by the couple and to involve extended families and community members in the future marital success of the couple? If so, are the large and growing expenses involved in carrying out the lavish white wedding ceremony really necessary for this success? Or, as many scholars suggest, are they embraced by wedding consumers because of the extensive and effective market campaigns of the producers and providers of wedding products and services?

See also Prenuptial Agreements; Preparation for Marriage; Wedding and Eloping.

Further Reading: Chessler, Barbara Jo. "Analysis of wedding rituals: An attempt to make weddings more meaningful." *Family Relations* 29, no. 2 (1980): 204–209; Ingraham, Chrys. *White Weddings: Romancing Heterosexuality in Popular Culture*, 2nd ed. New York: Routledge, 2008; Jellison, Katherine. *It's Our Day: America's Love Affair with the White Wedding 1945–2005*. Lawrence, KS: University of Kansas Press, 2008; Mead, Rebecca. *One Perfect Day: The Selling of the American Wedding*. New York; Penguin Books, 2007; Otnes, Cele C., and Elizabeth J. Pleck. *Cinderella Dreams: The Allure of the Lavish Wedding*. Berkeley: University of California Press, 2003; Wallace, Carolyn McD. *All Dressed in White: The Irresistible Rise of the American Wedding*. New York: Penguin Books, 2004.

Constance L. Shehan

BIBLIOGRAPHY

Adams, Carol, and Marie Fortune, eds. *Violence against Women and Children: A Christian Theological Sourcebook.* New York: Continuum, 1995.

Adams, Leslie. "The Effects of Birth Order on Procrastination." Missouri Western State University, 2008. Available at: http://clearinghouse.missouriwestern.edu/manuscripts/14.asp.

Adler, A. *What Life Should Mean to You.* New York: Perigree Books, 1931.

Administration for Children and Families. *Trends in Foster Care and Adoption.* Washington D.C., 2007. Available at: http://www.acf.hhs.gov/programs/cb/stats_research/afcars/trends.htm.

Adoption History: National Association of Black Social Workers. "Position Statement on Trans-Racial Adoption." September 1972. Available at: http://darkwing.uoregon.edu/~adoption/archive/NabswTRA.htm.

Adoption History Project. *Timeline of Adoption History.* Eugene, OR: University of Oregon, 2007. Available at: http://www.uoregon.edu/~adoption/timeline.html.

Ahluwalia, I., Morrow, B., & Hsia, J. "Why Do Women Stop Breastfeeding? Findings from the Pregnancy Risk Assessment and Monitoring System." *Pediatrics* 116 (2005): 1408–1412.

Ahrons, Constance. *The Good Divorce: Keeping Your Family Together When Your Marriage Comes Apart.* New York: Harper Collins, 1994.

Ahrons, Constance. *We're Still Family: What Grown Children Have to Say about Their Parents' Divorce.* New York: Harper Collins, 2004.

Aitken, Lynda, and Gabriele Griffin. *Gender Issues in Elder Abuse.* London: Sage, 1996.

Akerman, Sherri. "Young Caregivers Face Many Challenges." *Tampa Tribune,* January 29, 2007.

Albanese, Jay S. *Criminal Justice.* 3rd ed. Boston, MA: Pearson Education, 2005.

Aldridge, Jo. "The Experiences of Children Living with and Caring for Parents with Mental Illness." *Child Abuse Review* 15, no. 2 (2006): 79–88.

Aldridge, Jo, and Saul Becker. "Befriending Young Carers: A Pilot Study." Loughboro University, 1996. Available at: http://www.lboro.ac.uk/departments/ss/centres/YCRG/young CarersDownload/pilot%20study.pdf.

Aldridge, Jo, and Saul Becker. "Inside the World of Young Carers." Loughboro University, 1993. Available at: http://www.lboro.ac.uk/departments/ss/centres/YCRG/young CarersDownload/ Children%20who%20care.pdf.

Alsdurf, James, and Phyllis Alsdurf. *Battered into Submission: The Tragedy of Wife Abuse in the Christian Home.* Downers Grove, IL: Intervarsity Press, 1989.

Alwani, Zainab, and Salma Abugideiri. *What Islam Says about Domestic Violence: A Guide for Helping Muslim Families.* Herndon, VA: Foundation for Appropriate and Immediate Temporary Help, 2003.

Amato, Paul R., and Alan Booth. *A Generation at Risk: Growing Up in an Era of Family Upheaval.* Cambridge, MA: Harvard University Press, 2000.

Amato, Paul R., Alan Booth, David R. Johnson, and Stacy J. Rogers. *Alone Together: How Marriage in America is Changing.* Cambridge, MA: Harvard University Press, 2007.

Ambert, Anne-Marie. *Cohabitation and Marriage: How Are They Related?* Ottawa, Ontario, Canada: The Vanier Institute of the Family, 2005.

American Academy of Child and Adolescent Psychiatry. *Facts for Families: Foster Care.* Washington, D.C., 2005. Available at: http://www.aacap.org/cs/root/facts_for_families/foster_care.

American Bar Association. *The American Bar Association Legal Guide for Women: What every Woman Needs to Know about the Law and Marriage, Health Care, Divorce, Discrimination, Retirement, and More.* New York: Random House, 2004.

Ammerman, R., and M. Hersen. *Case Studies in Family Violence.* New York: Plenum Press, 1991.

Anderson, Elizabeth. Is Women's Labor a Commodity? *Philosophy and Public Affairs* 19 (1990): 71–92.

Andrews, Lori. Beyond Doctrinal Boundaries: A Legal Framework for Surrogate Motherhood. *Virginia Law Review* 81(1995): 2343–2375.

Anetzberger, Georgia J. *The Clinical Management of Elder Abuse.* New York: The Haworth Press, 2003.

Armstrong, Thomas. "ADD: Does It Really Exist?" In *Taking Sides: Clashing Views on Controversial Issue in Abnormal Psychology,* ed. Richard P. Halgin, 3rd ed., 63–72. Dubuque, IO: McGraw-Hill/Duskin, 2005.

Austin, LeAne. "Children as Caregivers." Caregiver.com. Available at: http://www.caregiver.com/ articles/children/children_as_caregivers.htm.

Bailey, Beth. *From Front Porch to Back Seat: Courtship in Twentieth Century America.* Baltimore, MD: Johns Hopkins University Press, 1988.

Baker, Amanda. Eloping: An Overview Taking a Look at the Basics of Eloping. Associated Content Web site, 2006. Available at: http://www.associatedcontent.com/article/48647/eloping_an_overview.html.

Barkley, Russell A. *Attention-Deficit Hyperactivity Disorder: A Handbook for Diagnosis and Treatment.* 3rd ed. New York: The Guilford Press, 2006.

Barlow, Anne, Simon Duncan, Grace James, and Alison Parks. *Cohabitation, Marriage and the Law: Social Change and Legal Reform in the 21st Century.* Oxford: Hart Publishing, 2005.

Barnett, O., C. L. Miller-Perrin, and R. D. Perrin. *Family Violence Across the Lifespan: An Introduction.* 2nd ed. Thousand Oaks, CA: Sage Publications, 2005.

Bartholet, Elizabeth. *Nobody's Children: Abuse, Neglect, Foster Drift, and the Adoption Alternative.* Boston, MA: Beacon Press, 2000.

Bartkowski, John. *Remaking the Godly Marriage: Gender Negotiation in Evangelical Families.* New Brunswick, NJ: Rutgers University Press, 2001.

Bartkowski, John. *Promise Keepers: Servants, Soldiers, and Godly Men.* New Brunswick, NJ: Rutgers University Press, 2004.

Bartlett, Jane. *Will You Be Mother? Women Who Choose to Say No.* New York: New York University Press, 1995.

Bauman, Laurie J., Ellen J. Silver, Barbara H. Draimin, and Jan Hudis. "Children of Mothers With HIV/AIDS: Unmet Needs for Mental Health Services." *Pediatrics* 120, no. 5 (November 2007). Available at: http://pediatrics.aappublications.org/cgi/reprint/peds.2005-2680v1.

Baumeister, Alfred A. *Mental Retardation: Appraisal, Education, and Rehabilitation.* Chicago: Aldine, 1968.

Baumhover, Lorin A., and S. Colleen Beall. *Abuse, Neglect, and Exploitation of Older Persons.* Baltimore, MD: Health Professions Press, 1996.

Baumrind, Diana. "Parental disciplinary patterns and social competence in children." *Youth and Society* 9 (1978): 239–276.

Baumslag, N., and D. Michels. *Milk, Money, and Madness: The Culture and Politics of Breastfeeding.* Westport, CT: Bergin and Garvey, 1995.

Baxter, Janeen, and Edith Gray. *For Richer or Poorer: Women, Men and Marriage.* Retrieved September 1, 2006, from http://lifecourse.anu.edu.au/publications/Discussion_papers/NLCDP012.pdf.

Beaman-Hall, Lori, and Nancy Nason-Clark. "Translating Spiritual Commitment into Service: The Responses of Evangelical Women to Wife Abuse." *Canadian Women's Studies/Les Cahiers De La Femme* 17 (1997): 58–61.

Bearman, Peter S., and Hannah Bruckner. "After the Promise: The STD Consequence of Adolescent Virginity Pledges." *Journal of Adolescent Health* 36 (2005): 271–278.

Becker, Saul. "Young Carers in Europe: An Exploratory Cross-National Study. Young Carers Research Group." Loughboro University, 1995. Available at: http://www.lboro.ac.uk/ departments/ss/centres/YCRG/youngCarersDownload/Young%20Carers%20in%20Europe1.pdf.

Beer, Alan E., Julia Kantecki, and Jane Reed. *Is Your Body Baby-Friendly: Unexplained Infertility, Miscarriage, and IVF Failure.* LaSalle, Ontario, Canada: AJR Publishing, 2006.

Behm, Lisa. "Legal, Moral, and International Perspectives on Surrogate Motherhood: The Call for a Uniform Regulatory Scheme in the United States." *DePaul Journal of Health Care Law* 2(1999): 557–603.

Bellafante, Gina. "In the U.S., Assisted Marriages for South Asians." *The International Herald Tribune,* August 24, 2005, news section p. 2.

Belsky, Jay, and John Kelly. *The Transition to Parenthood: How a First Child Changes a Marriage; Why Some Couples Grow Closer and Others Apart.* New York: Delacorte Press, 1995.

Bennion, Janet. *Women of Principle: Female Networking in Contemporary Mormon Polygyny.* New York: Oxford University Press, 1998.

Benson, Dale. "Providing Health Care to Human Beings Trapped in the Poverty Culture." *The Physician Executive* 26 (2000): 28–32.

Berg-Weger, Marla. *Caring for Elderly Parents.* New York: Garland Publishing, 1996.

Berk, Laura E. *Infants, Children, and Adolescents.* 5th ed. Boston: Pearson, 2005.

Berman, Eleanor. *Grandparenting ABC's: A Beginners Handbook.* New York: A Perigee Book, 1998.

Bernard, Jessie. *The Future of Marriage.* 2nd ed. New Haven, CT: Yale University Press, 1982.

Bernstein, Nina. *The Lost Children of Wilder: The Epic Struggle to Change Foster Care.* New York; Vintage Books, 2001.

Berquist, Kathleen Ja Sook. *International Korean Adoption: A Fifty-year History of Policy and Practice.* Binghamton, NY: Haworth Press, 2007.

Berry, Judy O., and Michael L. Hardman. *Lifespan Perspectives on the Family and Disability.* Boston: Allyn and Bacon, 1998.

Bertrand, Marianne, Sendhil Mullainathan, and Eldar Shafir. "Behavioral Economics and Marketing in Aid of Decision Making Among the Poor." *American Marketing Association* 25 (2006): 8–23.

Bialik, Carl. "Calculating the Cost of Weddings." Wall Street Journal Web site. Available at: http://blogs.wsj.com/numbersguy/calculating-the-cost-of-weddings-175/.

Bidwell, Lee D. Millar, and Brenda J. Vander Mey. *Sociology of the Family: Investigating Family Issues.* Boston: Allyn and Bacon, 2000.

Biggs, Simon, Chris Phillipson, and Paul Kingston. *Elder Abuse in Perspective.* Buckingham, UK: Open University Press, 1995.

Bistine, Benjamin. *Colorado City Polygamists: An Inside Look for the Outsider.* Scottsdale, AZ: Agreka Books, 2004.

Bitensky, Susan H. *Corporal Punishment of Children: A Human Rights Violation.* Ardsley, NY: Transnational Publishers, 2006.

Blacher, Jan, and Bruce L. Baker. "Positive impact of intellectual disability on families." *American Journal on Mental Retardation* 112 (2007): 330–348.

Black, Henry Campbell. *Black's Law Dictionary.* Abridged 6th ed. St. Paul, MN: West Publishing Co., 1991.

Blackstone-Ford, Jann, and Sharyl Jupe. *Ex-Etiquette for Weddings: The Blended Families' Guide to Tying the Knot.* Chicago: Chicago Review Press, Inc., 2007.

Blades, Joan, and Kristin Rowe-Finkbeiner. *The Motherhood Manifesto: What America's Moms Want: and What To Do About It.* New York: Nation Books, 2006.

Blair-Loy, Mary. *Competing Devotions: Career and Family among Women Executives.* Cambridge, MA: Harvard University Press, 2003.

Blake, J. *Family Size and Achievement.* Berkeley: University of California Press, 1989.

Blank, Rebecca, and Ron Hoskins, eds. *The New World of Welfare.* The Brookings Institution, 2001.

Blankenship, Kim, Suzanne Onorato, Beth Rushing, and Kelly White. Reproductive Technologies and the U.S. Courts. *Gender and Society* 7(1993): 8–31.

Blau, David M. *The Child Care Problem: An Economic Analysis.* New York: Russell Sage Foundation, 2001.

Blum, Jonathan. "Caring for Dad." *Scholastic Action* 30, no. 1 (2006): 14–16.

Blum, L. *At the Breast: Ideologies of Breastfeeding and Motherhood in the Contemporary United States.* Boston: Beacon Press, 1999.

Blumstein, Philip, and Pepper Schwartz. *American Couple: Money, Work, Sex.* New York: Simon and Schuster Adult Publishing Group, 1985.

Bonnie, Richard J., and Robert B. Wallace, eds. *Elder Mistreatment: Abuse, Neglect, and Exploitation in an Aging America.* Washington, D.C.: The National Academic Press, 2003.

Bosch, Kathy, and Walter R. Schumm. "Accessibility to Resources: Helping Rural Women in Abusive Partner Relationships Become Free from Abuse." *Journal of Sex and Marital Therapy* 30 (2004): 357–370.

Boyce, Glenna C., Brent C. Miller, Karl R. White, and Michael K. Godfrey. "Single Parenting in Families of Children with Disabilities." *Marriage and Family Review* 20 (1995): 389–409.

Brabant, Christine, Sylvain Bourdon, and France Jutras. "Home Education in Quebec: Family First." *Evaluation and Research in Education* 17 (2003): 112–131.

Braver, Sanford L. *Divorced Dads: Shattering the Myth.* New York: Putnam Special Markets, 1998.

Brewster, Karin, and Irene Padavic. "Change in Gender-Ideology, 1977–1996: The Contributions of Intracohort Change and Population Turnover." *Journal of Marriage and the Family* 62 (2000): 477–487.

Brinkerhoff, Merlin, Elaine Grandin, and Lupri, Eugene. "Religious Involvement and Spousal Violence: The Canadian Case." *Journal of the Scientific Study of Religion* 31 (1992): 15–31.

Brown A. W., and B. Bailey-Etta. "An Out of Home Care System in Crisis: Implications for African-American Children in the Foster Care System." *Child Welfare* 76 (1997): 65–83.

Brown, Kevin D., and Catherine Hamilton-Giachritsis. "The Influences of Violent Media on Children and Adolescents: A Public Health Approach." *Lancet* 365 (2005): 702–710.

Browne, Joy. *Dating for Dummies.* Hoboken, NJ: Wiley Publishing, 2006.

Brownell, Patricia J., and Stuart Bruchey, eds. *Family Crimes Against The Elderly: Elder Abuse and the Criminal Justice System.* New York: Garland Publishing, 1998.

Bryson, Ken, and Lynne M. Casper. "Coresident Grandparents and Grandchildren." *US Census Bureau: US Department of Commerce Economic and Statistics Administration* (1999): 1–10.

Bull, Chris, and John Gallagher. *Perfect Enemies: The Battle Between the Religious Right and the Gay Movement.* Lanham, MD: Madison Books, 1996.

Buri, John R. *How to Love Your Wife.* Mustang, OK: Tate Publishing and Enterprises, 2006.

Burkett, Elinor. *The Baby Boon: How Family-Friendly America Cheats the Childless.* New York: The Free Press, 2000.

Burnett, Myrna. "Suffering and Sanctification: The Religious Context of Battered Woman's Syndrome." *Pastoral Psychology* 44 (1996): 145–149.

Buzawa, Eve S., and Carl G. Buzawa. *Domestic Violence: The Criminal Justice Response*, 3rd ed. Thousand Oaks, CA: Sage, 2003.

Cabaniss, Emily, and Jill Fuller. "Ethnicity, Race, and Poverty." *Race, Gender, and Class* 12 (2005): 142–162.

Caffaro, J., and A. Conn-Caffaro. *Sibling Abuse Trauma*. New York: Haworth Maltreatment and Trauma Press, 1998.

Cain, A. O. "Pets as Family Members." *Marriage and Family Review* 8 (1985): 5–10.

Cain, Madelyn. *The Childless Revolution*. Boston: Perseus Publishing, 2001.

Caldwell, Roslyn M., Susan M. Sturges, and N. Clayton Silver. "Home Versus School Environments and their Influences on the Affective and Behavioral States of African American, Hispanic, and Caucasian Juvenile Offenders." *Journal of Child and Family Studies* 16 (2007): 119–132.

Calvo, Emily T., and Laurence Minsky. *25 Words or Less: How to Write Like a Pro to Find That Special Someone Through Personal Ads*. New York: McGraw-Hill, 1998.

Campbell, Suzanne B. "Taking Race out of the Equation: Transracial Adoption in 2000." *Southern Methodist University Law Review* 53 (2000): 1599.

Caplan, Arthur L., and Rosalie A. Kane. *Everyday Ethics: Resolving Dilemmas in Nursing Home Life*. New York: Springer Publishing, 1990.

Caporaso, James A., and David P. Levine. *Theories of Political Economy*. New York: Cambridge University Press, 1992.

Carlson, Allan C. *Love is not Enough: Toward the Recovery of a Family Economics*. The Family Research Council Web Site, September 2007. Available at: www.frc.org.

Carpenter, Laura. *Virginity Lost: An Intimate Portrait of First Sexual Experiences*. New York: New York University Press, 2005.

Carroll, Jason S., and William J. Doherty. "Evaluating the Effectiveness of Premarital Prevention Programs: A Meta-analytic Review of Outcome Research." *Family Relations* 52 (2003): 105–118.

Cartwright, Lisa, Kay Johnson, Laurel Kendall, and Barbara Yngvesson. *Culture of Transnational Adoption*. Durham, NC: Duke University Press, 2005.

Casper, Lynne M., and Suzanne M. Bianchi. *Continuity and Change in the American Family*. Thousand Oaks, CA: Sage, 2001.

Centers for Disease Control and Prevention. Breastfeeding Practices: Results from the National Immunization Survey, November 2007. Available at: http://www.cdc.gov/breastfeeding/data/NIS_data/data_2004.htm.

Centers for Disease Control and Prevention. Mental Health in the United States: Prevalence of Diagnosis and Medication Treatment of Attention-Deficit/Hyperactivity Disorder: United States, 2003. Centers for Disease Control and Prevention Web Site. Available at: http://www.cdc.gov/mmwr/preview/mmwrhtml/mm5434a2.htm.

Chapman, Gary. *The Five Love Languages: How to Express Heartfelt Commitment to Your Mate*. Chicago: Northfield Publishing, 2004.

Chessler, Barbara Jo. "Analysis of Wedding Rituals: An Attempt to Make Weddings More Meaningful." *Family Relations* 29 (1980): 204–209.

Chichetti, Dante, and Vicki Carlson. *Child Maltreatment: Theory and Research on the Causes and Consequences of Child Abuse and Neglect*. New York: Cambridge University Press, 1997.

Chideya, Farai. "When Children Must Care for Others." *NPR News and Notes,* October 12, 2006. Available at: http://www.npr.org/templates/story/story.php?storyId=6253049.
Child Welfare League of America. *CWLA Standards of Excellence for Family Foster Care.* Washington DC: Child Welfare League of America, 2005.
Child Welfare League of America. *CWLA Standards of Excellence for Services for Abused or Neglected Children and Their Families.* Washington DC: Child Welfare League of America, 1999.
Child Welfare League of America. *Special tabulation of the Adoption and Foster Care Analysis Reporting System.* Washington, DC: Child Welfare League of America, 2006. Available at: http://ndas.cwla.org/data_stats/access/predefined/Report.asp?PageMode=1&%20ReportID=379&%20GUID={4859F5C2-DD74-4AF0-AD55-8360140347E3}#Table.
Child Welfare League of America. *Quick Facts about Foster Care.* Washington DC: Child Welfare League of America, 2007. Available at: http://www.cwla.org/programs/fostercare/factsheet.htm.
Clarke-Stewart, A., and V. Allhusen. *What We Know About Childcare.* Cambridge, MA: Harvard University Press, 2005.
Claxton, Reid P. "Empirical Relationships Between Birth Order and Two Types of Parental Feedback." *The Psychological Record* 44 (2002): 475–500.
Cohen, Abby. "A Brief History of Federal Financing for Child Care in the United States." *Financing Child Care 6.* Available at: http://www.futureofchildren.org.
Coleman, J. W., and H. R. Kerbo. *Social Problems.* 9th ed. Upper Saddle River, NJ: Pearson Prentice Hall, 2006.
Coleman, Malna. "Gestation, Intent, and the Seed: Defining Motherhood in the Era of Assisted Human Reproduction." *Cardoza Law Review* 17 (1996): 497–530.
Coleman, Marilyn, Mark Fine, and Lawrence Ganong. "Reinvestigating Remarriage: Another Decade of Progress." *Journal of Marriage and Family* 62 (2000): 1288–1307.
Coleman, Marilyn, and Lawrence H. Ganong. *Stepfamily Relationships: Development, Dynamics, and Interventions.* New York: Kluwer Academic/Plenum Publishers, 2004.
Collins, Patricia Hill. *Black Feminist Thought: Knowledge, Consciousness, and the Politics of Empowerment.* Boston: Unwin Hyman, 1990.
Collins, Particia Hill. *Black Feminist Thought: Knowledge, Consciousness, and the Politics of Empowerment,* 2nd ed. New York: Routledge, 2000.
Collom, Ed. "The Ins and Outs of Homeschooling." *Education and Urban Society* 37 (2005): 307–335.
Coltrane, Scott. *Family Man: Fatherhood, Housework, and Gender Equity.* New York: Oxford University Press, 1996.
Coltrane, Scott. *Gender and Families.* Thousand Oaks, CA: Pine Forge Press, 1998.
Coltrane, Scott, and Michele Adams. *Gender and Families.* Lanham, MD: Rowman and Littlefield Publishers, 2008.
Comer, James P., and Alvin F. Poussant. *Raising Black Children.* New York: Penguin Group, 1992.
Commission on Leave. *A Workable Balance: Report to Congress on Family and Medical Leave Policies.* Washington D.C.: U.S. Department of Labor, 1996.
Congalton, David, and C. Alexander. *When Your Pet Outlives You: Protecting Animal Companions After You Die.* Troutdale, OR: New Sage Press, 2002.

Connell, Elizabeth B. *The Contraception Sourcebook.* New York: McGraw-Hill, 2002.

Conrad, Peter, and Joseph W. Schneider. *Deviance and Medicalization: From Badness to Sickness.* Philadelphia: Temple University Press, 1992.

Constable, Nicole. *Romance on a Global Stage: Pen Pals, Virtual Ethnography, and "Mail-Order" Marriages.* Berkeley, CA: University of California Press, 2003.

Cooke, Barbara, and Carleton Kendrick. *Take Out Your Nose Ring, Honey, We're Going to Grandma's.* Bloomington, IN: Unlimited Publishing, 2003.

Cooke, P., and P. J. Standen. "Abuse and Disabled Children: Hidden Needs?" *Child Abuse Review,* 11(2002): 1–18.

Coontz, Stephanie. *The Way We Never Were: American Families and the Nostalgia Trap.* New York: Harper Collins, 1992.

Coontz, Stephanie. *The Way We Really Are: Coming to Terms with America's Changing Families.* New York: Basic Books, 1997.

Coontz, Stephanie. *Marriage, a History: From Obedience to Intimacy or How Love Conquered Marriage.* New York: Penguin Group, 2005.

Coontz, Stephanie, and Nancy Folbre. 2002. "Marriage, Poverty, and Public Policy." Available at: http://www.prospect.org/cs/articles?article=marriage_poverty_and_public_policy.

Cooper, Bruce S., and John Sureau." The Politics of Homeschooling-New Developments, New Challenges." *Educational Policy* 21 (2007): 110–131.

Cooper, Paul, and Katherine Bilton. *ADHD: Research, Practice and Opinion.* London: Whurr Publishers, 1999.

Corkum, Penny V., M. Margaret McKinnon, and Jennifer C. Mullane. "The Effect of Involving Classroom Teachers in a Parent Training Program for Families of Children with ADHD." *Child and Family Behavior Therapy* 27 (2005): 29–49.

Courtney, M. E., R. P. Barth, J. D. Berrick, D. Brooks, B. Needell, and L. Park. "Race and Child Welfare Services: Past research and Future Directions." *Child Welfare* 76 (1996): 99–137.

Cowles, K. V. "The Death of a Pet: Human Responses to the Breaking of the Bond." In *Pets and Family,* ed. M. B. Sussman. New York: Haworth Press, 1985.

Crary, Elizabeth. *Without Spanking or Spoiling: A Practical Approach to Toddler and Preschool Guidance.* Seattle, WA: Parenting Press, 1993.

Crittenden, Ann. *The Price of Motherhood: Why the Most Important Job in the World is Still the Least Valued.* New York: Henry Holt and Company, 2001.

Crittenden, Ann. *If You've Raised Kids, You Can Manage Anything: Leadership Begins at Home.* New York: Gotham Press, 2005.

Crosson-Tower, Cynthia. *Understanding Child Abuse and Neglect.* Boston: Allyn and Bacon, 2007.

Crowley, Jocelyn. *The Politics of Child Support in America.* New York: Cambridge University Press, 2003.

Cullen, L. T., and L. Grossman. Fatherhood 2.0. *Time* (October 4, 2007). Available at: http://www.time.com.

Cunradi, Carol, Raul Caetano, and John Schafer. "Religious Affiliation, Denominational Hegemony, and Intimate Partner Violence Among U.S. Couples." *Journal for the Scientific Study of Religion* 41 (2002): 139–152.

Currie, Janet M. *The Invisible Safety Net.* Princeton, NJ: Princeton University Press, 2006.

Curtis, Patrick A., G. Dale, and J. Kendall. *The Foster Care Crisis Translating Research into Policy Practice.* Lincoln, NE: University of Nebraska Press, 1997.

Darrock, J. E., and S. Singh. "Why is Teenage Pregnancy Declining? The Roles of Abstinence, Sexual Activity, and Contraceptive Use." *Occasional Report* 1 (1999). New York: The Alan Guttmacher Institute.

Daston, Lorraine, and Gregg Mitman. *Thinking with Animals: New Perspectives on Anthropomorphism.* New York: Columbia University Press, 2005.

Davenport, Dawn. *The Complete Book of International Adoption: A Step by Step Guide to Finding Your Child.* New York: Broadway Press, 2006.

Davis, Deborah. *You Look Too Young to be a Mom: Teen Mothers on Love, Learning, and Success.* New York: Perigree, 2004.

Davis, Lennard J. *The Disability Studies Reader.* New York: Routledge, 2006.

Davis-Floyd, Robbie E. *Birth as an American Rite of Passage.* Berkeley, CA: University of California Press, 2004.

DeAngelis, Barbara. *The Real Rules: How to Find the Right Man for the Real You.* New York: Dell Books, 1997.

Dearden, Chris, and Saul Becker. "Young Carers and Education." *Carers UK*, 2002. Available at: http://www.lboro.ac.uk/departments/ss/centres/YCRG/youngCarers Download/yceduc[1].pdf.

Defago, Nicki. *Childfree and Loving It!* London: Vision, 2005.

Demos, John. 1970. *A Little Commonwealth.* New York: Oxford University Press, 1970.

Demos, John. *Past, Present, and Personal: The Family and the Life Course of American History.* New York: Oxford University Press, 1986.

Department of Health and Human Services. "Cohabitation, Marriage, Divorce, and Remarriage in the United States." *Vital and Health Statistics* 23, no. 22. Hyattsville, MD: Department of Health and Human Services. Available at: www.cdc.gov/nchs/data/series/sr_23/sr23_022.pdf.

Descartes, Rene. "Animals are Machines." In *Animal Rights and Human Obligations,* ed. Regan T. and P. Singer. Upper Saddle River, NJ: Prentice Hall, 1976.

Deyo, Yaacov, and Sue Deya. *Speed Dating: A Timesaving Guide to Finding Your Lifelong Love.* New York: HarperCollins Publishers, 2003.

Dickson, Lynda. "The Marriage and Family in Black America." *Journal of Black Studies* 23 (1993): 472–491.

Digregorio, Charlotte. *Everything You Need to Know about Nursing Homes.* Portland, OR: Civetta Press, 2005.

Divakaruni, Chitra. "Arranged Marriages Can Provide Couples Stronger Relationships: South Asian Families Are Adopting an Updated Version of the Old Custom." *The Standard,* June 23, 2001, Viewpoint section, St. Catherines, Ontario, edition: A13.

Dobson, James C. *Marriage Under Fire: Why We Must Win This Battle.* Colorado Springs, CO: WaterBrook Multnomah Publishing Group, 2007.

Doherty, William J. *Take Back Your Marriage: Sticking Together in a World that Pulls Us Apart.* New York: Guilford Publications, 2001.

Domar, Alice. *Conquering Infertility.* New York: Penguin Books, 2002.

Dowling, Scott. *The Psychology and Treatment of Addictive Behavior.* Madison, CT: International Universities Press, 1995.

Downs, Donald Alexander. *More Than Victims: Battered Women, the Syndrome Society, and the Law.* Chicago: The University of Chicago Press, 1996.

Downs, Susan Whitelaw, Ernestine Moore, Emily Jean McFadden, and Susan Michaud. *Child Welfare and Family Services: Policies and Practices,* 7th ed. New York: Allyn-Bacon, 2003.

Doyle, Laura. *The Surrendered Wife: A Practical Guide to Finding Intimacy, Passion, and Peace.* New York: Fireside, 2001.

Drake, Jennifer. "Pro's and Con's of Eloping versus Planning a Wedding Ceremony," 2007. Associated Content Web site. Available at: http://www.associatedcontent.com/article/185413/the_pros_and_cons_of_eloping_versus.html.

Drescher, Jack, and Deborah Glazer. *Gay and Lesbian Parenting.* Binghamton, NY: The Haworth Medical Press, 2001.

Durkheim, Emile. *The Elementary Forms of Religious Life.* Translated from French by Joseph Ward Swain. New York: Free Press, 1965.

Dutton, Donald G. *Rethinking Domestic Violence.* Vancouver, BC: UBC Press, 2006.

Duvall, Steven F., Joseph C. Delquadri, and D. Lawrence Ward. "A Preliminary Investigation of the Effectiveness of Homeschool Instructional Environments for Students with Attention-Deficit/Hyperactivity Disorder." *School Psychology Review* 33 (2004): 140–158.

Ebaugh, Helen Rose, and Mary Curry. "Fictive Kin as Social Capital in New Immigrant Communities." *Sociological Perspectives* 43 (2000):189–209.

Edgarton, Robert B. *The Cloak of Competence: Stigma in the Lives of the Mentally Retarded.* Berkeley: University of California Press, 1967.

Edwards, O. "Teachers' Perceptions of the Emotional and Behavioral Functioning of Children Raised by Grandparents." *Psychology in the Schools* 43 (2006): 565–572.

Ehrensaft, Diane. *Parenting Together: Men and Women Sharing the Care of Their Children.* Champaign: University of Illinois Press, 1990.

Eitzen, Stanley, and Maxine Baca Zinn. "Contemporary Family Policy: An Alternative Vision." *Michigan Family Review* 2 (1997): 7–24.

Eitzen, Stanley, and Maxine Baca Zinn. "The Missing Safety Net and Families: A Progressive Critique of the New Welfare Legislation." *Journal of Sociology and Social Welfare* 27 (2000): 53–73.

Elkind, David. *The Hurried Child: Growing Up Too Fast Too Soon: 25th Anniversary Edition.* Cambridge, MA: Perseus Books, 2006.

Elkind, David. *The Power of Play: How Spontaneous, Imaginative Activities Lead to Happier, Healthier Children.* Cambridge, MA: Perseus Books, 2006.

Ellison, Christopher, and Kristin Anderson. "Religious Involvement and Domestic Violence among U.S. Couples." *Journal for the Scientific Study of Religion* 40 (2001): 260–286.

Ellison, Christopher, John Bartkowski, and Kristin Anderson. "Are There Religious Variations in Domestic Violence?" *Journal of Family Issues* 20 (1999): 87–113.

Ellison, Christopher, Jenny Trinitapoli, Kristin L. Anderson, and Byron Johnson. "Race/ethnicity, Religious Involvement, and Domestic Violence." *Violence against Women* 13 (2007): 1094–1112.

Emery, Robert E. *Marriage, Divorce and Children's Adjustment,* 2nd ed. Thousand Oaks, CA: Sage Publications, 1999.

England, Paula, and Nancy Folbre. "The Cost of Caring." *The Annals of the American Academy of Political and Social Sciences* 561(1999): 39–51.

Enss, Chris. *Hearts West: True Stories of Mail-Order Brides on the Frontier.* Guilford, CT: TwoDot Press, 2005.

Epstein, Fuchs Cynthia. "Great Divides: The Cultural, Cognitive, and Social Bases of the Global Subordination of Women." *American Sociological Review* 72 (2007):1–22.

Eriksen, S., and V. Jensen. "All in the Family? Family Environment Factors in Sibling Violence." *Journal of Family Violence* 21 (2006): 497–507.

Ernst, C. *Birth Order: It's Influence on Personality.* New York: Springer Publishing, 1983.

Evan B. Donaldson Adoption Institute. "Adoption by Lesbians and Gays: A National Survey of Adoption Agency Policies, Practices, and Attitudes." Evan B. Donaldson Adoption Institute, 2002. Available at: www.adoptioninstitute.org.

Evans, Richard C., and Elder Joseph P. Smith Jr. *Blood Atonement and the Origin of Plural Marriage: Church of Jesus Christ of Latter Day Saints.* Whitefish, MT: Kessinger Publishing, 2007.

Fagan, P., and R. Rector. "The Effects of Divorce on America." *Heritage Foundation Backgrounder* 1373 (June 2000). Available at: www.heritage.org/research/family/BG1373.cfm.

FaithTrust Institute. Working Together to End Sexual and Domestic Violence, 2008. FaithTrust Institute Web site. Available at: http://www.faithtrustinstitute.org/.

Falbo, Toni. *The Single-Child Family.* New York: Guilford, 1984.

Falk, Ursula A., and Gerhard Falk. *Grandparents: A New Look at the Supporting Generation.* Amherst, NY: Prometheus Books, 2002.

Falkner, Elizabeth Swire. *The Ultimate Insider's Guide to Adoption: Everything You Need to Know About Domestic and International Adoption.* New York: Wellness Central Publishing, 2006.

Faria, Alison. When to Consider Eloping, 2005. Happy Living Web site. Available at: http://www.happynews.com/living/eventtips/consider-eloping.htm.

Farmer, Steven. *Adult Children of Abusive Parents: A Healing Program for Those Who Have Been Physically, Sexually, or Emotionally Abused.* New York: Ballantine Books, 1989.

Fay, Jim. *Grandparenting with Love and Logic: Practical Solutions to Today's Grandparenting Challenges.* Golden, CO: Love and Logic Press, 1998.

Fein, E., and S. Schneider. *The Rules: Time-Tested Secrets for Capturing the Heart of Mr. Right.* New York: Warner Books, 1996.

Feldman, Maurice A., and Shannon E. Werner. "Collateral Effects of Behavioral Parent Training on Families of Children with Developmental Disabilities and Severe Behavior Disorders."*Behavioral Interventions* 17 (2002): 75–83.

Feldman, Maurice A., L. McDonald, L. Serbin, D. Stack, M. L. Secco, and C. T. Yu. "Predictors of Depressive Symptoms in Primary Caregivers of Young Children with or at Risk for Developmental Delay." *Journal of Intellectual Disability Research* 51 (2007): 606–619.

Ferber, Richard, M. D. *Solve Your Child's Sleep Problems: New, Revised and Expanded Edition.* New York: Fireside, 2006.

Feshbach, S. "The Function of Aggression and the Regulation of Aggressive Drive." *Psychological Review* 71 (1964): 257–272.

Fidelman, Charlie. "Arranged Marriages Still Very Popular: New Generation Years for Their Roots." *The Gazette,* April 27, 2003, News section, Montreal, Quebec, edition: A10.

Fields, Jason, and Lynne M. Casper. "America's Families and Living Arrangements: 2000." *Current Population Reports* 20–537 (2001): Figure 1.

Fineman, Martha Albertson. *Marriage Proposals; Questioning a Legal Status.* New York: New York University Press, 2006.

Fiorenza, E. Schussler. *Bread not Stone: The Challenge of Biblical Feminist Interpretation.* New York: Beacon Press, 1995.

Fisher, Bruce, and Robert E. Alberti. *Rebuilding: When Your Relationship Ends,* 3rd ed. Atascadero, CA: Impact Publishers, 2006.

Fisher, Laurel. Eloping vs. a Family Wedding, 2005. Happy Living Web site. Available at: http://www.happynews.com/living/eventtips/eloping-vs-family.htm.

Fisher, Seymour, and Rhonda Fisher. *What We Really Know About Child Rearing.* New York: Basic Books, 1976.

Fisher, S. W. The Stay at Home Dad: Why Some Christian Couples are Choosing to Reverse Roles and How it Affects Their Marriage. *Marriage Partnership* 17 (2000): 24.

Flowers, R. Barri. *Domestic Crimes, Family Violence and Child Abuse: A Study of Contemporary American Society.* Jefferson, NC: McFarland and Company, 2000.

Fowers, Blaine J. *Beyond the Myth of Marital Happiness: How Embracing the Virtues of Loyalty, Generosity, Justice, and Courage Can Strengthen Your Relationship.* New York: Jossey-Bass, 2000.

Fogle, B., and A. Edney. *Interrelations between People and Pets.* Chicago: Charles C. Thomas, 1981.

Fogel, Robert W., and Stanley Engerman. *Time on the Cross: The Economics of American Negro Slavery.* Boston: Little Brown, 1974.

Fogg-Davis, Hawley. *The Ethics of Transracial Adoption.* Ithaca, NY: Cornell University Press, 2002.

Folbre, Nancy. "Rethinking the Child Care Sector." *Community Development* 37 (2006): 38–53.

Folks, Homer. *The Care of Destitute, Neglected, and Delinquent Children.* London: The Macmillan Company, 1978.

Ford, D. A., and S. Breall. Violence against Women: Synthesis of Research for Prosecutors. National Institute of Justice, 2003. Available at: http://www.ncjrs.gov/pdf files1/nij/grants/199660.pdf.

Francis, Leslie Pickering, and Anita Silvers. *Americans with Disabilities: Exploring Implications of the Law for Individuals and Institutions.* New York: Routledge, 2000.

Frazier, Franklin. *The Negro Family in the United States.* Chicago: The University of Chicago Press, 1966.

Frinz, Iris, and Steven Frinz. *Secret Sex: Real People Talk About Outside Relationships They Hide from Their Partners.* New York: St. Martin's Press, 2003.

Fry Konty, Melissa, and Jonathan Harrison. *Child Care in Appalachian Kentucky: Financial Sustainability in a Low-income Market.* Berea, KY: Mountain Association for Community Economic Development, 2007.

Furstenberg, Frank. "Good Dads: Bad Dads: Two Faces of Fatherhood." In *The Changing American Family and Public Policy*, ed. Andrew J. Cherlin. Washington, D.C.: Urban Institute Press, 1988.

Furstenberg, Frank F., and Andrew Cherlin. *Divided Families: What Happens to Children When Parents Part.* Cambridge, MA: Harvard University Press, 1991.

Furstenberg, Frank E., and Christopher C. Weiss. "Intergenerational Transmission of Fathering Roles in At Risk Families." *Marriage and Family Review* 29 (2000): 181–202.

Gadberry, James H. "Pet Cemeteries Help Recognize Pet Bereavement." *Mortuary Management* 86 (2000): 18–19.

Galinsky, Ellen. *Ask the Children: The Breakthrough Study that Reveals How to Succeed at Work and Parenting.* New York: HarperCollins, 1999.

Galinsky, Ellen, and Judy David. *Ask the Children: What America's Children Really Think About Working Parents.* New York: William Morrow, 1999.

Garcia, Juanita L., and Jordan I. Kosberg, eds. *Elder Abuse: International and Cross-Cultural Perspectives.* New York. The Haworth Press, 1995.

Geffner, Robert A., and Alan Rosenbaum, eds. *Domestic Violence Offenders: Current Interventions, Research, and Implications for Policies and Standards.* Binghamton, NY: The Haworth Press, 2002.

Gelles, Richard J. *Intimate Violence in Families.* Thousand Oaks, CA: Sage, 1997.

Gelles, R. J., and C. P. Cornell. *Intimate Violence in Families,* 2nd ed. Thousand Oaks, CA: Sage, 1990.

Gelles, Richard J., and Donileen Loseke. *Current Controversies in Family Violence.* Thousand Oaks, CA: Sage Publications, 1993.

Gelles, R. J. "Violence in the Family: A Review of Research in the Seventies." *Journal of Marriage and the Family* 42 (1980): 873–885.

George, R. M., F. H. Wulczyn, and A. W. Harden. *Foster Care Dynamics 1983–1993: California, Illinois, Michigan.* Chicago: University of Chicago, Chapin Hall Center for Children, 1995.

Gest, Ted. "Divorce: How the Game is Played Now." *U.S. News and World Report,* November 21, 1983, 39–42.

Gibbs, Nancy, Hilary Hylton, and Peta Owens-Liston. "Polygamy Paradox." *Time,* October 7, 2007, 48–50.

Gillespie, Cynthia K. *Justifiable Homicide: Battered Women, Self-Defense and the Law.* Columbus: Ohio State University Press, 1989.

Ginsberg, Faye, D. *Contested Lives: The Abortion Debate in an American Community.* Berkeley: University of California Press, 1989.

Glenn, Norval D. With This Ring: A National Survey on Marriage in America. National Fatherhood Initiative Web Site, January 2008. Available at: www.smartmarriages.com/nms.pdf.

Godsall, Robert E., Gregory J. Jurkovic, James Emshoff, Louis Anderson, and Douglas Stanwyck. "Why Some Kids Do Well in Bad Situations: Relation of Parental Alcohol Misuse and Parentification to Children's Self-Concept." *Substance Use and Misuse* 39, no. 5 (2004): 789–809.

Goer, Henci. *The Thinking Woman's Guide to a Better Birth.* New York: A Perigee Book, 1999.

Goer, Henci. *Obstetric Myths Versus Research Realities: A Guide to the Medical Literature.* Westport, CT: Bergin and Garvey, 1995.

Goffman, Erving. *Stigma: Notes on Management of Spoiled Identity.* Englewood Cliffs, NJ: Prentice Hall, 1963.

Goldstein, Avram. *Addiction: From Biology to Drug Policy.* New York: Oxford University Press, 2001.

Gordon, Jay, M. D., and Maria Goodavage. *Good Nights (The Happy Parents' Guide to the Family Bed).* New York: St. Martin's Press, 2002.

Gordon, Sara Barringer. *The Mormon Question: Polygamy and Constitutional Conflict in Nineteenth Century America.* Chapel Hill: The University of North Carolina Press, 2002.

Gornick, Janet C., and Marcia K. Meyers. *Families that Work.* New York: Russell Sage Foundation, 2003.

Gosciewski, F. William. *Effective Child Rearing: The Behaviorally Aware Parent.* New York: Human Sciences Press, 1976.

Gottfried, Ted. *Teen Fathers Today.* Brookfield, CT: Twenty-First Century Books, 2001.

Gottman, John M. *What Predicts Divorce?: The Relationship Between Marital Processes and Marital Outcomes.* Hillsdale, NJ: Lawrence Erlbaum Associates, 1994.

Gottman, John M. *Why Marriages Succeed or Fail and How You Can Make Yours Last.* New York: Fireside, 1994.

Gottman, John M., and Nan Silver. *The Seven Principles for Making Marriage Work.* New York: Three Rivers Press, 1999.

Gottman, John. *And Baby Makes Three: The Six-Step Plan for Preserving Marital Intimacy and Rekindling Romance After Baby Arrives.* New York: Three Rivers Press, 2008.

Gowan, Mary A., and Raymond A. Zimmerman. "The Family and Medical Leave of 1993: Employee Rights and Responsibilities, Employer Rights and Responsibilities." *Employee Responsibilities and Rights Journal* 9 (1996): 57–71.

Grant, Gilbert J. *Enjoy Your Labor: A New Approach to Pain Relief for Childbirth.* White Plains, NY: Russell Hastings Press, 2005.

Gray, Deborah. *Attaching in Adoption: Practical Tools for Today's Parents.* Indianapolis: Perspective Press, 2002.

Green, Christa L., and Kathleen V. Hoover-Dempsey. "Why Do Parents Homeschool?" *Education and Urban Society* 39 (2007): 264–285.

Greenstein, T. N. "Gender Ideology, Marital Disruption, and the Employment of Married Women." *Journal of Marriage and the Family* 57 (1995): 31–42.

Grier, Katherine. *Pets in America: A History.* Chapel Hill, NC: University of North Carolina Press, 2006.

Grogger, Jeffrey, and Lynn A. Karoly. *Welfare Reform: Effects of a Decade of Change.* Cambridge, MA: Harvard University Press, 2005.

Gross, James J. *Fathers' Rights: A Legal Guide to Protecting the Best Interests of Your Children.* Naperville, IL: Sphinx Legal Publishing, 2004.

Gross, Michael. *The More Things Change: Why the Baby Boom Won't Fade Away.* New York: Harper Collins Publishers, 2000.

Guastello, Denise D., and Stephen J. Guastello. "Birth Category Effects on the Gordon Personal Profile Variables." Reyson Group Web Site. 2002. Available at: http://www.jasnh.com/a1.htm.

Gubrium, Jaber F., and James A. Holstein. *What is Family?* Mountain View, CA: Mayfield Publishing Co., 1990.

Hajnal, John. "Two Kinds of Preindustrial Household Formation System." *Population and Development Review* 8 (1982):449–494.

Halbig, Marlene C. *Personal Ads: Never Be Lonely Again.* LaPuente, CA: Baron Publications, 1992.

Hales, Brian C. *Mormon Polygamy and Mormon Fundamentalism: The Generation After the Manifesto.* Draper, UT: Greg Kofford Books, 2007.

Hall, Beth, and Gail Steinberg. Adoptism: A Definition. Pact, an Adoption Alliance Web site, 1998. Available at: www.pactadopt.org.

Hallowell, Edward M. "What I've Learned from ADD." In *Taking Sides: Clashing Views on Controversial Issue in Abnormal Psychology,* ed. Richard P. Halgin, 3rd ed. Duque, IO: McGraw-Hill/Duskin, 2005.

Han, E. L. Mandatory Arrest and no Drop Policies: Victim Empowerment in Domestic Violence Cases, 2002. Available at: http://www.bc.edu/schools/law/lawreviews/meta-elements/journals/bctwj/23_1/04_TXT.htm (accessed May 19, 2007).

Han, WenJui, and Jane Waldfogel. "Parental Leave: The Impact of Recent Legislation on Parents' Leave Taking." *Demography* 40 (2003): 191–200.

Harris, Fred R. *The Baby Bust: Who will do the Work? Who will Pay the Taxes?* Lanham, MD: Rowman and Littlefield Publishers, 2005.

Harris, Leslie M. *After Fifty: How the Baby Boom will Redefine the Mature Market.* Ithaca, NY: Paramount Market Publishing, 2003.

Hartlaub, P. Full-time Dad and Fine with It. July 23, 2006. Available at: http://www.sfgate.com.

Hartmann, Heidi. "The Unhappy Marriage of Marxism and Feminism: Towards a More Progressive Union." In *Social Stratification: The Sociological Perspective,* ed. D. Grusky. Boulder, CO: Westview Press, 2001.

Haskins, C. "Treating Sibling Incest Using a Family Systems Approach." *Journal of Mental Health Counseling* 25(2003): 337–351.

Hass, Aaron. *The Gift of Fatherhood: How Men's Lives are Transformed By Their Children.* New York: Fireside Publications, 1994.

Hastings, Richard P., and Helen M. Taunt. "Positive Perceptions in Families of Children with Developmental Disabilities." *American Journal on Mental Retardation* 107 (2002): 116–127.

Hausman, Bernice. *Mother's Milk: Breastfeeding Controversies in American Culture.* New York: Routledge, 2003.

Hawkins, Alan J., Steven L. Nock, Julia C. Wilson, Laura Sanchez, and James D. Wright. "Attitudes about Covenant Marriage and Divorce: Policy Implications from a 3-stage Comparison." *Family Relations* 51 (2002): 166–175.

Hawkins, Alan J., Lynn D. Wardle, and David O. Coolidge, eds. *Revitalizing the Institution of Marriage for the 21st Century: An Agenda for Strengthening Marriage.* New York: Praeger, 2002.

Hayden, Mary F., and Brian H. Abery. *Challenges for a Service System in Transition: Ensuring Quality Community Experiences for Persons with Developmental Disabilities.* Baltimore, MD: Paul H. Brookes, 1994.

Hays, Sharon. *The Cultural Contradictions of Motherhood.* New Haven, CT: Yale University Press, 1996.

Hayslip Jr., Bert, and Robin Goldberg-Glen, eds. *Grandparents Raising Grandchildren: Theoretical, Empirical, and Clinical Perspectives.* New York: Springer Publishing, 2000.

Hegeman, Mary Theodore. *Developmental Disability: A Family Challenge.* New York: Paulist Press, 1984.

Helburn, Suzanne Wiggons, and Barbara Bergmann. *America's Child Care Problem: The Way Out.* New York: Palgrave Macmillan, 2003.

Herrera, N. "Beliefs about Birth Rank and Their Reflection in Reality." *Journal of Personality and Social Psychology* 85 (2003): 142–150.

Hertel, Bradley, and Michael Hughes. "Religious Affiliation, Attendance, and Support for 'Pro-Family' Issues in the United States." *Social Forces* 65 (1987):858–883.

Hesse-Biber, Sharlene, and Gregg Lee Carter. *Working Women in America: Split Dreams.* New York: Oxford University Press, 2000.

Hetherington, E. Mavis, and John Kelly. *For Better or Worse: Divorce Reconsidered.* New York: W. W. Norton and Company, 2003.

Hewitt, Sylvia Ann. *Creating a Life: Professional Women and the Quest for Children.* New York: Miramax Books, 2002.

Higuera, V. C. Modern Weddings: Planning a Marriage Elopement. Associated Content Web site, 2006. Available at: http://www.associatedcontent.com/article/36493/modern_weddings_planning_a_marriage.html.

Hindin, Michelle, and Arland Thornton. *The Ties That Bind: Perspectives on Marriage and Cohabitation (Social Institutions and Social Change).* Piscataway, NJ: Aldine Transaction, 2000.

Hirschman, E. C. "Consumers and Their Companion Animals." *Journal of Consumer Research* 20 (1994): 616–632.

History of Domestic Violence: A Timeline of the Battered Women's Movement. Minnesota Center Against Violence and Abuse, 1999. Available at: http://www.mincava.umn.edu/documents/herstory/herstory.html (accessed May 26, 2007).

Hochschild, Arlie Russell, and Anne Machung. *The Second Shift: Working Parents and the Revolution at Home.* New York: Viking, 1989.

Hochschild, Arlie Russell. *The Time Bind: When Work Becomes Home and Home Becomes Work.* New York: Henry Holt and Company, 1997.

Hoffman, Allan M., and Summers, Randal W., eds. *Elder Abuse: A Public Health Perspective.* Washington, D.C.: American Public Health Association, 2006.

Hoffman, K. L., and J. N. Edwards. "An Integrated Theoretical Model of Sibling Violence and Abuse." *Journal of Family Violence* 19 (2004): 185–200.

Hooper, Lisa. M. "Expanding the Discussion Regarding Parentification and Its Varied Outcomes: Implications for Mental Health Research and Practice." *Journal of Mental Health Counseling* 29, no. 4 (2007): 322–37.

Horton, Anne, and Judith Williamson. *Abuse and Religion: When Praying Isn't Enough.* Lexington, MA: D.C. Heath and Company, 1988.

Houts, Leslie A. "But Was It Wanted? Young Women's First Voluntary Sexual Intercourse." *Journal of Family Issues* 26 (2005): 1082–1102.

Hoyt, Peggy R. *All My Children Wear Fur Coats: How to Leave a Legacy for your Pet.* West Conshohoken, PA: Infinity Publishing, 2002.

Human Rights Campaign. *HRC: Domestic Partners.* Washington, D.C.: Human Rights Campaign, 2008. Available at: http://www.hrc.org/issues/marriage/domestic_partners.asp.Human Rights Campaign. *HRC: Civil Unions.* Washington, D.C.: Human Rights Campaign, 2008 Available at: http://www.hrc.org/issues/marriage/civil_unions.asp.Human Rights Campaign. *Massachusetts Marriage/Relationship Recognition Law.* Washington, D.C.: Human Rights Campaign, 2008. Available at: http://www.hrc.org/laws_and_elections/926.htm.Hyman, Irwin A. *Reading, Writing, and the Hickory Stick. The Appalling Story of Physical and Psychological Abuse in American Schools.* Lexington, MA: Lexington Books, 1990.

Ibsen, Charles, and Patricia Klobus. "Fictive Kin Term Use and Social Relationships: Alternative Interpretations." *Journal of Marriage and Family* 34(1972):615–620.

In The Name of Love: Modern Day Mail Order Brides, dir. Shannon O'Rourke, 2005. Harriman, NY: New Day Films. (Film)

Ingraham, Chrys. *White Weddings: Romancing Heterosexuality in Popular Culture,* 2nd ed. New York: Routledge, 2008.

Intimate Partner Violence: Overview. Centers for Disease Control and Prevention. August 26, 2006. Available at: http://www.cdc.gov/ncipc/factsheets/ipvoverview.htm.

Isabella, Kalee. Elope. Love to Know Weddings, 2006. Available at: http://weddings.lovetoknow.com/wiki/Elope.

Jagannathan R., M. Camasso, and S. McLanahan. "Welfare Reform and Child Fostering: Pinpointing Affected Child Populations." *Social Science Quarterly* 86 (2005): 1081–1103.

Jellison, Katherine. *It's Our Day: America's Love Affair with the White Wedding 1945–2005.* Lawrence: University of Kansas Press, 2008.

Jendrek, Margaret P. "Grandparents Who Parent Their Grandchildren: Effects on Lifestyle." *Journal of Marriage and the Family* 55 (1993):609–621.

Jenks, Richard J. "Swinging: A Review of the Literature." *Archives of Sexual Behavior* 27 (1998): 507–520

John, Jaiya. *Black Baby, White Hands: A View from the Crib.* Silver Spring, MD: Soul Water Rising, 2005.

Johnson, Colleen. "Perspectives on American Kinship in the Later 1990s." *Journal of Marriage and Family* 62 (2000):623–639.

Johnson, Leanor Boulin, and Robert Staples. *Black Families at the Crossroads: Challenges and Prospects.* San Francisco: John Wiley and Sons, 2005.

Johnson, M. P. "Patriarchal Terrorism and Common Couple Violence: Two Forms of Violence Against Women." *Journal of Marriage and Family* 57 (1995): 283–294.

Johnson, M. P., and K. J. Ferraro. "Research on Domestic Violence in the 1990s: Making Distinctions." *Journal of Marriage and Family* 62 (2000): 948–963.

Jones, Ann. *Next Time She'll Be Dead: Battering and How to Stop It.* New York: Beacon Press, 2000.

Jost, Kenneth. "*Gay Marriage.*" *Issues for Debate in American Public Policy,* 5th ed. Washington, D.C.: CQ Press, 2004.

Kakar, Suman. *Domestic Abuse: Public Policy/Criminal Justice Approaches Towards Child, Spousal and Elderly Abuse.* San Francisco: Austin and Winfield, 1998.

Kamp Dush, Claire M., Catherine L. Cohan, and Paul Amato. "The Relationship between Cohabitation and Marital Quality and Stability: Change Across Cohorts." *Journal of Marriage and Family* 63 (2003): 539–549.

Karp, Harvey. *The Happiest Baby on the Block.* New York: Bantam Dell, 2002.

Katcher, A. H., and A. M. Beck. *New Perspectives on our Lives with Companion Animals.* Philadelphia: University of Pennsylvania Press, 1983.

Kaufman, Carole. *Sins of Omission: The Jewish Community's Reaction to Domestic Violence.* Boulder, CO: Westview Press, 2003.

Kay, W., Nieburg H. A., Kutscher, A. H., Grey, R. M., and C. E. Fudin. *Pet Loss and Human Bereavement.* Ames, IA: Iowa State University Press, 1984.

Kelly, Erin. "The Strange History of Employer-Sponsored Child Care: Interested Actors, Uncertainty, and the Transformation of Law in Organizational Fields." *American Journal of Sociology* 109(2003): 606–649.

Kelly, Kristin A. *Domestic Violence and the Politics of Privacy.* Ithaca, NY: Cornell University Press, 2003.

Kennedy, Allison M., and Deborah A. Gust. "Parental Vaccine Beliefs and Child's School Type." *Journal of School Health* 75 (2005): 276–280.

Kennedy, John S. *The New Anthropomorphism.* New York: Cambridge University Press, 1992.

Kettrey, H., and B. Emery. "The Discourse of Sibling Violence." *Journal of Family Violence* 22 (2007): 769.

Khandelwal, Madhulika S. *Becoming American, Being Indian: An Immigrant Community in New York City.* Ithaca, NY: Cornell University Press, 2002.

Kirsh, Steven J. *Children, Adolescents, and Media Violence: A Critical Look at the Research.* Thousand Oaks, CA: Sage Publications, 2006.

Kiselica, A., and M. Morril-Richards. "Sibling Maltreatment: The Forgotten Abuse." *Journal of Counseling and Development* 85 (2007): 146–160.

Kitzinger, Sheila. *The Complete Book of Pregnancy and Childbirth,* 4th ed. New York: Knopf, 2003.

Knickmeyer, Nicole, Heidi Levitt, Sharon Horne, and Gary Bayer. "Responding to Mixed Messages and Double Binds: Religious Oriented Coping Strategies of Christian Battered Women." *Journal of Religion and Abuse* 5 (2003): 29–54.

Knoll, Jean, and Mary-Kate Murphy. *International Adoption: Sensitive Advice for Prospective Parents.* Chicago: Chicago Review Press, 1994.

Koppelman, Andrew. *The Gay Rights Question in Contemporary American Law.* Chicago: The University of Chicago Press, 2002.

Kornblum, Janet. "When Child Cares for Parent." *USA Today,* September 14, 2005. Student Research Center Database.

Kornhaber, Arthur. *The Grandparent Guide: The Definitive Guide to Coping with the Challenges of Modern Grandparenting.* New York: Contemporary Books, 2002.

Kotlowitz, Alex. *There Are No Children Here: The Story of Two Boys Growing Up in The Other America.* New York: Anchor Books, 1991.

Krakauer, Jon. *Under the Banner of Heaven.* London: Pan Books, 2004.

Kranz, Rachel, and Tim Cusick. *Gay Rights. Library in a Book,* rev ed. New York: Facts on File, 2005.

Krause, Harry D., and David D. Meyer. *Family Law in a Nutshell,* 5th ed. St. Paul, MN: Thomson West, 2007.

Kreisher, Kristen. "Gay Adoption." *Children's Voice Magazine* 17. Child Welfare League of America, January/February 2002. Available at: http://www.cwla.org/articles/cv 0201gayadopt.htm.

Kroeger, Catherine, and James Beck. *Healing the Hurting: Giving Hope and Help to Abused Women.* Grand Rapids, MI: Baker Books, 1998.

Kroeger, Catherine, and Nancy Nason-Clark. *No Place for Abuse: Biblical and Practical Resources to Counteract Domestic Violence.* Downers Grove, IL: Intervarsity Press, 2001.

Kuriansky, Judith. *Complete Idiot's Guide to Dating.* Indianapolis, IN: Alpha Books, 2004.

Kurst-Swanger, Karel, and Jacqueline L. Petcosky. *Violence in the Home: Multidisciplinary Perspectives.* New York: Oxford University Press, 2003.

Lackey, Nancy R., and Marie F. Gates. "Adults' Recollections of their Experiences as Young Caregivers of Family Members with Chronic Physical Illnesses." *Journal of Advanced Nursing* 34, no. 3 (2001): 320–328.

La Leche League International, Inc. *The Womanly Art of Breast Feeding,* 6th ed. Schaumberg, IL: LaLeche League International, 1997.

Lamb, Kathleen A., Gary R. Lee, and Alfred DeMaris. "Union Formation and Depression: Selection and Relationship Effects." *Journal of Marriage and Family* 65 (2003): 953–962.

Lanci-Altomare, Michele. *Good-Bye My Friend: Pet Cemeteries, Memorials, and Other Ways to Remember.* Irvine, CA: Bowtie Press, 2000.

Landry, Bart. *Black Working Wives: Pioneers of the American Family Revolution.* Berkeley: University of California Press, 2000.

Landry-Meyer, Laura, Jean M. Gerard, and Jacqueline R. Guzell. "Caregiver Stress Among Grandparents Raising Grandchildren: The Functional Role of Social Support." *Marriage and Family Review* 37 (2005): 171–190.

Laner, Mary Reige. *Dating: Delights, Discontents and Dilemmas.* Salem, WI: Sheffield Publishing Co., 1992.

Lareau, Annette. *Unequal Childhoods: Class, Race, and Family Life.* Berkeley: University of California Press, 2003.

Larsen, Wanwadee. *Confessions of a Mail-Order Bride: American Life through Thai Eyes.* Far Hills, NJ: New Horizon Press, 1989.

Laufer-Ukeles, Pamela. Gestation: Work for Hire or the Essence of Motherhood? A Comparative Legal Analysis. *Duke Journal of Gender Law and Policy* 9 (2002): 91–134.

LaViolette, Alyce D., and Ola W. Barnett. *It Could Happen to Anyone: Why Battered Women Stay.* Thousand Oaks, CA: Sage, 2000.

Leavitt, Jacqueline. "Where's the Gender in Community Development?" *Journal of Women in Culture and Society* 29(2003): 207–231.

Leman, Kevin. *The New Birth Order Book: Why You Are the Way You Are.* Grand Rapids, MI: Revell Books, 1998.

Leo, Jonathan. "American Preschoolers on Ritalin." *Society* 39 (2002): 52–60.

Leonard, Karen I. *The South Asian Americans.* Westport, CT: Greenwood Press, 1997.

Lessinger, Johanna. *From the Ganges to the Hudson: Indian Immigrants in New York City.* Boston: Allyn and Bacon, 1995.

Levin, Irene, and Jan Trost. "Understanding the Concept of Family." *Family Relations* 41 (1992): 348–351.

Lewis, Oscar. *La Vida: A Puerto Rican Family in the Culture of Poverty: San Juan and New York.* New York: Vintage Books, 1966.

Lewis, Oscar. *A Study of Slum Culture: Backgrounds for La Vida.* New York: Random House, 1968.

Li, R., F. Fridinger, and L. Grummer-Strawn. "Public Perceptions on Breastfeeding Constraints." *Journal of Human Lactation* 18 (2002): 227–235.

Liebow, Elliot. *Tally's Corner.* Boston: Brown and Company, 1967.

Linares, L. O. "An Understudied form of Intra-family Violence: Sibling-to-Sibling Aggression among Foster Children." *Aggression and Violent Behavior* 11 (2006): 95–109.

Lindsey, D. *The Welfare of Children.* New York: Oxford University Press, 1994.

Lindsey, Linda L. *Gender Roles: A Sociological Perspective,* 3rd ed. Upper Saddle River, NJ: Prentice Hall, 1997.

Lisle, Laurie. *Without Child: Challenging the Stigma of Childlessness.* New York: Ballantine Books, 1996.

Lowe, Heather. What You Should Know If You're Considering Adoption for Your Baby. Concerned United Birthparents Web site, 2006. Available at: www.cubirthparents.org.

Lowery, Fred. *Covenant Marriage: Staying Together For Life.* West Monroe, LA: Howard Publishing Co., 2002.

Luker, Kristen. *Abortion and the Politics of Motherhood.* Berkeley: University of California Press, 1984.

Luker, Kristin. *Dubious Conceptions: The Politics of Teenage Pregnancy.* Cambridge, MA: Harvard University Press, 1996.

MacGregor, Cynthia. *Mommy Rescue Guide: Getting Your Baby to Sleep.* Avon, MA: Adams Media, 2007.

Magnusson, Tony. "What's Love Got to Do With It?" *Sunday Herald Sun* (Melbourne Australia), February 12, 2006, Magazine section: 20.

Malacrida, Claudia. "Alternative Therapies and Attention Deficit Disorder: Discourses of Maternal Responsibility and Risk." *Gender and Society* 16 (2002): 366–383.

Mallon, Gerald P. *Lesbian and Gay Foster and Adoptive Parents: Recruiting, Assessing, and Supporting an Untapped Resource for Children and Youth.* Washington, DC: Child Welfare League of America Inc., 2006.

Mancillas, A. "Challenging the Stereotypes about Only Children: A Review of the Literature and Implications for Practice." *Journal of Counseling and Development* 84 (2006): 268–275.

March, Karen, and Charlene E. Miall. "Reinforcing the Motherhood Ideal: Public Perceptions of Biological Mothers Who Make an Adoption Plan." *The Canadian Review of Sociology and Anthropology* 43 (2006): 367–386.

Markman, Howard J., Scott M. Stanley, and Susan L. Blumberg. *Fighting for Your Marriage: Positive Steps for Preventing Divorce and Preserving a Lasting Love.* New York: Jossey-Bass, 2001.

Marks, Michelle Rose. "Party Politics and Family Policy." *Journal of Family Issues* 18 (1997): 55–70.

Marks, Michelle Rose. *Business, Labor, Gender, and the State: The Shaping of the Family and Medical Leave Act of 1993.* Akron, OH: University of Akron Press, 1995.

Marshner, Connie. Reform the Nation's Foster Care System Now. Family Research Council Web site, 2005. Available at: www.frc.org.

Marsiglio, William, Paul Amato, Randal D. Day, and Michael E. Lamb. "Scholarship on Fatherhood in the 1990s and Beyond." *Journal of Marriage and the Family* 62(2000): 1173–1191.

Marsiglio, William, and Sally Hutchinson. *Sex, Men, and Babies: Stories of Awareness and Responsibility*. New York: New York University Press, 2004.

Marston, Allison. "Planning for Love: The Politics of Prenuptial Agreements." *Stanford Law Review* 49 (1997): 887–916.

Maschke, Karen J. *The Legal Response to Violence Against Women*. New York: Garland Publishing, 1997.

Mason, Mary Ann, Arlene Skolnick, and Stephen D. Sugarman, eds. *All Our Families: New Policies for a New Century*. New York: Oxford University Press, 1998.

Mattox, Renee, and Jeanette Harder. "Attention Deficit Hyperactivity Disorder (ADHD) and Diverse Populations." *Child and Adolescent Social Work Journal* 24 (2007): 195–207.

Maushart, Susan. *The Mask of Motherhood: How Becoming a Mother Changes Everything and Why We Pretend It Doesn't*. New York: New Press, 1999.

Maushart, Susan. *Wifework: What Marriage Really Means for Women*. New York: Bloomsbury, 2001.

Maxwell, Carol J. C. *Pro-Life Activists in America: Meaning, Motivation, and Direct Action*. Cambridge: Cambridge University Press, 2002.

Mayntz, Melissa. Places to Elope. Love to Know Weddings, 2007. Available at: http://weddings.lovetoknow.com/wiki/Places_to_Elope.

McCarthy, Barry, and Emily J. McCarthy. *Getting It Right the First Time: Creating a Healthy Marriage*. New York: Brunner-Routledge, 2004.

McCullough, Derek, and Hall, David S. Polyamory-What it Is and What it Isn't. Electronic Journal of Human Sexuality, February 27, 2003. Available at: http://www.ejhs.org/volume6/polamory.htm.

McGrath, E. *My One and Only: The Special Experience of the Only Child*. New York: Morrow, 1989.

McKenna, James J. *Sleeping with Your Baby: A Parent's Guide to Cosleeping*. Washington, DC: Platypus Press, 2007.

McLellan, David. "Contract Marriage: The Way Forward or Dead End?" *Journal of Law and Society* 23 (1996): 234–246.

McRae, William J. *Preparing for Your Marriage*. Grand Rapids, MI: The Zondervan Corporation, 1980.

Mead, Rebecca. *One Perfect Day: The Selling of the American Wedding*. New York: The Penguin Press, 2007.

Meisels, Joseph, and Martin Loeb, "Foster Care and Adoption: Unanswered Questions About Foster Care" *The Social Service Review* 30, no. 3 (1956): 239–246.

Meyers, Marcia K., and Janet C. Gornick. "Public or Private Responsibility? Early Childhood Education and Care, Inequality, and the Welfare State." *Journal of Comparative Family Studies* 34 (2003): 379–406.

Miller, Laurie C. *The Handbook of International Adoption Medicine: A Guide for Physicians, Parents, and Providers*. New York: Oxford University Press, 2004.

Mills, Linda G. *Insult to Injury: Rethinking Our Responses to Intimate Abuse.* Princeton, NJ: Princeton University Press, 2003.

Mills, L. G. "Mandatory Arrest and Prosecution Policies for Domestic Violence: A Critical Literature Review and the Case for More Research to Test Victim Empowerment Approaches." *Criminal Justice and Behavior* 25 (1998): 306–319.

Mincy, Ronald B. "Marriage, Child Poverty, and Public Policy." 2001. Available at: http://www.americanexperiment.org/uploaded/files/aeqv4n2mincy.pdf.

Minervini, Bibiana Paez, and Francis T. McAndrew. "The Mating Strategies and Mate Preferences of Mail Order Brides." *Cross Cultural Research* 40 (2006): 111–129.

Minkler, Meredith, and Kathleen M. Roe. "Grandparents as Surrogate Parents." *Generations* 20 (1996): 34–39.

Mitford, Jessica. *The American Way of Birth.* New York: Penguin, 1992.

Mobilia, Marcia, and Joel Bulmil. *Deadbeat Dads: A National Child Support Scandal.* Westport, CT: Praeger Publishers, 1996.

Monteleone, James A. *A Parent's and Teacher's Handbook on Identifying and Preventing Child Abuse.* St. Louis, MO: G.W. Medical Publishing, 1998.

Morgan, Marabel. *The Total Woman.* New York: Pocket Books, 1990.

Moynihan, Daniel Patrick. "The Negro Family: The Case for National Action." In *The Moynihan Report and the Politics of Controversy,* ed. Lee Rainwater and William L. Yancey. Cambridge, Massachusetts: The M.I.T. Press, 1967.

Nason-Clark, Nancy. *The Battered Wife: How Christians Confront Family Violence.* Louisville, KY: Westminster John Knox Press, 1997.

Nason-Clark, Nancy. "When Terror Strikes at Home: The Interface Between Religion and Domestic Violence." *Journal for the Scientific Study of Religion* 42 (2004): 303–310.

National Alliance on Caregiving and the United Hospital Fund. "Young Caregivers in the U.S.," 2005. Available at: http://www.caregiving.org/data/youngcaregivers.pdf.

National Coalition for Child Protection Reform. Foster Care vs. Keeping Families Together: The Definitive Study. National Coalition for Child Protection Reform Web site, 2006. Available at: www.nccpr.org.

National Coalition for Child Protection Reform. What is "Family Preservation"? National Coalition for Child Protection Reform Web site, 2005. Available at: www.nccpr.org.

National Institute of Child Health and Human Development, NIH, DHHS. *The NICHD Study of Early Child Care and Youth Development (SECCYD): Findings for Children up to Age 4 1/2 Years (05–4318).* Washington, DC: U.S. Government Printing Office, 2006.

Nelson, T. J., S. Clampet-Lundquist, and K. Edin. "Sustaining Fragile Fatherhood": Father Involvement among Low-income, Noncustodial African American Fathers in Philadelphia. In *A Handbook of Father Involvement,* ed. Catherine S. Tamis-LeMonda, and Natasha Cabrera. Mahwah, NJ: Lawrence Erlbaum, 2002.

Netting, Nancy S. "Two-Lives, One Partner: Indo-Candian Youth Between Love and Arranged Marriages." *Journal of Comparative Family Studies* 37, no. 1 (2006): 129–146.

Neufeld, B. "SAFE Questions: Overcoming the Barriers to Detecting Domestic Violence." *American Family Physician* 53 (1996): 2575–2581.

Neugarten, B., and Weinstein, K. "The Changing American Grandparent." *Journal of Marriage and Family* 26, no. 2 (1964): 199–204.

Newton, Betty, and Saul Becker. "The Capital Carers: An Evaluation of the Capital Carers Young Carers Project." Loughboro University, 1999. Available at: http://www.lboro.ac.uk/departments/ss/centres/YCRG/youngCarersDownload/capital%20carers.pdf.

NICHD Early Child Care Research Network. "The Effects of Infant Child Care on Infant-Mother Attachment Security: Results of the NICHD Study of Early Child Care." *Child Development* 68 (October 1997): 860–879.

NICHD Early Child Care Research Network. "The Relation of Child Care to Cognitive and Language Development." *Child Development* 71 (July-August 2000): 960–980.

Nichols, Joel A. "Louisiana's Covenant Marriage Law: A First Step Toward a More Robust Pluralism in Marriage and Divorce Law?" *Emory Law Journal* 47 (1998): 929–930.

NIJ's Violence Against Women Research and Evaluation Program: Selected Results. VAWFV: Violence Against Women and Family Violence. Available at:http://www.ojp.gov/nij/vawprog/selected_results.html (accessed May 16, 2007).

Nock, Steven L., James D. Wright, and Laura Sanchez. "America's Divorce Problem." *Society* 36 (1999): 43–52.

Nordstrom, Byron. *The History of Sweden.* Westport, CT: Greenwood Press, 2002.

Nordstrom, N. "When Dad Stays Home." *Jugglezine,* June 12, 1998. Available at: http://www.hermanmiller.com.

Olfson, Mark, Marc J. Gameroff, Steven C. Marcus, and Peter S. Jensen. "National Trends in the Treatment of Attention Deficit Hyperactivity Disorder." *The American Journal of Psychiatry* 160 (2003): 1071–1076.

Oliver, Mary Beth, and Janet Shibley Hyde. "Gender Differences in Sexuality: A Meta-analysis." *Psychological Bulletin* 114 (1993): 29–52.

Olsson, Malin B., and C. P. Hwang. "Depression in Mothers and Fathers Rearing Children with Intellectual Disabilities." *Journal of Intellectual Disability Research* 45 (2001): 535–545.

Orel, Nancy A., and Paula Dupuy. "Grandchildren as Auxiliary Caregivers for Grandparents with Cognitive and/or Physical Limitations: Coping Strategies and Ramifications." *Child Study Journal* 32, no. 4 (2002): 193–213.

Ortiz, C. G., and Ena Vasquez-Nuttal. "Adolescent Pregnancy: Effects of Family Support, Education, and Religion on the Decision to Carry or Terminate Among Puerto Rican Teenagers." *Adolescence* 22 (1987): 897–917.

Otnes, Cele C., and Elizabeth J. Pleck. *Cinderella Dreams: The Allure of the Lavish Wedding.* Berkeley: University of California Press, 2003.

Owen, S. *Numbers of Stay-at-Home-Fathers Are Rising.* Available at: http://www.thenothwestern.com (accessed March 5, 2008).

Padavic, Irene, and Barbara Reskin. *Women and Men at Work.* Thousand Oaks, CA: Pine Forge Press, 2002.

Pagelow, Mildred. "Secondary Battering and Alternatives of Female Victims of Spouse Abuse." In *Women and Crime in America,* ed. Lee Bowker. New York: MacMillan, 1981.

Pagnini, Deanna, and Philip Morgan. "Racial Differences in Marriage and Childbearing: Oral History Evidence from the South in the Early Twentieth Century." *The American Journal of Sociology* 101 (1996): 1694–1718.

Panksepp, Jaak. "Attention Deficit Hyperactivity Disorders, Psychostimulants, and Intolerance of Childhood Playfulness: A Tragedy in the Making?" *Current Directions in Psychological Science* 7 (1998): 91–98.

Pargament, Kenneth. *The Psychology of Religion and Coping: Theory, Research, and Practice.* New York: Guilford Press, 1997.

Parrott, Les, and Leslie Parrot. *Saving Your Second Marriage Before It Starts.* Grand Rapids, MI: Zondervan, 2001.

Patton, Sandra. *BirthMarks: Transracial Adoption in Contemporary America.* New York: New York University Press, 2000.

Paul, Pamela. *The Starter Marriage and the Future of Matrimony.* New York: Villard, 2002.

Payne, Brian K. *Crime and Elder Abus: An Integrated Perspective.* Chicago: Charles C. Thomas, 2005.

Peele, Stanton. *Seven Tools to Beat Addiction.* New York: Three Rivers Press, 2004.

Peisner-Feinberg, E. S., M. R. Burchinal, R. M. Clifford, M. L. Culkin, C. Howes, S. L. Kagan, N. Yazehian, P. Byler, J. Rustici, and J. Zelazo. *The Children of the Cost, Quality, and Outcomes Study go to School: Executive Summary.* Chapel Hill: University of North Carolina at Chapel Hill, Frank Porter Graham Child Development Center, 1999.

Perry, Brea. "Understanding Social Network Disruption: The Case for Youth in Foster Care." *Social Problems* 53 (2006): 371–391.

Peskowitz, Miriam. *The Truth Behind the "Mommy Wars": Who Decides What Makes a Good Mother?* Berkeley, CA: Seal Press, 2005.

Phillips, R. *Untying the Knot: A Short History of Divorce.* New York: Cambridge University Press, 1991.

Pillemer Karl A., and Rosalie S. Wolf. *Helping Elderly Victims: The Reality of Elder Abuse.* New York: Columbia University Press, 1989.

Pinello, D. R. *America's Struggle for Same-sex Marriage.* New York: Cambridge University Press, 2006.

Place, Jeffery. "Gestational Surrogacy and the Meaning of 'Mother': Johnson v. Calvert." *Harvard Journal of Law and Public Policy* 9 (1994): 907–918.

Polakow, Valerie. *Who Cares for Our Children?* New York: Teachers College Press, 2007.

Poling, James, and Christie Neuger. *Men's Work in Preventing Violence against Women.* Binghamton, NY: The Haworth Press, 2003.

Pollack, Eunice G. "The Children We Have Lost: When Siblings were Caregivers, 1900–1970." *Journal of Social History* 36, no. 1 (2002): 31.

Popenoe, David. *Disturbing the Nest: Family Change and Decline in Modern Societies.* Piscataway, NJ: Transaction Publishers, 1988.

Popenoe, D. *State of Our Unions: The Social Health of Marriage in America, 1999.* New Brunswick, NJ: The National Marriage Project, 1999.

Popenoe, David, and Barbara Defoe Whitehead. *Should We Live Together? What Young Adults Need to Know About Cohabitation Before Marriage: A Comprehensive Review of Recent Research*, 2nd ed. New Brunswick, NJ: The National Marriage Project, Rutgers University, 2002.

Postman, Neil. *The End of Education: Redefining the Value of School.* New York: Alfred A. Knopf, 1995.

Postman, Neil. *The Disappearance of Childhood.* New York: Vintage Books, 1994.

Prohaska, Ariane. *The Gendered Division of Leave Taking.* Akron, OH: University of Akron Press, 2006.

Ptacek, James. *Battered Women in the Courtroom: The Power of Judicial Responses.* Boston: Northeastern University Press, 1999.

Purdie, Nola, John Hattie, and Annemaree Carroll. "A Review of the Research on Interventions for Attention Deficit Hyperactivity Disorder: What Works Best?" *Review of Education Research* 72 (2002): 61–99.

Quinn, William H. *Family Solutions for Youth at Risk: Applications to Juvenile Delinquency, Truancy, and Behavior Problems.* New York: Brunner-Routledge, 2004.

Quinn, William H., and Richard Sutphen. "Juvenile Offenders: Characteristics of at-risk Families and Strategies for Intervention." *Journal of Addictions and Offender Counseling* 15 (1994): 2–23.

Quiroz, Pamela Ann. *Adoption in a Color-Blind Society.* Lanham, MD: Rowman and Littlefield. 2007.

Rainwater, Lee, and William L. Yancey. "The Moynihan Report and the Politics of Controversy." In *The Moynihan Report and the Politics of Controversy,* ed. Lee Rainwater and William L. Yancey. Cambridge, MA: The M.I.T. Press, 1967.

Randall, K. University of Texas Stay-at-Home Father Survey Results. Austin, TX: University of Texas Department of Educational Psychology, 2008. Available at: http://www.utexas.edu.

Rangaswamy, Padma. *Namasté America: Indian Immigrants in an American Metropolis.* University Park: The Pennsylvania State University Press, 2000.

Regnerus, Mark. "Religion and Positive Adolescent Outcomes: A Review of Research and Theory." *Review of Religious Research* 44 (2003): 394–313.

Reichman, Nancy E., Hope Corman, and Kelly Noonan. "Effects of Child Health on Parents' Relationship Status." *Demography* 41 (2004): 569–584.

Remez, Lisa. "Oral Sex Among Adolescents: Is It Sex or Is It Abstinence?" *Family Planning Perspectives* 32 (2000): 298–304.

Renick, Mari Jo, Susan L. Blumberg, and Howard J. Markman. "The Prevention and Relationship Enhancement Program (PREP): An Empirically Based Preventive Intervention Program for Couples." *Family Relations* 41 (1992): 141–147.

Rich, Adrienne. *Of Woman Born: Motherhood as Experience and Institution.* New York: W.W. Norton and Co., 1986.

Riddle, John M. *Eve's Herbs: A History of Contraception and Abortion in the West.* Cambridge, MA: Harvard University Press, 1997.

Rimmerman, Craig A., and Clyde Wilcox. *The Politics of Same-Sex Marriage.* Chicago: The University of Chicago Press, 2007.

Risdal, Don, and George H. S. Singer. "Marital Adjustment in Parents of Children with Disabilities: A Historical Review and Meta-analysis." *Research and Practice for Persons with Severe Disabilities* 29 (2004): 95–103.

Risman, Barbara, and Pepper Schwartz. "After the Sexual Revolution: Gender Politics in Teen Dating." *Contexts* 1 (2002): 16–24.

Roberts, Albert R., ed. *Handbook of Domestic Violence Intervention Strategies: Policies, Programs, and Legal Remedies.* New York: Oxford University Press, 2002.

Robinson, Evelyn Burns. *Adoption and Loss: the Hidden Grief.* Christies Beach, Australia: Clova Publications, 2000.

Rooks, Judith Pence. *Midwifery and Childbirth in America.* Philadelphia, PA: Temple University Press, 1997.

Ross, Cheri Barton, and J. Baron-Sorenson. *Pet Loss and human Emotion: a Guide to Recovery,* 2nd ed. London: Brunner-Routledge, 2007.

Rothman, Barbara Katz, Wendy Simonds, and Beri Meltzer Norman. *Laboring On: Birth in Transition in the United States.* New York: Routledge, 2006.

Rothman, E. A. *Hands and Hearts: A History of Courtship in America.* New York: Basic Books, 1984.

Rubin, Roger H. "Alternative Lifestyles Revisited, or Whatever Happened to Swingers, Group Marriages, and Communes?" *Journal of Family Issues* 22 (2001): 711–726.

Saake, Jennifer. *Hannah's Heart: Seeking God's Hope in the Midst of Infertility.* Colorado Springs, CO: NavPress, 2005.

Safer, Jennifer. *Beyond Motherhood: Choosing Life without Children.* New York: Pocket Books, 1996.

Schilling, Renee M. "The Effects of Birth Order on Interpersonal Relationships." 2001. McKendree University Web site. Available at: http://faculty.mckendree.edu/scholars/2001/Schilling.htm.

Schoen, Robert, and Robin Weinick. "Partner Choice in Marriages and Cohabitors." *Journal of Marriage and the Family* 55 (1993): 408–414.

Schuck, Peter. COLLOQUY: Some Reflections on the Baby M Case. *Georgetown Law Review* 76 (1988): 1793–1810.

Schwartz, Felice N. "Management Women and the New Facts of Life." *Harvard Business Review* 67 (1989): 65–76.

Schwartz, Margaret L. *The Pumpkin Patch: A Single Woman's Adoption Journey.* Chicago: Chicago Spectrum Press, 2005.

Schwarz, Pepper. *Peer Marriage.* New York: The Free Press, 1994.

Schwartz, Pepper. *Love Between Equals: How Peer Marriage Really Works.* New York: Simon and Schuster Adult Publishing Group, 1995.

Schweitzer, Arlette. *Whatever It Takes.* Mandan, ND: Crain Grosinger Publishing, 2004.

Sears, William, and Martha Sears. *The Birth Book: Everything You Need to Know to Have a Safe and Satisfying Birth.* New York: Little, Brown, and Co., 1994.

Sears, William, and Martha Sears. *The Pregnancy Book: A Month-by-Month Guide.* New York: Little, Brown, and Co., 1997.

Sears, W., and Sears, M. *The Breastfeeding Book.* New York: Little, Brown and Company, 2000.

Sears, William, and Martha Sears. *The Attachment Parenting Book.* New York: Little, Brown and Company, 2001.

Sember, Brette McWhorter. *Gay and Lesbian Parenting Choices: From Adopting or Using a Surrogate to Choosing the Perfect Father.* Franklin Lakes, NJ: The Career Press Inc., 2006.

Serpell, J. "People in Disguise: Anthropomorphism and the Human-Pet Relationship." In *Thinking with Animals: New Perspectives on Anthropomorphism,* ed. Daston, L. and G. Mitman. New York: Columbia University Press, 2005.

Shalev, Carmel. *Birth Power: The Case for Surrogacy.* New Haven, CT: Yale University Press, 1989.

Shannon-Lewy, Collen, and Valerie Dull. "The Response of Christian Clergy to Domestic Violence: Help or Hindrance?" *Aggression and Violent Behavior* 10 (2005): 647–659.

Shaver, K. "Stay at Home Dads Forge New Identities, Roles." *Washington Post*, June 17, 2007.

Shawne, Jennifer L. *Baby Not on Board: A Celebration of Life without Kids.* San Francisco: Chronicle Books, 2005.

Sheehan, Michele. "Dancing With Monica: Personal Perceptions of a Home-School Mom." *Roeper Review* 24 (2002): 191.

Shehan, Constance L. "No Longer a Place for Innocence: The Re-Submergence of Childhood in Post-Industrial Societies." In *Through the Eyes of the Child: Revisioning Children as Active Agents of Family Life,* ed. Constance L. Shehan, vol. 1. Stamford, CT: JAI Press, 1999.

Sherman, L. W., and R. A. Berk. "The Minneapolis Domestic Violence Experiment." *Police Foundation Reports,* April, 1984, Washington, DC.

Sheth, P. *Indians in America: One Stream, Two Waves, Three Generations.* Jaipur, India: Rawat Publications, 2001.

Shifren, Kim, and Lauren V. Kachorek. "Does Early Caregiving Matter? The Effects on Young Caregivers' Adult Mental Health." *International Journal of Behavioral Development* 27, no. 4 (2003): 338–346.

Shoop, J. G. "Children in Violent Homes Need Better Protection, Report Says." *Trial* 30 (1994): 114–116.

Siegal, Larry J., and Joseph J. Senna. *Essentials of Criminal Justice,* 4th ed. Belmont, CA: Wadsworth/Thomson Learning, 2004.

Simkin, Penny. *Pregnancy, Childbirth and the Newborn, Revised and Updated: The Complete Guide.* Minnetonka, MN: Meadowbrook Press, 2001.

Simon, Rita J., and Rhonda M. Roorda. *In Their Own Voices Transracial Adoptees Tell Their Stories.* New York: Columbia University Press, 2000.

Simon, Rita J., and Rhonda M. Roorda. *In Their Parents' Voices: Reflections on Raising Transracial Adoptees.* New York: Columbia University Press, 2007.

Simpson, Kathleen. Formula Companies and their "Free" Gifts. 1999. Available at: http://www.breastfeedingonline.com/free.shtml (accessed November 2007).

Simring, Steven S., Sue Klavans Simring, and Gene Busnar. *Making Marriage Work for Dummies.* New York: Hungry Minds, 1999.

Singh, Ilina. "Boys Will Be Boys: Fathers' Perspectives on ADHD Symptoms, Diagnosis, and Drug Treatment." *Harvard Review of Psychiatry* 11 (2003): 308–316.

Smith, Dorothy E. "The Standard North American Family: SNAF as an Ideological Code." *Journal of Family Issues* 14 (1993): 50–65.

Smith, J. David. *In Search of Better Angels.* Thousand Oaks, CA: Corwin Press, 2003.

Smith, J. Walker, and Ann Clurman. *Generation Ageless: How Baby Boomers are Changing the Way We Live Today . . . And They're Just Getting Started.* New York: HarperCollins, 2007.

Smith, Lona. *Help! He Wants Me to Sign a Prenup.* Miami Beach, FL: Help Publishing, 2007.

Smith Ruiz, Dorothy. *Amazing Grace: African American Grandmothers as Caregivers and Conveyors of Traditional Values.* Westport, CT: Praeger Publishers, 2004.

Smith, Susan. Safeguarding the Rights and Well-being of Birthparents in the Adoption Process. Evan B. Donaldson Adoption Institute Web site, 2006. Available at: www.adoptioninstitute.org.

Smock, Pamela. "Cohabitation in the United States: An Appraisal of Research Themes, Findings, and Implications." *Annual Review of Sociology* 26 (2000): 1–20.

Social Care Institute for Excellence. "The Health and Well-Being of Young Carers." *Research Briefing Number 11,* 2005. Available at: http://www.scie.org.uk/publications/briefings/briefing11/ index.asp.

Solomon, Dorothy Allred. *Daughter of Saints: Growing Up in Polygamy.* New York: W.W. Norton and Company, 2004.

Solot, Dorian, and Marshall Miller. *Unmarried to Each Other: The Essential Guide to Living Together as an Unmarried Couple.* New York: Marlowe and Company, 2002.

Spinelli, Margaret G. *Infanticide: Psychosocial and Legal Perspectives on Mothers Who Kill.* Arlington, VA: American Psychiatric Publishing, 2002.

Sprecher, Susan, Anita Barbee, and Pepper Schwartz. "'Was it Good For You, Too?': Gender Differences in First Sexual Intercourse Experiences." *Journal of Sex Research* 32 (1995): 3–15.

Sprecher, Susan, and Pamela C. Regan. "College Virgins: How Men and Women Perceive Their Sexual Status." *The Journal of Sex Research* 33 (1996): 3–15.

Sprechcer, Susan, Pamela C. Regan,and Kathleen McKinney. "Beliefs About the Outcomes of Extramarital Relationships as a Function of the Gender of the 'Cheating Spouse.'" *Sex Roles* 38 (1998): 301–311.

Sprecher, Susan, and Rachita Chandak. "Attitudes about Arranged Marriages and Dating among Men and Women From India." *Free Inquiry in Creative Sociology* 20, no. 1 (1992): 59–69.

Stack, Carol B. *All Our Kin: Strategies for Survival in a Black Community.* New York: Harper and Row, 1974.

Stahmann, Robert F., and William J. Hiebert. *Premarital and Remarital Counseling: The Professional's Handbook.* San Francisco: Jossey-Bass, 1997.

Stainton, Tim, and Hilde Besser. "The Positive Impact of Children with an Intellectual Disability on the Family." *Journal of Intellectual and Developmental Disability* 23 (1998): 57–70.

Stanley, Scott M. "Making a Case for Premarital Education." *Family Relations* 50 (2001): 272–280.

Stanley, Scott M. *The Power of Commitment: A Guide to Active, Lifelong Love.* San Francisco: Jossey-Bass, 2005.

Stanley, Scott M., Paul R. Amato, Christine A Johnson, and Howard J. Markman. "Premarital Education, Marital Quality, and Marital Stability: Findings from a Large, Random Household Survey." *Journal of Family Psychology* 20 (2006): 117–126.

Stark, Barbara. "Marriage Proposals: From One-Size-Fits-All to Post-modern Marriage Law." *California Law Review* 89 (2001): 1479–1548.

Stearns, Cindy A. "Breastfeeding and the Good Maternal Body." *Gender and Society* 13 (1999): 308–325.

Steil, Janice M. *Marital Equality: Its Relationship to the Well-Being of Husbands and Wives.* Thousand Oaks, CA: SAGE Publications, 1997.

Stark, Marg. *What No One Tells the Mom: Surviving the Early Years of Parenthood With Your Sanity, Your Sex Life and Your Sense of Humor Intact.* New York: Penguin, 2005.

Steiner, Leslie Morgan. *Mommy Wars: Stay-at-Home and Career Moms Face Off on Their Choices, Their Lives, Their Families.* New York: Random House, 2007.

Stewart, K. A., Christian P. Gruber, and Linda M. Fitzgerald. *Children at Home and in Day Care.* Hillsdale, NJ: Lawrence Erlbaum Associates Publishers, 1994.

Stone, Helen D. *Foster Care in Question: A National Reassessment by Twenty-One Experts.* New York: Child Welfare League of America, 1970.

Stone, Pamela. *Opting Out? Why Women Really Quit Careers and Head Home.* Berkeley: University of California Press, 2007.

Stoner, Katherine E., and Shae Irving. *Prenuptial Agreements: How to Write a Fair and Lasting Contract.* Berkeley, CA: Nolo, 2005.

Straus, M. A. "Forward." In *The Violent Home: A Study of Physical Aggression between Husbands and Wives,* ed. R. J. Gelles. Thousand Oaks, CA: Sage Publications, 1974.

Straus, Murray A. *Beating the Devil Out of Them: Corporal Punishment in American Families and its Effects on Children.* New Brunswick, NJ: Transaction Publishers, 2001.

Straus, Murray A., Richard J. Gelles, and Suzanne K. Steinmetz. *Behind Closed Doors: Violence in the American Family.* New York: Doubleday/Anchor, 1980.

Straus, Murray A., and Richard J. Gelles. *Physical Violence in American Families: Risk Factors and Adaptations to Violence in 8,145 Families.* New Brunswick, NJ: Transaction Publishers, 1989.

Stritof, S., and B. Stritof. Full Time Dads and Marriage. 2007. Available at: http://marriage.about.com.

Strong, B., C. DeVault, B. W. Sayad, and T. F. Cohen. *The Marriage and Family Experience,* 8th ed. Belmont, CA: Wadsworth, Thomson Learning, 2001.

Sulloway, Frank J. *Born to Rebel: Birth Order, Family Dynamics, and Creative Lives.* New York: Vintage Books, 1997.

Swallow, Wendy. *Breaking Apart: A Memoir of Divorce.* New York: Hyperion, 2001.

Swize, Jennifer. "Transracial Adoption and the Unblinkable Difference: Racial Dissimilarity Serving the Interests of Adopted Children." *Virginia Law Review* 88 (2002): 1079–1118.

Szinovacz, Maximiliane E., ed. *Handbook on Grandparenthood.* Westport, CT: Greenwood Press, 1998.

Tabb, Lisa, and Susan Breslow Sardone. Top Five Reasons to Elope. About.com, 2008. Available at: http://honeymoons.about.com/cs/toppicks/a/letselope_2.htm.

Tabb, Lisa, and Sam Silverstein. *Beyond Vegas.* Chicago: Contemporary Books, 2000.

Taylor, Verta. *Rock-a-bye Baby: Feminism, Self-Help, and Postpartum Depression.* New York: Routledge, 1996.

Territo, Leonard, James B. Halsted, and Max L. Bromley. *Crime and Justice in America: A Human Perspective,* 6th ed. Upper Saddle River, NJ: Pearson Education, 2004.

Tesler, Pauline, and Peggy Thompson. *Collaborative Divorce: The Revolutionary New Way to Restructure Your Family, Resolve Legal Issues, and Move on With Your Life.* Los Angeles: Regan Books, 2006.

Thevenin, T. *The Family Bed: An Age Old Concept in Childrearing.* Wayne, NJ: Avery Publishing Group, 1987.

Thomas, Darwin, and Marie Cornwall. "Religion and Family in the 1980s: Discovery and Development." *Journal of Marriage and the Family* 52 (1990): 983–992.

Thomas, J., L. Sperry, and M. Yarborough. "Grandparents as Parents: Research Findings and Policy Recommendations." *Child Psychiatry and Human Development* 31 (2000): 3–22.

Thomas, William I., and Dorothy S. Thomas. *The Child in America: Behavior Problems and Programs*. New York: Alfred A. Knopf, 1928.

Thornton, Arland. "Changing Attitudes Toward Family Issues in the United States." *Journal of Marriage and the Family* 51 (1989): 873–893.

Thurer, Shari L. *The Myths of Motherhood: How Culture Reinvents the Good Mother*. New York: Penguin Books, 1994.

Timimi, Sami. *Naughty Boys: Anti-Social Behavior, ADHD and the Role of Culture*. New York: Palgrave Macmillan, 2005.

Toman, Walter. *Family Constellation: It's Effects on Personality and Social Behavior*. New York: Springer Publishing Group, 1992.

Toth, Attila. *Fertile vs. Infertile: How Infections Affect Your Fertility and Your Baby's Health*. Tucson, AZ: Fenestra Books, 2004.

Treas, J., and D. Giesen. "Sexual Infidelity among Married and Cohabiting Americans." *Journal of Marriage and the Family* 62 (2000): 48–60.

Tremblay, R. E., D. S. Nagin, J. R. Séguin, M. Zoccolillo, P. D. Zelazo, M. Boivin, D. Pérusse, and C. Japel. "Physical Aggression During Early Childhood: Trajectories and Predictors." *Pediatrics* 114 (2004): 43–50.

Trenka, Jane Jeong. *Outsiders Within: Writing on Transracial Adoption*. Cambridge, MA: South End Press, 2006.

Tucker, P. Stay at Home Dads: At-home Dads Can Benefit Children and Mothers. *Futurist*, 2005. Available at: http://www.allbusiness.com (accessed June 15, 2008).

Turner, Bryan S., ed. *Islam: Critical Concepts in Sociology Volume III Islam, Gender, and the Family*. New York: Routledge, Taylor and Francis Group, 2003.

Uddin, Mohammad S. "Arranged Marriage: A Dilemma for Young British Asians." *Diversity in Health and Social Care* 3 (2006): 211–219.

Uekert, Barbara. *10 Steps to Successful International Adoption: A Guided Workbook for Prospective Parents*. New York: Third Avenue PR, 2007.

Urban, Wayne, and Jennings Wagoner Jr. *American Education: A History*. New York: McGraw Hill, 1996.

U.S. Bureau of Labor Statistics, Consumer Expenditure Survey, and U.S. Census Bureau, *Statistical Abstract of the United States, 2008*. Available at: http://www.census.gov/compendia/statab/.

U.S. Census Bureau. Census 2000, Table DP-1, *Profile of General Demographic Characteristics*, 2001. Available at: http://www.census.gov/prod/cen2000/doc/ProfilesTD.pdf.

U.S. Census Bureau. March 2006. *America's Families and Living Arrangements, 2006*. Current Population Survey and Report. Available at: http://www.census.gov/population/www/socdemo/hh-fam/cps2006.html.

U.S. Census Bureau. "QT-P18. Marital Status by Sex, Unmarried-Partner Households, and Grandparents as Caregivers: 2000." U.S. Census Bureau, 2006. Available at: http://factfinder.census.gov/home/saff/main.html.

U.S. Census Bureau. "Adopted Children and Stepchildren: 2000." U.S. Department of Commerce: Economic and Statistics Administration, 2003. Available at: www.census.gov/population/www/socdemo/ms-la.html.

U.S. Census Bureau. "Marital Status: 2000." U.S. Department of Commerce: Economic and Statistics Administration, 2003. Available at: www.census.gov/population/www/socdemo/marr-div.html.

U.S. Congress. *Family and Medical Leave Act of 1987*. House Committee on Education and Labor. Congressional Information Service (CIS). Washington, DC: US General Accounting Office, 1987.

U.S. Congress. *Parental and Disability Leave Act of 1985*. House Committee on Post Office and Civil Service. 99th Congress. Congressional Information Service (CIS). Washington, DC: GPO, 1985.

U.S. Department of Health and Human Services. Preventing Violence against Women, 2001. Available at: http://www.hhs.gov/news/press/2001pres/01fsdomviolence.html.

U.S. Department of Health and Human Services Office on Women's Health. Violence against Women: Domestic and Intimate Partner Violence Prevention, 2005. Available at: http://www.womenshealth.gov/violence/index.cfm.

Vaidyanathan, Prabha, and Jospehine Naidoo. "Asian Indians in Western Countries: Cultural Identity and the Arranged Marriage." In *Contemporary Issues in Cross-Cultural Psychology*, ed. N. Bleichrodt and P. J. Drenth. Amsterdam: Swets and Zeitlinger, 1990.

VanGoethem, Jeff. *Living Together: A Guide to Counseling Unmarried Couples*. Grand Rapids, MI: Kregel Publications, 2005.

Vega, William. "Hispanic Families in the 1980s: A Decade of Research." *Journal of Marriage and Family* 52 (1990): 1015–1024.

Viesson, Marika. "Depression Symptoms and Emotional States in Parents of Disabled and Non-disabled Children." *Social Behavior and Personality* 27 (1999): 87–97.

Waldfogel, Jane. "Family and Medical Leave: Evidence from the 2000 Surveys." *Monthly Labor Review* (September 2001): 17–23.

Waite, Linda, and Maggie Gallagher. *The Case for Marriage: Why Married People are Happier, Healthier, and Better-off Financially*. New York: Broadway Books, 2001.

Walker, Lenore E. A. *The Battered Woman Syndrome*, 2nd ed. New York: Springer Publishing Company, 2000.

Walker, Lenore E. *Terrifying Love: Why Battered Women Kill and How Society Responds*. New York: Harper and Row, 1989.

Wallace, Carolyn McD. *All Dressed in White: The Irresistible Rise of the American Wedding*. New York: Penguin Books, 2004.

Wallerstein, J., and J. B. Kelly. *Surviving the Breakup: How Children and Parents Cope With Divorce*. New York: Basic Books, 1980.

Wallerstein, Judith S., Julia M. Lewis, and Sandra Blakeslee. *The Unexpected Legacy of Divorce: The 25 Year Landmark Study*. New York: Hyperion, 2000.

Warner, Mildred. "Overview: Articulating the Economic Importance of Child Care for Community Development." *Community Development* 37 (2006): 1–6.

Warner, Mildred, Shira Adriance, Nikita Barai, Jenna Hallas, Bjorn Markeson, Taryn Morrissey, and Wendy Soref. *Economic Development Strategies to Promote Quality Child Care*. Ithaca, NY: Cornell Cooperative Extension, 2004.

Warren, Elizabeth. *The Two-Income Trap: Why Middle-Class Parents are Going Broke.* New York: Basic Books, 2004.

Wattenberg, Ben J. *The Birth Dearth: What Happens When People in Free Countries Don't Have Enough Babies.* New York: Ballantine Books, 1987.

Wedam, Elfriede. "Splitting Interests or Common Causes: Style of Moral Reasoning in Opposing Abortion." In *Contemporary American Religion: An Ethnographic Reader,* ed. Penny Edgell Becker and Nancy Eisland. Walnut Creek, CA: Alta Mira Press, 1997.

Wegandt, Lisa L. *An ADHD Primer,* 2nd ed. Mahwah, NJ: Laurence Erlbaum Associates, 2007.

Weiner-Davis, Michele. *The Sex-Starved Marriage: Boosting Your Libido: A Couple's Guide.* New York: Simon and Schuster, 2004.

Weiss, Jessica. *To Have and To Hold: Marriage, the Baby Boom and Social Change.* Chicago: The University of Chicago Press, 2000.

Weiztman, Lenore J. *The Divorce Revolution.* New York: Free Press, 1985.

Wells, L. Edward, and Joseph H. Rankin. "Families and Delinquency: A Meta-Analysis of the Impact of Broken Homes". *Social Problems* 38 (1991): 71–93.

Wenham, Gordon, William A. Heth, Craig S. Keener, and Mark L. Strauss. *Remarriage After Divorce in Today's Church: 3 Views.* Grand Rapids, MI: Zondervan, 2006.

Wertheimer, Alan. "Two Questions About Surrogacy and Exploitation." *Philosophy and Public Policy* 21 (1992): 211–239.

Weschler, Toni. *Taking Charge of Your Fertility.* New York: Harper Collins, 2006.

West, Traci. *Wounds of the Spirit: Black Women, Violence, and Resistance Ethics.* New York: New York University Press, 1999.

Westman, Jack C. "Grandparenthood." In *Parenthood in America: Undervalued, Underpaid, Under Siege,* ed. Jack C. Westman. Madison: The University of Wisconsin Press, 2001.

Whisman, Mark A., and Tina Pittman Wagers. "Assessing Relationship Betrayals." *Journal of Clinical Psychology* 61 (2005): 1383–1391.

Whitehead, Barbara Dafoe. *The Divorce Culture: Rethinking Our Commitments to Marriage and Family.* New York: Vintage Books, 1998.

Whitman, Stacy, and Wynne Whitman. *Shacking Up: The Smart Girl's Guide to Living in Sin without Getting Burned.* New York: Broadway Books, 2003.

Wiehe, V. R. *SiblingAbuse: Hidden Physical, Emotional, and Sexual Trauma.* Thousand Oaks, CA: Sage Publications, 1997.

Wiehe, V. R. *What Parents Need to Know About Sibling Abuse.* Springville, UT: Bonneville Books, 2002.

Wilcox, Bradford. "Good Dads: Religion, Civic Engagement, and Paternal Involvement in Low-Income Communities. CRRUCS Report." New York: Manhattan Institute for Policy Research, 2001.

Willetts, M. C. "An Exploratory Investigation of Heterosexual Licensed Domestic Partners." *Journal of Marriage and Family* 65 (2003): 939–952.

Willliams, H. K., and R. E. Bowen. "Marriage, Same-Sex Unions, and Domestic Partnerships." *The Georgetown Journal of Gender and Law* 1 (2000): 337–359.

Williams, Joan. *Unbending Gender: Why Family and Work Conflict and What To Do About It.* New York: Oxford University Press, 2000.

Williams-Wheeler, Dorrie. *The Unplanned Pregnancy Book for Teens and College Students.* Virginia Beach, VA: Sparkledoll Productions Publishing, 2004.

Wilson, Chris M., and Andrew J. Oswald. *How Does Marriage Affect Physical and Psychological Health? A Survey of the Longitudinal Evidence.* May 2005. Available at: http://papers.ssrn.com/sol3/papers.cfm?abstract_id=735205 (accessed September 19, 2006).

Wilson, James Q. *The Marriage Problem.* New York: HarperCollins, 2002.

Wilson, William Julius. *The Declining Significance of Race: Blacks and Changing American Institutions.* Chicago: University of Chicago Press, 1978.

Wilson, William Julius. *The Truly Disadvantaged: The Inner City, the Underclass, and Public Policy.* Chicago: University of Chicago Press, 1990.

Wilson, William Julius. *When Work Disappears: The World of the New Urban Poor.* New York: Vintage Books, 1997.

Winking, Jeffery, Hillard Kaplan, Michael Gurven, and Stacey Rucas. "Why Do Men Marry and Why Do They Stray?" *Proceeding: Biological Sciences* 274 (2007): 1643–1649.

Wolf, Naomi. *Misconceptions: Truth, Lies, and the Unexpected Journey to Motherhood.* New York: Doubleday, 2001.

Wright, David W., and Earl Wysong. "Family Friendly Workplace Benefits: Policy Mirage, Organizational Contexts, and Worker Power." *Critical Sociology* 24 (1998): 244–276.

Wright, Erik Olin, Karen Shire, Shu-Ling Hwang, Maureen Dolan, and Janeen Baxter. "The Non-Effects of Class on the Gender Division of Labour in the Home: A Comparative Study of Sweden and the United States." *Gender and Society* 6 (1992):252–282.

Wright, Kevin N., and Karen E. Wright. *Family Life, Delinquency, and Crime: A Policymaker's Guide. Research Summary.* Washington, D.C.: Office of Juvenile Justice and Delinquency Prevention, 1994.

Wu, Zheng. *Cohabitation: An Alternative Form of Family Living (Studies in Canadian Population).* New York: Oxford University Press, 2001.

Wyckoff, Jerry L., and Barbara C. Unell. *Discipline Without Shouting or Spanking: Practical Solutions to the Most Common Preschool Behavior Problems.* Minnetonka, MN: Meadowbrook Press, 2002.

Young, J. "Babies and Bedsharing . . . Cosleeping." *Midwifery Digest* 8 (1998): 364–369.

Zaidi, Arsha U., and Muhammad Shuraydi. "Perceptions of Arranged Marriage by Young Pakistani Muslim Women Living in a Western Society." *Journal of Comparative Family Studies* 33, 4 (2002): 495–514.

Zimmerman, Marc A., Deborah A. Salem, and Paul C. Notaro. "Make Room for Daddy II: The Positive Effects of Fathers' Role in Adolescent Development." In *Resilience Across Contexts: Family, Work, Culture, and Community,* ed. R. Taylor and L. Wang. Mahwah, NJ: Lawrence Erlbaum Associates, 2000.

Web Site Resources

8minute Dating. The Leader in Speed Dating: 8minutedating.com

AARP (American Association for Retired Persons): aarp.org

Administration for Children and Families: Healthy Marriage Initiative: www.acf.hhs.gov/healthymarriage/about/factsheets_hm_matters.html

Adoption.com:
    Background on China Adoption and One Child Policy: china.adoption.com.
    Statistics. Cost of Adopting: statistics.adoption.com

Adoptive Families Magazine online: adoptivefamilies.com

Alaska Men Magazine: alaskamen-online.com

Alcohol and Drug Treatment Referrals: alcohol-drug-treatment.net/causes_of_addiction.html

All Family Resources: familymanagement.com

Alliance for Non-custodial Parent s Rights: ancpr.org

Almanac of Policy Issues: policyalmanac.org

Alternatives to Marriage Project: unmarried.org

American Academy of Pediatrics. Cosleeping Policy: aappolicy.aappublications.org/cgi/content/full/pediatrics%3B105/3/650

American Animal Hospital Association. 2004 Pet Owner Survey: aahanet.org

American Civil Liberties Union: aclu.org

American College of Nurse-Midwives: acnm.org

American College of Obstetrics and Gynecology: acog.org

American Homeschool Association: americanhomeschoolassociation.org

American Pet Products Manufactures' Association. Industry Trends and Statistics: appma.org/press_industrytrends.asp

American Pregnancy Association: americanpregnancy.org

American Pregnancy Association. Infertility: americanpregnancy.org/infertility/whatisinfertility.html

American Psychological Association. Marriage Promotion: apa.org/monitor/sep04/marriage.html

American Surrogacy Center, Inc.: surrogacy.com

American Veterinary Medical Association. U.S. Pet Ownership & Demographics Sourcebook: avma.org

Americans for Divorce Reform: divorcereform.org

The Annie E. Casey Foundation: aecf.org

Answers.com. Infertility: answers.com/topic/infertility

At home dad.com. The Stay at Home Dad Oasis: athomedad.org

Attachment Parenting International: attachmentparenting.org

Aware Parenting Institute: awareparenting.com

Baby Center: babycenter.com

The Barna Group: barna.org

Break the Cycle, Empowering Youth to end Domestic Violence: breakthecycle.org

Breastfeeding. American Academy of Pediatrics: aap.org/healthtopics/breastfeeding.cfm

Breastfeeding. World Health Organization: who.int/topics/breastfeeding/en/

Breastfeeding vs. Formula Feeding. KidsHealth: kidshealth.org/parent/food/infants/breast_bottle_feeding.html

Brigham Young University. Latter Day Saints Questions: ldsfaq.byu.edu

California Cryobank, Inc.: cryobank.com

Catholic Answers: catholic.com/library/Birth_Control.asp

The Cato Institute, a Libertarian think tank explanation of two basic motivations for home schooling: cato.org/pubs/pas/pa-294.html

Center for Adoption Support and Education: adoptionsupport.org

Centers for Disease Control and Prevention. Understanding Child Maltreatment, 2006: www.cdc.gov/injury.

Childhelp USA Foundation: childhelpusa.org

Children's Defense Fund: childrensdefense.org

Children's Home Society of Washington: chswpirc.org
Children's Hospital, Boston, MA: childrenshospital.org
Child Welfare Information Gateway: childwelfare.gov
Child Welfare League of America: cwla.org
Christian Coalition: cc.org
Citizens for Midwifery: cfmidwifery.org
Coming Together: A Proposal for Social Progress. Public Assistance: comingtogether.info
Defense of Marriage Act: Legal Resources and Information: domawatch.org
Department of Health & Human Services. Fatherhood Reports: http://aspe.os.dhhs.gov/_/topic/subtopic.cfm?subtopic=376
Divorce Net: Family Law Information, Solutions, News and Community: divorcenet.com
Doulas of North America: dona.org
Dr. Philip McGraw, Psychologist and talk show host: drphil.com
Dr. James McKenna, Medical Anthropologist and CoSleeping researcher: nd.edu/~jmckenn1/lab
Dr. Laura Schlessinger, Marriage and Family Counselor and radio talk show host: drlaura.com
Dr. William Sears: askdrsears.com
The Doctor Will See You Now: thedoctorwillseeyounow.com
eHarmony.com. America's number one relationship site: eharmony.com
Endo-Online. The Voice of the Endometriosis Association: endometriosisassn.org/
Equality in Marriage Institute: equalityinmarriage.org
Evan B. Donaldson Adoption Institute: adoptioninstitute.org
Families and Work Institute: familiesandwork.org
Family Research Council: frc.org
Family Violence Prevention Fund: endabuse.org
Fatherhood Foundation: fathersonline.org
Father's Rights: fathersrightsinc.com
Feminist Majority Foundation: Working for Women's Equality: feminist.org
Feminist Women's Health Center: Fwhc.org
Fertile Thoughts.com- Supporting Your Family Building Challenges: fertilethoughts.com
Focus on the Family, a Christian organization dedicated to promoting a traditional perspective on the family: family.org and focusonthefamily.org
Foster Care Month: fostercaremonth.org
The Foundation for Grandparenting: grandparenting.org
Gay and Lesbian Association Against Defamation: glaad.org
Georgia Reproductive Specialists: ivf.com
Grandparents Raising Grandchildren: raisingyourgrandchildren.com
The Heritage Foundation: heritage.org
Home School Legal Defense Association: hslda.org/Default.asp?bhcp=1
Houston Women's Center: intendedparents.com
Human Rights Campaign: hrc.org
I Do Take Two. Guide to Second Weddings, Second Marriages, and Vow Renewals: idotaketwo.com
Institute for Women's Policy Research: iwpr.org
International Adoption Center: adoptionclinic.org

International Association of Pet Cemeteries and Crematories: iaopc.com
Interpreting Social Science Research: camden.rutgers.edu:8080/ramgen/wood/causation.rm
iParenting Media. Internet Communities for Parents: iparenting.com
An Introduction to Men's Liberation: http://www.gelworks.com.au/MENDOCUM.NSF/504ca249c786e20f85256284006da7ab/befd776247d76f99ca2566430043201b!OpenDocument
IVF-Infertility.com: ivf-infertility.com
Jeevansathi Indian Matrimonials: jeevansathi.com
Joint Council on International Children's Services. Guatemala 5000: jcics.org
Kids' Health. Nemours Foundation: kidshealth.org
La Lache League International: llli.org
Labour of Love. The Web Magazine for Conscious Parenting.: labouroflove.org
Learned Helplessness information: familyshelterservice.org/pdf/survivor.pdf
Legal Momentum, Advancing women's rights: legalmomentum.org
Maryland Black Family Alliance: www.marylandbfa.org
Match.com: match.com
Matrimonials India. Com. Indian Matrimonials: matrimonialsindia.com
Media Awareness Network: media-awareness.ca/english/issues/violence/index.cfm
Midwives Alliance of North America: mana.org
Mormonism Research Ministry: mrm.org
National Adoption Information Clearinghouse: naic.acf.hhs.gov
National Aging In Place Council: naipc.org
National and World Religion Statistics: adherents.com
National Association for Social Workers: socialworkers.org
National Association of Former foster care children of America: naffcca.org
National Association to Protect Children: protect.org
The Nation Campaign to Prevent Teen and Unplanned Pregnancy: thenationalcampaign.org
The National Center for Victims of Crime. Stalking Fact Sheet 2004,: ncvc.org/Src
The National Children's Advocacy Center: nationalcac.org
National Coalition Against Domestic Violence: ncadv.org
National Conference of State Legislatures: ncsl.org
National Council for Adoption: adoptioncouncil.org
The National Domestic Violence Hotline: www.ndvh.org
National Foster Parents Association: nfpainc.org
National Gay and Lesbian Task Force: thetaskforce.org
National Home Education Network: nhen.org
National Home Education Research Institute: nheri.org
National Institute on Media and the Family: mediafamily.org
National Marriage Project: marriage.rutgers.edu
National Network to end Domestic Violence: nnedv.org
National Organization for Women: now.org
National Sexual Violence Resource Center: nsvrc.org
North American Mission Board. "Extramarital Sex: A Christian Perspective": namb.net

Office of Juvenile Justice and Delinquency Prevention, a component of the Office of Justice Programs, U.S. Department of Justice: ojjdp.ncjrs.org

Only Child. Advocates for Only Children: onlychild.com

Ontario Consultants on Religious Tolerance: religioustolerance.org

Parental Alienation Syndrome information: leadershipcouncil.org/1/pas/faq.htm

Partners Task Force for Gay and Lesbian Couple: buddybuddy.com/partners.html

Perfect Match. Online Dating and Relationship Service.: perfectmatch.com

Pew Commission on Children in Foster Care: pewfostercare.org

Pew Forum on Religion and Public Life. Same-Sex Marriage in California: pewforum.org/events/?EventID = 138

The Pew Research Center for the People and the Press: people-press.org

Planned Parenthood Federation of America, Inc.: plannedparenthood.org

The Polyamory Society: polyamorysociety.org

Prenuptial Agreements: prenuptialagreements.org

Prevent Child Abuse America: preventchildabuse.org

The Princess Royal Trust for Carers. "Who Does What?: Young Carers Projects": http://www.youngcarers.net/who_can_help_me/86/92.

Pumping and Bottle Feeding. Kellymom: kellymom.com/bf/pumping/index.html

Rebeldad.com. A father puts the stay-at-home dad trend under the microscope: rebeldad.com

Religion and Ethics News Weekly: pbs.org/wnet/religionandethics/index_flash.html

Religious Coalition for Reproductive Choice: rcrc.org/about/index.cfm.

Resolve: The National Infertility Association: resolve.org/

Smart Marriages: The Coalition for Marriage, Family, and Couples Education: smartmarriages.com

Society for Assisted Reproductive Technology: sart.org

State of Alabama Sanctity of Marriage Amendment # 744: alisdb.legislature.state.al.us/acas/CodeOfAlabama/Constitution/1901/Constitution1901_toc.htm

Stop Family Violence: stopfamilyviolence.org

Strength for Caring. Caregiving help, resources, and community: strengthforcaring.com

Suitablematch.com. Matrimonials for Indians and South Asians.: suitablematch.com

Support Network for Battered Women: snbw.org

Surrogate Mothers Online, LLC: surromomsonline.com

Surrogacy UK: surrogacyuk.org

Take Back the Night: takebackthenight.org.

Transracial Adoption Research and Consultation: transracialadoption.net

Uniform Crime Reports. Federal Bureau of Investigation.: fbi.gov/ucr/cius2006/data/table_38.html

United States Department of Health and Human Services: hhs.gov

United States Department of Labor, Office of Policy Planning and Research, Moynihan Report March 1965: dol.gov/oasam/programs/history/webid-meynihan.htm

University of Pennsylvania Health System. Stairway to Recovery: uphs.upenn.edu/addiction/berman/treatment/

The Urban Institute: urban.org

U.S. Citizenship and Immigration Services: uscis.gov

U.S. Department of Labor. *The Family and Medical Leave Act*.: dol.gov/esa/whd/fmla/.

U.S. Department of State, Bureau of Consular Affairs: travel.state.gov

U.S. Supreme Court Cases and Opinions, See United States Supreme Court Meister v. Moore 1877: supreme.justia.com/us/96/76/index.html

The White House: Marriage Protection Week: http://www.whitehouse.gov/news/releases/2003/10/20031003-12.htm

The Young Carers Initiative. "Projects A-Z Index": http://www.youngcarer.com/showPage. php?file=projects.htm

ABOUT THE EDITOR AND CONTRIBUTORS

Kimberly P. Brackett is Distinguished Teaching Associate Professor of Sociology and Head of the Sociology Department at Auburn University at Montgomery. She received her undergraduate degrees in Sociology and Psychology from Jacksonville University in Jacksonville, FL and MA and Ph.D. degrees from University of Florida. Her specialties include Family, Gender, and Social Psychology, and it is in these areas that she teaches. Her most recent work has focused on the link between religious homogeneity and the divorce rate.

Victoria Adams is a junior at Auburn University at Montgomery majoring in secondary education with a social sciences emphasis. She and her husband of three years, Kyle Adams, are parenting a two-year-old son, Parker. An honor student who is perennially on the Dean's list, Victoria is very interested in families and parenting styles. In her leisure time, she enjoys photography and reading.

Rachel Birmingham is currently a doctoral student in Human Development and Family Studies at Auburn University. She completed her Master's Degree in Family Youth and Community Sciences at the University of Florida, with a specialization in family violence studies. She has been certified by the Florida Coalition Against Domestic Violence as a Victim's Advocate.

Britten Allison Brooks hails from Greenville, Alabama. She is a senior undergraduate at Auburn University at Montgomery, finishing her degree in Sociology with a marriage and family concentration. Britten plans to further her education at Auburn University at Auburn by earning a Master's Degree in therapy.

Santarica Buford received an Associates degree from Alabama Southern Community College before attending Auburn University at Montgomery where she is majoring in Sociology with dual concentrations in Marriage and Family and

Pre-Social Work. Upon completion of degree requirements at AUM, she will transfer to Auburn University to complete the Social Work degree. Her future goals involve counseling and work with pregnant teens and domestic violence victims.

Susan Cody-Rydzewski has a Ph.D. from the University of Florida and is an Associate Professor of Sociology at LaGrange College, a small, private liberal arts college in Georgia. She teaches courses in Marriage and Family, Gender and Society, Social Problems, and Sociology of Religion. She has published articles on work and family conflict and women's experiences working within male-dominated occupations, such as ministry. Her current research involves a consideration of the experiences and attitudes of women rabbis as well as a content analysis comparison of Christian and Jewish family and women's magazines.

Hayley Cofer is from Dothan, Alabama. She is currently pursuing an undergraduate degree in Sociology with a concentration in marriage and family at Auburn University at Montgomery.

Margeaux Corby is currently attending Elon University and majoring in Biology and Journalism. She hopes to become a pediatric surgeon and join Doctors Without Borders. She plans to chronicle her experiences treating impoverished people for medical journals to raise awareness of health issues in developing countries. Margeaux believes in the importance of family, as hers has provided constant guidance and strength.

Lane Destro. A Penn State alumni, Lane Destro received her Bachelor's Degrees in Anthropology and English in 2003. She is currently a graduate student in the sociology program at Duke University. Lane's research interests include demography, mixed-methodologies, and the racial disparities in wealth acquisition.

Sarah Fish was born in Newark, California and moved to Wetumpka, Alabama in 1998. Since then, she has become fascinated with southern culture and motherhood and plans to combine those studies into her Ph.D. She holds her Bachelor's in English (2004) and her Master's of Liberal Arts (2007) from Auburn University at Montgomery. She currently teaches English to some of the most amazing high school students she has ever met.

Christy Haines Flatt received a B.A. degree from Midwestern State University in Wichita Falls, Texas, and a M.A. degree from Texas Technological University in Lubbock, Texas both in the field of Sociology. Following the completion of these degrees, she taught Sociology classes at Hinds Community College. Today she is a Doctoral Candidate in Sociology at Mississippi State University specializing in Comparative Family and Gender. She is currently working on a dissertation exploring how women's employment influences attitudes toward gender roles or gender ideologies across countries. Upon completion of her degree she plans to pursue a faculty position at a university.

Aaron D. Franks was born to Anthony D. Franks and Annie Glenn in Mobile, Alabama in 1982. From a humble and religious upbringing he attended and graduated from Murphy High school and attended Bishop State Community

College in Mobile, Ala. He then pursued a Bachelor of Liberal Arts from Auburn University at Montgomery. Aaron is currently sole proprietor and CEO of A1 Health and Fitness. His interests include furthering his academic pursuits as well as improving the lives of others in any way possible.

James H. Gadberry is an Assistant Professor of Sociology at Athens State University in Athens, Alabama. He has written several articles in the areas of family and death and dying. His work has been published in both peer-reviewed and professional journals. Dr. Gadberry's recent research focuses on the changing structure of funeral practices to include the growth in pet death care.

Selina Gallo-Cruz is a graduate student in sociology at Emory University. Her research interests lie in culture, social movements, and global change. Broadly, she asks how collectively shared belief systems emerge and effect social transformations. In addition to studying the effects of the natural birth movement upon the commoditization of maternity care, she is also currently conducting a study of strategy and meaning in the debate over the School of the Americas.

Nicole D. Garrett is a graduate of Auburn University at Montgomery. She is a student in the Marriage and Family Therapy Master's Degree program at the University of Kentucky. Her research interests include couple dynamics, methods of improving relationship quality, and adolescent behavior and emotional health. In 2007, she was named an AUM Chancellor's Scholar for outstanding academic achievement.

Jeanne Holcomb is completing her Ph.D. in sociology at the University of Florida. Her project is focused on women's experiences with breastfeeding and, more specifically, challenges women might face as they breastfeed over time. Her interests include work and family issues, sociology of childhood, and social change. She lives with her husband, Greg, and their daughter and son.

Jonelle Husain is a doctoral student in Sociology at Mississippi State University. Her research interests focus on the diversity and negotiation that characterizes pro-life activism, the turning points that propel activists into public activism, the multivalent ways pro-life activists construct abortion as a moral problem, and the ways activists create and use action strategies to disseminate their worldviews and to stop abortion. Her dissertation will explore the intersection of race, gender, and religious diversity among pro-life activists engaged in public activism.

Jeffrey Jones is a senior Liberal Arts student at Auburn University at Montgomery. Jeffrey's research interests include representations of homosexuality in contemporary art, pagan symbolism in Renaissance art, queer theory, and gay rights advocacy. His plans after graduation include graduate school, where he will continue working on research regarding queer studies in various areas of curriculum. In his spare time, Jeffrey likes to read biographical texts and reference materials on various artists, as well as conduct his own research based on various facts learned through his art historical studies at AUM. Jeffrey currently resides in Prattville, Alabama but hopes his educational goals will take him around the country and eventually around the world.

Linda Pope Jones is a Drama and Speech graduate from Judson College (1981) in Marion, AL. After retirement from the Alabama Governor's staff, she received a Liberal Arts degree from Auburn University at Montgomery (2008). As a wife and mother of six children she is continuing her education in Criminal Justice and Legal Studies.

Tonya Lowery Jones holds a Master of Arts in Sociology (2001) and a Bachelor of Arts in Criminology (1997), both from Auburn University in Auburn, Alabama. She is currently an Adjunct Sociology Instructor at Auburn University, Auburn University at Montgomery, Southern Union State Community College, and Chattahoochee Valley Community College. Her publications include *Serial Homicide: Examining Differences in Sexual and Non-Sexual Offenders* (Thesis 2001). In addition, she is a lifetime member of The National Scholars Honor Society, Alpha Kappa Delta (Honor Society for Sociology), and Alpha Phi Sigma (National Honor Society for Criminal Justice).

Njeri Kershaw completed her undergraduate degree in Sociology and Legal Studies from the University of Massachusetts—Amherst. She is now at Virginia Tech pursuing a Ph.D. in Sociology with concentrations in Crime and Deviance and Gender. She lives in Blacksburg, VA all year long.

Katie Kerstetter is a Research Associate at the DC Fiscal Policy Institute. Her work focuses on improving tax and budget policy to benefit low-income residents in Washington DC. Previously, she worked as a third grade teacher in Greenville, Mississippi, where several of her students were caregivers for siblings or other relatives. She would like to dedicate this entry to those very smart and caring students.

Nataylia Ketchum is a Graduate student at Auburn University at Montgomery in the Public Administration Division and mother of twin girls aged three. She is a native Chicagoan and a graduate of Roosevelt University with a Master's of Science in Journalism. Her undergraduate degree is in Communication, Journalism and Education. She is currently residing in Montgomery Alabama and in her spare time she enjoys playing sports, cooking, and baking. In the future she hopes to receive a Ph.D. in Communication and teach Journalism and Communications Studies.

Melissa Fry Konty is a Research and Policy Associate at the Mountain Association for Community Economic Development (MACED) in Berea, Kentucky. Her work involves research, program evaluation, policy analysis and advocacy. Melissa has a Ph.D. in Sociology from the University of Arizona with teaching and research interests in social inequality, public policy and organizations. She is co-author of the 2008 report *Child Care in Appalachian Kentucky: Financial sustainability in a low-income market*.

David G. LoConto is an associate professor of Sociology, and Program Coordinator of the Sociology Program at Jacksonville State University in Alabama. His current research interests include pragmatism, particularly as it relates to people with developmental disabilities. He also is conducting research on the origins of American Sociology. He has published on a wide variety of topics such as developmental disabilities, grieving, dreams, college athletics, Italian Americans, multiculturalism, and pragmatism.

Shaquona Malone is a 2008 graduate of Auburn University at Montgomery with a Bachelor of Liberal Arts Degree. She is currently working as a certified phlebotomist. Future plans include a Master's Degree and a career in forensics.

Namita N. Manohar is a doctoral candidate in the sociology department at the University of Florida. Her research interests include race and ethnicity, gender, migration, and family sociology with a particular focus on Indians in the United States. She currently has two papers exploring dating and marriage among Patel-Americans under review at the *Journal of Comparative Family Studies* and the *International Journal of Sociology of the Family*.

Stephanie "Christy" McCalman is an only child who was born and raised in Montgomery, AL. She is a single mother of one daughter. She has an Associates Degree from Troy State University in Psychology and graduated from Auburn University at Montgomery with a Liberal Arts degree.

Shondrah Tarrezz Nash received her doctorate in Sociology from the University of Kentucky and conducted postdoctoral work at the University of Illinois at Chicago in the Department of African American Studies. She is currently an Assistant Professor of Sociology in the Department of Sociology, Social Work, and Criminology at Morehead State University. Dr. Nash's research examines the intersection of religion, gender, and intimate partner violence, particularly abused women's strategies of religious coping.

Maria J. Patterson was born and raised in Montgomery, Alabama. Maria graduated from Brewbaker Technology Magnet High School in 2004. She received the Bachelor of Science degree in Justice and Public Safety coupled with a Paralegal Certificate from Auburn University at Montgomery in spring 2008. Maria would like to thank her family, especially her parents for their continued support throughout this arduous process. It has been a pleasure to be a part of this endeavor.

Carolyn F. Pevey. After eighteen years as a nurse, Dr. Pevey became a sociologist, completing her doctoral dissertation at the University of Texas at Austin. Her primary research areas are religion, death, and gender. She teaches courses on death, theory, religion and social problems. Currently, Dr. Pevey is using in-depth interviews with Muslim women to explore their understandings of gender and religion.

Leslie Houts Picca is Assistant Professor of Sociology at the University of Dayton. She has publications in the areas of racial relations and adolescent sexuality. She is co-author of the book *Two Faced Racism: Whites in the Backstage and Frontstage* (2007 with Joe Feagin). Her research on racial relations has been nationally recognized, and she has been interviewed by CNN, the Associated Press, *Congressional Quarterly*, National Public Radio, *Journal of Blacks in Higher Education*, the *Dayton Daily News*, among others.

Ariane Prohaska is an Assistant Professor in the Department of Criminal Justice at the University of Alabama. Her dissertation looked at women's leave taking from work after the birth or adoption of a child. Her research interests include work and family and the sociology of gender.

Ruby R. Reed is from Montgomery, AL where she graduated from Robert E. Lee High School in 2005. She currently attends Auburn University at Montgomery majoring in secondary education/social science. Ruby has tentative plans to graduate in the fall of 2009. After receiving her bachelor's degree, Ruby plans to continue her education by pursuing her masters and specialist degrees in education. She plans to be a high school teacher and eventually have an administrative position within a school system.

Lasita Rudolph is currently a senior at Auburn University at Montgomery majoring in Psychology with a minor in Sociology (Marriage & Family Concentration). She plans to graduate in May 2009 and then to further her education by receiving a Master's in Marriage and Family Counseling and Therapy. Her career goal is to become a Marriage and Family Therapist and open her own private practice.

Linda J. Rudolph is a married mother of three daughters and grandmother of two grandchildren. She is currently a junior Sociology major at Auburn University at Montgomery. Her area of concentration is Marriage and Family.

Virginia Rutland is an undergraduate student at Auburn Montgomery. She is planning to pursue a Master's Degree in Education following graduation. Virginia enjoys researching topics in the fields of Sociology, Psychology, and Human Development.

Tera Rebekah Scott graduated in May 2008 from Auburn University at Montgomery with a Bachelor's Degree in Psychology. Her future educational goals include a Master's Degree in Clinical Psychology and a career in therapy or teaching. Ms. Scott's current job is with PreHab Diabetes of Montgomery, Alabama. Her personal interests revolve around pottery, soccer, movies, and music.

Jessica Sexton received a Bachelor of Science Degree in the field of Psychology in May 2008 at Auburn University at Montgomery. She will attend graduate school to obtain a Master's Degree in the same field. Jessica hopes to use her Psychology training with families and children.

Derrick Shapley is currently working toward his Ph.D. in Sociology at Mississippi State University. He earned a Bachelor of Arts degree in Political Science and History from Auburn University and a Bachelor of Science degree in Sociology from Athens State University. His research interests include rural sociology, poverty, political sociology, sociology of religion, and social theories. He is currently researching political ideology from 1972 to 2006.

Constance L. Shehan is Professor of Sociology at the University of Florida. Her research and teaching focus on families and gender. She is the editor of the *Jour-*

nal of Family Issues, author of several books and numerous articles and chapters pertaining to women's roles in work and families.

Amanda Singletary graduated from Auburn University at Montgomery in December 2006 with an undergraduate degree in Sociology and minor in Psychology. Amanda currently works with the Alabama Department of Human Resources (DHR) as a foster care social worker. She is pursuing a Master's in Community Counseling at Troy State University Montgomery.

Angela Sparrow is a Human Services major, Exercise/Sports Science minor student at Elon University. Originally from Ithaca, New York, Angela has plans to be a nurse in the future, and is also interested in doing work with Teach for America. She has a passion for sociology and helping others. Angela is very excited about her first publication, and what the post-graduation future holds.

Patricia A. Thomas is a graduate student at Duke University. Her research interests include sociology of the family, aging, and the impact of social factors on health outcomes. After she receives her Ph.D. in Sociology, she hopes to teach sociology and do research at a university as a professor.

Courtney Blair Thornton is currently employed with East Alabama Mental Health, Family and Children's Services and plans to continue working with children and adolescents in community mental health before eventually going into private practice. Courtney is a 2005 B. A. graduate of Auburn University at Montgomery where she majored in Sociology and minored in Justice and Public Safety. Areas of interest in research and practice include human sexuality, trauma, and addictive behaviors such as alcoholism, drug addiction, eating disorders and self-injury. She is also interested in the development and implementation of programs to divert involvement in at-risk behaviors or in juvenile court.

Taralyn Watson and her husband lived in several different states before settling in the South to be near family. She then decided to finish her college degree and received a Bachelor of Liberal Arts from Auburn University at Montgomery in the spring of 2007. She enjoys reading all types of books whether it is to learn something new or just a fun story.

Marion C. Willetts is an Associate Professor of Sociology at Illinois State University. Her areas of specialization include families, particularly cohabitation and coupling policies, and stratification, most notably poverty. She has published numerous articles in journals such as *Journal of Marriage and Family*, *Journal of Family Issues*, and *Journal of Divorce and Remarriage*. Her most recent research is a policy analysis of licensed domestic partnership ordinances.

Donald Woolley completed his doctoral work in Sociology at North Carolina State University. He has since worked at Duke University as a researcher in the Fast Track study within the Center for Child and Family Policy and in the Healthy Childhood Brain Development and Developmental Traumatology Research Program within the Department of Psychiatry and Behavioral Sciences, Division of Child and Adolescent Psychiatry. Dr. Woolley also teaches as an

Adjunct Assistant Professor, Department of Sociology and Anthropology, Elon University.

Annice Yarber, Assistant Professor at Auburn University at Montgomery, teaches Sociology of Health and Illness, Human Sexuality, Divorce and Remarriage, and Human Behavior and the Social Environment. Current research interests include adolescent sexual health, African American male sexual behavior, as well as the influence of neighborhood context on the health of various groups.

Orli Zaprir is a graduate student in the Sociology Department at the University of Florida, Gainesville. Her research interests include intergenerational relations, caregiving, and grandparenthood.

INDEX

AARP (American Association of Retired Persons), 311, 314
Abortion, 1–9; birth dearth and, 94; first-trimester, 1, 2; laws, early, 3–5; laws, restrictive, 8–9; medical, 1, 2–3; partial birth, 7–8; personhood of fetus and, 8; procedures, 1–3; religion and, 495–96; second-trimester, 1, 2–3; as social issue, 3; surgical, 1, 2, 3. *See also* Birth control
Absent fathers, 24, 26, 27–30, 283
Abstinence, 70, 546
Achievement motivation theory, 435
Addiction, 9–15; causes, 12–13; described, 10–11; domestic violence and, 14; effects within family, 13–14; family and recovery, 14–15; incarceration and, 9–10, 14; medical debates, 12; physical, 11; psychological, 11–12; Social Learning model of, 13. *See also* Domestic violence behaviors and causes
ADHD. *See* Attention deficit hyperactivity disorder
Adler, Alfred, 76, 79, 432, 434
Adolescent pregnancy. *See* Teen pregnancy
Adoption: biological privilege and, 66; of child abuse victims, 104; second-parent, 298; surrogacy and, 540–41; teen pregnancy and, 551. *See also* Gay parent adoption; International adoption; Transracial adoption
Adoption and Foster Care Analysis and Reporting System (AFCARS), 297–98, 346

Adoption and Safe Families Act (1996), 561
Ads, personal, 404–5
Adult day care, 248
Adultery. *See* Extramarital sexual relationships
Adversarial divorce. *See* Divorce, adversarial and no-fault
AFCARS (Adoption and Foster Care Analysis and Reporting System), 297–98, 346
AFDC. *See* Aid to Families with Dependent Children
Affairs. *See* Extramarital sexual relationships
African American fathers, 24–33; absenteeism, 24, 26, 27–30; black family awareness, 26–27; causes of paternal delinquency, 26; historical influence, 24–25; involvement of, 31–32; present concerns, 26–27; statistics, formal, 27–29; statistics, informal, 29–30; stay at home dads, 528; in television programs, 25. *See also* African Americans; Fathers
African Americans: child care policy and, 106; cohabitation, 427; corporal punishment, 156; culture of poverty, 167–68, 169–70, 171, 172–73; divorce, 209; extended families, 172; fictive kin, 287, 288; foster care, 290; grandparenthood, 307, 315, 316; housework allocation, 329; marriage and childbearing, 143; matriarchy and, 168, 172–73; overscheduled children, 439, 440; parenting styles, 445–46; premarital sexual

625

relationships, 474; remarriage, 506, 508; teen pregnancy, 545, 549; white wedding industry, 575. *See also* African American fathers; Transracial adoption
Agency argument, and marital power, 381
Aging in place, 251–52
Aging out, of foster care, 294
Ahrons, Constance, 207, 213
Aid to Families with Dependent Children (AFDC): culture of poverty, 169, 174; day care, 188; foster care, 291; poverty and public assistance, 467. *See also* Temporary Assistance for Needy Families
Ain't I a Woman (hooks), 25
Alabama: cohabitation, 424; common law marriage, 147, 150; divorce, 18
Alcohol abuse, 12–13, 99. *See also* Addiction
Alimony, 20, 22
Alternatives to Marriage Project, 141, 425
Alzheimer's Disease, 137
AMA (American Medical Association), 409
American Academy of Family Physicians, 410
American Academy of Pediatrics, 81–82, 161–62, 300
American Association of Retired Persons (AARP), 311, 314
American College of Nurse Midwives, 411, 412
American College of Obstetrics and Gynecology, 410, 411, 412
American Medical Association (AMA), 409
Ante-nuptial agreements. *See* Prenuptial agreements
Anthropomorphism, 451–52
Apprentices, 186, 286
Arizona: covenant marriage, 164; divorce, 18; prenuptial agreements, 480; same-sex marriage, 517
Arkansas: covenant marriage, 164; divorce, 18
Arranged marriage, 33–40; current controversies, 37–39; described, 33–35; love marriages, 36–37; mate selection alternatives, 402–3; semi-arranged marriages, 35–36. *See also* Mail order brides; Mate selection alternatives
Arrest laws, mandatory. *See* Mandatory arrest laws
Asian Americans: divorce, 209; parenting styles, 445; teen pregnancy, 545. *See also* Arranged marriage
Assisted living facilities, 248, 249–50
Assisted marriages, 35–36
Attachment parenting, 159–60
Attention deficit hyperactivity disorder (ADHD), 40–48; as disease, 41–42; future issues, 47–48; genetic factor, 42; homeschooling and, 325; medicalization of, 42–44; medication for, 43–44; neurological markers, 41–42; parents and ADHD children, 45–47; as social construction, 44–45; statistics, 40. *See also* Developmental disability and marital stress
Attractiveness, and marital power, 379
Authoritarian parenting, 445–46
Authoritative parenting, 444–45

Baby abandonment, 114, 116–17
Baby and Child Care (Spock), 152–53
Baby boomers, 89–93; adolescence, 91–93; adulthood, 93; baby boom family, 90–91; childhood, 91; effects of, 95–96
Baby boomlet, 97
Baby bust, 93–95, 96
Baby echo, 97
Baby Jessica case, 66
Baby M case, 533–34, 536, 539
Baby-sitting, as term applied to fathers, 419
Baehr, Ninia, 517
Baker, Jack, 516
Balanced parenting, 444–45
Baltimore Parenthood Study, 29
Bangladesh, fictive kin in, 287
Baptists: corporal punishment, 154–55; divorce, 211; marital power, 378
Barrier methods of birth control, 71–72
Bartkowski, John, 381
Battered woman syndrome (BWS), 49–56; battering cycle, 50–51; history, 49–50; as legal defense, 53–55; legal system and, 52–53; opposition to battered-woman defense, 53–54; patterns, 51–52; shelter-seeking, 51; stereotypes about abused women, 55–56; support for battered-woman defense, 54–55. *See also* Domestic violence; Domestic violence behaviors and causes; Domestic violence interventions; Mandatory arrest laws; Religion, women, and domestic violence
Bed sharing. *See* Cosleeping
Beneficiaries, reciprocal, 216
Benefits of marriage. *See* Marriage, benefits of
Benson, Dale S., 170
Berger, Oscar, 349
Berman, Howard, 265
Bernard, Jessie, 57, 277
Best interest argument: biological privilege and, 64, 66; foster care and, 292; gay parent adoption and, 299, 300
Beyond Existing (organization), 246
Biblarz, Timothy, 299
Bible: family roles and, 275; on monogamy, 262; polygamy in, 460
Bigamy. *See* Plural marriage
Binuclear families, 307, 511–12
Biological privilege, 63–67; child custody, 65; foster care and adoption, 65–66, 291–92; future, 66–67; social policy, 64; views of motherhood, 64–65. *See also* Foster care; Surrogacy

Birth control, 67–76; birth dearth and, 94; emergency, 9, 75; history, 69–70; new technologies, 72–74; permanent, 74–75; premarital sexual relationships and, 475; religion and, 495; traditional methods, 70–72. *See also* Abortion
Birth control pill, 70, 72
Birth dearth, 93–95, 96
Birth order, 76–81; debate over, 79–80; first-born children, 76, 77, 79–80; middle-born children, 76, 77–78, 80; youngest children, 76, 78–79, 80. *See also* Only children
Birth parents, and gay parent adoption, 302
Birth plans, 123–24
Black fathers. *See* African American fathers
Blacks. *See* African Americans
Blended families, 307, 511–12
Boarders, as fictive kin, 286
Boarding out. *See* Foster care
Bottle feeding. *See* Breastfeeding or formula feeding
Brace, Charles Loring, 291
Bradley Method, 122
Brazelton, T. Berry, 161
Breastfeeding or formula feeding, 81–87; breastfeeding benefits, 81–82; breastfeeding challenges, 82–84; cosleeping and, 159, 162; formula feeding advantages, 84–85; formula feeding disadvantages, 85; issues, 85–87
Bride price, 403, 479, 484–85
Bush, George W.: marriage promotion, 396; same-sex marriage, 518
BWS. *See* Battered woman syndrome

California: divorce, 18, 208, 385; domestic partnerships, 216, 217; foster care, 290; gay parent adoption, 298; prenuptial agreements, 479, 480; same-sex marriage, 520; surrogacy, 534–36, 539, 541
Calvert, Crispina, 534–35, 539
Calvert, Mark, 534–35
Caregivers. *See* Children as caregivers; Elder care; Grandparents as caregivers
Cartoon violence, 359
Cascade effect, of domestic violence, 525
Cash assistance. *See* Temporary Assistance for Needy Families
Catholics: abortion, 496; battered woman syndrome, 52; birth control, 495; cohabitation, 424; corporal punishment, 155; covenant marriage, 165; divorce, 16, 207, 211; fictive kin, 286–87; gay parent adoption, 301, 302; homeschooling, 321; international adoption, 347; preparation for marriage, 487; remarriage, 510; teen pregnancy, 545; United States, 494. *See also* Christianity
Caucasians. *See* Whites

Cell phone program, for domestic violence victims, 227
Centers for Disease Control and Prevention: breastfeeding recommendations, 81–82; domestic violence statistics, 371; infertility, 334; spouse abuse categories, 230–31
Certified professional midwives, 118, 124–25, 406, 407, 410, 412
Cervical caps, 72
Cesarean section, 120, 409
Chapin, Henry, 291
Cheating. *See* Extramarital sexual relationships
Child abuse, 98–105; causes, 98–100; consequences, 100–101; controversies, 101–4; corporal punishment and, 102, 154; defining abuse, 102; defining abusers and settings, 102–3; homeschooling and, 325; interventions, 103–4. *See also* Corporal punishment; Domestic violence
Child Abuse Prevention and Treatment Act (1974), 103
Child advocates, 115–17, 194–95
Childbirth options, 117–25; birth plans, 123–24; future, 124–25; healthcare providers, 118–19; midwifery and medicalization, 119–21; pain control, 119–20, 121–22; prepared childbirth, 121–22; safety and risk, 411–12; witnesses to birth, 122–23. *See also* Midwifery and medicalization
Child care policy, 105–12; benefits of child care, 107–8; current policy, debates, and future prospects, 109–10; dysfunctional child care market, 108; race, class, and gender, 105–7; state support, 108–10. *See also* Day care; Employed mothers
Child custody, 65, 226
Childfree, as term, 126–27
Childfree relationships, 125–34; acceptability of, 343–44; movement, 130–31; organizations, 130; reasons for, 127–30; reproductive issues, 132; social issues, 133; terms, 126–27, 130–31; workplace issues, 132–33. *See also* Infertility; Transition to parenthood
Childless, as term, 126, 127
Child neglect, 98, 114–15, 116, 325. *See also* Child abuse
Childrearing: juvenile delinquency and, 357–58; marriage and, 143; prenuptial agreements and, 484; religion and, 497–98
Children: benefits of marriage for, 59; as domestic violence witnesses, 233–34; employed mothers and, 255; first-born, 76, 77, 79–80; housework allocation and, 328–29; marital satisfaction and, 421; middle-born, 76, 77–78, 80; remarriage and, 507, 508, 511–12; youngest, 76, 78–79,

80. *See also* Only children; Overscheduled children
Children and divorce. *See* Divorce and children
Children as caregivers, 134–39; care receiver characteristics, 136; child caregiver characteristics, 135; defined, 134; effects on children, 136–38; negative effects on children, 137–38; parentification and, 134–35; positive effects on children, 137; prevalence, 135. *See also* Elder care; Grandparents as caregivers
Children having children. *See* Teen pregnancy
Child rights advocates, 115–17, 194–95
Child support, 112–17; African American fathers and, 29, 30; baby abandonment, 114, 116–17; child neglect, 114–15, 116; child rights advocates and, 115–17; deadbeat parents and, 191–94; encouraging parental responsibility, 112–13; father absence and, 283; fathers' rights advocates and, 113–15; infanticide and, 115, 117; prenuptial agreements and, 484; private, 191–92; public, 192, 195; shared parenting and, 116; transformation of, 192–94. *See also* Deadbeat parents
Child Welfare League of America, 290
China: day care, 186; transracial adoption, 564; wedding industry workers, 575
Christianity: abortion, 496; childfree relationships, 133; cohabitation, 140; common law marriage, 150; corporal punishment, 154–55; covenant marriage, 164–65; divorce, 16, 207, 211, 497; domestic violence, 499–503; family roles, 275; gay parent adoption, 297; infertility, 343; monogamy, 261–62; premarital sexual relationships, 475–76; remarriage, 510–11; United States, 494. *See also* Catholics; Protestants; *specific denominations*
Church of Jesus Christ of Latter-day Saints, 458–61, 462
Citizens for Midwifery, 412
Civil marriage, 145, 146, 148
Civil Rights struggle, 92
Civil unions, 215
Class. *See* Social class
Clergy, 487, 501–2. *See also* Religion
Clinton, Bill, 467
Cognitive development, 189–90
Cohabitation, effects on marriage, 139–45; comparisons of married and nonmarried cohabitants, 140–41; future marriage, 144; selection *versus* experience effect, 143–44; strengthening effects, 141–42; weakening effects, 142–44. *See also* Cohabitation, nonmarital
Cohabitation, nonmarital, 423–29; as alternative to marriage, 427–29; before remarriage, 512; birth dearth and, 94; common law marriage *versus*, 146, 149; divorce and, 213; evolution of, 424–25; motives for, 428–29; religion and, 497; as stage in courtship, 425–28; statistics, 423–24. *See also* Cohabitation, effects on marriage; Common law marriage
Coitus interruptus, 70–71
Colonial era: child support, 192–93; divorce, 207; fatherhood, 280; fictive kin, 286; homeschooling, 319; housework allocation, 327; maternity care, 408; mate selection, 178
Colorado: abortion, 5; same-sex marriage, 517, 518
Colorblindness, and transracial adoption, 564
Come On, People (Cosby and Poussaint), 27
Commercial surrogacy, 533
Common couple violence, 223
Common law marriage, 145–52; common law states, 147; debate over, 148–51; history, 146–47; law, 147–48. *See also* Cohabitation, nonmarital; Domestic partnerships
Communication: in foster care, 293; marital satisfaction and, 390–91; transition to parenthood and, 555
Community property states, 480
Compadrazgo, 286–87
Companion animal death and family. *See* Pet death and the family
Comstock Laws, 4
Conciliation period, 51
Condoms, 71
Conflict management, and marital satisfaction, 391
Conflict perspective, on domestic violence, 231
Confluence model of only children, 434–35
Conley, Dalton, 80
Connecticut, domestic partnerships in, 215
Consent-intent argument, 535, 539
Consumer Product Safety Commission, 161
Contested divorce. *See* Divorce, adversarial and no-fault
Continuous care communities, 248
Contraception. *See* Birth control
Contraceptive patches, 73
Coontz, Stephanie, 213, 276–77, 425
Copernicus, 78
Corporal punishment, 152–57; attitudes toward, 153–54; child abuse and, 102, 154; effects, 156–57; parenting styles and, 153–54, 445, 446, 447; regional differences, 155–56; religion and, 154–55, 498. *See also* Child abuse; Parenting styles
Cosby, Bill, 27, 174
The Cosby Show, 25
Cosleeping, 157–63; advantages, 159–61; background, 158–59; disadvantages, 161; future, 161–62. *See also* Parenting styles

Council on Contemporary Families, 57, 425
Counseling, as preparation for marriage, 486–87
Courtship, 35–36, 178–79, 401, 425–28
Covenant marriage, 163–67; characteristics of participants, 164–65; concerns with, 165–66; definitions and provisions, 164; future trends, 166–67; history, 163–64; proponents, 165. *See also* Divorce, adversarial and no-fault; Divorce, as problem, symptom, or solution
Creation science, teaching of, 498
Crèches, 186
Crude divorce rate, 208
Cult of true womanhood, 272–73, 328
Cultural spillover theory, 157
Culture: homeschooling and, 324; marital power and, 379; transracial adoption and, 559–60
Culture of poverty, 167–75; applying in American society, 169–70; behavioral traits, 168, 173–74; origins, 167–68; pathology, 172–73; structural approach *versus*, 170–74; way of life, 171–72. *See also* Poverty and public assistance
Culture wars, abortion in, 3
Current Population Study, 29
Custody, 65, 226

Daddy track, 417. *See also* Mommy track
Dancel, Genora, 517
Dating, 177–84; baby boomers and, 92; courtship, 178–79; current trends, 180–81; as game, 183–84; group, 181, 182; history, 178–81; mate selection alternatives, 400–402; as preparation for marriage, 181–83; speed, 405; traditional, 179–80. *See also* Mate selection alternatives; Premarital sexual relationships; Preparation for marriage
Dating services, 404
Dating tours, 365, 368
Day care, 185–91; effects, 189–90; history (Europe), 186; history (United States), 186–88; institutionalized care of children, 185–86. *See also* Child care policy
Ddharmaatmyor, 287
Deadbeat parents, 191–96; African American fathers, 26, 29, 30; child advocates and, 194–95; child support and, 191–94; defined, 112, 191; fathers' rights activists and, 195–96. *See also* Child support
Deadbeat Parents Punishment Act (1998), 112, 113, 191, 194
Decker, Jonathan P., 483
Defense of Marriage Act (1996), 215–16, 517–18
Dementia, 244
Democracy, 323–24, 386

Dependence. *See* Addiction
Depression: developmental disability of children and, 198, 199; family roles and, 275, 278; in grandparents as caregivers, 315; in wives, 61; in working women, 275, 278
Desensitization, and mass media, 358–59
Destructive parentification, 135
Developmental disability and marital stress, 196–201; attention deficit hyperactivity disorder, 47; background, 197; future prospects, 200; negative effects on married life, 197–99; positive effects on married life, 199–200. *See also* Attention deficit hyperactivity disorder (ADHD); Marital satisfaction
Diagnostic and Statistical Manual of Mental Disorders, 41, 54
Diaphragms (birth control method), 71–72
Dick-Read, Grantly, 121
Direct-entry midwives, 118, 124–25, 406, 407, 410, 412
Disability, developmental. *See* Developmental disability and marital stress
Discipline: authoritarian parenting and, 445, 446; birth order and, 79; parenting styles and, 445, 446, 447. *See also* Corporal punishment
Disease, attention deficit hyperactivity disorder as, 41–42
Disenfranchised grief, 454
Displaced homemakers, 20
Distant figure (grandparenting style), 306
District of Columbia: domestic partnerships, 216, 217; same-sex marriage, 517
Divorce: African American fathers and, 26; after remarriage, 507–8, 509; birth dearth and, 94; cohabitation after, 428; cohabitation and, 143–44; common law marriage and, 148; developmental disability of child and, 199; domestic violence interventions and, 235; family roles and, 274, 277; fathers' rights activists and, 195; fictive kin and, 288; financial issues, 20, 22, 203–4, 205–6, 210, 211; grandparenting style and, 307; history, 16–17, 207–8; parenting styles and, 448; premarital sexual relationships and, 474; religion and, 497; statistics, 208–9. *See also* Divorce, adversarial and no-fault; Divorce, as problem, symptom, or solution; Divorce and children; Prenuptial agreements; Remarriage
Divorce, adversarial and no-fault, 15–24; adversarial approaches, 16, 21–23; divorce as problem, symptom, or solution, 208, 212; extramarital sexual relationships and, 262; history of divorce, 16–17; no-fault approaches, 16, 18–21, 23. *See also*

Covenant marriage; Divorce; Divorce, as problem, symptom, or solution; Divorce and children

Divorce, as problem, symptom, or solution, 206–14; divorce as problem, 209–11; divorce as solution, 213–14; divorce as symptom, 211–13; divorce statistics, 208–9; history of divorce, 207–8. *See also* Covenant marriage; Divorce; Divorce, adversarial and no-fault; Divorce and children

Divorce and children, 201–6; divorce, as problem, symptom, or solution, 210–11, 213; economic factors, 204, 205–6; long-term effects, 202; minimizing effects of divorce, 204–6; overview, 20–21; processes of divorce effects, 203–4. *See also* Divorce; Divorce, adversarial and no-fault; Divorce, as problem, symptom, or solution

Dobson, James: benefits of marriage, 56; corporal punishment, 155; divorce, 206, 497; same-sex marriage, 519

Doe v. Bolton (1973), 5

DOMA. *See* Defense of Marriage Act (1996)

Domestic partnerships, 215–20; civil unions, 215; common law marriage *versus*, 145–46; controversies, 218–20; legal options, 215–18; licensed, 216–18; reciprocal beneficiaries, 216; same-sex marriage as type of, 215–16. *See also* Common law marriage; Same-sex marriage

Domestic violence: basic facts, 370–71; causes, 232–33; as disadvantage to marriage, 61; divorce and, 213; history of attitudes toward, 369–70; mail order brides and, 365, 368–69; sibling violence/abuse and, 525; statistics, 231–32. *See also* Battered woman syndrome; Child abuse; Domestic violence behaviors and causes; Domestic violence interventions; Religion, women, and domestic violence; Sibling violence and abuse

Domestic violence behaviors and causes, 221–28; abuse behaviors, 221–23, 230–31; addiction and, 14; barriers to seeking help, 224–26; common couple violence *versus* intimate terrorism, 223–24; learned helplessness, 226–27; resources for victims, 227. *See also* Battered woman syndrome; Domestic violence; Domestic violence interventions; Religion, women, and domestic violence

Domestic violence interventions, 229–38; arrest of offender, 235–36; battered woman syndrome and, 50; categories of spouse abuse, 230–31; causal influences, 232–33; child abuse and, 103; compound effects, 233–34; divorce, 235; domestic violence statistics, 231–32; future directions, 238; government policies and programs, 236; interventions, 235–38; mandatory arrest, 236–37; shelter movement, 230, 237; sibling violence/abuse, 525. *See also* Battered woman syndrome; Domestic violence; Domestic violence behaviors and causes; Mandatory arrest laws; Religion, women, and domestic violence

Donaldson Institute, 301–3
Dornan, Robert K., 539
Doulas, 122–23
Dowries, 403
Drug abuse, 99. *See also* Addiction
Duluth Domestic Abuse Intervention Project, 373
Durkheim, Emile, 453

Early Childhood Education and Care (ECEC), 106
Economic issues. *See* Financial issues
Economic power, 377–78
Educational attainment, 170, 202, 322, 547–48
Educational marriage preparation programs, 486–87
Education laws, 320
Elder abuse, 239–46; contributing factors, 243–44; defined, 239–40; elder care and, 250; gender issues, 244; history, 242; interventions, 244–46; types, 240–42. *See also* Domestic violence; Elder care
Elder care, 247–52; caregiver stress, 248–49; future directions, 251–52; history, 247–48; home care issues, 250–51; nursing home issues, 249–50. *See also* Children as caregivers; Elder abuse
Elizabethan Poor Laws (1601), 112–13, 192
Ellis, Coleen, 454
Eloping. *See* Wedding and eloping
Emergency contraception, 9, 75
Emotional abuse, 222, 241, 522
Emotional parentification, 135
Emotional problems: children and divorce, 202, 205; grandparents as caregivers, 309, 315–16; infertility, 344
Employed mothers, 252–57; balancing work and family, 254–55; economic issues, 253; history and trends, 252–53; housework allocation and, 255–56; impact on children, 255; minimizing effects of motherhood on employment, 417–18; overscheduled children and, 439–40; stay at home dads and, 527; in World War II and after, 282. *See also* Child care policy; Housework allocation; Mommy track; Stay at home dads; Working women
Endometriosis, 337
Engagement, 567, 569
Engagement rings, 576

Engels, Friedrich, 377
England. *See* United Kingdom
English Common Law, 3–4, 146, 370
English Poor Laws (1601), 112–13, 192
Enrichment workshops, 486–87
Environmental contaminants, and infertility, 343
Environmental reasons, for childfree relationships, 129
Epidural anesthesia, 120, 121
Episcopalians: marital power, 378; same-sex marriage, 518–19
Episiotomy, 120
Eron, Leonard, 359
Ethnicity. *See* Race and ethnicity; *specific racial and ethnic groups*
Euphemisms, for death, 452
Europe: cohabitation, 423; common law marriage, 146; day care, 186; fictive kin, 286
European Americans. *See* Whites
Evaluation and diagnosis stage, of infertility, 340–41
Evan B. Donaldson Adoption Institute, 301–3
Evangelicals: abortion, 495; birth control, 495; homeschooling, 320; marital power, 381. *See also* Christianity
Evolution, teaching of, 498
Experience effects, of cohabitation, 144
Explicit anthropomorphism, 451
Expressive view of marriage, 386
Extended families, 172
Extramarital sexual relationships, 257–64; dealing with, 262–63; legal aspects, 262; monogamy *versus*, 261–62; open marriages, 259–61; reasons for involvement, 258–59

Falbo, Toni, 432–33
Familism, in Latino families, 172
Family and Medical Leave Act (FMLA), 255–69; development of, 255–67; employee attitudes toward, 267–68; future directions, 268; gender issues, 265–66, 267, 531. *See also* Employed mothers
Family bed. *See* Cosleeping
Family Constellation (Toman), 79
Family Law Act (California, 1969), 18
Family life cycle model, 391–92
Family Research Council: benefits of marriage, 56, 59; divorce, 212; family roles, 275; gay parent adoption, 303; remarriage, 504; same-sex marriage, 519–20
Family roles, 269–79; debate over, 274–78; egalitarian model, 270–71, 276–78; future, 278–79; history, 271–73; models, 270–71; religion and, 496–97; traditional model, 270, 274–76; transition to parenthood and, 555. *See also* Employed mothers; Housework allocation; Stay at home dads
Family size, 389
Family structure, 309, 496–97
Family Support Act (1988), 188
Family values, 356–57
Family wage economy, 275
Father-Daughter Purity Balls, 476–77
Fathers, 279–85; absent, 24, 26, 27–30, 283; ADHD children and, 46–47; as childbirth witnesses, 122; in colonial period, 280; corporal punishment by, 154; divorced, 205; in modern era, 281–83; poverty and public assistance and, 472; present, 284–85; as providers, 281; religion and, 498; resident, 284–85; social history of roles, 280–83; traditional expectations of, 415; in Victorian era, 280–81. *See also* African American fathers; Stay at home dads
Fathers' rights advocates, 113–15, 195–96
Fault divorce. *See* Divorce, adversarial and no-fault
Federal Marriage Amendment, 518
Female reproduction, 334–35
Females. *See* Women
Fence sitters, as term, 127
Ferber, Richard, 161
Fertility assistance, 344–45
Fertility patterns, 89–98; baby boom, 89–93, 95–96; birth dearth, 93–95, 96; effects of fluctuations in fertility, 95–97
Fetal monitors, 119
Fetus, personhood of, 8
Fictive kin, 285–89; cross-culturally, 286–87; future, 287–89; history, 286; terms for, 287. *See also* Biological privilege; Domestic partnerships; Pet death and the family
Financial abuse, 222–23, 241
Financial issues: birth dearth, 94–95, 96; child abuse and, 99–100; childfree relationships, 129–30; cohabitation and, 429; divorce, 20, 22, 203–4, 205–6, 210, 211; domestic violence victims, 225; employed mothers, 253; grandparents as caregivers, 309, 314–15; marriage, benefits of, 58–59, 61; prenuptial agreements, 479–81; remarriage, 509–10; surrogacy, 536–38; teen pregnancy, 547–48; transition to parenthood, 556–57; white wedding industry, 573–74
Fineman, Martha Albertson, 150
First-born children, 76, 77, 79–80
First-trimester abortions, 1, 2
Five Families (Lewis), 168
FLDS (Fundamentalist Latter-day Saints), 461–62
Florida: covenant marriage, 163–64; divorce, 18; gay parent adoption, 298, 303
FMLA. *See* Family and Medical Leave Act

Focus on the Family: benefits of marriage, 59; cohabitation, 142, 425; divorce, 206, 211; gay parent adoption, 299; same-sex marriage, 519
Follicle stimulating hormone, 335, 336, 338
Food stamps, 468–69
Forbidden sexual relationships. *See* Extramarital sexual relationships
Forceps, during childbirth, 120
Formal grandparenting style, 306
Formula feeding. *See* Breastfeeding or formula feeding
Foster care, 289–96; aging out, 294; biological privilege and, 65–66; child abuse victims in, 103–4; future prospects, 294–95; history, 290–91; tips for foster families, 292–94; values underlying, 291–92. *See also* Biological privilege; Poverty and public assistance
Four Horsemen of the Apocalypse model, 389, 390
"A Framework for Understanding Poverty," 170
France: day care, 186; mail order brides, 364
Frazier, E. Franklin, 167–68, 170, 172
Freedom of Access to Clinic Entrance Act, 6
Fuchs, Cynthia, 376–77
Full-time fathers. *See* Stay at home dads
Fundamentalist Latter-day Saints (FLDS), 461–62
Fun seeker (grandparenting style), 306
Furstenberg, Frank, 285

Gallagher, Maggie, 22, 56, 62, 206
Gay parent adoption, 297–304; agencies, 300–303; background, 297–98; effects of, 299–300; future directions, 303–4; religion and, 496; state laws, 298, 303. *See also* International adoption; Same-sex marriage; Transracial adoption
Gender: child care policy and, 106–7; cohabitation motives and, 428; divorce and children and, 202; elder abuse and, 244; extramarital sexual relationships and, 257–58; Family and Medical Leave Act and, 265–66, 267, 531; grandparenting style and, 307; premarital sexual relationships and, 475; remarriage and, 507; transition to parenthood and, 553–54. *See also* Men; Women
Gender equality, 93, 265–66, 376–77, 382–83
Gender ideology, 269, 378, 381–82. *See also* Family roles
Gender roles, 231, 269–70. *See also* Family roles
Generation gap, 316–17
Genetic contribution test for legal motherhood, 539
Gestational surrogacy, 533

Gestation test for legal motherhood, 539
Goodtimes, 25
Gottman, John, 389–90
Grandparenthood, 304–11; background, 304–5; child custody and, 65; grandparenting styles, 306–7; grandparents as caregivers, 308–9; grandparent visitation rights, 309–11; stereotypes, 305–6. *See also* Grandparents as caregivers
Grandparents as caregivers, 311–17; background, 312; emotional concerns, 309, 315–16; financial concerns, 309, 314–15; future prospects, 317; health concerns, 309, 313–14, 316; legal concerns, 316; negative aspects, 312–16; overview, 308–9; positive aspects, 316–17. *See also* Children as caregivers; Grandparenthood
Great Depression: day care, 188; divorce, 209; poverty and public assistance, 466; working women, 281
Green, Tom, 461–62
Grief, disenfranchised, 454
Group dating, 181, 182

Hague Treaty on International Adoptions, 353
Hartsdale Pet Cemetery and Crematory, 454
Hawaii: domestic partnerships, 216; grandparent visitation rights, 310; same-sex marriage, 517
Head Start, 109
Healthcare providers, 118–19, 246
Health issues: childfree relationships, 127–28; culture of poverty, 170; grandparents as caregivers, 309, 313–14, 316; homeschooling, 325; marriage, benefits of, 57–58, 61; open marriages, 261; poverty, 465–66; teen pregnancy, 546–47
Healthy Marriage Initiative, 396, 398–99, 472
Hinckley, Gordon B., 461
Hispanics. *See* Latinos
Hochschild, Arlie, 269, 275
Holt, Bertha, 348
Holt, Harry, 348
Holt International Children's Services, 348
Home care issues, in elder care, 250–51
Home charter school students, 321
Homemakers, displaced, 20
Homeschooling, 319–26; arguments concerning, 321–22; culture and, 324; democracy and, 323–24; fairness and, 324; health concerns, 325; history, 319–20; parental motives for, 320–21; religion and, 498; research studies, 322–23; student performance and, 322; welfare of children and, 325
Homicide, 225, 232
Honeymoon effect, in engaged couples, 489

"Honeymoon" phase, of battered woman syndrome, 51
hooks, bell, 25
Hormonal implants, 73
Horoscope matching, 34
Housework allocation, 326–32; children and household labor, 328–29; consequences, 330–31; employed mothers and, 255–56; marital power and, 378; marital satisfaction and, 331; options and strategies, 331; overview of women and work, 327–28; race, ethnicity, and social class, 329–30; transition to parenthood and, 555. *See also* Employed mothers; Family roles
Housing programs, 471
Huesmann, Rowell, 359
Human Rights Campaign, 297, 298, 519
Hurried child syndrome. *See* Overscheduled children
Hyde Amendment (1977), 5
Hyper-parenting. *See* Overscheduled children
Hysterectomy, 75
Hystreosalpingogram, 337

Immigrants, 295. *See also* Mail order brides
Immunization, 325
Incarceration, 9–10, 14, 113–14
Independent living (elder care), 248
Indians and Indian Americans, 33–40; arranged marriages, 33–35; current controversies about arranged marriages, 37–39; love marriages, 36–37; semi-arranged marriages, 35–36
Industrialization: child support and, 193; dating and, 180; day care and, 186; family roles and, 272–73; motherhood tasks and, 419–20; parenthood and, 280–81
Infanticide, 115, 117
Infant schools, 186
Infertility, 333–46; childfree relationships, acceptability of, 343–44; controversies, 341–45; couple, effects on, 340; defined, 334; emotions, stages of, 340–41; fault, assigning, 342–43; female factors in, 335–37; female reproduction, 334–35; international adoption and, 347; male factors in, 338–39; male reproduction, 338; prevalence, 334; reproductive technology and, 344–45. *See also* Childfree relationships; Surrogacy
Infidelity. *See* Extramarital sexual relationships
Informal marriage. *See* Common law marriage
Institute for American Values, 56, 142, 206, 212
Instrumental parentification, 135
Instrumental view of marriage, 385–86

Intent-based test for legal motherhood, 535, 539
Intercountry adoption. *See* International adoption
Intercountry Adoption Act (2000), 353
International adoption, 346–54; benefits of, 351; Chinese adoptions, 346–47, 348, 350; concerns about, 347, 351–52; former Soviet States, 346–47, 348, 350–51; Guatemalan adoptions, 346–47, 348, 349; history, 347–48; reasons for, 346–47; South Korean adoptions, 346–47, 348–49; transracial adoption and, 564; trends, 252–353; Vietnamese adoptions, 349. *See also* Gay parent adoption; Transracial adoption
International marriage brokering. *See* Mail order brides
International Marriage Broker Regulation Act (2005), 365, 368
Internet: dating and, 404; extramarital sexual relationships and, 263; mail order brides and, 365, 369; matrimonial Web sites, 36; stay at home dads and, 530, 531
Interpersonal violence. *See* Domestic violence
Interracial adoption. *See* Transracial adoption
Intersexuality Theory, 174
Intimate partner violence. *See* Domestic violence
Intimate terrorism, 223–24
Intravenous infusion, during childbirth, 119
Introduced marriages, 35–36
Islam: abortion, 495–96; plural marriage, 464; prenuptial agreements, 483
Isolation: domestic violence victims and, 224–25; grandparents as caregivers and, 309, 316; stay at home dads and, 528
IUDs, 72

Jails, 9–10, 14, 113–14
Jane Project, 4–5
Jaycee B. case, 535–36
Jealousy: in open marriages, 260, 261; in plural marriage, 463
Jeff, Morris, Jr., 560
The Jeffersons, 25
Jeffs, Warren, 457, 462
Jews: abortion, 495–96; gay parent adoption, 301, 302; marital power, 378; prenuptial agreements, 483; speed dating, 405
Johnson, Anna, 534–35, 539
Johnson, Lyndon B., 466
Johnson, Michael, 223–24
Johnson v. Calvert, 534–35, 537, 539
Judaism. *See* Jews
Juvenile delinquency, 355–61; arenas for debate, 356–60; child-rearing and, 357–58; defined, 356; family values and, 356–57; mass media influence on, 358–59; parental responsibility and, 360; statistics, 355–56

Keane, Noel, 532
Kennedy, John F., 92
Kinderdult phenomenon, 437–38
Kruger morphology test, 339

Labor coaches, 122–23
Lafayette, Leslie, 126
Laissez-faire parenting, 446–47
La Leche League International, 160
Lamaze, Ferdinand, 121–22
Language development, 189–90
Laparoscopy, 337
Las Vegas weddings, 570
Latin America, fictive kin in, 286–87
Latinos: culture of poverty, 168, 172, 173; divorce, 209; familism, 172; fictive kin, 287; housework allocation, 329; patriarchy, 173; teen pregnancy, 545, 549; white wedding industry, 575
Learned helplessness, 52, 226–27
Legal concerns: extramarital sexual relationships, 262; grandparents as caregivers, 316
Levonorgestrel intrauterine systems, 73
Lewis, Oscar, 167, 168
Licensed domestic partnerships, 216–18
Licensed midwives, 118, 124–25, 406, 407, 410, 412
Linguistic development, 189–90
Living together. *See* Cohabitation, nonmarital
Lodgers, as fictive kin, 286
Louisiana: covenant marriage, 164; divorce, 18; mail order brides, 364; prenuptial agreements, 480
Love marriages, 36–37
Lowery, Fred, 165
Luken, Thomas A., 538–39
Luker, Kristin, 549–50
Lutenizing hormone, 335, 338
Lutherans: gay parent adoption, 302; international adoption, 347

Mail order brides, 363–69; agencies, 364–65; arguments against, 367–68; arguments for, 367; parties involved in, 365–67. *See also* Mate selection alternatives
Maine, domestic partnerships in, 216, 217
Male reproduction, 338
Males. *See* Men
Mandatory arrest laws, 369–75; battered woman syndrome and, 50; domestic violence interventions, 236–37; domestic violence overview, 370–71; paradigm shifts in attitudes, 372–73; victim empowerment models, 373–74. *See also* Battered woman syndrome; Domestic violence interventions
Mandatory prosecution policies, 50, 372–73
"Manifesto" (Woodruff), 461, 462

Marital contracts. *See* Prenuptial agreements
Marital power, 375–83; battered woman syndrome and, 54–55; cultural norms and, 379; economic power and, 377–78; gender ideology and, 378, 381–82; gender inequality and, 376–77; negotiating, 380–81; physical attributes and, 379; relationship dynamics and, 379–80; religion and, 496–97; sources of, 377–80. *See also* Family roles; Housework allocation
Marital quality, 384–85
Marital satisfaction, 383–94; children and, 421; correlates, 389–91; debate over, 387–89; evolution of marriage, 385–86; family roles and, 277; future directions, 392–93; housework allocation and, 331; life course considerations, 391–92; marital success measures, 384–85; remarriage and, 508; stay at home dads and, 529; then *versus* now, 386–89; transition to parenthood and, 553, 555. *See also* Developmental disability and marital stress; Marriage, benefits of
Marital stability, 384
Marital stress and developmental disability. *See* Developmental disability and marital stress
Marital success measures, 384–85
Marriage: childrearing and, 143; civil, 145, 146, 148; cohabitation as alternative to, 427–29; dating as preparation for, 181–83; democracy and, 386; developmental disability of child and, 198–99; evolution of, 385–86; expressive view of, 386; instrumental view of, 385–86; patriarchy and, 386; peer, 382; protection effects, 59–60; rights as discriminatory, 62; selection effects, 62; statutory, 145, 146, 148; teen pregnancy and, 550–51. *See also* Marriage, benefits of; Marriage promotion; *specific types of marriage*
Marriage, benefits of, 56–63; benefits for children, 59; financial aspects, 58–59, 61; future debate, 62–63; health aspects, 57–58, 61; marriage protection effects, 59–60; marriage rights as discriminatory, 62; marriage selection effects, 62; pro-alternative relationships argument, 60–62; pro-marriage argument, 57–60; psychological aspects, 58, 61; as unequal between men and women, 60–61. *See also* Marital satisfaction; Marriage; Marriage promotion; *specific types of marriage*
Marriage, common law. *See* Common law marriage
Marriage, covenant. *See* Covenant marriage
Marriage, effects of cohabitation on. *See* Cohabitation, effects on marriage

Marriage, open. *See* Open marriages
Marriage, preparation for. *See* Preparation for marriage
Marriage, same-sex. *See* Same-sex marriage
Marriage brokering, international. *See* Mail order brides
Marriage by habit and repute. *See* Common law marriage
Marriage promotion, 394–400; arguments against, 398–99; arguments for, 397–98; poverty, public assistance and, 398–99, 472; single-parent families, 394–95; welfare reform and, 395–96. *See also* Marriage; Marriage, benefits of; Poverty and public assistance; *specific types of marriage*
Marriage Proposals (Fineman), 150
Marriage squeeze, 506
Marx, Karl, 376, 377, 378
Masculinity, and stay at home dads, 529
Massachusetts: domestic partnerships, 215–16, 219; foster care, 291
Matchmakers, 404
Maternal age, and infertility, 343
Maternity care, history of, 407–11
Maternity leave, 554
Mate selection alternatives, 400–405; arranged marriage, 402–3; dating, 400–402; matchmaker and dating services, 404; personal ads, 404–5; speed dating, 405. *See also* Arranged marriage; Dating; Mail order brides
Matriarchy, 168, 172–73
McConnell, Mike, 516
McKenna, James, 158, 160
McRae, William J., 150
Media: juvenile delinquency and, 358–59; marital satisfaction and, 393; pregnancy in, 554–55; weddings in, 576
Mediation, 23, 311
Medicaid, 470–71
Medical abortions, 1, 2–3
Medicalization. *See* Midwifery and medicalization
Medical pain control, during childbirth, 121
Medicare, 95–96
Medication, for attention deficit hyperactivity disorder, 43–44
Meister v. Moore (1877), 148, 149
Men: cohabitation motives, 428; dating, role in, 181–82, 183–84; Family and Medical Leave Act and, 267, 531; financial benefits of marriage, 58–59; grandparenting style of, 307; health benefits of marriage, 57; infertility, effects on, 340; premarital sexual relationships and, 475; remarriage and, 507; transition to parenthood, 553–54. *See also* Fathers; Gender; Women

Mental health: child abusers, 98; child caregivers, 137, 138; family roles and, 275–76; grandparents as caregivers, 315; marriage, benefits of, 58, 61. *See also* Depression
Mental health workers, and preparation for marriage, 487
Merritt, William T., 560
Methotrexate, 2
Mexico, fictive kin in, 288
Michigan, surrogacy in, 532
Middle-born children, 76, 77–78, 80
Middle-class families. *See* Social class
Midwifery and medicalization, 405–14; childbirth options, 119–21; history of maternity care, 407–11; midwifery described, 406–7; midwifery model of care, 119–21, 412–13; midwives as childbirth healthcare providers, 118–19, 124–25; safety and risk in childbirth, 411–12; training of midwives, 410. *See also* Childbirth options
Midwives Alliance of North America, 412–13
Mifepristone, 2, 9
Miller-Muro, Layli, 368
Minneapolis Domestic Violence Experiment, 50, 236–37, 372
Minnesota: same-sex marriage, 516; transracial adoption, 558
Minorities: discipline, 447; in foster care, 295; poverty and, 465. *See also* Race and ethnicity; Transracial adoption; *specific minorities*
Misoprostol, 2, 9
Mississippi: divorce, 19; gay parent adoption, 298, 303
Mock anthropomorphism, 451
Mommy track, 414–18. *See also* Employed mothers; Motherhood, opportunity costs
Monogamy, 261–62
Mormons, 458–61, 462
Morning after pill, 9, 75
Morrill Anti-Bigamy Act, 460
Motherhood, opportunity costs, 418–22; mothering tasks, 418–20; relationship opportunity costs, 421–22; structural opportunity costs, 420–21; transition to parenthood and, 557. *See also* Employed mothers; Mommy track; Mothers
Mothers: ADHD children and, 45; biological privilege and, 64–65; breastfeeding benefits to, 82; child abuse by, 100; in colonial era, 280; corporal punishment by, 154; cosleeping and, 159, 160; day care and, 189; single, 465, 496; surrogacy and, 540–41; views of, 64–65, 540–41. *See also* Employed mothers; Motherhood, opportunity costs
Movies, stay at home dads in, 529

Moynihan, Daniel Patrick, 169–70
Moynihan Report, 169–70
Multi Ethnic Placement Act (1994), 561
Murder, 225, 232
Music, 92
Muslims. *See* Islam

National Association of Black Social Workers, 559, 560
The National Campaign to Prevent Teen and Unplanned Pregnancy, 546
National Center for Injury Prevention and Control, 221–23
National Center on Elder Abuse, 245
National Coalition Against Domestic Violence, 227
National Directory of New Hires, 193–94
National Domestic Violence Hotline, 227
National Education Association, 170
National Institute of Human Health and Development Early Child Research Network, 189
National Longitudinal Survey of Labor Market Experience of Youth, 28–29
National Marriage Project, 212, 425
Native Americans, opposition to transracial adoption, 559
Natural childbirth, 121–22
Neglect: child, 98, 114–15, 116, 325; elder, 242
Negligent parenting, 447
The Negro Family in the United States (Frazier), 167–68
"The Negro Family" (Moynihan), 169–70
New Jersey: domestic partnerships, 215, 216; gay parent adoption, 298; surrogacy, 533–34, 539
New York: divorce, 18, 19; midwife licensing, 408
No-drop policies, 50, 372–73
No-fault divorce. *See* Divorce, adversarial and no-fault
Noncommercial surrogacy, 533
Nonmarital cohabitation. *See* Cohabitation, nonmarital
Nurse midwives, 118–19, 124
Nurses, 246, 247
Nursing homes, 247, 248, 249–50

Obstetricians, 118, 406–7, 409. *See also* Childbirth options; Midwifery and medicalization
Oettinger, Katherine, 348
Oklahoma, divorce in, 23
Old Deluder Satan Act (1647), 319
Oneida Community, 187–88
Only children, 431–36; achievement motivation theory, 435; Adler's theory, 434; confluence model, 434–35; factors promoting, 431–32; famous, 436; future directions, 436; stereotypes, 432–33. *See also* Birth order; Fertility patterns
Open marriages, 259–61; health related dangers, 261; polyamory, 260; styles, 259; swinging, 260–61
Operation Baby Lift, 349
Opportunity costs of motherhood. *See* Motherhood, opportunity costs
Oral contraceptive pills, 70, 72
Ordinal position. *See* Birth order
Orphanages, 188
Ovarian function tests, 336–37
Overscheduled children, 436–41; benefits of activity participation, 441; debate over, 439–41; history, 437–39. *See also* Parenting styles
Ovulation, 335

Pain control, during childbirth, 119–20, 121–22
Parental Alienation Syndrome, 226
Parental and Disability Leave Act, 265. *See also* Family and Medical Leave Act
Parental and Medical Leave Act, 265. *See also* Family and Medical Leave Act
Parental responsibility, 112–13, 360. *See also* Child support; Deadbeat parents
Parenthood, transition to. *See* Transition to parenthood
Parentification, 134–35
Parenting styles, 443–50; authoritarian, 445–46; authoritative, 444–45; birth order and, 79–80; corporal punishment and, 153–54, 445, 446, 447; cosleeping and, 158–59; discipline and, 445, 446, 447; factors affecting, 448–49; permissive, 446–47; sibling violence/abuse and, 523–25; uninvolved, 447. *See also* Corporal punishment; Cosleeping
Partial birth abortions, 7–8
Part-time employment for parents, 415
Patriarchal terrorism, 223–24
Patriarchy, 173, 379, 386
Paul, Pamela, 212
Peabody, Shelley, 261
Peer marriage, 382
Peer Marriage (Schwartz), 382
Pelvic adhesions, 337
Pennsylvania: abortion, 7; foster care, 291; housing programs, 471
Peritoneal factors, in infertility, 337
Permanent contraception, 74–75
Permissive parenting, 446–47
Personal ads, 404–5
Personal Responsibility and Work Opportunity Reconciliation Act (1996): child support, 112, 113, 193–94; foster care, 295; marriage promotion, 394, 395–96; poverty and public assistance, 467
Pet Angel Memorial Center, 454

Pet cemeteries and cremation, 453–54
Pet death and the family, 450–57; anthropomorphism, 451–52; debate over, 454–56; euphemisms, 452; pet cemeteries and cremation, 453–54; pet health care, 453; teachable moments, 452–53. *See also* Fictive kin
Pet health care, 453
Philippines, mail order brides from, 363–64
Physical abuse: domestic violence, 221–22, 231–32; elder abuse, 240; sibling violence and abuse, 521–22, 523–24
Physical addiction, 11
Physical attributes, and marital power, 379
Physicians, 246, 487. *See also* Obstetricians
Picture brides. *See* Mail order brides
Pincus, Charles, 70
Plan B (emergency contraception), 9, 75
Planned Parenthood of Southeastern Pennsylvania v. Casey, 7
Plural marriage, 457–64; current status, 461–62; future, 463–64; history, 459–61; negative aspects, 462–63; polyandry, 458; polygyny, 458; positive aspects, 463; types, 457–58. *See also* Religion
Polyamory, 260
Polyamory Society, 260
Polyandry, 458
Polygamy. *See* Plural marriage
Polygyny, 458
Poor Laws (England, 1601), 112–13, 192
Popenoe, David, 425
Post-coital contraception, 9, 75
Postindustrial era, family roles in, 273
Poussaint, Alvin, 27
Poverty and public assistance, 464–72; characteristics of impoverished, 465; child abuse and, 99–100; culture of poverty and, 169–70, 174; fathers and, 472; food stamps, 468–69; history, 466–67; housing programs, 471; marriage promotion and, 398–99, 472; Medicaid, 470–71; public child support, 192, 195; statistics, 465; Temporary Assistance for Needy Families, 467–68; WIC program, 469–70. *See also* Culture of poverty; Marriage promotion; Social class
Power in marriage. *See* Marital power
Pregnancy: prevention programs, 545–46; transition to parenthood and, 554–55; unplanned, 68. *See also* Teen pregnancy
Preindustrial era, family roles in, 271–72
Pre-kindergarten movement, 110
Premarital Personal and Relationship Evaluation (PREPARE), 212, 487, 488, 489, 490
Premarital preparation. *See* Preparation for marriage
Premarital sexual relationships, 472–78; age of first sexual intercourse, 474–75; context of first sexual intercourse, 475; dating and, 179, 183, 184, 401, 402; first sexual intercourse, 473–74; strategies to delay sex, 475–78; teen pregnancy and, 543. *See also* Dating; Teen pregnancy
Prenuptial agreements, 478–85; arguments against, 482–83; arguments for, 483–84; costs, 481; cultural aspects, 484–85; history, 479; purposes, 479–81; states' interests, 484. *See also* Divorce
Preparation for marriage, 485–91; argument for, 487–89; deciding about, 491; goals, 485; history, 486; inadequate research on, 490; Premarital Personal and Relationship Evaluation, 212, 487, 488, 489, 490; Prevention and Relationship Enhancement Program, 486, 488–89, 490; selection effect hypothesis, 489–90; skeptical argument, 489–90; types, 486–87; wedding and eloping, 568, 569. *See also* Dating
Prepared childbirth, 121–22
PREPARE (Premarital Personal and Relationship Evaluation), 212, 487, 488, 489, 490
Prevention and Relationship Enhancement Program (PREP), 486, 488–89, 490
Professional midwives, 118, 124–25, 406, 407, 410, 412
Promise Keepers, 378, 528
Proposals, in arranged marriage, 34, 35, 36
Prosecution policies, mandatory, 50, 372–73
Protestants: abortion, 495; corporal punishment, 154–55; domestic violence, 499–500, 502–3; United States, 494. *See also* Christianity; *specific denominations*
Pseudo-kin. *See* Fictive kin
Psychological addiction, 11–12
Psychological health. *See* Mental health
Psychostimulants, 43–44
Public assistance. *See* Poverty and public assistance; *specific programs*
Public housing, 471
Purity balls, 476–77

Quality, marital, 384–85
Quasi-kin. *See* Fictive kin

Race and ethnicity: child care policy and, 106; divorce and, 209; homeschooling and, 321; housework allocation and, 329; power and, 376; premarital sexual relationships and, 474; remarriage and, 506; teen pregnancy and, 545; white wedding industry and, 575. *See also* Minorities; Transracial adoption; *specific racial and ethnic groups*
Racial identity, and transracial adoption, 563
Realization stage, of infertility, 340
Reciprocal beneficiaries, 216
Reconstituted families, 307, 511–12

Refined divorce rate, 208
Relationship issues: childfree relationships, 133; children and divorce, 202; marital power, 379–80; motherhood, opportunity costs, 421–22; transition to parenthood, 552–54
Religion, 493–99; abortion and, 495–96; birth control and, 495; childfree relationships and, 130, 133; childrearing and, 497–98; cohabitation and, 140, 143, 424, 425, 497; corporal punishment and, 154–55, 498; covenant marriage and, 164–65; defined, 493–94; divorce and, 235, 497; domestic partnerships and, 218; domestic violence and, 235; eloping and, 570; family matters and, 494–95; family roles and, 275, 496–97; family structure and, 496–97; fathers and, 498; gay parent adoption and, 297, 301, 302, 496; gender ideology and, 378; homeschooling and, 320, 498; housework allocation and, 326; infertility and, 343, 345; international adoption and, 347; marital power and, 381, 496–97; pet death and, 451; premarital sexual relationships and, 474, 475–76; prenuptial agreements and, 483; preparation for marriage and, 487; remarriage and, 510–11; reproduction and, 495–96; same-sex marriage and, 496, 518–19; social support and, 498; stay at home dads and, 528; United States, 494; unmarried mothers and, 496. *See also* Religion, women, and domestic violence
Religion, women, and domestic violence, 499–504; battered woman syndrome, 50; institutional responses, 501–2; resources, 502–3; women's responses, 500–501. *See also* Battered woman syndrome; Domestic violence; Domestic violence behaviors and causes; Domestic violence interventions; Religion
Remaking the Godly Marriage (Bartkowski), 381
Remarriage, 504–13; consequences, 509–11; eloping, 571; factors affecting rates of, 506–7; fictive kin and, 288; first marriages compared to, 507–8; future directions, 512; prenuptial agreements and, 480; religion and, 510–11; stepfamilies and, 511–12. *See also* Divorce
Remarried families, 307, 511–12
Repercussion fears, of domestic violence victims, 225, 235
Replacement level, of population, 97
Reproduction: childfree relationships and, 132; female, 334–35; male, 338; religion and, 495–96
Reproductive technology, 344–45
Reservoir of family wisdom (grandparenting style), 306

Resolution stage, of infertility, 341
Resource distribution, and economic power, 377–78
Restraining orders, 52
Reverse mortgages, 314
Rhythm method of birth control, 71
Rings, wedding and engagement, 576
Rituals, wedding, 574, 575–76
Rochlen, Aaron, 529, 530
Roe v. Wade (1973), 5, 6, 7, 94
Rogov, Marc, 367
Roman Catholics. *See* Catholics
Roman Empire, divorce in, 16, 207
Roosevelt, Franklin Delano, 169, 466
Rorex, Clela, 517
RU-486, 2, 9
Rule of thumb law, 370
Russia: adoptions from, 346–47, 348, 350–51; mail order brides, 363–64; transracial adoption, 564

Safe haven laws, 114, 116–17
SAFE model, 525
Safety fears, of domestic violence victims, 225, 235
SAHDs. *See* Stay at home dads
Same-sex adoption. *See* Gay parent adoption
Same-sex marriage, 515–21; background, 515–16; Defense of Marriage Act and, 215–16, 517–18; as domestic partnership type, 215–16; groups opposing, 519–20; historic firsts and prominent cases, 516–17; marriage and family law, 516; recent accomplishments and future directions, 520; religion and, 496, 518–19; supporters of, 518–19. *See also* Domestic partnerships; Gay parent adoption
San Diego Pet Memorial Park, 454
Sanger, Margaret, 4, 67
Satisfaction in marriage. *See* Marital satisfaction
Schroeder, Pat, 266
Schwartz, Felice, 416–17
Schwartz, Pepper, 382, 404
Scotland: common law marriage, 146; day care, 186
Sears, William, 159, 160
Second-parent adoption, 298. *See also* Gay parent adoption
Second-shift phenomenon: employed mothers and, 256; family roles and, 275; housework allocation and, 326, 330–31; motherhood, opportunity costs, 421. *See also* Working women
Second-trimester abortions, 1, 2–3
Section 8 program, 471
Selection effects: cohabitation, 143–44; marriage, 62; preparation for marriage, 489–90

Self-esteem: child abuse and, 99; domestic abuse and, 233; family roles and, 277–78; transracial adoption and, 563
Self-neglect, elder, 242
Semen analysis, 338–39
Semi-arranged marriages, 35–36
Serial marriage, 505
Servant/leadership model of marital power, 381
Servants, as fictive kin, 286
Settlement houses, 188
Sex education, 498, 546
Sexual abstinence, 70, 546
Sexual abuse: domestic violence, 222, 232; elder abuse, 240–41; sibling violence and abuse, 522, 524
Sexual intercourse, first, 473–74; age at, 474–75; context of, 475
Sexually transmitted diseases, 68, 70, 71–72, 73–74, 261
Sexual relationship: cosleeping and, 161, 162; marital satisfaction and, 390
Sexual relationships, premarital. *See* Premarital sexual relationships
Shared parenting, 116, 557
Shelter movement, 51, 230, 237
Sibling violence and abuse, 521–26; emotional abuse, 522; intervention strategies, 525; physical abuse, 521–22, 523–24; problems in recognizing and responding to, 522–25; sexual abuse, 522, 524. *See also* Domestic violence
SIDS (Sudden Infant Death Syndrome), 158, 160, 161, 162
Simon-Altstein Longitudinal Study of adoption, 563–64
Simpson, O. J., 370
Single-parent families: income, 204; juvenile delinquency and, 357–58; poverty and, 465; religion and, 496. *See also* Marriage promotion
Skipped generation families. *See* Grandparents as caregivers
Skolnick, Arlene, 62, 66
Slavery, impact on consciousness of black males, 25
Sleep sharing. *See* Cosleeping
Smith, Joseph, 459–60
Social class: child abuse and, 99–100; child care policy and, 105–7; developmental disability and marital stress and, 199; housework allocation and, 329–30; overscheduled children and, 438–39, 440–41; power and, 376; premarital sexual relationships and, 474; remarriage and, 507
Social construction, attention deficit hyperactivity disorder as, 44–45
Social families. *See* Fictive kin
Social isolation. *See* Isolation

Social Learning model of addiction, 13
Social Security, 95
Social Security Act (1935), 196, 217
Social Security Administration, 195
Social stratification, 376–77
Social support: developmental disability, 198; first marriage *versus* remarriage, 508; grandparents as caregivers, 309; religion, 498; stay at home dads, 530, 531; teen pregnancy, 548; wedding and eloping, 570
Social workers, 290, 559, 560
Socioeconomic status. *See* Social class
South Dakota, divorce in, 18, 208
Spanking. *See* Corporal punishment
Special Supplemental Nutrition Program for Women, Infants, and Children (WIC), 469–70
Speed dating, 405
Sperm testing, 338–39
Spirituality, 493–94. *See also* Religion
Spiritual marriages. *See* Plural marriage
Spock, Benjamin, 152–53, 161
Spousal support, 20, 22
Spouse abuse. *See* Domestic violence
Spouse swapping, 260–61
Stability, marital, 384
Stacey, Judith, 299
Stack, Carol, 288
Stalking, 225, 232, 235
Stanley, Scott M., 487, 488
Statutory marriage, 145, 146, 148
Stay at home dads (SAHDs), 526–32; benefits, 529–30; challenges, 528–29; future, 530; history, 527; motivations of, 527–28; statistics, 527. *See also* Employed mothers; Family roles; Fathers
Stenberg v. Carhart, 7–8
Stepfamilies, 307, 511–12
Stereotypes: abused women, 55–56; grandparenthood, 305–6; only children, 432–33
Sterilization, 132
Stern, Elizabeth, 533–34, 536, 539
Stern, William, 533–34, 536
Stigma: adoption and, 560–61; developmental disability and, 198; eloping and, 571; teen pregnancy and, 544
Stress: child abuse and, 99; child caregivers and, 137; elder caregivers and, 248–49; family roles and, 275, 278; grandparents as caregivers and, 309, 313, 315; infertility and, 344; wedding and eloping and, 568–69, 570, 571; working women and, 275, 278. *See also* Developmental disability and marital stress
Structural functionalism, 231, 274
Structuralism, 170–74, 380–81, 382
Structural opportunity costs, of motherhood, 420–21

Substance abuse. *See* Addiction
Sudden Infant Death Syndrome (SIDS), 158, 160, 161, 162
Support. *See* Social support
Surgeon General, 51
Surgical abortions, 1, 2, 3
Surrogacy, 532–41; Baby M case, 533–34, 536, 539; debate over, 536–38; history, 532–36; Jaycee B. case, 535–36; *Johnson v. Calvert*, 534–35, 537, 539; legal motherhood and, 538–40; motherhood notions and, 540–41. *See also* Biological privilege; Infertility
Surrogate parent (grandparenting style), 306. *See also* Grandparents as caregivers
Sweden: cohabitation, 423; marital power, 382–83
Swinging, 260–61

Tahirih Justice Center, 368
Taiwan, mail order brides from, 367
Take Back the Night movement, 227
TANF. *See* Temporary Assistance for Needy Families
Target children, 525
Tax benefits: of marriage, 58; of parenthood, 132
Teen pregnancy, 543–52; adoption and, 551; controversies, 549–51; intervention, 545–46; marriage and, 550–51; positives of, 549; problems with, 546–48; race and ethnicity and, 545; statistics, 543–44. *See also* Premarital sexual relationships
Television programs: African American fathers in, 25; baby boomers and, 91, 92; juvenile delinquency and, 359
Temporary Assistance for Needy Families (TANF): child support, 195; culture of poverty, 169; grandparents as caregivers, 314; marriage promotion, 395–96; poverty and public assistance, 467–68
Tender years doctrine, 65
Tennessee, divorce in, 18, 19
Testing, cohabitation as, 428–29
Texas: abortion, 5; prenuptial agreements, 480
Thomas Theorem, 451
Toman, Walter, 79
Traditional surrogacy, 533
Trained childbirth assistants. *See* Midwives
Transition to parenthood, 552–58; communication issues, 555; cosleeping and, 157, 159; employment issues, 554; financial issues, 556–57; pregnancy issues, 554–55; relationship issues, 552–54; shared parenting, 557. *See also* Childfree relationships
Transnational adoption. *See* International adoption
Transracial adoption, 558–65; arguments against, 559–61; arguments for, 561–64; debate over, 559; future, 564; history, 558–59; statistics, 559. *See also* International adoption
Treatment stage, of infertility, 341
Trewhella, Matt, 150
Trial marriage, 428–29
True Love Waits campaign, 476
True womanhood, cult of, 272–73, 328
The Truly Disadvantaged (Wilson), 171
Trust, and extramarital sexual relationships, 262–63
Tubal ligation, 74, 132
Tubman, Harriet, 78

Ukraine: adoptions from, 348, 350; mail order brides, 363–64
Ultrasound examinations, 337
Uncontested divorce. *See* Divorce, adversarial and no-fault
Uniform Parentage Act (California), 539, 541
Uniform Reciprocal Enforcement of Support Act, 113, 193
Uninvolved parenting, 447
United Church of Christ, 518
United Kingdom: cohabitation, 423; day care, 186; fictive kin, 286; surrogacy, 538
Urbanization: child support and, 193; dating and, 179–80; fictive kin and, 286
U.S. Citizenship and Immigration Service, 352
Utah: common law marriage, 147; gay parent adoption, 298, 303
Uterine factors, in infertility, 337–38

Vaccination, 325
Vacuum aspiration, 2
Vacuum extraction, 120
Vaginal contraceptive rings, 73
Vaginal sponges, 72
Vasectomy, 75, 132
Vermont, domestic partnerships in, 215
Victim empowerment models, 373–74
Victorian era: courtship, 178–79; fatherhood, 280–81
Vietnam, mail order brides from, 367
Violence Against Women Act (1994), 51, 221
Virginity pledges, 476, 477
Volunteer work, 128

Waite, Linda J., 56, 62
Walker, Lenore, 50, 53, 55, 226
Wallerstein, Judith, 206, 211
Washington, D.C.: domestic partnerships, 216, 217; same-sex marriage, 517
Washington State: grandparent visitation rights, 310; prenuptial agreements, 480
Water births, 120
Weber, Max, 376, 378
Webster v. Reproductive Health Services (1989), 6–7

Wedding and eloping, 567–72; eloping negatives, 571; eloping positives, 570–71; wedding negatives, 568–69; wedding positives, 567–68. *See also* White wedding industry

Wedding rings, 576

Welfare Extension and Marriage Promotion Act, 394

Welfare reform. *See* Personal Responsibility and Work Opportunity Reconciliation Act (1996)

Whitehead, Barbara Dafoe, 19, 206

Whitehead, Mary Beth, 533–34, 536, 539

Whites: corporal punishment, 156; discipline, 447; divorce, 209; fictive kin, 287; parenting styles, 445; poverty, 465; remarriage, 506; teen pregnancy, 545; white wedding industry, 575. *See also* Transracial adoption

White wedding industry, 572–77; financial costs of weddings, 573–74; global exploitation of wedding industry workers, 575; ideology, 576–77; rituals, 574, 575–76; wedding and eloping, 568, 569; wedding debt, 574–75; wedding goods and services, 573. *See also* Wedding and eloping

WIC (Special Supplemental Nutrition Program for Women, Infants, and Children), 469–70

Wiehe, Vernon, 525

Wife swapping, 260–61

Wilson, William J., 26, 171, 376

Witnesses to birth, 122–23

The Woes of the Inner-City African-American Father (Wilson), 26

Women: cohabitation motives, 428; dating, role in, 181–82, 183, 184; divorce and, 213; elder abuse and, 244; Family and Medical Leave Act and, 267; grandparenting style of, 307; infertility, effects on, 340; marriage, benefits of, 57–58, 59; marriage, disadvantages of, 60–61; premarital sexual relationships and, 475; remarriage and, 507; Sweden, 382–83; transition to parenthood, 553. *See also* Gender; Men; Mothers; Working women

Woodruff, Wilford, 460–61, 462

Working-class families. *See* Social class

Working women: baby boomers, 93; birth dearth and, 94; breastfeeding or formula feeding, 86; in Great Depression, 281; infertility and, 342–43; marital satisfaction and, 387, 388; in World War II, 281–82. *See also* Employed mothers; Housework allocation; Second-shift phenomenon

Work issues: childfree relationships, 128, 132–33; grandparents as caregivers, 309, 314–15; traditional assumptions in workplace, 414–15, 417; transition to parenthood, 554. *See also* Family and Medical Leave Act

World War II: baby boom, 89–90; child care policy, 108; day care, 188; divorce, 209; family roles, 273; housework allocation, 328; working women, 281–82

Youngest children, 76, 78–79, 80

Zero population growth, 96–97